The Economic Effects of
Taxing Capital Income

The Economic Effects of
Taxing Capital Income

Jane G. Gravelle

The MIT Press
Cambridge, Massachusetts
London, England

This book was set in Palatino by The MIT Press and was printed and bound in the United States of America.

Library of Congress Cataloging-in-Publication Data

Gravelle, Jane.
    The economic effects of taxing capital income / Jane G. Gravelle.
    p.   cm.
    Includes bibliographical references and index.
    ISBN 0-262-07158-4
    1. Capital levy—United States. 2. Income tax—United States.
I. Title.
HJ4133. U5G73   1994
336. 24'24'0973—dc20   94-10553
                                                                CIP

to Jennifer

Contents

List of Tables and Figures

Tables

Figures

Preface

The taxation of capital income is a topic both narrow and vast. It has spawned an extensive economics literature and garnered considerable attention in the public policy debate, while remaining a complex and, at times, arcane subject.

This book is, in the broadest sense, written for anyone who is interested in the economic effects of capital income taxes and in the design of tax policies that affect capital income. It is written not only for public finance economists (whether practitioners or students) but also for a broader academic and policy community with a need to understand these economic issues. I have attempted to explain issues that are often complex in nontechnical language. While this work could be described most simply as a survey of the economics literature, it is written within the framework of existing tax institutions and the political debate over capital income taxation.

Writing a book to appeal to a disparate audience entails some compromises. Those researchers interested primarily in technical issues may find this book more useful as a starting point for locating the existing literature or as a reference source for data (especially on effective tax rates). Still I hope that these readers will find the summaries of economic research and the information about institutions, history, and policy debates to be of interest and that they will bear with me when I occasionally detour to explain basic economic concepts or present my own conclusions about what the literature says for the general reader. For this latter audience I have endeavored to explain economic theory and evidence in terms that can be understood by the general reader. When the topic sometimes unavoidably becomes difficult, I have tried to ensure that basic conclusions of an economic analysis are nevertheless clearly stated.

Acknowledgments

I owe a special debt to Ron Boster, veteran Capitol Hill staffer, and Joseph Cordes, of George Washington University. Their extensive comments on the initial draft of this book were invaluable to me. I also thank my colleagues at the Congressional Research Service— David Brumbaugh, Don Kiefer, Alfred Reifman, Jack Taylor, and Dennis Zimmerman—who made comments, shared their expertise and their files, and provided lots of encouragement. I am further grateful to Henry Aaron and Bill Gale of the Brookings Institution, Charles Ballard of Michigan State University, Larry Kotlikoff of Boston University and the National Bureau of Economic Research, Larry Ozanne of the Congressional Budget Office, and Gene Steuerle of the Urban Institute, for helpful comments, suggestions, and discussions.

Finally, I am indebted to the Congressional Research Service of the Library of Congress, an institution that provides nonpartisan assistance to the U.S. Congress. Working for the Congressional Research Service has given me the opportunity over the years to observe the intersection between the academic world of economics and the practical world of policy-making from a unique vantage point. That experience has influenced this book enormously. The views in this book of course are mine, and they do not necessarily reflect those of the Service or the Library.

The Economic Effects of
Taxing Capital Income

1   Overview

Income from capital is only a quarter of all income. Yet the taxation of capital income is at the center of some of the most long-standing and spirited debates about federal income tax policy. The tax treatment of capital income is, rightly or wrongly, seen by many policymakers to be at the heart of a number of fundamental questions of public policy. Indeed, considerations of taxes on investment and saving quickly enter the fray in public debate over issues such as savings and economic growth, international competitiveness, and fairness.

Some Illustrations from the Policy Debate

Savings and Economic Growth

Discussions of savings and economic growth rarely get very far without proposals for tax incentives to increase savings becoming a centerpiece. Proponents of cutting taxes on capital income argue that such taxes reduce the return individuals can earn on their savings. Thus reducing capital income taxes will make saving more attractive. They may cite research that suggests cutting taxes on capital income would induce a significant savings response and promote greater economic growth.

Skeptics argue that economic theory does not provide a clear case for a positive effect on savings as rate of return rises, and find the body of empirical evidence on the effects ambiguous. Merely labeling something a saving incentive, they suggest, does not necessarily make it successful in achieving an objective. They eschew tax changes in exchange for a more certain route to increasing savings—through reductions in the deficit.

International Competitiveness

As pressure on basic manufacturing jobs from imports has increased, the issue of "international competitiveness" has taken center stage— and it is not long before capital income taxation makes an entrance. The claim made here is that the United States should cut capital income taxes to become more competitive in international trade, since lower taxes will reduce the cost of production. A related notion is that replacing the corporate tax with a value-added tax will increase net exports, since value-added taxes are rebated on exports and corporate taxes are not.

On the other side of this issue is the argument that the very notion of competitiveness in international trade for a country as a whole is an example of incorrect reasoning. (Economists term this error a fallacy of composition.) Cutting the taxes of one firm or industry will make that firm or industry more competitive. If taxes of all firms are cut, then the competitive advantage for a given firm is reduced, eliminated, or reversed (depending on how important the tax is in the cost structure of the firm as compared to the average). This outcome should be obvious in a domestic market, but it also occurs in the international market because exchange rates will adjust to offset the *average* cost reduction. Cutting capital income taxes will simply change the mix of exports and imports—some industries will lose market share while others will gain. Because of the offsetting effects of exchange rates, net exports will not increase. Indeed, if the tax reduction attracts capital from abroad, net exports will decrease in the short run.

Fairness

Capital income taxes are also viewed as having important implications for fairness, especially the corporate income tax. One of the more dramatic illustrations of how this issue plays out in the public debate was the reaction to the failure of many corporations, otherwise reporting profits, to pay income tax in the early 1980s. The upshot of this publicity was the adoption of a "minimum" tax on corporate income. If a corporation's tax liability was low relative to its book income, the minimum tax rules would ensure that some tax was paid. This minimum tax was justified by supporters largely based on the notion that taxes on different firms should be made more equal in order to achieve fairness among taxpayers.

Critics of the minimum tax suggested that while this approach may make tax payments more equal across firms, it does not necessarily make taxation more equitable to investors. Investors will respond to tax differentials by altering their investments and in the long run will earn the same rate of return. (The change itself, however, may produce some windfall gains and losses in the short run.) The policy issue in evaluating the minimum tax, they suggest, is efficiency—whether investments are allocated to their most productive uses. On those grounds the minimum tax does not necessarily appear to be a good idea.

Sorting Out the Issues

A colleague of mine was fond of remarking, when pressed for precision in stating the economic effects of tax policies, that "economics ain't physics." One might also add that economics is not theology. Too often the admittedly uncertain answers that economic theory and evidence provide must vie with what seem to be articles of faith. Indeed, it often seems that these articles of faith have become the guiding principles of the tax policy debate. What economic research has to say about policy issues is often lost in the heat of the political debate. This body of literature, at the very least, raises questions about some of the statements frequently made in support of various tax breaks.

Economics is a science containing a set of theories to be tested against observation. These theories are derived from simple ideas such as the basic scarcity of resources, the preference for more rather than less, and the desire to consume a mixture of goods. Economic theory is constrained by certain propositions, for instance, that firms will not continually produce more than they sell (supply must, eventually and perhaps with some fluctuations, equal demand). The theoretical and accounting structure of economics imposes a discipline on the expected outcome of various policies. Some of these outcomes can be stated with precision, others with strong likelihood, and still others with considerable uncertainty—but in many cases they conflict with "popular wisdom."

Separating what is known or suggested from the science of economics, as uncertain as that science sometimes is, from the mythology that often seems to dominate the popular debate is especially important because following the enactment of the 1986 tax reform, we are at a crossroads in tax policy regarding capital income taxation.

Clearly the Tax Reform Act (TRA) of 1986 was a watershed event in the taxation of capital income. Reversing twenty-five years of tax policy, it focused on narrowing the differences between tax burdens on different types of capital and evening out the treatment of different taxpayers. It rejected a growing clamor in some quarters for moving further in the direction of a consumption-based tax and instead took its theme from the views of policy oriented economists such as Joseph Pechman and Richard Musgrave who stressed an income tax. Provisions thought to be firmly ensconced in the tax law, such as the investment credit and differential treatment of capital gains, were traded in favor of lower tax rates and uniformity in taxation. Under the guidance of economists Charles McLure and Eugene Steuerle of the Treasury Department, TRA 1986 virtually demolished tax shelters and tackled complex elements of accounting for income such as uniform capitalization rules that had heretofore mismatched income and expense.

How important it was to even up tax rates across capital income as opposed to lowering the tax rate on capital income was a fundamental disagreement during consideration of the act, and it has remained so. Indeed, the central theme of TRA 1986 was the movement toward a more efficient *income* tax. A much different path might have been taken had lowering the overall tax rate on capital income been considered central.

In the years following the act, one camp has continued to criticize the TRA for raising the overall tax rate on capital income (although evidence presented in this book suggests that there was no increase). This argument has expressed itself in proposals to lower the tax rate on capital gains and to restore Individual Retirement Accounts (IRAs). There has also been discussion of restoring some form of investment credit or substituting consumption taxes for *income* taxes. This viewpoint—that the most compelling issue is to lower overall taxes on capital income—seems to pay scant attention to most questions of the neutrality of taxes across investments.

The other side of the issue, evening up tax rates, has primarily involved a holding action to keep the TRA provisions in place. Yet substantial variations across tax rates remain even in the post-TRA law—differences between corporate capital, noncorporate capital, and owner occupied housing; differences between debt and equity finance; differences between retained and distributed corporate profits; and uneven treatment of capital invested at home and abroad. Addressing some of these issues are thought to be stymied by political constraints—an example is the treatment of owner occupied housing. Others are under discussion—the Treasury Department has recently completed a study of corporate tax integration—but none is the immediate subject of tax legislation.

The central questions in the formulation of tax policy toward capital income taxation are: How important is it to lower tax rates on capital income? And how important is it to minimize the differences in taxation of different types of capital? As with any policy issue, these questions need to be guided by issues of economic efficiency, equitable distribution of the tax burden, simplification of the tax law for both administrative and compliance purposes, and revenue needs. Yet, the debate often proceeds without regard for evidence economists can bring to bear on the issue. And, numerous unsettled questions about the allocational and distributional consequences of tax changes remain. This book attempts to bring some order to the debate over what the next steps, if any, in improving the taxation of capital income, might be taken, along with cautions about missteps.

What's to Come

There are two underlying policy questions around which this book is organized—whether capital income should be taxed at all, and if so, what is the best way to do it? Chapter 2 addresses the first question, whether the capital income tax belongs in the tax structure. In this discussion the policy debate—over savings—has been different from what normative economics suggests that the debate should be—over efficiency and distribution.

While increasing savings may be a laudable goal, there is no certainty that eliminating taxes on capital income will achieve the goal. The chapter explains why theory is ambiguous as to whether raising the rate of return will increase savings, leaving the answer to the question a matter of empirical evidence. But empirical evidence does not consistently support the view that reducing tax rates on capital income will exert a strong influence on private savings behavior. Indeed, recent events raise further doubts—although private savings rates were at an historical low for the post–World War II period during the 1980s, interest rates were high and effective tax burdens on capital income low. And, even if a reduction in the tax on capital income would increase savings, it is by no means clear that it is the best route to doing so.

Moreover an increase in savings is not identical to an increase in well-being. An increase in savings trades present consumption for future consumption, and it is the value of that trade-off that determines economic efficiency. Likewise, if revenues lost by lowering the rates on one tax are to be made up by raising other taxes, the increased distortions from the increased taxes must be weighed against the decreased distortions from the lowered taxes. In addition substituting other tax sources for taxes on capital income has distributional consequences that should be considered. The issues of economic efficiency and an equitable distribution of income suggest that capital income taxes may well play a role in an optimal and fair tax system.

The remaining chapters of the book are devoted to the issue of how capital income should be taxed to achieve efficiency and equity. Chapter 3 sets up the overall framework for considering the design of the capital income tax. Calculations of effective tax rates suggest that with the exception of owner-occupied housing, taxes across physical types of investments and across industries are relatively even, whereas tax rates across organizational (corporate versus noncorporate) and financial forms of investment remain highly diverse. Various rationales for tax benefits to particular types of activities are reviewed. The conclusion is that with the exception of certain departures from neutrality arising from administrative and compliance concerns, it is difficult to justify most of the departures from tax neutrality.

Chapter 4 addresses a central structural feature of the income tax that may be most responsible for tax distortions—the separate application of tax on corporate income. The analysis of efficiency in this chapter suggests that there is a case for relieving the additional tax on corporate income. Indeed, under plausible assumptions the economic costs of distortions from the corporate income tax may be as large as the yield of the tax. Even if full relief from the tax is not feasible, some partial relief measures may well be so and could yield a higher ratio of efficiency gain to revenue cost.

Chapter 5 considers the fundamentals of measuring capital income. In addition to considering the basic system for capital cost recovery, this chapter also discusses the neutrality of investment incentives. Although capital cost recovery appears to conform largely to a correct measure of income under current law, significant changes in inflation could cause distortions. Restoration of previous incentives could also produce large tax differentials across different types of business capital. For example, the investment tax credit of pre-1987 tax law favored some types of assets over others. This chapter also discusses how tax incentives might be structured to produce more even tax rates. This analysis also suggests that it is important to consider how the incentive affects the corporate/noncorporate differentials. To minimize the differential, incentives should be allowed in the form of deductions, not credits.

Chapter 6 grapples with an issue that has had a high profile in the policy debate over the past few years—the capital gains tax. The treatment in this chapter is, however, broader—it considers as well the tax consequences to sale that arise from changes in capital cost recovery, which is restarted with the sale of an asset. The latter is often ignored, but clearly influences the tax consequences of the sale of depreciable assets. The consequences of different types of gains relief are shown to be quite different. The efficiency case for providing general capital gains relief is mixed, since cutting the capital gains tax would decrease some distortions and increase others. Trading off relief for corporate stock in favor of taxing capital gains at death seems the policy option most likely to yield favorable efficiency effects. (Such an approach would, however, face major political obstacles.) This chapter also discusses the confusion in the debate about how to assess the distributional effects of a capital gains tax cut.

Chapter 7 examines two appendages to the capital income tax system, the alternative corporate minimum tax and the passive loss restriction. Both provisions were adopted as part of TRA 1986. The alternative minimum tax (especially as it applies to corporations) was designed to ensure some minimum payment of tax. The passive loss restriction was aimed primarily at real estate and other tax shelters. In the case of the alternative minimum tax, there is not a clear case for retaining this tax on either equity or efficiency grounds, particularly for corporations. The popular support for this provision reflects misunderstanding of questions of distributional equity. While there may be a case for the passive loss restriction, which was enacted in part in response to the alarming explosion in tax shelters, the passive loss restriction can prevent the deduction of real economic losses. Recent tax policy revisions have been narrowly aimed at lifting the restrictions for a narrow class of taxpayers (those involved in the real estate business) rather than tackling any fundamental problems with this provision.

Chapter 8 turns to tax exemption of income for retirement savings. The major form of this exemption is through private pension plans or deferred income plans. There are also some benefits from the accumulation of value in life insurance policies and from Individual Retirement Accounts. While these provisions are often justified as a means of increasing savings, there is not a great deal of evidence that these tax benefits have much effect on savings behavior, particularly since they are inframarginal in nature. The benefits for pension plans are unevenly allowed. There may be a case for increasing the taxes on earnings of pension funds and similar tax favored vehicles, and perhaps using the revenues to accomplish some efficiency gains. Indeed, certain schemes for corporate tax integration that would accomplish this result indirectly might be considered.

Chapter 9 catalogs and briefly discusses a variety of special tax treatments for particular types of investments not reviewed elsewhere in this study. These items include some specialized issues surrounding the tax treatment of housing, the treatment of intangible investments, benefits for the extractive industries, tax-exempt bond financing, special treatment for the financial and nonprofit sectors, small business incentives, and incentives for geographical location. These activities have been singled out for special treatment, the rationales commonly being to adjust for spillover effects, to simplify tax administration, or some combination of the two.

Chapter 10 reviews tax policies that have been debated largely for reasons of so-called international competitiveness. In this chapter two somewhat separate issues are considered. The first is an issue that has loomed large in the public debate—the effect of corporate taxes on "international competitiveness" through increases in the cost structure. This is a misleading and fruitless objective, since exchange rate adjustments act to offset any overall price effects. The second, and more relevant, issue is the tax treatment of inbound and outbound investment. Unfortunately, the most sensible system of taxation for the purposes of tax neutrality is a system that has never been adopted— residence based taxation. This section reviews "second-best" choices and, suggests that there may be a justification for eliminating deferral of taxes on foreign source income, for imposing a foreign tax credit limitation on a per country basis, and for eliminating certain specialized provisions in the tax law.

The final chapter reviews the role that economic analysis has played and should play in the legislative process. It concludes that gains in economic welfare are most likely to arise from continuing tax reform— achieving greater uniformity in the taxation of investment within the framework of an income tax. Among the changes it suggests in the policy-making process that might lead to better analysis are a greater focus on efficiency implications, a longer revenue-estimating time horizon, and more sophisticated distributional studies, including attention to intergenerational distribution issues and distribution across incomes.

Two appendixes provide a history of the U.S. capital income tax system and the underlying formulas and data on which quantitative measures in the book rest.

2   Should We Tax Income from Capital?

Whether capital income should be taxed has long been debated by academic economists. Despite the popularity of the income tax with most governments and many economists, there have been many distinguished proponents of using consumption rather than income as a tax base.[1]

Switching to a consumption base is not the only method of eliminating taxes on capital income: Another approach is shifting to a wage tax base. Both bases are smaller than the income tax base. Income is the sum of wage income and capital income; it is also the sum of consumption and savings. Both tax bases effectively eliminate the tax on the return to new savings. Shifting from a tax on income to a tax on wages directly eliminates taxes on the return to capital in place as well as any new capital added in the future. Shifting from a tax on income to a tax on consumption effectively eliminates the tax on the return to new savings by allowing such savings to be excluded from the tax base (owners of existing capital suffer a windfall loss in the purchasing power of their capital). For the U.S. economy the consumption tax base would be larger than the wage tax base, since the fraction of income saved (less than 10 percent) is smaller than the fraction of income received from capital (about 25 percent).[2]

The economic consequences of reducing the tax on capital actually depends on how such reduction is accomplished—through increased wage taxes, increased consumption taxes, or through deficit finance. Recent studies of savings behavior in life-cycle models have, for example, focused on the different consequences of removing taxes on capital income via a switch to consumption rather than wage taxation (Summers 1981; Auerbach and Kotlikoff 1987).

Replacing some or all of capital income taxes with consumption taxes has been a more widely discussed direction for broad revision. However, there are different types of consumption taxes—indirect taxes (notably sales and value-added taxes) and direct taxes imposed on income less net saving. These two consumption taxes differ primarily because only direct taxes can be imposed at graduated rates.

In practice many smaller-scale tax reductions on capital income are proposed without a specific tax replacement, and virtually all of them provide some reduction in tax on returns to existing capital as well as new savings. Actually the federal income tax code has contained, and continues to contain, elements of both wage and consumption taxation. Although the major federal tax for general revenues has always been called an income tax base, in practice the income tax has frequently provided special benefits for certain types of capital income.

During the late 1970s and 1980s, the debate about whether to tax income or consumption was joined explicitly, first in the Treasury Department's Blueprints for Basic Tax Reform (1977) and then in the debate about tax reform that preceded the Treasury's Tax Reform Study (1984). The Tax Reform Act (TRA) of 1986 (as well as the initial proposals made by the Treasury) came squarely down on the side of an income tax framework. A whole range of tax benefits to capital—such as the investment credit, various tax deferrals, individual retirement accounts, and partial exclusions for capital gains—were eliminated. As an offset for jettisoning these provisions, and others, tax rates were lowered for both corporations and individuals.

The debate was resolved, for the time being, in favor of the income tax. But the issue of whether the tax rate on capital income is too high, or even whether the tax base should include capital income, was by no means set to rest. Academic economists have continued to debate the issue of consumption versus income as the proper base for taxation. In the policy arena some of the major tax debates that followed were over reducing the tax burden on capital via tax incentives and, in particular, resurrecting some of the lost tax benefits. The most prominent of these debates were over capital gains taxes, individual retirement accounts, and reenacting an investment tax credit. In addition bills that would substitute a value-added tax (a form of consumption tax) for the corporate income tax have continued to be introduced.

While both the popular and the academic debates deal with issues of savings and fairness, the focus of the popular debate is slightly different from the debate in the professional economics literature. In the popular debate the argument for reducing the tax on capital income taxation typically has to do with issues of savings, economic growth, and so called international competitiveness. The notion that people should be taxed on consumption—what they are taking out of society—and not on savings—what they are putting back into the economy for the future—is also heard.

The main argument here for maintaining the tax on capital income has to do largely with progressivity. Higher-income individuals typically have a much larger fraction of their income from capital and a lower ratio of consumption to total income. Substitution of either a tax on wages or a tax on consumption would tend to be less progressive with respect to an annual income than an income tax, absent a steeper graduation in rates.

In the economics literature, the issues are different. Economic analysis of capital income tax often focuses on optimal (or efficient) tax systems. Efficiency is related to the savings response (since both the savings effects and the efficiency effects are influenced by the same fundamental behavioral responses), but the efficiency analysis recognizes that savings trades present for future consumption. It is possible for increases in savings to reduce welfare rather than increase it. In general, increased saving raises welfare if the rate of return is sufficient to compensate the saver for the delay in consumption. Economic analysis of the distributional effects recognizes that annual incomes are imperfect proxies for lifetime income and that substituting consumption or wage taxation for income taxation can redistribute tax burdens across age as well as income groups.

It is not possible to answer precisely the question of whether the tax rate on capital income is too high or too low. To throw some light on the question, this chapter reviews the savings impact, the economic efficiency issue, the distributional consequences, and differences in administering the different tax bases.

As discussed below, the effect on savings of eliminating capital income taxes is ambiguous in theory. The empirical evidence does not appear to support a strong relationship between the rate of return and savings. The discussion of efficiency also examines the important differences between wage and consumption tax bases. As with the savings issue, the evidence on whether reducing the tax on capital income would increase efficiency is not clear, but there are some distributional consequences, both across incomes and across age groups. The discussion of distribution also further addresses the difference between various types of consumption taxes frequently discussed—progressive consumption taxes, value-added and similar taxes levied on commodities, and some hybrid treatments. Finally, while consumption or wage taxes would be simpler to administer for some taxpayers, they might be more complicated for others.

Taxation of Capital Income and Savings

The main argument made in the popular debate for taxing capital income lightly, if at all, is the supposed negative effect of capital income taxes on savings. Reduced savings, in turn, results in lower economic output and a lower future standard of living. Arguments in the public debate for lowering tax burdens on capital income frequently cite the loss of tax incentives and rise in corporate tax revenues from the 1986 TRA, the purportedly high cost of capital in the United States compared with other countries, the dismal U.S. savings rate, a slowing of economic growth, and a perception that the United States is losing its competitive position in international markets. The latter three issues are frequently linked to both the low savings rate and the high tax burdens on capital. Some of these arguments are long-time staples of those who support a tax system that, at most, falls lightly, or not at all on capital. Others, especially those focused on the low savings rate and the loss of tax incentives in 1986, have given the argument for lowering tax burdens on capital a new boost. Such a reaction is perhaps not surprising given the Tax Reform Act's shift away from long-standing tax incentives such as the investment credit and the preferential taxation of capital gains.

Some of these issues are of course linked more closely to domestic investment than to savings. In a closed economy, savings and investment are identical concepts; in an open economy, an increased rate of domestic savings can lead partially to investments abroad. Moreover some taxes and tax benefits primarily affect domestic investment and others domestic savings. (Further elaboration on this issue is deferred until chapter 10.) Nevertheless, there are reasons to focus on savings rather than investment. It is domestic savings that will affect future standards of living, since domestic savers receive the return to investments made in other countries, while foreigners will reap the returns to U.S. investment that they own.

Before turning to the evidence on this issue, however, it is important to recognize that there is no reason to argue automatically that the savings rate should increase. Increasing savings reduces consumption in the present, in return for increased consumption in the future. It involves a shifting of consumption and welfare across our lifetimes and also from current to future generations.

There may, however, be some reason that the savings rate should be increased, perhaps because individuals are myopic or because government policies may have cut savings below levels that would otherwise have occurred. For example, large fiscal deficits and unfunded social security liabilities could explain undersaving in the United States, although the corrective policy prescription is more likely to be a reduction in the deficit (or even running a surplus) rather than altering capital income taxation. For the remainder of this section, however, the issue of why increasing savings is a desirable goal is set aside. The question rather is whether reducing taxes on capital can increase savings.

First, it is instructive to look at the pattern of tax burdens on capital over time. This pattern of tax burdens can shed light on the arguments that have assumed a new prominence—that our dismal rate of savings reflects too heavy a tax burden on capital and that recent legislation has inappropriately increased that tax burden.

Effective Marginal Tax Rates

The tax burden on new investment cannot be identified simply with reference to tax rates. To measure this burden, one must determine the "effective" marginal tax rate on earnings from investment. Simply put, the effective marginal tax rate measures what fraction of the real pre-tax rate of return to a new investment will be collected as taxes. This measure is derived from a somewhat complicated exercise that accounts for a myriad of tax features. Since this measure of the effective marginal tax rate will be used extensively to illuminate a number of economic issues in this and future chapters, it is important to understand this concept and how it differs from other measures of tax rates.

The Concept of Effective Marginal Tax Rate
If all income were measured correctly and taxed on a current basis, the effective marginal tax rate and the statutory marginal tax rate would be identical. The statutory marginal tax rate is the rate applied to the last dollar of *taxable* income. In the case of equity capital of large corporations (which are subject to a flat rate), it would also be identical to the effective average tax rate—tax payments divided by profits.

The effective marginal tax rate measure accounts for tax benefits and penalties on income from new investments that do not take the form of changes in the statutory marginal tax. Tax benefits may take other forms, including explicit tax subsidies such as investment tax credits (allowing a credit for a fraction of investment undertaken).

Tax benefits may also occur through accelerated depreciation. For investments in physical assets that wear out during production, the cost of the investment must be recovered tax free through deductions for depreciation so that the tax will be confined to the return. If depreciation deductions are allowed earlier than justified by the true decline in value of the asset, there is a tax benefit because taxes will be postponed. Similarly, if depreciation is allowed at too slow a rate, the effective marginal tax rate will be increased.

Another tax benefit results from delaying a tax on accruals of income because they have not been realized—this effect occurs in the case of the capital gains tax. The taxpayer's effective burden is smaller because tax payments are postponed. Capital gains that are held until death are never subject to tax.

Owner-occupied housing is also eligible for tax benefits because the implicit rental income is not included in income. If two families purchased homes and rented them to each other, each would report income (gross rent minus costs) that would reflect the return on their equity investment. When individuals purchase a home and occupy it, they do not have to include that return in income for tax purposes, even though that income is effectively received through the occupancy of the home and even though interest and property taxes may be deducted.

Inflation can also affect the effective marginal tax rate. Increases in tax burdens arise from inflation because the recovery of original investments is not adjusted by changes in the overall price level. Inflation can, however, lower tax rates on debt-financed investment. When income is correctly measured and there is no inflation, interest income is not taxed to the lender but not to the borrower. In the case of the borrower, the interest deduction offsets any normal profits on this capital. When inflation is present, the interest rate is composed of two parts: the real rate of return and the inflation premium necessary to compensate the lender because repaid nominal principal will not be indexed for inflation. To measure income correctly, this inflation premium should be neither deductible by the borrower nor taxable to the lender, since the inflation premium is simply an adjustment of the principal to reflect new price levels and real purchasing power.

A simple example can illustrate this point. If there were no inflation and an interest rate of 5 percent, an investor who begins with $100 would have $105 after a year. At the end of a year the investor's purchasing power has increased by $5. If the tax rate is 50 percent, half of the $5 would be paid in taxes for a net change in real purchasing power of $2.50. If there is an inflation rate of 5 percent, in order to have a change in real purchasing power of $5 before tax, the investor would earn $110.25 ($105 times 1.05). Since all prices are 5 percent greater, this amount will be required to purchase the equivalent of $105 in prior year prices. The equivalent of $5 in real purchasing power is now $5.25, and only this amount should be included in income, to yield the equivalent of $2.50 in after-tax real purchasing power. The remainder of the increase in value, $5, is simply the inflation premium which maintains the real purchasing power of the original $100 of principal. A similar adjustment should be made by the borrower, whose nondeductible principal should be increased by $5 in order to repay debt in real purchasing power.

If the lender's tax rate is lower than the borrower's tax rate, there is a net tax savings because the reduction of taxes of the borrower is greater than the increase in taxes of the lender. The influence of these features on the effective tax rate is also affected by the prevailing interest rates, since it is the size of the inflation premium relative to the interest rate that determines the size of the tax benefit relative to taxes on the real portion of interest.

The marginal effective tax rate calculation takes all of these features—along with the statutory marginal tax rate—and converts them into an equivalent effective marginal tax rate. Another way of putting it is that for a given investment, the marginal effective tax rate is the tax rate that would have to be applied to economic income in order to yield the same after-tax return as the investment yields with the combination of the statutory marginal tax rate and all of the other tax benefits/penalties.

Note that we cannot simply employ an average effective tax rate (taxes paid divided by income) as a proxy for this marginal effective tax rate. The tax rate on new investment will be different from the average tax rate, since it associates tax subsidies and penalties provided for new investment only with income from that investment and not the flow of income from the existing capital stock. Of course some capital income taxes are imposed on entities (individuals and smaller corporations) subject to graduated tax rates, where marginal and average rates would diverge even if income were measured correctly. The effective marginal tax rate approach also allows the differentiation of tax burdens paid by the firm on different types of capital investments.

The method of calculating the marginal effective tax rate can be illustrated by a simple example. Suppose that an investment of $100 produces output after a year and then becomes worthless. Receipts at the end of the year are $110, a rate of return of 10 percent. If a 50 percent income tax is imposed, the investor will have taxable income of $10, which is gross earnings minus recovery of the principal (or depreciation). A 50 percent tax will result in a tax of $5 and receipts after tax of $105. If $105 is earned on a $100 investment, the rate of return is 5 percent, and the effective tax rate is equal to the statutory rate, since 50 percent of the return is paid in taxes.

Suppose now that the taxpayer is allowed an investment credit of 1 percent without otherwise altering the depreciation allowed. The cost of the investment is then $99. The investor's $105 constitutes a rate of return on $99 of approximately 6 percent (1.05/0.99 − 1 equals 0.0606). The fraction of the 10 percent pretax return paid in taxes is now only 40 percent ((0.10 − 0.0606)/0.10). In other words, allowing the investment credit is the equivalent of reducing the tax rate to 40 percent.

The same example can be used to illustrate the effects of inflation as it interacts with depreciation when depreciation is based on historical cost. Suppose that the inflation rate is 5 percent so that the price level after a year is 5 percent higher. Gross receipts will now be $115.50 ($110 times 1.05). Allowing $100 of depreciation will result in taxable income of $15.50, a tax of $7.75 and receipts after tax of $107.75. The original investment of $100 is now $105 (to make the same real investment in current dollars would require $105). The $107.75 is approximately a 2.6 percent return on $105. The effective tax rate is 74 percent ((0.10 − 0.026)/0.10), since that fraction of the 10 percent return has been paid in taxes. But, if depreciation deductions had been boosted by the rate of inflation to $105, the effective tax rate would have remained at 50 percent—taxable income would have been $10.50, tax $5.25, and after tax receipts $110.25, which is a 5 percent return on $105.

The effects of accelerated depreciation on tax rates and the operation of various tax penalties and features in multiperiod investments are more complex. Chapter 5 contains additional elaborations on the concept of economic depreciation. Some further numerical examples of the calculation of effective tax rates are provided in appendix B, which also provides the specific formulas and assumptions for computing tax rates found in this and following chapters.

Effective Marginal Tax Rates: 1953–89
As noted earlier, marginal effective tax rates depend not only on the statutory marginal tax rates but also on the rules regarding depreciation and investment credits, inflation, and the relationship of inflation to the interest rate. Corporate equity income, however, is taxed twice. Profits are taxed at the firm level, and dividends and capital gains are taxed to the stockholder as well. The flow of implicit income from owner occupied housing is not taxed, although mortgage interest and property taxes are deducted if the taxpayer itemizes deductions.

Table 2.1 presents some of the underlying data for variables used to calculate the effective tax for the period 1953 to 1989. These data include the statutory corporate tax rate, the estimated marginal individual tax rate (which affects the taxation of corporate income at the individual level, the taxation of noncorporate income, and the taxation of interest received), the estimated expected inflation rate, and the interest rate (the Baa bond rate is used).[3]

Table 2.1
Data used to estimate marginal effective tax rates

Year	Individual tax rate	Corporate tax rate	Inflation rate	Interest rate
1953	31	52	3.3	3.7
1954	29	52	1.6	3.5
1955	29	52	1.9	3.5
1956	29	52	2.5	3.9
1957	29	52	3.2	4.7
1958	29	52	3.0	4.7
1960	28	52	2.6	5.1
1961	28	52	1.7	5.1
1962	27	52	1.3	5.0
1963	26	52	1.1	4.9
1964	25	50	1.3	4.8
1965	24	48	1.3	4.9
1966	24	48	1.8	5.7
1967	25	48	2.8	6.2
1968	27	48	4.1	6.9
1969	28	48	5.0	7.8
1970	28	48	4.6	9.1
1971	28	48	4.8	8.6
1972	28	48	4.7	8.2
1973	29	48	4.5	8.2
1974	30	48	5.7	9.5
1975	30	48	7.5	10.6
1976	31	48	5.7	9.8
1977	31	48	5.2	9.8
1978	32	48	6.5	9.5
1979	34	46	6.8	10.7
1980	35	46	8.6	13.7
1981	36	46	7.8	16.1
1982	33	46	6.8	16.1
1983	31	46	6.6	13.6
1984	30	46	6.1	14.2
1985	30	46	5.6	12.7
1986	30	46	5.2	10.4
1987	23	34	5.2	10.6
1988	23	34	5.0	10.8
1989	23	34	4.8	10.2

Note: Based on calculations in appendix B.

Since effective tax rates are influenced by the level of the real rate of return, a higher after-tax rate of return was assumed for equity investment. Historical measures of the return to equity over long periods of time indicate that equity investment earns a persistently higher return, presumably to compensate for other differences in the characteristics of these investments (e.g., risk). Nevertheless, the equity return should fluctuate with the interest rate, and the method of adjusting for these differential returns was to assume that the after-tax return to equity is the sum of the after-tax return to debt plus a fixed after-tax premium.

The estimated inflation rate is a difficult variable to determine. For the period 1979–89 it is based on the Drexel-Burnham-Lambert decision makers poll of January 16, 1990. The estimated inflation rate for the previous years is based on a weighted average of the previous seven quarters of inflation (using the GNP deflator, as suggested by Hendershott and Hu 1981). The marginal effective tax rate series is affected by the marginal statutory personal tax rates; there rates are based on a series developed by Peek and Wilcox (1986), and updated with data from the Treasury Department (more details are provided in appendix B).

In addition to statutory tax rates and macroeconomic variables, marginal effective tax rates account for depreciation rules and estimates of economic depreciation, investment credits, and capital gains exclusions and deferrals (details are given in appendix B). These rules were significant determinants of effective tax rates and were changed considerably over the period.

The major changes in these rules include the move to accelerated depreciation methods in 1954, the shortening of tax lives and introduction of the investment credit in 1962, modifications of the investment credit in 1964, repeal of the investment credit and restrictions on accelerated depreciation for structures in 1969, restoration of the investment credit and depreciation methods in 1971, increases in the investment credit in 1975, larger capital gains exclusions in 1979, more accelerated depreciation methods in 1981, and restrictions on depreciation in 1982 and 1984. The 1986 Act further limited depreciation and repealed the investment credit. It also taxed capital gains in full and required full capitalization of inventories. (More detailed descriptions of these changes are given in the historical summary of the tax law in appendix A.)

The resulting estimated marginal effective tax rates for 1953–89 are displayed in figure 2.1 (see appendix B, table B.1, for the specific numbers). Effective tax rates are shown for reproducible capital (equipment, structures, and inventories) separated into corporate business, noncorporate business, and owner-occupied housing. Corporate tax rates reflect the total burden, both at the firm and individual level, of taxes. The tax rates on owner-occupied housing reflect the failure to tax imputed rent. (The formulas and assumptions underlying these calculations are given in appendix B.)

These estimated tax rates illuminate certain watershed events, as well as the effects of inflation on the capital income tax burden. The dramatic drop in effective tax rate from 1953 to 1954 in three of the four categories is largely due to the introduction of accelerated depreciation, and it illustrates the influence of such rules on tax burdens. The corporate tax rate dropped from 70 to 57 percent, the noncorporate tax rate dropped from 37 to 23 percent, and the overall tax rate dropped from 58 to 43 percent.

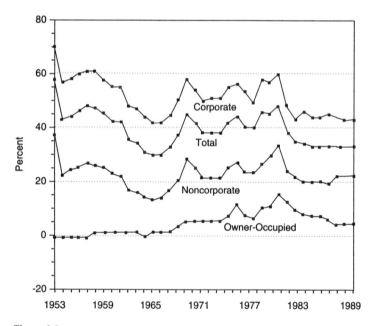

Figure 2.1
Estimated marginal effective tax rates. Based on table B.1, appendix B

After some minor fluctuations in the period 1954–61, reflecting variations in inflation, another major drop in the marginal effective tax rate occurred. This drop resulted from the introduction of the investment credit and the shorter 1962 tax lives, followed by the lowering of tax rates in 1964 and 1965. Marginal effective tax rates were lowest in the mid-1960s when significant tax incentives were allowed, but inflation remained low. In the late 1960s the inflation rate began to rise, and with it the tax rates. The marginal effective tax rate bumped up briefly during the repeal of the investment credit in 1969 and 1970. The credit was restored in 1971 and expanded in 1975, and the corporate tax rate and capital gains inclusion rate were lowered again in 1979. Nevertheless, the tax rate had moved back up to its level in the 1950s as inflation resulted in both higher statutory marginal tax rates for individuals and a greater overstatement of capital income. While the tax code had become much more generous than the law of the 1950s, this effect was undone by inflation.

The tax rate dropped substantially in 1981 following the more generous depreciation and lower individual tax rates enacted at that time. It also dropped in 1982 because the fall in inflation was more significant than the restrictions on depreciation enacted in that year. The rate fell further as inflation fell but was unchanged by the 1986 provisions. The current low tax rates are similar to the lower tax rates of the mid-1960s—that is, tax rates have never been much lower than they are currently.

These lower tax rates should continue. Under legislation adopted in 1993, the corporate statutory tax rate on large firms will rise to 35 percent and average statutory individual tax rates will rise as well. These changes will slightly increase effective tax rates (by a percentage point or so). At the same time the persistence of low inflation may lead to further declines in the anticipated inflation rate. These effects will slightly lower the effective tax rates.

These calculations illustrate several important points. First, the treatment of depreciation and presence of investment incentives can powerfully affect tax burdens on investment. Second, the marginal effective tax rate is influenced by the failure to account for inflation; although the effect of inflation is theoretically ambiguous due to its effects on debt, as a matter of history higher inflation tends to raise marginal effective tax rates. Moreover it is possible to trade off lowering the tax rate with broadening the tax base to keep overall marginal effective tax rates constant.

Indeed, this latter effect occurred with the Tax Reform Act of 1986. By these calculations, TRA 86 did not increase the marginal effective tax rate on reproducible capital; indeed, it kept the tax rates on various broad aggregates of the capital stock relatively fixed. While its focus remained on a system that taxed capital income, the lower tax rates made up for the loss of tax benefits such as the investment credit. Thus the claim for a need to lower capital income tax burdens on the grounds that increases in the 1986 TRA were excessive is not support- ed by this measure of effective tax rate. A similar finding of no increase in the overall effective tax rate was reported by Fullerton, Gillette, and Mackie (1987).[4]

Effects of Taxes on Savings

The marginal effective tax rate on capital income has bounced around considerably over the years. What relationship is there between these movements and private savings in the United States? Taxes affect the after-tax rate of return, and it is the after-tax rate of return that in turn affects savings. To explore this question, first, economic theory is reviewed and, second, the empirical evidence is considered.

Theoretical Considerations

Although the conclusion may seem surprising, economic theory is ambiguous as to whether raising the rate of return will increase the savings rate. This theoretical result is, however, quite straightforward. Saving itself is not a commodity; rather the commodity is consump- tion at some future time. The rate of return affects the price of that future commodity. If the interest rate is 10 percent, one has to forgo consumption of slightly over 90 cents this year to consume a dollar next year, since that amount will grow to a dollar in a year. The "price" of future consumption is 90 cents. If the interest rate falls to 5 percent, one has to forgo 95 cents of consumption (i.e., save more) to consume a dollar in the future.

If future consumption is unchanged, a drop in the after-tax rate of return, for example, from increased capital income taxation, will *raise* saving. For each dollar of future consumption, savings rises from 90 to

95 cents. But at lower rates of return, the price of future consumption (forgone current consumption) is higher, and this higher price will discourage future consumption. A sufficient drop in future consumption will offset this tendency of higher capital taxation to raise saving. Thus, if desired consumption drops to 93 cents, only 89 cents needs to be saved. Whether a drop in the rate of return raises or lowers savings depends on how much planned future consumption changes.

In sum, economic theory cannot establish the direction of the effect of a tax reduction on savings. Empirical evidence must be used to assess the direction as well as the size of any effect on savings.

Empirical Research
Empirical research on the responsiveness of the savings rate to the rate of return has been based on examining the pattern of savings over time and how it relates to changes in the after-tax rate of return, as well as to other variables that might affect savings rates such as economic downturns. Such research is inexact, since there are errors in measuring savings rates and the expected after-tax rate of return, which depends not only on expected future tax rates but on expected future before-tax returns and inflation. None of these variables can be observed directly.

Figure 2.2 displays the estimated saving rate and after-returns for the time period 1953–89 (the underlying data are in appendix B, table B.7). The savings rate shown is the one consistent with the concepts in the previous theoretical discussion—net private savings divided by after-tax private income. The measure of net savings (taken from gross private savings less capital consumption allowances as reported in the *Economic Report of the President*) includes both personal savings undertaken by individuals and savings done on behalf of individuals by corporations, but it does not include public sector savings (i.e., the deficits or surpluses of federal, state, and local governments). The denominator is gross domestic product less capital consumption allowances and taxes (also as reported in the *Economic Report of the President*), and it represents the direct income of individuals plus profits earned on their behalf and retained by corporations. These savings rates are slightly higher than those commonly mentioned, largely because the denominator is net of taxes.

The rate-of-return series is computed directly from the data in table 2.1—the interest rate minus the fraction of interest paid in taxes (which yields the nominal after-tax interest rate) minus inflation, plus a fixed 4 percent premium for equity. The series only varies, however, with variations in interest rates, tax rates, and inflation rates, as the premium is fixed.

While there are fluctuations in both measures, one is struck by the observation that the drop in the savings rate in the 1980s is, accompanied by a rise in the after-tax rate of return. This is precisely the opposite of what one would expect if saving rates increased with the rate of return. Pretax returns were relatively high, and tax rates on capital were relatively low by historical standards. Thus, as a simple exercise, it is hard to argue that increased tax rates had much to do with the low current savings rates.

Economists try to bring to bear some statistical tests of the relationship between variables such as these. Of course savings rates tend to be affected by other variables as well. One variable that is quite likely to affect savings rates is economic downturns, when individuals are normally expected to reduce their savings rates to maintain current

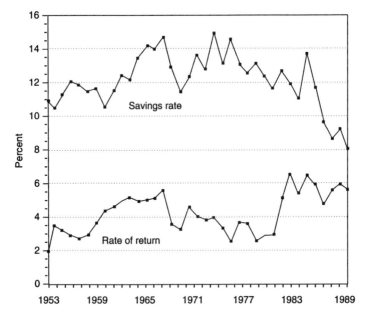

Figure 2.2
Savings rates and estimated rates of return. Based on table B.7, appendix B

consumption levels in the face of a temporary reduction in income. Many other factors can affect savings rates as well. For example, increased social security coverage might be expected to reduce savings over time, while an increased life span or earlier retirement might be expected to increase it.

A number of attempts to examine this relationship between savings and rates of return through multivariate statistical analysis have produced ambiguous evidence; Bovenberg (1989) and Ballard (1990) survey much of the recent literature. Some studies failed to account for inflation and/or taxes, and their results must be suspect.[5] After correcting for these factors, Boskin (1978) found a positive coefficient for the rate of return, which ranged between 0.2 and 0.6. This coefficient was statistically significant, indicating that it was not a result of random relationships. While these responses are not huge, they are not insignificant, particularly at the upper range.

In subsequent work, however, Howrey and Hymans (1980) found that Boskin's results were not very robust. Making some minor changes in specification or altering the time period caused the relationship found by Boskin to disappear. Carlino (1982) found an insignificant (and negative) relationship between savings and interest rates. Friend and Hasbrouck (1983) find no evidence that there is a significant positive savings response to rate of return—indeed, many of their regressions reveal a negative relationship between savings and rate of return. Bosworth (1984) also reported results similar to those of Howrey and Hymans. In general, his results suggested that one could obtain small positive elasticities with some specifications and time periods but not with others. Skinner and Feenberg (1991) find a negative relationship between savings and rate of return with a simple regression that spanned four decades, though they obtained different results for other time periods.

The traditional empirical studies, which suggest that rates of return have little effect on the savings rate, are all based on studies in which rates of savings and rates of return for the aggregate economy along with other variables are examined over time. Another empirical approach compares savings rates and rates of return across individuals in a single period or over a brief period of time. Unfortunately, such studies are extremely hard to perform because it is so difficult to observe savings and permanent income, or to take account of life-cycle differences in savings. Moreover, since all individuals face the same pretax rates of return, tax rates determine the variation in after-tax return across individuals. In a progressive tax system these tax rates are correlated with income. Thus it is difficult to disentangle the effects on savings arising from differences in after-tax return from the effects arising from differences in incomes. For these reasons cross-sectional analysis has generally not been used to study savings behavior.[6]

Conclusion

The insights of economic theory and empirical evidence suggest that though increasing the savings rate is an important and desirable goal, approaches that reduce taxes and increase after-tax rates of return appear to be dubious options. Theory provides no clear direction, suggesting that increasing taxes on capital income could increase or decrease private savings. The empirical evidence is mixed and inadequate to justify any certainty about the direction—or magnitude—of effects.

While this research does not provide evidence of a strong savings response to a reduction of taxes on capital income, the conclusions should be modified by the issue of how the tax reduction is financed. Earlier it was shown that an increase in the rate of return can, in theory, decrease savings. When considering changes in the rate of return caused by changes in taxes, this effect arises from an "income effect"—the fact that individuals keep more of the earnings of their investments and can potentially consume more both in the present and in the future. Such an income effect would occur if the reduction in taxes is financed from increased deficits. Indeed, a reduction in national (overall) savings is even more likely to take place because the government is dissaving as well. If the tax reduction is financed by substituting an alternative tax, the income effects that tend to decrease private savings could be altered. In that case the effects depend on whose income is altered, a topic discussed in the following section.

There may be a more direct route to increasing savings—increasing government savings. National savings is the sum of government savings and private savings. Assuming that changes in government savings do not produce offsetting increases in private savings, this is a straightforward route to increasing the overall savings rate.[7]

Capital Income Taxation and Economic Efficiency

Normative or prescriptive economics is concerned with what types of policies tend to maximize welfare. If a tax is distorting, then economic efficiency may be improved by substituting a different type of tax that is less distorting.

What Is Economic Efficiency?

The argument from normative economics for eliminating capital income taxes would focus not on savings but on the distortions (inefficiencies) introduced by capital income taxes. Several concepts of efficiency are frequently used, occasionally without clarifying them. On occasion "efficiency" is used interchangeably with the notion of effectiveness or "bang for the buck." Thus a tax incentive is efficient when it accomplishes its purpose at a minimal cost in revenues regardless of whether the purpose is worth pursuing.

A second use of the term relates to the administration and compliance costs. Thus a tax system is efficient if it collects taxes without large administrative costs to the government and without large compliance costs to the taxpayer. While such issues are clearly relevant to the design of tax structures and are discussed in the final section of this chapter, administrative cost is a different concept from the issue of minimizing the cost of economic distortions.

The third and primary definition of efficiency refers to minimizing the distortions in the allocation of resources caused by taxes and on using the tax system to correct failures of private markets to allocate resources efficiently. The cost of any misallocation of resources, however generated (through taxes or private market failures), is called a "deadweight loss." When this deadweight loss refers to the distortions resulting from taxes, it is often called an "excess burden," referring to the excess of the cost of the tax (in reduced welfare) over the revenue collected. For example, if collecting $100 in revenue makes individuals $110 worse off, then the excess burden is $10.

Two factors tend to make an excess burden large relative to revenue collected—a high tax rate and a relatively large behavioral response to a tax rate. For a given responsiveness, increasing the tax increases the excess burden more than proportionately. The basic reason that the excess burden rises proportionally faster than the tax wedge can be illustrated by the example of a consumption distortion, such as might occur with differential excise taxes. The excess burden measures the change in the value of consumer surplus. Consumer surplus is the excess of the value of a commodity above the price being paid. Units of a good that have a large consumer surplus will continue to be purchased at very high prices, while units with a small consumer surplus will no longer be purchased is the price rises by a small amount. Thus a small tax would eliminate from the market those commodities with a small consumer surplus on average, while a large tax would eliminate commodities with a large consumer surplus on average. Doubling the tax will more than double the consumer surplus.

For a market with many individuals in it, the excess burden rises roughly with the square of the tax wedge (it rises exactly with the square for linear relationships). The tax wedge is not necessarily the tax rate, since it refers to the percentage by which tax inclusive prices or incomes rise. For a sales tax on products, it is the tax rate itself. For a tax on income, the tax wedge is the tax rate divided by 1 minus the tax rate. Thus a tax rate on income of 25 percent will have a tax wedge of 1/3 (0.25/(1 − 0.25)). That is, the pretax rate of return will be one-third above the after-tax rate of return. The square of the tax wedge is 1/9. Doubling the tax rate to 50 percent will result in a tax wedge of 1 (0.5/(1 − 0.5)) and a square of the tax wedge of 1. Thus doubling the tax rate will triple the tax wedge in this case and will cause the excess burden to (roughly) increase ninefold (the square of the increase in the tax wedge). That is, doubling of an income tax will result in an excess burden that is nine times as large, since doubling the tax rate measured as a fraction of pretax return is the same as tripling the tax wedge, which is measured as a fraction of after-tax income.

This excess burden can take the form of encouraging individuals to consume a less desirable mix of products (e.g., an excise tax). Some taxes can also cause inefficient production processes (use of an uneconomic mix of labor and capital). An example would be a tax on capital that discourages not only the overall sales of a product but also the desirability of using capital to produce it. Capital income taxes might also result in individuals holding an undesirable mix of assets in their portfolios. When considering the aggregate level of taxes on capital income, it refers to encouraging individuals to consume more in the present and less in the future, since, as discussed above, taxes on capital income raise the "price" of future consumption.

Given some ability to substitute present for future consumption, the welfare of any individual would be increased if taxes could be collected in a lump sum (i.e., a fixed amount that will not vary with behavior). Such a lump-sum tax would not distort the choice between consuming in the present and in the future. Collection of taxes in this fashion is not feasible for distributional reasons, and all taxes cause some distortions. For example, even uniform consumption taxes (i.e., sales taxes) or wage taxes cause a distortion since they favor leisure over consumption.[8]

But revenues must be collected in some fashion, so the case for eliminating capital income taxes on efficiency grounds is uncertain. Taxing the return to capital causes individuals to favor current over future consumption. Lowering the tax rates on capital income for a given revenue requirement causes tax rates to be higher on either wages or consumption. Individuals can also choose between consuming goods or enjoying leisure, and wage or consumption taxes cause individuals to choose too much leisure (with income held constant). Raising the tax rate on wage or consumption taxes will cause an increase in this distortion.

Theory does not tell us, a priori, whether eliminating capital income taxes will increase overall efficiency, since it reduces one distortion at the price of increasing another. As in the case of the effect of taxes on inhibiting savings, the answer must come from empirical evidence. The following section discusses some of the existing models and the implications for efficiency that they found. This section is unavoidably complex. A capsule summary of this discussion is provided for the reader who is less interested in the details:

1. The efficiency effects depend on assumptions about behavioral effects. If individuals are relatively unwilling to substitute consumption over time and relatively willing to substitute leisure for consumption of goods, then a significant tax on capital income would constitute part of an optimal tax system. These behavioral effects are difficult to estimate empirically.

2. As a corollary, it is possible that eliminating capital income taxes causes a loss in welfare due to distortions in other taxes. Such results

can be obtained when using behavioral assumptions that are in the range of those empirically estimated. Thus these models cannot resolve the issue of whether eliminating the capital income tax is desirable. Yet these welfare effects appear to be relatively small in magnitude, and a partial elimination of capital income taxes may provide a larger benefit than a complete elimination.

3. In the more fully developed life-cycle models, substituting tax bases can cause significant redistribution across age cohorts and that may be the most important consequence from a policy standpoint. Indeed, even if there is an efficiency gain to eliminating capital income taxes, such a policy may not be desirable if these distributional effects are troubling. In this case an income tax may be favored simply because it already exists (had we begun with a consumption tax, it would be favored).

4. Despite the attention given to modeling intertemporal choices, there are many unsatisfactory aspects of all of these models as proxies of actual economic behavior. In particular, many of the more sophisticated models predict savings responses that are extremely large compared to fluctuations that have occurred historically. Thus the results of these models should be considered with some skepticism.

The Efficiency of Capital Income Taxation: The Models

The study of the efficiency effects of capital income taxation has turned out to be a major challenge, a mathematical and computational challenge, as well as an empirical one. Indeed, most of the models of this effect are relatively recent, largely because of the need for sophisticated computers to solve vast arrays of equations. These models also require estimates, presumably derived from empirical studies, of the willingness of individuals to substitute consumption across these time periods, a response that is difficult to measure.[9]

The models are not empirical research; rather, they incorporate some sort of empirical measures that must be obtained from some other source into a specific model of individual behavior, and then derive the welfare effects of taxation. The models themselves cannot provide evidence of an empirical relationship; rather empirical relationships derived through other research are required to use the model.

This point is occasionally confused even in the economics literature. For example, the Summers (1981) life-cycle model, which will be discussed subsequently, has been occasionally cited as evidence of a large savings elasticity because it is necessary if such a model to be consistent with other observed data such as the ratio of wealth to income. This study has sometimes been included with citations to the empirical literature on savings discussed in the previous section on tax policy and savings. But it is possible to fit any model to a given wealth to income ratio by choosing certain unknown parameters, in particular, the relative absolute valuation of consumption (referred to as a time rate of preference) in each period. Summers's model sets this valuation exogenously, and the model will then be consistent with wealth-to-income ratios only with a particular savings response. As Evans (1983) points out, such a model can be made consistent with a variety of savings responses by changing these unknown taste parameters or other features of the model (such as adding a bequest motive).

The welfare effects derived from these models reflect both the behavioral responses assumed and the fundamental structure of the model. An elaboration of these behavioral responses is in order. The savings elasticity is the percentage change in savings divided by the percentage change in the after-tax rate of return. The intertemporal substitution elasticity is the percentage change in the ratio of current to future consumption divided by the percentage change in the ratios of the prices of consumption today and consumption in the future. If the price of current consumption is a dollar, the price of consumption a year from now is less, specifically $1/(1 + r)$, where r is the after-tax rate of return. In very simple two-period models where all income is earned in the first period, the intertemporal substitution elasticity can be derived from the savings elasticity. In more complex models the savings response is a result of the intertemporal substitution elasticity.

Models of the efficiency effects of capital income taxation fall into two broad categories: representative-consumer models and overlapping-generations, life-cycle models. The representative-consumer model treats individuals in the economy as if there is one, infinitely lived, consumer. It is the easier model to work with computationally, but it does not distinguish between the welfare of different age cohorts of individuals in society. The life-cycle model separates individuals into representative age cohorts, so it seems to provide a more realistic picture of society. These life-cycle modeling efforts will be discussed in more detail. Before turning to life-cycle models, I well discuss some of the representative-consumer models.

Representative-Consumer Models
In part because of computational ease, one of the earliest and best known models of taxpayer behavior uses a form of the representative-consumer approach. This model is sometimes referred to as the Fullerton-Shoven-Whalley (or FSW) model after the researchers who initially developed and refined it. Many papers have been published using this model to study many different types of tax distortions (e.g., differential taxation of different types of capital income), but the modeling of consumption and savings are laid out in the most detail in Ballard et al. (1985).

Ballard and his coauthors further simplified the representative-consumer model by assuming myopic behavior and a relatively simple consumption/savings choice, much like the simple two-period model discussed earlier. Even though the representative individual in this model lives an infinite period of time, their modeling approach, for reasons of simplicity, is not derived from an explicit examination of choice over this time horizon but rather has the individual make choices one period at a time.

Ballard et al. found that a consumption tax as compared to a neutral income tax (one that taxed all capital income at the same rate) would increase welfare by slightly over 2 percent. Since the base for welfare included both the present value of consumption and the present value of leisure, the welfare gain as a fraction of consumption alone would be larger. Part of this welfare gain reflected a relatively large savings elasticity and, in the structure of the model, also reflected a relatively large intertemporal substitution elasticity—the elasticity that is crucial to measuring the excess burden of capital income taxation. The myopic, representative-consumer approach is recognized as less than perfect by the authors, who state: "Adoption of an explicit life cycle structure would be a welcome addition to the analysis of many intertemporal issues" (p. 242).

A different version of the representative-consumer model is one where a single infinitely lived consumer with foresight is used to represent individuals in the economy.[10] Examples of this infinite-time-horizon, representative-consumer model include Chamley (1981) and Jorgenson and Yun (1990). In such a model the utility of consumption over an infinite time horizon is added up with and without taxes. Because these models must eventually return to a steady state, the long run capital/labor ratio, and thus the long run savings rate, depend solely on the ease with which capital can be added to labor. This effect is measured by the "factor substitution elasticity" (the percentage change in the ratio of capital to labor divided by the percentage change in their relative prices). Savings rates in the transition are, however, affected by the intertemporal substitution elasticity.

Chamley's (1981) model found a tax of 30 percent (the general magnitude of the current estimated effective tax rate on capital) produces a welfare cost of 0.77 percent of consumption. These numbers assumed a factor substitution elasticity and an intertemporal substitution elasticity of one. While the study does not report results with different values of the elasticities for this particular tax rate, other results indicated that the welfare cost is not greatly affected by the intertemporal substitution elasticity. A replication of his model confirms this result for the discrete change—an intertemporal substitution elasticity of 0.25 reduces the welfare cost to 0.62 percent of consumption. Reducing the factor substitution elasticity appears to have more powerful effects; reducing it by one half appears to reduce the welfare effects by a similar magnitude.

Chamley's exercise assumed that elimination of capital income taxes would be replaced by lump sum payments. Although he considered the case of a variable labor supply, he did not consider the policy of replacing an income tax with a wage or consumption tax. This substitution can be important, since reducing taxes on capital income can cause the tax distortion between labor and leisure to be greater by raising the tax on consumption (or wages) which governs this distortion. Jorgenson and Yun (1990) incorporate this feature into a model that also looks at the effects of differential taxation of capital income. They found that moving from a pure income tax to a pure consumption tax reduced welfare. (They do not express these losses as percentages of consumption, but the losses appear to be in the neighborhood of 0.5 percent of consumption.)

One troubling aspect of the infinite-horizon, representative-consumer model is that the gains become extremely large when the factor substitution elasticity is very large. This result occurs because long run equilibrium in the model is always forced to a particular solution: namely that with the removal of tax the pretax rate of return must be driven down to the original after-tax rate of return in order to return the economy to steady state growth. When capital is easily substitutable with labor in production, a great deal of capital must eventually be added to drive the rate of return down to this point and the consequence is a great deal of savings response—and thus a large welfare effect.

Another troublesome point is that the savings rate would be expected to shift dramatically when the tax rate on capital income falls. With the unitary intertemporal elasticity assumption, the initial savings rate rises by 13 percentage points, and even with the lower 0.25 elasticity the rate rises by 5 percentage points. By historical standards these are very large shifts in the savings rates. In the long run the savings rate will depend solely on the capital/output ratio, which in turn depends on how easily capital can be substituted with labor in the production function. While these infinitely lived consumer models are computationally easier to deal with than the overlapping-generations, life-cycle models, they are troublesome as a method of representing behavior of many diverse economic agents.

Life-Cycle Models
Life-cycle models account for individuals of diverse ages, earning wages, and consuming over many years. A new adult entering the work force will face fifty to sixty years of life and will typically have an uneven pattern of labor income (low initially, then higher, and low or zero again during retirement). These models, which are also called "overlapping-generation models," also account for the fact that many generations coexist at any one time.

The fundamental proposition of such a model is that at any one time there are many generations, or cohorts, of individuals. The cohort just entering the work force will live for many years, part at work and part in retirement. This cohort must finance consumption in retirement by saving out of wage earnings. (In some versions of these models individuals expect to receive a bequest at some point, and they plan to leave a bequest when they die.) The next cohort has one year of life less, the next two years less, and so forth, until all of the generations are accounted for. Individuals in each generation differ in how they expect to receive income over their lifetimes: Younger generations receive most of their income from wages, while retired generations receive all income from capital. Each cohort differs in how much they save, with the greatest savings rates typically occurring in the high earning years of middle age. Each cohort also responds differently to tax changes.

An overlapping-generations, life-cycle model does not rely directly on an estimate of the savings response, as discussed above. Rather, the savings responses result from two factors. The first depends on whose income is being reduced or increased (a distribution or income effect). The second factor depends on how readily individuals are willing to trade future for present consumption and how readily they are willing to trade consumption for leisure. Again, such a model does not provide any information about the magnitude of the savings response of its own accord, since it can be made consistent with any savings response. That is, any such model can be made to fit observed facts about the economy (e.g., the ratio of capital to income) by appropriate choice of unobservable taste parameters, while allowing either a very large or a very small willingness to substitute between present and future consumption. To estimate the welfare effects of tax substitutions, it is necessary to introduce an estimate of the substitution effects.

Overlapping generations, life-cycle models may be more appealing than the representative-consumer models because they account for what really occurs in society—generations of individuals with finite lives. Nevertheless, as complex as these models are, they are still subject to a number of serious drawbacks. Some models have not allowed for bequests, although evidence indicates that bequests are very important in explaining the aggregate level of wealth. We do not fully understand the motives for leaving bequests. The empirical estimates of behavioral responses are uncertain and typically rely on different studies using different samples. They omit a great many factors, such as much of the detail of the tax code, uncertainty, investment in human capital, and the effects of government programs (including transfer programs that have life-cycle effects). With the exception of Fullerton and Rogers (1993), who do not report comparable efficiency effects,[11] they also treat individuals in a given age cohort as identical: The only source of variation in income, earnings, savings, and consumption is date of birth. Thus most such models cannot explore differences across individuals with each group. In addition not all of the models consider variable labor supply. They typically distinguish only between idealized forms of consumption, wage, and income taxes. These caveats should be kept in mind in assessing what these models suggest about the effects of capital income taxation.

Initial modeling of welfare effects of the capital income tax in an overlapping-generations model by Summers (1981) suggested large potential gains in welfare from eliminating the taxes on capital income. The gains reported by Summers are strongly affected by several important structural aspects and behavioral assumptions of his model, however. The following discussion is useful in stressing how various assumptions can alter the estimated efficiency costs of the capital income tax.

Summers's analysis demonstrated that the gain to future generations depended on whether capital income taxes were replaced by wage taxes or consumption taxes. A wage tax substitution would simply eliminate all taxes on capital income, including the capital that already exists; the tax base would be wage income. Substituting a consumption tax for the income tax would eliminate taxes on new capital but not existing capital. A sales tax or value-added tax could be directly substituted for the income tax.

Alternatively, allowing deductions for net additions to savings (and inclusions of net reductions in savings) under an income tax could accomplish the same result and convert the tax base to consumption. The deduction of the cost of net investment effectively subjects the return to a zero tax rate. For example, suppose that the tax rate is 50 percent and the interest rate is 10 percent. An individual who invests $100 under an income tax will have an account that grows to $110 after a year, pay taxes of $5 on the $10 of earning, and have a net return of 5 percent. By allowing the deduction of net savings, an individual who invests $100 under a consumption tax will receive a tax benefit of $50, reducing the net cost of the investment to $50. A year from now, the investment, which has grown to $110, is withdrawn. Since this amount is a net reduction in savings, it is included in taxable income. A tax of $55 is paid, and the remaining $55 is available for consumption. The $55 received after a year represents a rate of return of 10 percent—the pretax rate of return.

In understanding the potential effects of a reduction in taxes, it is important to know whether the substitution is in the nature of a wage tax substitution or a consumption tax substitution. Cutting the corporate tax rate and raising the individual tax rate to make up the revenue would be an example of a tax change that is in the nature of a partial wage tax substitution, since the overall tax on capital would fall and the overall tax on wage income would rise. Some tax changes, such as a tax credit allowed for investment, occupy an intermediate position between a wage and consumption tax substitution.[12] It is difficult to find tax proposals, other than those proposing wholesale replacement, that are completely in the nature of consumption tax substitution.

Summers found a large long-run welfare gain of 13.4 percent of lifetime income for a consumption tax replacement. This welfare gain did not relate to the increased level of consumption to be found in the long run. Rather it measured the increase in the value of lifetime income for individuals living in the long run with their adaptations to the new tax regime. The gains were much smaller for a wage tax, only 5 percent.

Summers's model had several limitations. One, which he acknowledged, was that it did not account for redistribution across the generations. A consumption tax increases the tax burden on older individuals and reduces it on young and future generations. A wage tax does the opposite. A switch to a consumption tax involves a one-time capital levy, and this capital is possessed by the old. A switch to wage taxation eliminates the tax on returns to existing capital, thereby reducing the taxes of those older individuals whose income is primarily from capital. Included in Summers's estimates of the welfare of individuals living in the long run steady state are redistributions between generations, which do not isolate the effects of distortions from the effects of income shifts. The welfare of future generations could be improved by taking money from the old and giving it to young and future generations, but this gain would not measure the distorting effects of taxes. If one could correct for these redistributional effects, the welfare gains in the Summers model (which does not allow for a labor response) would be identical and fall between those of his wage and consumption tax estimates. That is, his model indicates that the income-compensated efficiency gains fall between 5 percent and 13 percent, but not where in this broad range they fall.

Gravelle (1991b) developed a method for correcting for the direct redistribution that occurs as a result of changing the tax base and the resultant changes in wages and rates of return. This method implicitly sets compensation payments to each generation, which exactly offset the changes in income from the change in the tax base. Using this method to estimate efficiency gains in the Summers model would lead to a 6 percent welfare gain for both wage and consumption taxes for individuals living in the long run steady state (gains of transitional generations, particularly of existing older generations, would be smaller). This welfare gain would, however, be considered large—to gain an overall increase in welfare of 6 percent by shifting the tax base could be viewed as a proposition well worth undertaking.

There are other concerns about the Summers conclusions for evaluating current tax policy. The tax rate assumed by Summers (50 percent) is too high for current law and indeed is too high for pre-1981 law except in the case of very high inflation rates. Table B.1 in appendix B indicates a capital income tax rate of 33 percent, and even this rate is overstated because of the exclusion of lightly taxed intangible assets (which are virtually impossible to measure). A rough, rounded, estimate of the current income tax rate is 30 percent. The tax wedge— the excess of the pretax return over the after tax return is 1, or $0.5/(1 - 0.5)$ in the case of a 50 percent tax rate but only 43 percent, or $0.3/(1 - 0.3)$ in the case of a 30 percent tax rate. Since the welfare gain rises in proportion to the square of the tax wedge, these tax measurement issues are crucial. Indeed a simulation of Summers's model with a 30 percent tax leads to a welfare increase (with income compensation) for individuals living in the long run, only one-fifth as large—1.2 percent. (This ratio of 1/5 is roughly equivalent to the ratio of the square of the tax wedge at a 30 percent rate to the square of the tax wedge at a 50 percent rate.) This illustration shows that a correct measure of the tax rate is crucial to the size of welfare costs.

A second important issue is the intertemporal substitution elasticity, set at one for the results reported above. Auerbach and Kotlikoff (1987) and Hall (1988) review current research in this area; Summers's measure would be at the high end of such estimates. Auerbach and Kotlikoff assumed a value of 0.25 based on their review; Hall argues that the value is probably below 0.10. Moreover, while such an estimate is notoriously difficult to determine, such high estimates are not plausible given the observations of limited response of the savings rates. Gravelle (1991b) using an elasticity of 0.25 finds an efficiency gain of 0.61 in the Summers model (using the 30 percent tax rate). The welfare effects of the life cycle model are more sensitive to this assumption than in the representative consumer model.

Second, the model employs a fixed labor supply. If labor supply were allowed to be responsive to taxes, the higher labor (or consumption) taxes necessary to make up revenue would increase other distortions. With a responsive labor supply, welfare gains could be either positive or negative. (Summers's model also assumes that all individuals in the economy earn the same wage rate.)

Auerbach and Kotlikoff (1987) subsequently developed a more sophisticated overlapping-generations model, which accounted for redistribution and also allowed labor supply to respond to tax rates. (They also allowed wages to vary over an individual's lifetime, so that individuals of different age cohorts earned different wages.) Based on a midpoint of the range in the literature, they used a smaller intertemporal substitution elasticity than Summers—0.25. Their finding was that a consumption tax would make future generations better off, by 2.32 percent of lifetime welfare, but that only about 10 percent of the gain is a true efficiency gain; most of it represented a transfer of income from prior generations. They also found that a wage tax substitution made future generations worse off and, even when the results were controlled for redistribution, eliminating taxes on capital income resulted in a less efficient system. (Their model used a tax rate on capital of 15 percent which is too low; at the same time the increase in the consumption/wage tax rate would be greater with a higher capital income tax rate.) The Auerbach and Kotlikoff model therefore suggested much smaller efficiency effects from eliminating capital income taxes than those suggested by the Summers model.[13]

Gravelle (1991b), further exploring the influence of estimated behavioral responses, found that the pure efficiency gains from either type of tax substitution in the model developed by Auerbach and Kotlikoff were ambiguous within the range of empirically estimated responses. If individuals are relatively unwilling to substitute present for future consumption but are relatively willing to substitute leisure for consumption of goods, then a significant tax on capital income would constitute part of an optimal tax system.

Given the difficulty in quantifying these empirical relationships, such an issue is not likely to be resolved. Like the infinite horizon models, however, these models imply a significant savings response to certain tax changes unless very low intertemporal substitution elasticities are used. In general, the consumption tax substitution always leads to an increase in the savings rate, as the income and price effects work in the same direction. (Older individuals who tend to be dissaving will have their income reduced.) The wage tax substitution can cause the savings rate to either rise or fall, as income and price effects work in opposite directions (older individuals who are dissaving will have their incomes reduced). In the short run these savings responses can be very pronounced. For example, Auerbach and Kotlikoff report that in their model, assuming a 0.25 intertemporal substitution elasticity, the savings rate initially quadruples with a switch to consumption tax, despite their use of a relatively low capital income tax rate. The implausibility of this result suggests that either some revision in the model or use of a much lower intertemporal substitution elasticity—and a lower efficiency gain—would be warranted. Ballard (1990) elaborates on this issue of the savings response, suggesting the need to develop models that are fundamentally realistic (as in the case of life-cycle models) but that also yield more reasonable savings responses.

These types of life-cycle simulation experiments basically suggest several conclusions. First, a switch to a consumption tax should increase the savings rate, while a switch to a wage tax has ambiguous effects. Second, eliminating capital income taxes leads to efficiency effects that are ambiguous in direction but seem likely to be small, particularly if small intertemporal substitution elasticities that seem more consistent with observed variations in savings behavior are used. Third, the primary consequences of tax substitutions are not in gains in economic efficiency but rather redistribution of income across generations. A primary consequence of substituting a wage tax base for an income tax base is a windfall for current older generations, while a primary consequence of substituting a consumption tax base for income taxes is a lump sum tax on current older generations.

Practically speaking, it is impossible to design a large tax change that would not have significant redistribution effects; even if such a change could be devised it would have to be a mix of a wage tax and a consumption tax substitution, where efficiency gains would be doubtful (recall that Auerbach and Kotlikoff found a loss from the switch to a wage tax). On the whole, the results of these modeling efforts do not appear to establish a compelling reason to eliminate capital income taxation on efficiency grounds, particularly if there is a preference for avoiding intergenerational redistribution.

The intergenerational redistribution effects of going to a consumption tax—which is more likely to yield an efficiency gain—might be considered acceptable if, for example, current government programs have been viewed as providing excessive benefits to the elderly. At the same time of course there may be a natural concern about altering the tax burden on older individuals who are no longer able to adjust their work and savings behaviors to respond to their new tax burdens.

Second, even if distributional effects are undesirable, there may be a more compelling case for reductions in capital income taxes which stopped short of complete elimination. Since other taxes must be increased to offset lost revenues, a partial reduction of capital income taxes could yield a larger gain than complete substitution. That is, the optimal capital income tax rate may be greater than zero but still less than the current tax rate. For example, using the Gravelle (1991b) model, eliminating all capital income taxes in favor of a wage tax would yield a long run gain of about 0.1 percent of consumption in one set of simulations. Eliminating only a third of the tax—approximately the amount for a policy to integrate corporate and individual income taxes—would yield a gain of 0.23 percent of consumption. Moreover complete substitution may yield a loss, but partial substitution a small gain. At the same time the intergenerational shifts in income would be much smaller.

Finally, shifting to a consumption or wage tax base might be more beneficial because it would also eliminate differentials across different types of assets, an issue taken up in future chapters. Much of this gain from reducing differentials across different types of assets might, however, be accomplished within the framework of an income tax, as discussed in chapter 4. Some problems, however, such as the favorable treatment of owner-occupied housing or precision in the measurement of economic depreciation, cannot be easily solved in the framework of an income tax.

Distributional Issues and Equity Issues

There are a variety of distributional consequences to substituting wage or consumption taxes for capital income taxes. In the popular debate the focus is frequently on the distributional effects across incomes. The discussion of distributional considerations in the economics literature includes the distribution across incomes, the distribution across age groups, the interrelationship between these two, and also the issue of horizontal equity.

Consider first the distributional effects across incomes. Individuals with high annual incomes are characterized by both higher savings rates and a larger fraction of income received from capital. Table 2.2 shows the dramatic differences across annual income levels in the share of income from capital, illustrating the importance of capital income at the higher income levels. Thus reducing or eliminating capital income taxation in favor of higher wage taxes would make the tax system less progressive with respect to annual income unless the rate structure is made more graduated. This fact plays an important role in the public debate over tax policy (although, as will be discussed subsequently, the use of annual incomes is somewhat misleading).

Shifting to a consumption tax base could also make the tax system less progressive because low-income individuals tend to consume a

Table 2.2
Distribution of family income by source

Decile	Capital	Labor	Transfer	Other
First	6.7	23.9	62.4	7.0
Second	6.3	39.9	47.0	6.8
Third	7.8	60.3	24.8	7.1
Fourth	9.5	67.3	16.1	7.2
Fifth	9.7	72.2	11.3	6.8
Sixth	9.8	76.9	8.0	5.4
Seventh	10.3	78.8	5.9	5.0
Eighth	9.4	82.3	4.3	4.0
Ninth	10.0	83.4	2.8	3.8
Tenth	28.9	66.7	1.4	3.0
Top 5%	35.5	60.7	1.1	2.7
Top 1%	47.8	50.5	0.4	1.2
All deciles	16.6	72.3	6.8	4.4

Source: Congressional Budget Office, *The Changing Distribution of Federal Taxes: 1975–1990*, p. 67.

larger fraction of their incomes than higher income individuals. The importance of this factor can be shown with data on the distribution of a value-added tax (these data are meant to show the importance of disposition of income in influencing distribution, since a consumption tax could be enacted as a direct tax at graduated rates). The Treasury Department (1984) estimated that a flat rate value added tax of 10 percent, even after allowing for indexed transfers, would impose a burden of 9.6 percent in the $0 to $10,000 income class, 6.9 percent in the $10,000 to $15,000 class, 6.0 percent in the $15,000 to $20,000 class, 5.2 percent in the $20,000 to $30,000 class, 4.5 percent in the $30,000 to $50,000 class, 3.6 percent in the $50,000 to $100,000 class, and 1.8 percent in the $200,000 and over class. These differences reflect a rising savings rate with income, which becomes very pronounced at the high end of the income scale.

This distributional issue would not, however, necessarily preclude a tax substitution given the ability to restructure tax rates to maintain the progressivity of the tax system. For example, the rate structure of a tax could be made more progressive as a distributional offset if a wage tax base were desired. Similarly consumption taxes could be imposed in many different ways, which could have very different effects on distribution across annual incomes. One method would be to replace the current income tax base with a consumption tax base by allowing the deduction of additions to savings and the taxation of reductions in savings. (Corporate taxes would also need to be placed on a consumption tax base by allowing deductions for increases in investment and taxes on net borrowing, or they could be repealed altogether.) The rate structure could then be further graduated to offset distributional changes, although the graduation would have to be very steep to avoid significant redistribution.

A direct consumption tax (i.e., a tax imposed directly on individuals rather than indirectly through a tax on consumption goods) is, however, more difficult to implement than an indirect consumption tax, as it requires measurement of net savings. Moreover a consumption tax would include funds borrowed in income (to the extent that they are used for consumption). Including loans in the tax base is an unfamiliar concept that might be resisted by taxpayers when a direct consumption tax is imposed.

In fact much of the popular discussion of consumption taxes has focused on indirect taxes. The simplest of such taxes conceptually would be a national sales taxes. An equivalent tax would be a European style value-added tax (VAT), which uses a credit mechanism. Such a VAT would impose a tax on gross receipts and provide a credit for taxes paid by suppliers of either intermediate goods or capital goods. A VAT is equivalent to a sales tax; it merely collects the tax in stages. Another equivalent tax, if a single rate is applied, is a subtraction method VAT, where firms pay a tax on gross receipts minus purchases. This tax is also occasionally referred to as business transfer tax (BTT). While these taxes are familiar and relatively easy to implement, they would dramatically alter the distribution of the tax burden across incomes.

There are also some hybrid methods. For example, a proposal by Bradford (1986) would combine a graduated tax on wages as a direct tax by eliminating capital income such as interest, dividends, and capital gains from the current income tax base with a business tax on the difference between the wage and consumption tax base. Businesses would be subject to a tax on gross receipts minus purchases minus wages. For a complete elimination of capital income taxes—through this hybrid tax, a direct wage tax, or a direct consumption tax—marginal tax rates on labor income or consumption would have to be more steeply graduated to preclude redistribution across taxpayers of different income levels.

The distributional consequences of eliminating or reducing taxes on capital have come to be seen as considerably more complex than the issue of progressivity of taxes in a simple cross section of incomes. The distributional consequences across generations have already been noted. Table 2.3 illustrates the variations in income sources for different age groups (although the underlying measurement of income concept is quite different from that in table 2.2). As this table indicates, the share of income from capital rises as age increases.

In addition life-cycle models make it clear that considering distribution of income in a cross section may provide an incomplete picture of tax progressivity. For example, even if all individuals in the economy had the same lifetime income, so that a wage tax and an income tax would produce equal lifetime tax burdens, we would observe individuals with higher incomes or lower incomes simply because of their stage in the life cycle. Young individuals with low wages and little savings would be characterized by low incomes, a higher consumption to income ratio, and little or no capital income. Individuals in the middle years would have higher incomes, a lower ratio of consumption to income, and a higher ratio of capital income to total income. Retired individuals would have no labor income, lower incomes, and higher ratios of consumption to income.

At this time the lack of data on wealth and the evolution of income and wealth over the life cycle makes it difficult to assess the long run distributional consequences of excluding capital income from the tax base. Moreover individuals experience transitory increases and decreases in income as well. Individuals with transitory decreases in income will likely have low savings rates out of current income, while those with transitory increases will likely have high savings rates. These factors influence the measured differences in savings rates across current incomes and overstate the differences relative to normal incomes. Thus, owing to both life cycle and transitory reasons, the distributional effects arising from the income or savings behavior across the income classes are likely overstated as compared to a distribution that took into account lifetime income.

Nevertheless, it seems likely that individuals with low lifetime incomes would tend to save proportionally less. Social welfare programs such as social security, medicare, unemployment compensation, and welfare accommodate the needs of lower income individuals to protect themselves from transitory income losses and to provide for retirement to a much larger extent than for high-income individuals. Menchik and David (1983) find that lower income individuals are also

Table 2.3
Distribution of family income by age

Age	Capital	Labor	Transfer	Other
15–24	2.7	86.3	10.7	0.3
25–44	4.3	91.6	3.2	0.9
45–64	9.5	79.3	6.6	4.6
65 and over	26.6	14.9	52.0	6.6
All ages	8.0	77.8	10.1	4.4

Source: Calculated from U.S. Department of Commerce, Bureau of the Census, *Current Population Reports, Money Income of Households, Families and Persons in the United States,* table 34. Self-employment income allocated 25 percent to capital and 75 percent to labor; other income includes alimony, child support, and pensions. Capital gains are not included. Mean income is $7,853 in the 15–24 group, $22,788 in the 25–44 group, $25,310 in the 45–64 group, $15,079 in the over 65 group, and $19,842 overall.

less likely to leave bequests than wealthy individuals. Thus it seems likely that including capital income in the tax base would tend to lead to a more progressive tax system, and these distributional issues would have to be considered in eliminating the tax on capital income, perhaps requiring a more steeply graduated rate structure if progressivity were to be retained.

A final distributional issue is whether taxing savings is unfair to those individuals, with otherwise identical lifetime resources, who have a greater preference for future consumption. Perhaps the oldest argument for consumption taxes, dating back to Thomas Hobbes, is that individuals should be taxed on what they take from society (consumption) rather than what they contribute to society (income). Such an argument appeals to a different philosophy from that of normative economics, which stresses that value derives from the welfare of individuals, which is turn derives from consumption. In normative economics, consumption is not "evil" but rather the basis of the fundamental utilitarianism that is at the root of the economist's way of looking at the world (although consumption can be defined broadly to include altruism, enjoyment of leisure, and many other aspects of human nature).

Economic theory cannot be employed to answer the question of which tax base is fair in the context of equal treatment of equals. If individuals have different tastes for consumption over time their utility functions are, of course, different and there would be no way to determine what policy tends to make their welfare more or less equal. There does seem to be a general consensus that taxation should not be arbitrarily applied across individuals. For example, there would be little support for a tax differentiating across individuals because of physical characteristics such as height or eye color. Rather, some capacity to pay taxes appears to underlie the current notions of horizontal equity, and both income and consumption might be accepted as reasonable proxies for this capacity to pay.

Administrative Issues

A final issue concerning the desirability of taxing capital income is the administrative feasibility and compliance costs. An income tax system does encounter a number of administrative difficulties. The proper measurement of income requires rules for depreciation that are complex and imprecise. It also requires, in theory, measurement of items of imputed income. Since these imputed items have not been included in income, the income tax cannot be imposed on all income. One result is likely distortions in the consumption of housing.

But the other types of tax bases are not simple either. While wage taxation may appear to be quite straightforward, it is extremely diffi-cult—indeed, probably impossible—to separate capital income from labor income for closely held businesses where the owner may supply both capital and labor services. (The current payroll tax simply ignores this problem and thus taxes some of the capital income of these busi-nesses.)

Consumption taxes are easier for businesses, since they involve simply the expensing of capital acquisitions. (Difficulties would remain, however, for firms involved in financial activities such as banking, investment, and life insurance; these problems exist in the income tax as well.) But direct consumption taxes encounter numerous difficulties for most individuals. The consumption tax would begin with wages and then be supplemented by loans and withdrawals from savings and investment accounts, but with contributions to savings accounts and repayments of loans subtracted. Moreover gifts and inheritances should be included; currently these items must be accounted for only in the case of large transfers. Finally, a proper con-sumption tax would need to account for the changing value of owner occupied housing, since, unlike other directly held business assets, there is no measured flow of income from these assets.

Indirect consumption taxes, such as sales taxes, would be easier to administer, although any gains in administration must be weighed against the differences in the distribution of these taxes from the cur-rent income tax. Hybrid tax systems, such as the system proposed by Bradford which would subtract wages from business receipts and include them in a graduated individual tax, might be a compromise to reduce the complexities of a direct consumption tax.

Summary

Existing economic research and analysis suggests that the conse-quences of reducing the tax on capital income are mostly uncertain. Even stipulating that increasing the U.S. saving rate is desirable, there seems little evidence that decreasing tax rates on capital income would have much of an effect, especially if a revenue loss is created that is not made up in some other fashion. Shifting the tax base from income to consumption taxes is more likely to increase savings than shifting the tax base to wage taxes. But the magnitude of this effect is also uncertain, and it arises in part from imposition of a windfall tax on old people. If the objective of government policy is to increase savings, a more certain route may be to directly increase the government savings rate.

The efficiency effects of shifting to wage or consumption taxes are also uncertain in magnitude and direction. Moreover there are important distributional consequences, across age cohorts and across incomes, that would need to be considered in contemplating a shift in tax base. While such a tax shift may be desirable, the certitude with which arguments are often advanced for doing so appears unwarranted.

If the decision to move to a pure consumption- or wage-based tax were made, there would of course be no further issue of analyzing the effects of capital income tax. For the remainder of the book the assumption of a capital income tax base is given, and the analysis focuses on the economic issues surrounding the nature of a tax on capital.

3

Is the Capital Income Tax Structure Efficient?

In the economics literature, as well as in the tax policy debate, considerable attention has been focused on the efficiency of U.S. capital income taxation. The issue can be cast in these terms: Is it better to tax all capital income as uniformly as is administratively possible, or is it better to tax some forms of capital income more heavily than others? The changes enacted in the Tax Reform Act of 1986 clearly were intended to achieve more uniform taxation of capital, but the changes stopped short in several crucial respects. What is to be made of this? Did TRA 1986 move in the right direction, and should more be done? Or, would there be some payoff, as some have suggested, to moving away from uniform taxation of capital income?

To begin, it is important to recognize the difference between tax neutrality and efficiency. A capital income tax system is neutral if it taxes all investments at the same rate and hence, for a given capital stock, would not alter the allocation of capital. In an efficient tax system, taxes are collected in a fashion that produces the optimal allocation of resources. If there are no external (spillover) effects from one economic activity to another, no other policy-induced distortions or other "market failures," and if the economy is characterized by competitive behavior, a neutral capital income tax system would also be an efficient one. In such a system all investments are taxed at the same rate. Given equal taxes and the assumed equating of after-tax returns on investment, all investments will earn the same pretax or social rate of return, and capital will be allocated to its most valuable uses. The analysis of the current tax system and the evaluation of reforms can then proceed straightforwardly, since sources of tax differentials can be identified and their efficiency costs estimated.

Thus evaluating the efficiency of the tax system involves both an investigation of the neutrality of the system and an exploration of whether any deviations from neutrality are justified.

Deviations of the Current Tax System from Neutral Taxation

Judged by the standard of neutral taxation, the U.S. capital income tax system falls short. The effective marginal tax rates reported in figure 2.1 in the preceding chapter demonstrate one of the main flaws in the current capital income tax system: a significant difference in the marginal effective tax rates on capital income in different sectors. Corporate capital income is taxed at an effective rate of 43 percent, about twice the rate of the noncorporate sector; owner-occupied housing is subject to a negligible rate of income taxation. Moreover these aggregated measures obscure other differentials—uneven treatment of debt and equity financed investment, uneven treatment across industries, and uneven treatment of different assets within a firm. These tax differentials reflect both fundamental structural aspects of the tax system and mismeasurement of income for tax purposes.

The first fundamental feature of the tax system is the taxation of corporate sector equity income at both the firm level, through the corporate income tax, and at the personal level, through individual taxes on dividends and capital gains. The second fundamental feature is the failure to tax imputed income. One important example of this effect is the failure to tax owner-occupied housing. Income tax burdens on the return to owner-occupied housing vary depending on the form of finance and on whether the owner-occupant itemizes deductions. The costs of mortgage interest and property taxes are deductible by individuals who itemize on their tax returns.

The treatment of owner-occupied housing results in a variety of tax burdens. For equity financed investments in owner-occupied housing, when the taxpayer does not itemize deductions, the effective tax rate is zero, since the imputed return to the equity investment is not subject to tax. (The estimates assume that only 40 percent of property tax and interest deductions are itemized.) If the taxpayer does itemize deductions, the income tax rate is negative because property taxes are deductible. (There will, however, be a positive property tax imposed, which is not reflected in income tax rates.)

The tax burden is positive for debt-financed investments in housing where the individual does not itemize. Although the imputed rent is not included in income, interest payments are not deducted. The cost of the investment to the owner is the interest rate, and the pretax real return is the real interest rate. The lender includes mortgage interest in income; thus a tax is collected in the amount of the taxes imposed on interest to the lender. Since nominal interest is taxed, the effective tax burden can be quite high.

The tax burden is negative for debt-financed investment where the individual itemizes, if the tax rate of the borrower and the lender are identical. In this case the deduction of the lender and the inclusion of interest income by the borrower offset each other, but the ability to deduct property taxes leads to a tax savings and a negative tax rate.

After weighting the effective tax rates by the proportion that itemize and the proportion that is borrowed, the treatment overall results in very low tax rates on owner-occupied housing. This effect of failure to tax imputed income also extends to other types of consumer durables, such as automobiles, home furnishings, and other consumer items with extended useful lives. There are a variety of other items of income that escape or largely escape taxes. The change in value of assets is only taxed when realized as a capital gain; gain on assets passed on at death and a large fraction of realized gains on owner-occupied housing also are not taxed, the latter due to tax-free roll-overs and exclusions for the elderly.

These two features of the tax system—the failure to tax imputed income and the presence of a separate corporate tax—are the major features of the tax law causing differentials in the taxation of physical asset investments in the economy.

In addition to the differences across corporate, noncorporate, and owner-occupied houses, a number of other nonneutralities exist. Different assets within a firm are subject to different tax rates, and as a result different industries within each sector of the economy are subject to different taxation. These differentials were considerably narrowed, under current inflation rates, by the Tax Reform Act of 1986.

These differences between assets and industries result from an imperfect measurement of capital income. First, depreciation rates and useful lives are typically more generous than those implied by estimates of the economic rate of depreciation. This treatment results in a deferral of tax liability, with too little income subject to tax in the early years of an investment, and marginal effective tax rates that fall below statutory rates for depreciable assets. Second, depreciation allowances and deductions of costs of inventory are not indexed for inflation (restated in current dollars), so depreciation allowances and inventory costs tend to be understated over time.[1] This effect causes tax rates to be higher than the statutory tax rate. Finally, there are certain industry specific tax benefits, one of the most important being the relatively generous treatment for oil and gas extraction (where costs of dry holes and tracts and intangible drilling costs are allowed to be expensed or written off quickly).

Tables 3.1 and 3.2 illustrate tax differentials for both the corporate and the noncorporate sector and how they are affected by the tax rules as well as statutory tax rates. These tables show the marginal effective tax rate at the firm level (i.e., they report tax rates for the firm without considering the taxes at the personal level on dividends, capital gains, interest, or the deductibility of interest by the firm). If income were

Table 3.1
Marginal effective tax rates (firm level) by broad asset type

	1980	1981	1986	Current
Corporate				
Land	46	46	46	34
Equipment	14	–32	8	30
Structures	39	29	34	32
Inventories	54	54	54	41
Apartments	36	31	43	30
Noncorporate				
Land	30	30	30	23
Equipment	–13	–45	–20	21
Structures	24	15	19	22
Inventories	38	38	38	30
Apartments	22	18	20	20

Note: Based on calculations in appendix B. The calculations do not take into account the 1993 increase in the corporate tax rate from 34 to 35 percent. This change increased the corporate tax burdens by about one percentage point. Noncorporate tax burdens also rose slightly. These provisions also do not take into account the increase in depreciation write–off periods for nonresidential buildings, which increased the effective tax rate for structures by approximately one additional percentage point.

Table 3.2
Marginal effective tax rates: Structures and equipment, 1986 and present

Asset type	Corporate 1986	Corporate Current	Noncorporate 1986	Noncorporate Current
Equipment				
Autos	6	39	−29	28
Office/computing equipment	7	35	−46	25
Trucks, buses, and trailers	7	33	−43	25
Aircraft	5	33	−30	24
Construction machinery	5	27	−28	19
Mining/oilfield equipment	5	32	−27	23
Service industry equipment	5	32	−27	23
Tractors	5	31	−27	21
Instruments	10	32	−19	22
Other	5	31	−24	21
General industrial equipment	9	29	−15	20
Metalworking machinery	4	27	−19	18
Electric transmission equipment	21	36	−5	26
Communications equipment	4	22	−20	15
Other electrical equipment	4	27	−20	19
Furniture and fixtures	4	36	−19	18
Special industrial equipment	4	25	−18	16
Agricultural equipment	3	25	−17	17
Fabricated metal	15	32	−7	23
Engines and turbines	28	39	6	28
Ships and boats	3	27	−14	18
Railroad equipment	23	21	2	14
Structures				
Mining/oil and gas	11	11	5	6
Other	43	36	26	25
Industrial	40	36	26	25
Public utility	24	30	7	20
Commercial	38	34	23	23
Farm	38	28	24	19

Note: Based on calculations in appendix B. The calculations do not take into account the 1993 increase in the corporate tax rate from 34 to 35 percent. This change increased the corporate tax burdens by about one percentage point. Noncorporate tax burdens also rose slightly. These provisions also do not take into account the increase in depreciation write-off periods for nonresidential buildings, which increased the effective tax rate for other, industrial, and commerical by (respectively) four, two, and one percentage points.

measured correctly, all effective tax rates would be equal to the statutory rate.

Table 3.1 reports effective tax rates for broad categories of assets for four different recent states of the tax law: 1980 law, the permanent provisions of the Economic Recovery Tax Act of 1981 (ERTA), the law in 1986 immediately before the enactment of the Tax Reform Act of 1986, and the current law as enacted in 1986. All statutory tax rates are the same for 1980, 1981, and 1986 (46 percent for the corporate sector and 30 percent for the noncorporate sector), but depreciation rules varied substantially. Tax rates vary across these broad classes—30 percent to 41 percent for the corporate sector and 20 percent to 30 percent for the noncorporate sector. These variations are, however, much smaller than those in prior law. (Recent changes enacted as part of the 1993 tax legislation will slightly raise tax rates.) Table 3.2 reports these marginal effective tax rates before and after the Tax Reform Act for disaggregated categories of equipment and structures, illustrating the further vari-

Table 3.3
Marginal tax rates and corporate/noncorporate tax wedges

Industry	Prior to tax reform			After tax reform		
	t_c	t_n	Wedge[a]	t_c	t_n	Wedge[a]
Rental housing	0.47	0.23	0.59	0.40	0.20	0.42
Agriculture	0.52	0.28	0.69	0.44	0.23	0.49
Oil and gas	0.34	0.11	0.39	0.33	0.13	0.34
Mining	0.37	0.20	0.34	0.42	0.20	0.47
Construction	0.38	0.09	0.51	0.44	0.23	0.49
Transportation	0.34	0.11	0.39	0.41	0.19	0.46
Trade	0.52	0.28	0.69	0.47	0.26	0.54
Services	0.41	0.22	0.41	0.44	0.23	0.49
Manufacturing	0.49			0.46		
Utilities	0.37			0.40		
Owner-occupied housing		0.04			0.04	

Note: Based on calculations in appendix B. The calculations do not take into account the 1993 increase in the corporate tax rate from 34 to 35 percent, the increase in individual tax rates, nor the increase in depreciation write-off periods for nonresidential buildings, which slightly increased tax rates.

a. The wedge is the difference between the corporate marginal effective tax rate expressed as a percentage of net return ($t_c/(1 - t_c)$) and the noncorporate marginal effective tax rate expressed as a percentage of net return ($t_n/(1 - t_n)$).

ation within the broad categories. Within a sector, tax rates can be twice as high on some assets as on others, even under current tax law.

Table 3.3 aggregates the tax rates by industry and also incorporates personal level taxes and the deductibility of debt, demonstrating tax differentials across industries and forms of organization. This table reports the tax rates in each sector, and also the corporate/noncorporate tax wedge for each industry—the percentage increase in the required return before tax for the corporate sector in excess of the noncorporate sector.

As this table suggests, the tax rates across industries within each type of organizational form, which were highly uneven before the 1986 Act, are now more even. In most cases, in addition, the corporate tax wedge decreased. This evening up of tax rates and reduction of tax wedges occurred largely because the investment credit was traded for lower tax rates, evening out the tax treatment of different assets and providing larger benefits for the corporate sector relative to the noncorporate sector in most industries, other than those in which equipment was important.

There are also a number of specialized treatments that are either difficult to measure or relatively narrow in scope. Perhaps the most important of these is the treatment of intangible assets such as goodwill and technological know-how. The costs to create these assets (e.g., advertising, research and development, and job training) are largely expensed when incurred, and such assets are thus subject to a zero tax rate at the firm level. In addition there are a series of special tax benefits for certain narrow types of economic activities. Many of these special tax benefits are enumerated in the tax expenditure budget produced as part of the budget documents and measure the revenue cost of various special deviations from the standard tax structure. The primary beneficiaries are agriculture, timber, investments in certain renewable energy sources or energy conservation investments, research and development, and shipping.

In owner-occupied housing as well, aggregate tax burdens can vary between itemizers and nonitemizers, with the former experiencing negative tax rates due to the deduction of property taxes. Tax rates on owner-occupied housing are much larger for individuals who do not itemize.

Moreover, within each sector, tax burdens on debt can differ from those on equity. Interest deductions and payments do not include adjustments for inflation, and deductions for interest payments are too large, since they include both the real portion of the interest rate and the inflation premium. In a neutral tax system the reduction in the real value of debt (a gain for borrowers and a loss for lenders) would be included in income, so only the real portion of the interest payment would be deducted from or included in income. If the tax rate of the borrower is higher than the tax rate of the lender, this treatment provides a tax benefit for investment.

This deductibility of nominal interest along with the additional personal level tax results in a large difference between the tax rates on debt and equity in the corporate sector. Effective tax rates can also differ in the noncorporate sector if the tax rates of lenders and borrowers are different; similarly debt-financed owner-occupied housing is subject to differing tax rates. Tax rates on owner-occupied housing can vary depending on whether or not individuals itemize.

The differences in tax rates across individuals and across forms of finance are shown in table 3.4. These differences are dramatic in some cases. For example, using the average marginal tax rate of 23 percent, the tax burden on corporate equity is 48 percent, but there is actually a negative tax burden (or a subsidy) on debt of 4 percent. These calculations reveal that much of the difference stems from the two fundamental structural differences in the tax law—the corporate tax and failure to tax imputed income. Debt-financed investments are frequently subject to a negative tax rate because the tax rate of the creditor is higher than the tax rate of the debtor; with inflation this treatment can easily lead to a tax subsidy rather than a tax payment. Of course most of the investments at the zero tax rate are made by tax-exempt institutional investors, primarily pension funds. It is not clear whether these investments are marginal investments, and therefore whether any efficiency loss occurs; rather, there may simply be a loss of revenue without any effects on incentives. The tax rates reported previously in this and the preceding chapter are constructed assuming that these investments do not affect the margin. (This issue is addressed in chapter 8).

Finally, tax rates on corporate equity can vary depending on the share of income paid out as dividends rather than realized as capital gains, as well as the holding period for capital gains. Capital gains are not taxed until realized, and the longer the holding period, the lower the effective rate of capital gains tax. For an individual with a 31 percent statutory tax rate, the effective tax rate at the personal level can vary from 43 percent at the personal level when all income is distributed as dividends and capital gains (consisting of inflationary gains) are realized immediately to zero if no dividends are distributed and stocks are held until death.

These tax differentials capture the major differences in tax treatment of different assets, both real and financial. There are, however, numerous other aspects of the tax differentials. Income that is invested in pension plans and individual retirement accounts (IRAs) is not subject to tax, except at corporate rates when these funds are invested in corporate stock. Intangible assets, which are difficult to measure and are not included in the above tables, are generally expensed when incurred, yielding a zero tax at the firm level. There are a variety of special benefits for certain types of investments, including agriculture

Table 3.4
Marginal effective tax rates: Debt and equity finance

	Tax rate of individual investor			
	0	15	23	31
Corporate				
Debt	–84	–31	–4	24
Equity	34	43	48	53
Noncorporate[a]				
Debt	–38	1	22	43
Equity	0	14	22	30
Owner-occupied housing[a]				
Itemizers				
Debt	–97	–42	–12	18
Equity	0	–3	–5	–6
Nonitemizers				
Debt	0	28	43	59
Equity	0	0	0	0

Note: Based on calculations in appendix B. The calculations do not take into account the 1993 increase in the corporate tax rate from 34 to 35 percent, the increase in individual rates, nor the increase in depreciation write-off periods for nonresidential buildings. These changes had only a small effect.

a. Debt investments in the noncorporate sector and owner-occupied housing assume that the firm or owner-occupant's tax rate is 23 percent, the average marginal tax rate.

(where much of the cost of inventory is expensed for unincorporated farms and the return on some investments is taxed as a capital gain), timber growing (where income is not taxed until realized and many of the costs are expensed), low income housing, and research and development costs which, in addition to being expensed when incurred, are eligible for a tax credit.

When judged against neutrality in taxation, these effective tax rates display an enormous variation in effective rates. For the top statutory marginal tax rate of 31 percent, effective tax rates can range from 62 percent on FIFO (first-in-first-out) inventories financed by equity investment which is wholly paid out in dividends with gains currently realized to a tax rate of *minus* 180 percent on an intangible corporate asset that is financed by borrowing from a tax-exempt entity. (FIFO means that the cost of a good sold will reflect the oldest item in inventory, which is of course valued in prior period price levels. As a result taxable income includes a nominal, rather than a real, return on capital tied up in inventory.) Fullerton, Gillette, and Mackie (1997) find similar wide variances in the tax rates applied to different types of investments, although their measures include state and local income and property taxes as well as federal income taxes.

Justifications for Nonneutral Taxation

If a neutral tax is an efficient one, the next step in assessing the tax law is to examine the costs of existing distortions. There have, however, been a number of reasons advanced for arguing that some kinds of investment deserve better treatment than others, and thus that a neutral tax system may not necessarily be the most efficient one. These tax differentials could be an appropriate part of an efficient tax system. In this section these different arguments are assessed. This assessment suggests that there are some types of assets that might be favorably treated but that they are limited in scope. Moreover the magnitude of any desirable tax differences is highly uncertain.

In traditional economic analysis, there are three standard rationales for differential treatment—those stemming from optimal tax theory, those stemming from the possibility of market failures (including positive or negative externalities), and those arising from onerous administrative and compliance costs. Economic theory also recognizes that if a departure from neutral taxation is made for administrative reasons, we are now in a "world of the second best" where other departures may then become justified. There are also some arguments which, though they have entered the policy debate and even the economics literature, seem to fall far short of justification on any conventional economic grounds. Some of these arguments have been used to justify benefits focused on equipment investment, or in some way they have been associated with more "productive" or more "desirable" investment.

Optimal Tax Theory

Optimal tax theory is usually associated with the imposition of differential excise taxes. If revenue is to be raised, and if individual consumers can be viewed as identical, the most efficient tax system will be one applied to goods that are in relatively inelastic demand such as food and medicine. A set of taxes of this nature are often referred to as *Ramsey taxes*, following the exploration of the concept by Ramsey (1927). Corlett and Hague (1953) also suggested that because consumption can be taxed, but not leisure, higher excise taxes on goods that are complementary with leisure (e.g., sporting goods) might be more efficient than uniform taxes on all commodities. If excise taxes do not play a major role in the tax system—as is the case of the federal income tax system—then an argument might be made that differential capital income taxes could play some role in this optimal tax system.

In theory, some degree of nonneutral taxation of capital income would be optimal in a second-best world if direct excise taxation is not possible and consumers are identical. Capital income taxes have "excise tax effects." That is, they affect the price of products and can be used as an indirect excise tax mechanism. But it is more difficult to increase welfare with differential capital income taxes because these differential taxes would distort production. While higher capital income taxes may conceivably produce a system of desirable product prices, they would also lead to inefficient mixes of inputs (labor and capital) in the productive process. Nevertheless, there is almost certainly some set of deviations from uniform taxation that, in theory, could increase welfare. Despite this theoretical outcome, nonneutrality in capital income taxes cannot be justified on the grounds of optimal tax theory for several reasons.

Perhaps the most important reason for rejecting this narrowly defined notion of optimal taxes has to do with distribution. Optimal tax theory has not been considered particularly useful in structuring tax policy because of the distributional consequences and administrative barriers. The simplest form of optimal tax theory treats individuals as identical. A broader concept of this theory recognizes that individuals differ in their incomes (and in other ways). A socially optimal tax would take into account distributional consequences. Goods such as food that "should" be taxed more heavily for efficiency reasons under a narrow concept often are the necessities that figure heavily in the budgets of the poor; such a tax system would be highly regressive. Indeed many state sales taxes allow exemptions for food, illustrating the social concerns about regressive taxation.

Second, the magnitude of such efficiency gains is probably very small. Auerbach (1989b) explores the proposition of differential capital income taxes and, concludes that nonuniform taxes would be optimal. He uses a model of the economy to search for an optimal set of taxes on capital income. He concludes, however, that the welfare gain from moving from neutral to optimal taxes is negligible.

Finally (and related to the first point), the schedule of differential taxes depends on behavioral parameters that are difficult to assess. Given the uncertainty attached to setting differential rates, a neutral system may be the best outcome to aim for in practice. In any case the tax differentials described in the previous section were not created on the basis of demand elasticities for products; rather, they tend to reflect major underlying structural features of the income tax system.

Market Failures and Externalities

The case for equating neutral and optimal taxation also requires, in theory, an assumption of perfect private markets. Private markets can fail to achieve this ideal for a variety of reasons including externalities (or spillover effects), along with a variety of imperfections in operation of the capital and product markets.

Externalities
Some economic activities are likely to produce benefits or costs that accrue neither to producers nor consumers. For example, activities that

pollute the environment produce negative externalities—they impose costs on society at large or on specific individuals not reflected in the price of the goods. The allocation of resources would be improved if these goods were taxed to reflect these additional costs so that the efficient level of pollution is reached. Although pollution is undesirable, at the point where the additional economic costs of reducing pollution further are greater than the cost of the pollution itself, it is optimal to allow that level of pollution to continue.[2]

Investments in research and development, on the other hand, often produce positive externalities. Since the results of research may be copied by others, investments that earn high social returns may not earn private returns that justify undertaking them. Such activities could be encouraged by lower tax rates or subsidies.

Capital income tax differences are most frequently invoked as arguments for favorable tax treatment in the case of a positive externality (e.g., R&D), rather than the common negative spillovers, such as pollution, where corrective taxes would be imposed on the product. For example, the favorable treatment of owner-occupied housing has been defended on the grounds that home ownership makes individuals better citizens. Property ownership may give them a greater stake in their community. They may also maintain owned properties better than rented properties, thereby making their properties more pleasant for their neighbors to observe.

One reason that property ownership may result in better collective decision making is because homeowners, who pay the property tax, will take this tax burden into account in voting. Renters may vote for too many government services because they do not pay for them through property taxes. This argument presupposes that property taxes do not raise rents or that tenants do not perceive property taxes as increasing their rents. (It also presumes that individuals properly perceive the value of public goods and that voting leads to the optimal amount of these public goods). Individuals may in fact engage in voting choices that could be harmful rather than beneficial to the optimal provision of government services.

There may be some legitimacy to the argument that individuals maintain owned properties better, although such spillovers might be dealt with through private contractual arrangements (i.e., conferring some of these tasks on the landlord). The magnitude of these sup-

posed spillovers from owner-occupied housing have not been empirically measured, however, and tax relief for owner-occupied housing is
so generous that it seems doubtful that such spillover effects are sufficient to justify such generous tax treatment.

An argument for conferring benefits on certain industries is also
often made in the name of national defense. This argument has been
advanced to justify special tax benefits for the oil and gas industry,
where it was argued that preservation of an oil producing capability
was vital to national defense. Such an argument seems weak because
subsidies for oil production can deplete domestic resources more
quickly. Moreover the measurement of such external benefits was
never made (rather, the argument was asserted on qualitative
grounds) and other options such as a strategic oil reserve that might be
more efficient would have to be considered as well.

More recently such an argument has been asserted for a wide variety of industries such as computer chips and machine tools. The
weight one gives to such arguments should be based on a careful consideration of whether domestic production or production from friend-
ly sources is adequate for an emergency, how quickly an industry
might be expanded in the event of hostilities, the offsetting costs of
distorting production in the absence of such an emergency, and the
availability of alternative approaches such as stockpiles. Also, given
the broad range of goods used in the maintenance of a military capability, many industries could be arguably eligible for such subsidies.
Given limits on the total productive abilities of the economy, such
lower tax rates or subsidies may serve little purpose. For these reasons
justifications for special tax treatment on the grounds of national
defense seem weak.

Moreover these arguments are further weakened by the "new
world order." The end of the cold war, the breakup of the Soviet
Union, the prospect of joint international peacekeeping activities, and
the outlook for more harmonious relationships between East and West
all make a global war of the type that could severely interfere with
strategic supplies less likely.

Perhaps the one type of investment that might be argued to be
deserving of special tax treatment on the grounds of external benefits
is research and development, where evidence suggests that there are
large social returns to many of these investments. In theory, this is an

externality that could be corrected by a tax subsidy to investment. Indeed current tax law already confers subsidies on these investments by allowing the expensing of many costs of R&D (although such treatment was allowed primarily because of the difficulty of identifying expenses to be capitalized) and by allowing a research and experimentation tax credit.

Nevertheless, the use of tax subsidies or reduced tax rates to encourage investment in R&D is fraught with administrative difficulties. Tax law can only define some broad category of investment, and the tax benefits thus allowed may easily spill over to other investments. Nor can the government, in practice, identify and more heavily subsidize those projects with the largest externalities. For these reasons there may be a limited role for tax policy in correcting these external effects, and reliance on direct financing of research products and enforcement of patent laws may be a more appropriate solution.

This brief review of the externality issue suggests that the use of differential capital income taxes in correcting for externalities seems relatively limited. For many cases where substantial externalities are likely to occur, such as pollution and consumption of harmful substances, other remedies are more appropriate than varying the tax rate of capital income. Cases where an externality is associated directly with investment, such as investment in R&D, appear to be quite limited. Even in the case of R&D, it is not clear that government intervention through variable tax rates will achieve the objective of encouraging investment in those projects with large spillovers. In most cases corrective taxes would be extremely hard to determine, could create other distortions, and may be inferior to alternative government policies such as regulation and direct funding.

Other Market Imperfections
There are a variety of other market imperfections that cause private markets to operate in a fashion that is not optimal. One such market failure is the absence of perfect capital markets. Investors who lack the cash flow to invest may not be free to borrow or to raise equity capital funds from others in order to make investments that would earn the highest rate of return because of lack of collateral. This credit constraint is most likely to operate for small businesses. (It also is thought to interfere with optimal investment in human capital formation, since individuals cannot pledge future labor services against loans.)

Another market imperfection is that of agency cost—which applies to large firms where management and ownership are separated. Managers may not always be operating in the best interests of stockholders of firms or in the best interests of borrowers. There have been market responses to this agency cost problem that are intricately tied up in the tax treatment of different types of capital income (discussed in more detail in chapter 4). Private markets may also operate imperfectly because of lack of perfect competition—where monopoly profits are earned.

Although all of these market imperfections exist, it is not clear that differential taxation is the appropriate response. Market failures in borrowing are probably best addressed through government loan programs rather than differential tax treatment across firm size that would benefit established firms as well as new ones. It is not clear what purpose tax differentials would serve in rectifying the problems of agency cost other than allowing the mechanisms developed in the marketplace to work without the interference of taxation. Not is it clear that tax differentials can serve a useful role in dealing with the problems of industry concentration. (While monopoly profits could be taxed without interfering with market allocations, in practice there is virtually no way to isolate the monopoly profit from the normal return to capital.)

Risk

Another argument that is often made for special tax treatment is to encourage risk taking. This argument appears much more often in the popular debate than it does in the economics literature, in part because of the recognition in the professional economics literature that capital income taxation may well *encourage* risk taking. As shown by Domar and Musgrave (1944), although a tax reduces the expected return on an investment, it also reduces the variation in return of the investments (i.e., after-tax returns vary less than pretax returns). Indeed the imposition of taxes can actually increase investment in risky assets, depending on the responsiveness of behavior to risk and on the size of the risk-free return. As a simple illustration, if an individual is investing half his portfolio in a risky asset and half in a riskless asset with the riskless return of zero, and a 50 percent tax is imposed, he can restore his original risk and his original return by investing all of his assets in the risky form. Of course, if the riskless return is greater than zero, he may wish to invest somewhat less in the risky asset; nevertheless, the new portfolio may well contain more risky investments. Mossin (1968), Stiglitz (1969), and Gordon (1985) address these and related issues.

There are two arguments made in response to this observation. The first appears to be based on some notion that, in general, there is not enough risk taking in society. There is no obvious reason to believe that private markets do not undertake enough risk, particularly given the widespread opportunities for pooling capital in corporations and diversifying risk.

The second argument is a more valid one—that the tax law does not always allow for full deduction of losses. Overall capital losses of individuals are restricted to a $3,000 amount, although these losses can be carried forward indefinitely. The reason for this restriction on the deduction of capital losses is that realization and payment of the capital gains tax is under the control of the investor. Without such a restriction individuals who wish to sell assets for consumption purposes could simply sell assets with losses and receive tax benefits so that the tax would be asymmetric (losses would be deductible but gains would not be taxable).

Overall losses of a corporation or of an unincorporated business in excess of other income of the individual cannot be offset, although there are carry-back and carry-forward provisions. Bulow and Summers (1984) and Gordon and Wilson (1989) also address the issue of unrealized gains and losses, which would not normally be recognized and taxed.

Although these points are valid, they occasionally seem to be overstated. To the extent that riskiness shows up not in losses but in variation in the size of gains, the risk-reducing attributes of the tax law occur in full force. Moreover individuals may frequently have a portfolio of assets and losses on some assets can often be offset by gains on others. And, while the tax code does not provide full loss offset for a sustained period of overall loss for the firm, for a particular project undertaken by a firm in an otherwise profitable firm, loss offset is perfect. A temporary overall loss in an otherwise profitable firm is also offset, since losses can be carried back to offset previous taxable income. Finally, many, perhaps most, variations in asset value are a result of changes in the stream of income, where variations will be taxed.

Restrictions on loss offset, either by the firm or through restrictions on capital gains of the investors, remain for new firms. Indeed much of the concern about "venture capital" may be legitimate. Moreover every investor and firm faces some probability of a sustained period of overall loss. But, in general, the effective loss offset provisions of the tax law allow considerable sharing in gains and losses with individuals and with reducing private risk. There seems little argument for providing reduced tax burdens for investments that are identified as "risky." A special provision for venture capital might be desirable, but it is difficult to determine a method of effectively targeting such firms.

There is one specific provision of the tax law closely related to the issue of risk, and that is the passive loss restriction enacted as a part of the Tax Reform Act of 1986. This provision defers the deduction of losses on certain passive investments of individuals, primarily real estate. In general, individuals cannot realize losses on these investments, although these losses add to the basis of the asset when sold. The passive loss restriction was enacted in part as a response to the blossoming of tax shelter activities in the early 1980s, but its role in affecting risk taking was not addressed. This issue will be discussed in more detail in chapter 7.

Encouraging More "Productive" Investment

Discussion of tax policy toward investment often focuses on so-called productive investment. Productive investment is, in turn, often equated with investment in manufacturing or export industries, or equipment, especially equipment that is technologically sophisticated. It often excludes assets such as commercial buildings or certain businesses, such as trade and services. Indeed this preference for favoring equipment was embodied in the tax system for many years through the investment tax credit, which was in place, with occasional suspensions, for twenty-five years (1962–86).

Unless there are spillover effects, there is no reason to characterize certain assets as being more "productive." Manufacture of goods is no more valuable than distribution, and all types of assets—whether buildings, equipment, or inventories—contribute to production. The market will allocate investment efficiently and the tax system should not interfere with that choice. The most productive investment will be that investment the market economy undertakes on its own.[3]

There are at least two reasons for the focus on subsidizing equipment. The first is that equipment often embodies recent technological advances, and there is the notion that additional investment in equipment will result in a more technologically advanced productive process. Equipment should, however, be scrapped in favor of more advanced forms only when the return from replacing the equipment is high enough to justify such investment. The market will determine the desirable rate at which technology becomes embodied in the capital stock. (Again, this conclusion assumes there are no direct spillover effects from the equipment investment itself.)

The second is the association of equipment with manufacturing, which is also popularly associated with export industries and international trade, as well as a perceived decline in certain industries' share of international markets. Indeed "international competitiveness" has been invoked to justify tax benefits. Yet there is no rigorous meaning to the term "international competitiveness" when discussed from the point of view of the nation as a whole. (For an excellent discussion of this point, see Gradison 1991.) Often the successes of trading partners, such as Japan and Germany, are identified as resulting from government intervention to enhance this "international competitiveness."[4]

The classical economic theory of comparative advantage would dismiss this notion. Countries will, and should, for maximum efficiency, trade in those goods in which they have an advantage compared to other countries. Absent externalities and trade barriers, the market will automatically achieve an efficient outcome.[5] Patterns of international trade reflect these comparative advantages, as well as other factors such as the export or import of capital. It should not be surprising, for example, that a country like Japan, with a dearth of natural resources and a high savings rate, should be a net exporter of manufactured products. (The investments of the Japanese in other countries, a natural result of its high savings rate, can only be made real via a net export of goods.) An increase in net exports can be brought about in the short and intermediate run by increasing the national savings rates; not by subsidizing exports or export-intensive industries.

There are of course inefficient barriers to trade, such as tariffs and market restrictions. Subsidizing manufacturing in the United States would not likely improve our welfare but rather would worsen it.

Administrative and Compliance Considerations

One legitimate rationale for differential capital income taxation is that fully neutral taxation would require some prohibitive administrative and compliance costs. For example, neutral taxation of capital income would require the inclusion in income of all changes in the value of assets, whether real or financial—a treatment referred to as accrual-based taxation. Instead, the tax system only includes gains in the value of assets when they are sold—a realization basis. This treatment creates a deferral of tax with various attendant distortions such as favoring some assets over others or discouraging taxpayers from selling assets.

The failure to tax all income on an accrual basis may be justified on the grounds that such taxation might involve onerous problems of measurement. Taxpayers would be required to report changes in wealth when no market transactions had occurred. While such a system might be possible for frequently traded homogeneous assets, such as shares of stock, it would be difficult for assets such as businesses and real estate.

Similarly the failure to tax many types of imputed income, such as income of consumer durables, might be justified on the grounds that measurement of this imputed income would be extremely difficult. The most significant type of imputed income is the rental value of owner-occupied housing. In a pure economic sense, of course, any consumer item which has lasted a period of time earns some implicit income. Thus automobiles, household furnishings, and even clothing and sporting goods are in theory candidates for taxation. But measuring and reporting the flow of such income would be difficult. Indeed, even the taxation of imputed income on owner-occupied housing would be difficult in the absence of market transactions that could establish rents.

Another example of this differential taxation arising from administrative considerations is the failure to capitalize many costs, such as the costs of creating intangible assets. In general, these costs are difficult to measure, and their useful lives may be difficult to determine. Another example of tax benefits motivated by administration and compliance arguments is simplified accounting for farmers, an argument that was probably more valid when the farming sector was more concentrated among small, relatively unsophisticated farmers.

It has often been argued that the taxation of corporate income on a partnership basis, which is necessary to tax neutrality, is too complex. It is unclear whether this argument is true, but there are certainly some administratively simple ways to reduce this differential, the most straightforward being to eliminate the personal level tax on dividends and capital gains. Moreover, by certain simplifying devices, such as withholding tax at the corporate source and providing imputations of incomes and credits to individual shareholders (particularly, coupled with elimination of capital gains taxes), such a tax system could probably be implemented without onerous costs.

Tax Rules in the World of the Second Best

If deviations from tax neutrality occur due to overwhelming administrative and compliance costs, there may be some arguments for offsetting differences. One such example is the disallowance of many types of interest deductions. If all imputed income were taxed, it is proper to allow deductions for any interest paid (at least for real interest), just as it is proper to include all interest in income (White and White 1977). For example, suppose an individual borrows money to finance current consumption (e.g., a vacation). Income is the sum of consumption plus changes in wealth, a standard definition of income called *Haig-Simons income*. In the first period, when the money is borrowed, consumption rises by the amount of the loan while wealth falls by the amount of the loan, for no change in income. In the second period, when the loan plus interest is paid, consumption falls by the amount of the principal and interest, while wealth rises by the amount of the repaid loan, for a net reduction in income in the amount of the interest. Indeed only if interest is deductible does the borrower face the same price for future consumption as the lender.

Despite the fact that deduction of interest is appropriate in an income tax, consumer interest deductions are not allowed outside of mortgage interest. Moreover, only taxpayers who itemize are allowed to deduct mortgage interest, and there are arguments made that mortgage interest should also be disallowed. Since much of nonbusiness interest is incurred on funds used to purchase consumer durables where the imputed income is not taxed, it may be appropriate as a "second-best" solution to deny interest deductions. Although such a disallowance distorts the choice of financing mechanism, it may yield gains in efficiency because it increases the overall tax burden on these investments.

Another example of a second-best tax differential was the justification of a separate corporate tax to prevent the tax-free accumulation of income in corporations. When individual tax rates were much higher than corporate tax rates, it would have been possible to reduce taxes by investing in corporations that retained profits (and investing in one's own business through corporate form). If partnership taxation of corporations is deemed infeasible for administrative reasons, such a tax might be justified. Such a justification is, however, no longer relevant, since the current corporate tax rate is close to the top individual rate.

Another argument for generous tax benefits might be the offsetting in the federal tax system of differentials imposed at the state and local level. The most obvious of these tax differentials is in the property tax on different assets. Since real property is the primary basis for property taxation, this treatment may be a justification for allowing benefits for owner-occupied housing. There are, however, several reservations to this argument. First, this analysis does not take into account benefits from local public services, which under some theories of the property tax offset the cost of property taxation.[6] Second, this argument would apply to rental, as well as owner-occupied housing and nonresidential real estate. Finally, state and local taxes on corporations and on individual capital incomes burden those assets which are already subject to tax at the federal level.

Tax Capitalization

If taxes become capitalized in asset values or apply to an investment in inelastic supply, then revenue can be raised from such taxes without economic distortions (although there will be distributional consequences). One example of an asset in inelastic supply is land. Thus it may be efficient to tax land at a high rate. In practice, however, it is administratively difficult to do so. Moreover, since land used for owner-occupied housing is not subject to taxation, there will be distortions arising from the misallocation of land. Put another way, land is not inelastically supplied in each sector.

Another case where tax capitalization is argued to occur is in the taxation of dividends of corporations; whether this tax capitalization occurs is in considerable dispute. (This issue will be addressed in the following chapter.)

Summary

There seems to be relatively little evidence to justify the departure of the capital income tax from neutral taxation. Although tax differentials might, in theory, play some role in achieving an efficient tax structure, evaluations based on either optimal tax theory or the presence of externalities fail to make a strong case for deviations for tax neutrality. Perhaps the most compelling reasons are for those departures that arise from complications of administration and compliance.

Certainly the separate taxation of corporate sector income as currently practiced reveals little or no justification from any of these rationales. Nor do the special tax benefits for oil and gas, the failure to employ more realistic depreciation- and inflation-adjusted incomes, and the failure to account for inflation in measuring interest payments and deductions appear justified. Overall, most of the major departures from a neutral taxation must be viewed as causing an inefficient system of capital income taxation.

If the most compelling reasons for departure from neutral taxation are mainly administrative, then the rule of optimal tax design might be to tax capital income as evenly as possible as administrative and compliance considerations permit. In this respect the tax reform proposals originally outlined by the Treasury Department (1984) provide an illustration of what such a capital income tax system might look like if this principle were followed. One shortcoming of that set of proposals is that it provided an incomplete corporate tax integration plan; proposals outlined in the Treasury's integration study (1992) provide further examples of movement toward more uniform taxation tempered by administrative and compliance costs.

4   The Efficiency Cost of the Corporate Tax

No single aspect of the capital income tax system is more responsible for causing differential taxation of capital income than the existence of a separate corporate income tax. If corporate income were taxed on a partnership basis so that each stockholder simply paid a personal tax on his or her share of corporate income, differences between the taxation of corporate and noncorporate capital would be eliminated. Moreover differences between corporate capital and owner-occupied housing would be greatly lessened, and differences between debt and equity capital within the corporate sector virtually eliminated.

Since the 1986 Tax Reform Act largely eliminated tax differentials across assets within firms and industries within each sector, corporate tax integration would eliminate virtually all of the remaining tax differentials. Indeed, were the corporate tax to be integrated, the only remaining distortion of any magnitude would be the failure to tax imputed income on owner-occupied housing.

The previous chapter suggests little rationale for differential capital income taxation and none, other than administrative considerations, for a separate corporate tax in addition to personal level taxes. Moreover the administrative barriers would neither prevent relief at the individual level nor prevent partial relief through dividends (which has been implemented successfully in other countries). Nor is it clear that full integration is infeasible; if taxes are withheld at the corporation level, and then credited to stockholders, the imputation of corporate incomes to stockholders appears feasible.

The corporate tax does, however, raise substantial revenues, and this, as well as public perceptions of the "need" to tax large corporations, makes such a change difficult politically.[1] In the face of political reality, the case for reform of the corporate income tax depends in part on the efficiency cost of the tax. If these costs are large relative to revenue, then the policy goal of integrating the corporate income tax with the individual income tax is more worthy of consideration despite the political, administrative, and revenue difficulties to be encountered. How large, then, might these efficiency costs be?

As with many aspects of the tax system, such a question is not easy to answer. For many years the corporate tax and its distorting effects have been the principal subject of attention by economists studying the efficiency costs of nonneutral taxation. The tax produces a variety of distortions. As illustrated by table 3.3 of the preceding chapter, it raises the tax on corporate capital relative to both noncorporate businesses and owner-occupied housing, resulting in a misallocation of resources away from the corporate sector and into other sectors. These tax differentials are moderated only somewhat by advantages to corporate debt finance where the higher corporate tax rate produces low or even negative tax rates on corporate debt-financed investment. At the same time, this advantage to corporate debt involves another distortion of the corporate tax—favoring corporate debt over corporate equity (as is illustrated in table 3.4 of the previous chapter). Moreover, because dividends are taxed more heavily than capital gains, the corporate tax distorts the payout behavior of corporations, encouraging too little income to be paid out as dividends. Finally, because retained earnings are taxed at the personal level only when realized, the tax code encourages individuals to hold on to corporate stock longer than they otherwise would under a neutral system, locking stockholders into investments and, in the process, distorting their portfolios.

Despite the magnitude of the corporate tax differentials, there has been considerable debate about the efficiency effects of the corporate tax. Some of these debates have been going on for some time; some are relatively new. Moreover empirical estimates of behavioral response are frequently unsettled. These issues are discussed, followed by a review of policy options, in the following sections.

Distortions Arising from Corporate Taxation

There are four major types of distortions introduced by the separate corporate tax structure. The effects of the tax in discouraging the use of capital in the corporate sector have received the most attention in the academic literature. In addition the corporate tax causes a preference for debt over equity finance, a preference for retaining rather than distributing income (because the personal level tax on retained earnings is favored by the capital gains), and a lock-in effect for corporate stock. Each of these issues is considered in turn. The last issue, however, is given a cursory treatment in this section, as it will be considered in more detail in chapter 6.

The Misallocation of Physical Assets

Although the corporate tax is referred to as a *double* tax because income is taxed twice—once at the corporate level and once at the individual level—the degree of "excess" taxation depends on the marginal tax rate of the investor. For example, under current rules, the tax on corporate income (for large corporations) is roughly equal to the statutory rate of 35 percent, namely $100 of corporate income will yield $65 of after-tax income. If there were no inflation and all taxes were paid out as dividends, the $65 would then be subject to another tax. For a taxpayer in the 31 percent bracket, the additional tax would be 31 percent of $65, or $20.15, resulting in a total tax of $55.15. Such a tax rate is about 75 percent larger than the noncorporate rate of 31 percent. For a taxpayer in the 15 percent bracket, the corporate tax will be $44.75, about three times the noncorporate rate.

Distortions between corporate and noncorporate investment, however, depend on the *tax wedge*, or the excess of the corporate over the noncorporate pretax return. In the examples given thus far, this wedge would be the same for both investors—$0.35/(1 - 0.35)$, or slightly about 54 percent. There are, however, a number of other factors influencing this tax wedge. First, capital gains are not taxed until realized (corporate stock that is sold is typically held about seven years). Gains held until death are exempted entirely, and historical data suggest that about half of gains are never taxed for this reason. In addition there is a ceiling of 28 percent on individual capital gains. Partially offsetting these benefits to capital gains is the application to nominal rather than real gains. For example, consider a composite capital gain where half the stock is sold every seven years and the other half held until death. For the portion of earnings not paid out in dividends, the marginal effective tax rate on capital gains would be 13 percent with no inflation but 22 percent with the inflation of 4.8 percent (the anticipated inflation rate for 1989 in table 2.1). Overall, the tax rate on corporate equity at the personal level is slightly below the statutory rate for a high bracket individual.

A second factor mitigating the excess corporate tax is the tax treatment of debt. If there is no inflation and income is measured correctly at the firm level, the effective tax rate on debt is equal to the individual rate. With inflation, the effective tax rate can be below the individual rate because the inflation premium, while taxed at the individual level, is nevertheless deducted at the higher corporate tax rate. This aspect lowers the corporate tax wedge.[2]

Finally, the tax wedge can be affected by tax provisions that mismeasure income at the firm level. These provisions can act to lower tax rates at the firm level and the corporate wedge, or raise them. The tax wedges reported earlier in table 3.3 vary across industry, ranging from 34 to 47 percent.

Some of the earliest investigations of tax distortions in the academic literature focused on the corporate income tax. For many years the central model of these differential tax rates was that of Harberger (1962, 1966). In Harberger's original two-sector model the corporate tax causes capital to flow out of the corporate sector, driving down the pretax rate of return in the noncorporate sector and driving up the return in the corporate sector. The process continues until the after-tax returns are equated in the two sectors. The tax causes inefficient production because the corporate sector has too little capital relative to labor, while the noncorporate sector has too much. It also results in inefficient consumption because prices of corporate products are increased relative to the prices of noncorporate products.

Over the years, larger and more sophisticated multisector Harberger models were constructed and used. Shoven and Whalley (1972), Shoven (1976), Fullerton, Shoven, and Whalley (1983), and Ballard, Fullerton, Shoven, and Whalley (1985) presented Harberger-type models with many sectors, allowing for intermediate as well as final goods. Fullerton and Henderson (1989) introduced the marginal tax rates based on the rental cost of capital, similar to the marginal effective tax rates reported earlier. In general, most of these models produced welfare losses from the corporate tax in the neighborhood of

0.5 percent of GNP or slightly less, an amount that was not insignificant given the limited amounts of revenue collected from the tax.

Despite the sophistication of these models, there were troubling aspects of the Harberger model. Working independently, Gravelle (1981) and Ebrill and Hartman (1982) pointed out that the Harberger model is based on tax differentials across industries, while the corporate tax is based on the legal form of organization.

Corporations obtain equity capital by issuing stock, and equity investors in corporations enjoy limited liability.[3] If the firm fails, only the capital invested in the stock is at risk, and not the personal assets of the investors. Investors in noncorporate firms do not have limited liability (with the exception of limited partnerships, where only the general partner has liability that extends beyond equity investments). On the whole corporate businesses are much larger than noncorporate firms, and most corporate output is produced by corporations that have large volumes of publicly traded stock. Most noncorporate output is produced by proprietors and small partnerships.[4]

Given the constant-returns-to-scale production functions in the Harberger model, all firms should choose to operate in noncorporate form. That is, the costs of production do not, in this model, depend on whether the business is legally organized as a corporation. This observation has two unsettling conclusions. First, there is no reason in the model that businesses shouldn't avoid the double tax altogether by eschewing the corporate form, because it costs businesses nothing to do so. With constant returns to scale, all output could be produced by noncorporate firms. Second, there is no reason corporate and noncorporate businesses should coexist in the same industry, since noncorporate businesses enjoy an unambiguous tax advantage.

In empirical applications the Harberger model did not confront this problem of the coexistence of corporate and noncorporate firms in the same industry which, in some cases, produced completely identical products (e.g., crude oil). Rather, these applications generally finessed this issue by averaging corporate and noncorporate taxes within an industry, an approach that not only failed to consider choice of organizational form but also which diluted, through averaging, the tax differential.[5]

Fullerton and Henderson (1989), recognizing this problem, allowed some substitutability between corporate and noncorporate capital within each industry. That is, rather than each firm producing with a mix of labor and capital, each industry produced with a mix of labor, corporate capital, and noncorporate capital. This approach was not, however, based on an explicit modeling of the choice of operating in a corporate or a noncorporate form.

Several possibilities have been advanced for explaining the coexistence of corporate and noncorporate forms. To allow these firms to coexist both with and without taxes, there must be some advantages and disadvantages to each form of organization. Gravelle and Kotlikoff (1989b) proposed an explanation based on scale advantages in corporate firms and entrepreneurial skill in noncorporate firms, which they illustrated using a simple two sector model. This explanation was consistent with the legal differences in corporate and noncorporate firms, where the former are larger and rely on raising large amounts of capital in equity markets.

They found much larger estimated efficiency costs compared to the predictions of the Harberger model. A large-scale numerical model was also constructed (Gravelle and Kotlikoff 1989a). The welfare cost of nonuniform taxation in this model was over 1 percent of consumption, about twice the magnitude of that produced by the Harberger model. In a modification with rental housing disaggregated into a fully noncorporate single-family sector and a mixed multifamily sector (Gravelle 1989), the welfare cost was about 0.9 percent of consumption. Most of this cost derived from the differential treatment of corporate and noncorporate firms within a sector; only about 0.1 percent derived from the favorable treatment of owner-occupied housing in both models. This model does not weight the tax rates to reflect tax-exempt investment by individuals; with tax-exempt investment the welfare cost falls by about 0.2 percentage points, assuming that pension funds and other tax-exempt investors do not invest in noncorporate equity.[6]

Gravelle and Kotlikoff's approach also suggested a focus on distortions between corporate and noncorporate capital in those sectors with a large fraction of noncorporate capital. This focus indicated that the Tax Reform Act resulted in significant efficiency gains because it reduced the tax wedges in those sectors—agriculture, housing, and trade. This effect occurred primarily because the investment credit was offset by rate reductions. The loss of the investment credit did little to alter tax wedges in these industries because they use relatively small amounts of equipment, and because the credit provides larger benefits to noncorporate firms relative to corporate ones as compared to rate cuts—in that it is a credit rather than a deduction.

A second approach suggested by Gravelle and Kotlikoff (1993) would be to treat corporate and noncorporate products as differentiated; this approach also suggested much larger efficiency gains, particularly if corporate and noncorporate products were, as one might expect, close substitutes. No large-scale model using this approach has been developed; such a model would require abandoning the fixed input-output matrix for intermediate goods. Fullerton and Rogers (1993) use this approach, but only for final consumption goods. As in the case of the previous model developed by Gravelle and Kotlikoff, the industries that are characterized by large distortions are those with a large noncorporate component.

A third approach developed by Gravelle and reported in Gravelle and Mackie (1991) would allow after-tax rates of return to differ by treating the investments as subjectively different because of differences in risk or information. (Gravelle and Mackie report simulations of corporate integration in three models; a portfolio model developed by Gravelle is included in this study.) In this model investors choose among corporate equity, noncorporate equity, and debt in their portfolios, and relative prices are set by the corporate sector tax burdens. This approach could also explain, in part, the debt/equity choice of the firm as discussed in the next section. This model yields a much smaller distortion from the physical allocation of capital. If the corporate tax were integrated, the gain would be 0.28 percent of consumption. The gain from reducing the portfolio distortion would be more important, at 0.49 percent of consumption, for a total of 0.77 percent of consumption.

It is possible that all of these factors play some role in determining the corporate/noncorporate organizational choice. All of these new innovations suggest, however, that the efficiency cost of the corporate tax is large relative to revenue collected. Gravelle (1991a) reports that the extra revenue yielded by the corporate tax is only 1.38 percent of consumption. Therefore the cost of the misallocation of physical resources may be more than half the revenue gained from the corporate tax.

The size of the distortions produced by the corporate tax is subject to some uncertainty. Much depends on the explanation for the coexistence of corporate and noncorporate firms and how substitutable production is between them. Because so little attention has been focused on this issue, there are virtually no empirical studies of substitution of organizational form. Gravelle and Kotlikoff (1989a) show that the shares of corporate production have varied over time, and in some cases substantially; Gravelle (1989) also suggests that directional shifts in corporate shares in most industries over time are consistent with changes in relative marginal tax rates. Gordon and Mackie-Mason (1991) report modest estimates of substitution, but their study excludes the heavily noncorporate, capital intensive agriculture and housing sectors where the largest distortions might, in theory, occur.

But the welfare cost is large even if one assumes quite modest substitution between corporate and noncorporate firms—1 percent of GNP in 1991 amounted to $57 billion. Moreover, since the excess burden rises more than proportionally with changes in the tax wedge (and the tax rate) as discussed in chapter 2, a partial movement toward integration would yield an even higher ratio of welfare gain to revenue cost.

The Distortion between Debt and Equity Capital

Over the years attention has also been directed to explaining why corporations rely so heavily on equity. Corporations have never relied on debt as heavily as on equity (Blair and Litan 1990); a typical rule of thumb is that debt finance accounts for about one third of investment.

Table 3.4 from the previous chapter illustrates the substantial variations in tax burdens on debt and equity corporate capital. These differences are highly sensitive to inflation rates, since one of the benefits of debt is the deduction of the inflation portion of interest at the higher corporate tax rate. This distortion was decreased in the 1980s, not only because of lower statutory rates but also because of the fall in inflation. (The corporate/noncorporate distortion is also magnified by inflation but much less so, in part, because of the offsetting benefits for debt-financed corporate capital.)

Theoretical explanations for debt/equity choices include clientele effects, bankruptcy risk, agency cost, and portfolio effects. The "clientele" explanation advanced by Miller (1979) suggests that equity is

advantageous for high-income individuals if the personal tax rate is
higher than the corporate tax rate, and if most earnings are retained
and not realized as capital gains. This theory has a weak empirical
base because it implies that high-income individuals would hold only
equity and low income individuals would hold only debt, a result
unsupported by the data. Individuals hold mixed portfolios, and corporations tend to pay out substantial amounts of dividends. In any
case the 1986 legislation resulted in a corporate rate higher than the
top individual rate without apparently disturbing portfolios in a dramatic fashion.

Another possible explanation for firms' reliance on equity was the
bankruptcy risk argument advanced by Gordon and Malkiel (1981). In
their model, firms choose less than 100 percent debt finance because of
the risk of bankruptcy. They estimated the efficiency cost from this
distortion at about 0.24 percent of consumption. Fullerton and Gordon
(1983) incorporate this approach in a large-scale model. A difficulty of
the bankruptcy risk notion, however, is that it suggests that in the
absence of taxation firms should finance exclusively with equity, a
notion that is difficult to accept because firms clearly borrowed prior
to the imposition of corporate taxes.

An explanation for including debt in the capital structure even in
the absence of taxation is the agency cost problem advanced by Jensen
(1986). Stockholders cannot costlessly insure that managers maximize
firm value. Because of the separation of ownership and control and the
limits on information, stockholders may wish to limit managerial discretion by requiring managers to meet debt obligations. Complete
reliance on debt, however, may not be desirable, and equity allows a
cushion against changes in cash flow (Jensen 1986; Gertler and Hubbard
1990).

The bankruptcy risk and agency cost explanations imply that debt
and equity are substitutable and that some mix of both will be chosen,
varying, in part, with the tax differential. Given some substitutability,
the welfare cost of the differential can be estimated given an empirical
estimate of the substitution elasticity (percentage change in ratio of
debt to equity divided by the percentage change in the relative tax
burdens). Despite the interest in the debt/equity choice, there has been
little empirical work in this area. Some work has been undertaken estimating the responsiveness of debt acquisition to the ability to deduct
debt (i.e., based on whether adequate profitability is present to absorb

interest deductions); this work is reviewed in Gordon and MacKie-Mason (1990). Nadeau (1988) estimated the responsiveness of debt share to relative tax burdens, using time series data and obtaining a relatively modest elasticity; nevertheless, even a small substitution elasticity can yield a significant welfare effect because the tax differentials are so large. A recent time series study by Navin (1992) also found modest substitution elasticities between debt and equity. Time series empirical studies are, however, potentially plagued by the possibility that these relationships are not constant over time, in part, because various financial innovations appear over time (e.g., junk bonds).

Applying Nadeau's empirical estimate of the substitutability between corporate debt and corporate equity, as discussed in Gravelle and Mackie (1991), yielded a welfare cost of 0.17 percent of consumption from the debt/equity distortion. (This modification can be incorporated in a traditional Harberger-type model or into the Gravelle-Kotlikoff model.) If tax-exempt investors are averaged in, the existing distortion is larger and the cost is estimated at 0.23 percent of consumption. (The tax rates reported in earlier chapters treat tax-exempt pensions as not affecting the margin, under the assumption that individuals cannot make marginal decisions about pension assets.)

A final possible explanation of the debt equity choice is in a portfolio model discussed earlier, where individuals have subjective preferences for different types of assets. A portfolio approach was used by Galper, Lucke, and Toder (1988), although the physical side of that model is truncated. The Galper, Lucke, and Toder model allows individuals to choose assets in their portfolios based on after-tax returns, asset risk, and subjective preferences for risk.

Gravelle and Mackie (1991) also report results (as noted above) from a mixed portfolio/industry model developed by Gravelle. This model treats corporate equity, noncorporate equity, and debt as substitutable in the portfolio, using Nadeau's elasticity, but also contains disaggregated industries. This model is used to explain both the corporate and noncorporate distortions and the debt/equity choices.

Dividends versus Retentions

The question of why firms pay dividends has been a subject of heated debate because dividend payments present a genuine economic puzzle. Instead of paying dividends, the corporation could simply repurchase shares, which would cause all corporate income at the personal level to be taxed as capital gains rather than dividends. Since individuals pay taxes currently on dividends but can forgo paying taxes on capital gains until assets are realized, there is a tax penalty associated with paying dividends, even when there is no capital gains exclusion. Moreover, for most of the history of the income tax, capital gains were provided with preferential rates.

When comparing the tax burdens on dividends version retentions, it is appropriate to examine the capital gains tax on the real portion of the return rather than the entire gain considering inflation (since this choice involves the allocation of real income). With typical holding periods, the effective tax rate on real gains is less than half the tax rate on dividends (13 percent for the 31 percent bracket and 7 percent for the 15 percent bracket). Why, then, should firms pay dividends?

Three theories have been advanced to explain why firms pay dividends: agency costs, signaling, and the "trapped equity" view. The former two are lumped in the common name of the "traditional" or "old" view of dividends. The trapped equity view is also known as the "new" view. Zodrow (1991) provides a more extensive review of this issue.

The signaling view (Bhattacharya 1979; Miller and Rock 1985) is based on the notion that stockholders do not have full information about the earnings prospects of firms and dividend payments are used to communicate profitability about the firm. The tax is simply a necessary price paid for this information. The signaling view is supported by both casual observation (e.g., mutual funds that include only stocks that have a history of paying dividends) and by the relative constancy of dividend payments through temporary dislocations in the economy. Jensen and Meckling (1979) and Jensen (1986) suggest the agency cost mechanism discussed earlier with respect to debt; if managers are required to distribute dividends, their discretion in the disposition of profits is restrained.

The trapped equity view has been advanced by a number of economists—King (1977), Auerbach (1979a, 1979b), and Bradford (1981). In this view, dividend taxes are capitalized in the value of shares and have no effect on investments made out of retained earnings. The basic argument of the new view is this: If a dividend tax is imposed, a stockholder can choose to either receive the dividend and pay the tax or reinvest the dividend and defer the tax until the future when the dividend plus earnings are paid out and taxed. The present value of the future tax on dividends is equal to the tax that would be paid if the dividend is distributed immediately.

A brief example will illustrate this point, and can be simplified by assuming no tax on capital gains. Suppose that the firm has assets of $1,000, and earns a 10 percent rate of return on its assets, yielding a dividend of $100. If the investor's tax rate is 25 percent, $100 dollars of dividends paid today will yield $75 after tax. If the dividend is reinvested, say, at a 10 percent yield, the dividend available a year from now is $110, which will yield after tax $82.50. Since $82.50 represents a 10 percent return on the stockholder investment (the forgone dividends of $75), the rate of return is independent of the stockholder's tax rate. The current owner of the stock will have to pay the tax in either case; hence the tax is effectively imposed regardless of whether or not dividends are paid out.

The capitalization of the tax occurs because the stockholder must value dividends and capital gains equally. In the previous example, if the firm earned $100 on its capital stock, the replacement cost of the assets involved must be $1,000 for a 10 percent yield to earn $100. If the yield is 10 percent, then the value of the stock must rise by 10 percent. But the initial value of the stock does not necessarily have to be $1,000. In order for the investor to earn the same yield through a capital gain (which in this illustration is not taxed) as a dividend, the value of the stock must be 25 percent less, or $750. Indeed this is what the trapped equity view would predict (otherwise, individuals would wish to offer shares for sale and earn the higher return via capital gains). That is, under the trapped equity view, the market value of the firm is below the replacement cost of assets. (This ratio of market value to replacement cost is referred to as q.)

The new view does not preclude dividend payouts. The firm would keep making investments until the value of the stock is driven down to an equilibrium value which equates the return to dividends and the return to capital gains. Dividends paid out are the residual after the exhaustion of investment opportunities.

Economists have tried to assess whether the traditional view or the new view is the more appropriate one by turning to empirical evidence. This empirical evidence includes both statistical evidence and some fairly straightforward observations about the behavior of firms and asset values. For example, Gordon and Bradford (1980) find that market value of dividends is similar to that of capital gains, which would support the traditional view that these alternatives are valued equally (before tax) at the margin.

Several studies examine the relationship between dividends and dividend tax rates (Brittain 1966; Feldstein 1970a; Poterba and Summers 1985; Poterba 1987; Nadeau 1988). The interpretation of these relationships is not clear, however, since negative relationships between dividends and dividend tax rates could be consistent with either theory, as indicated by Auerbach (1979a). Dividends fall with an increase in dividend taxes under the traditional view because the use of dividends has become more costly. In the case of the new view, dividends fall with dividend tax increases because additional investment is necessary to drive down the value of the firm.

Poterba and Summers (1985) also, however, find a relationship between investment patterns and the market value of the firm that is more consistent with the traditional view. Under the traditional view firms should not be increasing investment when the value of q is less than one.

Auerbach (1984) finds a relationship between new share issues and higher earnings and argues that this implies new share issues are a higher cost source of funds consistent with new view. One problem with this conclusion, however, is that rapidly growing firms might rely more heavily on new share issues and might also be earning higher than average rate of return. Auerbach also finds higher personal tax rates of shareholders associated with lower earnings, which he suggests is inconsistent with the traditional view but consistent with the new view where high tax rates tend to expand investments to drive down market value.

These statistical studies have yielded mixed results. What is perhaps more compelling are some of the more straightforward empirical observations that are inconsistent with the new view. A crucial assumption to explain payment of dividends under the new view is that firms cannot repurchase shares; otherwise, firms could effectively pay out earnings by repurchasing shares from existing shareholders. This assumption is, however, inconsistent with both tax law requirements and with observed behavior of firms. There has never been any constraint on firms repurchasing their shares in the open market; moreover Bagwell and Shoven (1989) report evidence of considerable share repurchase activity. While the new view suggests that firms would repurchase shares if such an option is available, it precludes the continuing payment of dividends.

The new view is also inconsistent with the stability of dividend payments (which should fluctuate dramatically with changes in dividend tax rates) and with the value of asset prices relative to the capital stock (which should be depressed by the dividend tax). The theory underlying the payment of dividends and the translation of that theory into the measurement of the cost of capital are unsettled issues, but they have important ramifications for the efficiency effects of the corporate tax. If the new view is adopted, and if marginal investment is financed out of retained earnings, the effective tax rates on corporate equity and corporate capital in general are much lower and the distortions are smaller. Moreover, even though the old style "new view" that precludes share repurchases is inconsistent with observed behavior, it is possible to formulate a new "new view" if there are constraints on share repurchases or there is some fixed relationship between share repurchases and dividends (Sinn 1991; McLure et al. 1990). In such a model the effect of dividend taxes on cost of capital would be modified in a similar way to that of the original new view. These new theories do not, however, specify what might cause such constraints or fixed relationships. Bernheim (1991) has developed a model where dividends are used to signal profitability, and dividend taxes affect the level of dividends but have no implications for welfare or investment.

The more recent versions of the large-scale Harberger model incorporated the new view into the model. Not surprisingly, the result was a reduction of the estimated efficiency costs. (Some of these studies report the efficiency effects with both views.) Given the inconsistencies of the new view with observed behavior, the analysis in Gravelle (1989), Gravelle and Kotlikoff (1989a), and Gravelle and Mackie (1991) employ the traditional view. This traditional view was also adopted in the recent study of tax integration produced by the Treasury Department (1992).

How the dividend tax distorts the disposition of funds by corporations is also a relatively unsettled issue, given the uncertainties about theory in the first place. The signaling theory might suggest a relatively fixed dividend payment rate regardless of the tax, while the agency cost theory might suggest some substitutability between dividend

payments and retentions. Gravelle and Mackie (1991) report some estimated efficiency costs using the lower range of estimated elasticities
(Nadeau 1988); these efficiency gains are in the range of 0.04 to 0.11
percent of consumption. These estimates include tax-exempt investors
as marginal investors; without this assumption the welfare cost could
be as large as 0.2 percent of consumption.

Capital Gains Taxes on Corporate Stock and the Lock-in Effect

Along with the debate over the effect of tax incentives on savings, the
issue of the responsiveness of capital gains realizations to feedback
effects has been widely discussed in the popular tax policy debate.
This issue will be discussed in detail in chapter 6, but it is important to
recognize that part of the lock-in effect arises directly from the double
taxation of corporate income. If corporation income were taxed on a
partnership basis, the increase in value of the stock due to reinvest-
ment of retained earnings would be taxed currently. Even if a capital
gains tax were maintained, the basis would be increased to reflect
these earnings and thus would not be subject to a capital gains tax in
the future.

The empirical research has yielded an enormous range of capital
gains realizations responses. Gravelle (1991d) argued, however, that
the elasticity based on historical data on the ratio of realizations and
accruals could be no more that about 0.5. Gravelle (1991a) used the
midpoint between zero and the upper limit to estimate a welfare cost
for the capital gains lock-in effect for corporate stock arising from failure to tax on a partnership basis, which was measured at 0.06 percent
of consumption.

Summary of Efficiency Issues

Despite uncertainties surrounding the measurement of excess burden
from the imposition of a corporate income tax, there nevertheless
seems to be a fairly strong case on efficiency grounds for considering
revisions in this area. For example, using the higher measures of efficiency gain (0.9 percent for physical reallocation, 0.17 percent for debt
equity differentials, 0.2 percent for the dividend distortion, and 0.06
percent for the lock in effect), a welfare gain that is 1.36 percent of consumption can be obtained—this is approximately the size of the addi-

tional revenue collected from the tax. If we add some small intertemporal gain (Gravelle 1991b), the excess burden of collecting the corporate tax is larger than the direct revenue yield. But even more modest measures of efficiency gain suggest a large excess burden relative to revenue yield.

Even if full integration is not considered feasible, a partial relief measure that may avoid the administrative complications of full integration and lose less revenue might be considered. Recall that the welfare gain rises with the square of the tax rate. Thus, partial relief would actually yield larger welfare gains as a proportion of revenue loss than full relief. As an illustration of this important point, consider an excess of the corporate tax over the noncorporate tax of roughly around 30 percent. Eighty-three percent of the potential welfare gain associated with complete elimination would be achieved by cutting this tax in half; 66 percent of the gain would be achieved by cutting it by one-third. If the total gain were roughly equal to the extra revenue, then the welfare gain would be 1.6 times the lost revenue with the excess taxes cut in half and over twice the lost revenue with the excess tax cut by one-third.

Policy Options

One major reservation about revising the corporate tax has to do with redistribution—toward current elderly generations and toward higher-income individuals. As in the case of capital income taxation in general, corporate income taxes tend to be progressive because individuals' share of income in capital rises with income. There is another issue, however, to be addressed with reference to the corporate tax. Because of behavioral responses to the corporate tax, at least in the Harberger and related models, the tax can be shifted to labor as well as capital. Gravelle and Kotlikoff (1993) show that various types of models still find that the tax falls primarily on capital given reasonable assumptions about the ability of firms to substitute labor for capital and the ability of consumers to substitute different products. Gravelle (1991a) also shows that such incidence is likely in an open economy when account is taken of less than perfect substitutability between products in international trade.

Distribution across income classes can be remedied with a revision in the individual income tax rates to make up any lost revenue. And, while there would be some redistribution across generations, it would be much more modest with corporate tax integration than with full elimination of capital income taxes. Moreover the recent Treasury Department study (1992) suggests that it might be possible to design a system that would offset lower corporate sector taxes by raising capital income taxes on other assets. Hubbard (1992) also discusses the Treasury findings.

There are a wide variety of possible revisions that can reduce the corporate tax differential. These revisions are outlined below: Gravelle (1991a) provides some rough estimates of revenue consequences at FY 1992 income levels. McLure (1979) addresses many of the practical issues associated with corporate tax integration.

Full Integration

Full integration would simply tax all income to shareholders, although administratively the corporation might be used as a withholding device with individuals taking a credit against tax (the "credit method").[7] Capital gains on corporate stock could be eliminated entirely or allowed with the basis of stock increased by retained earnings attributed to the stockholder. The former would result in a revenue loss of $96 billion, and the latter would result in a revenue loss of $86 billion. Continuing to tax capital gains would result in a slightly smaller welfare gain because some lock-in effect would still occur. Eliminating capital gains on corporate stock altogether may be justified because the real gain would already be taxed under the full integration method and the remainder would simply be inflationary gains. This method would also be much simpler, since it would not require the constant adjustment of basis. The disadvantage is that windfall gains and losses on corporate stock would never be recognized.

If the credit method is used, tax-exempt shareholders could be denied the credit for a revenue loss of $70 billion without capital gains taxes. Under a credit method the corporation pays the tax, and the stockholder receives a credit against tax liability for taxes paid. If the credit is not refundable, it will not be available to tax-exempt shareholders. This approach will have no effect on the welfare gain if tax-exempt investments are not marginal, which seems a reasonable assumption (as outlined in chapter 8).

Elimination of Personal Level Tax

A partial, but simpler, approach would be to eliminate personal level taxes on dividends and capital gains for a revenue loss of $43 billion. This approach would not go as far as full integration but would reduce all of the distortions somewhat, and eliminate the dividend/retentions distortion and the lock-in effect entirely.

Dividend Relief

Another set of proposals would be directed only at dividends. These include a dividend deduction for a revenue loss of $59 billion. If a withholding/credit method is used with credits denied to tax exempts, the loss would be $38 billion. Another option is the dividend exclusion at the individual level. One of the difficulties with the dividend relief approaches is that they would now favor dividends over retentions and tend to gain much less at the dividends/retentions margin. Also lock-in effects on capital gains would not be affected, and the gains in the noncorporate/corporate distortion and debt distortion would be smaller.

Debt Advantages and the Comprehensive Business Income Tax

Debt advantages could be reduced and revenue gained in some of these partial systems by indexing interest deductions and payments, or by disallowing part of the interest deduction. The Treasury Department's integration study (1992) proposed a new method of reducing distortions by not only repealing the personal level taxes on corporate income but also disallowing interest deductions (while not taxing interest to creditors). This overall tax was proposed at a rate of 31 percent on both corporate and noncorporate business (with an exclusion for small noncorporate businesses). This approach, termed the *comprehensive business income tax* (CBIT), would not lose any revenue, yet should accomplish virtually all of the welfare gains of full integration.

CBIT is surely one of the most intriguing ideas for dealing with the corporate income tax and capital income to surface. Because it imposes only one level of tax that falls equally on corporate equity and corporate debt, it completely eliminates any distortion in favor of debt. If noncorporate income is taxed at the same rate, it would also eliminate the differences between corporate and noncorporate income. Finally, by eliminating the personal level taxes, CBIT would eliminate any incentive to retain earnings.

CBIT would indirectly increase taxes for pension funds and other tax exempt entities by disallowing interest deductibility, unless these funds have direct holdings of taxable mortgages. This outcome would be desirable if tax benefits for pension trusts do not affect tax burdens at the margin. Moreover it would be possible to preclude the shifting of these entities' asset holdings into taxable bonds by imposing a tax on mortgage interest at the corporate rate for these firms. It would create taxable and tax-exempt interest to investors, but this approach would effectively reduce the relative benefits to owner occupied housing since mortgage interest would remain taxable and thus carry a higher interest rate.

There are of course some drawbacks to CBIT, both political and economic. Disallowing interest deductibility might be resisted by firms, and the implicit increase in taxation of tax exempt entities would also create resistance. It might be necessary to phase in a CBIT approach because of the higher taxes on heavily leveraged firms. There would also be an incentive, absent some explicit tax correction, for tax exempt entities to hold taxable debt. Another problem with CBIT is the allocation of income between capital and labor for proprietorships. Even if, however, these entities were allowed to continue with their current individual rates, the distortions between corporate and noncorporate investments would be considerably narrowed. There are also some uncertainties about the rules for taxation of foreign source income and some complexities with taxing financial intermediaries.

An important advantage of CBIT or a modified version of the proposal is that it would avoid some of the equity concerns about reducing capital income taxes, since the revenue would be largely offset by increased tax burdens on other investments. CBIT could also be easily converted into a consumption tax base by repealing depreciation and inventory accounting and allowing expensing of investments. Such a system would then become equivalent to the x-tax (mentioned at the end of chapter 2), with labor income taxed under the graduated rates of the personal tax, old capital subject to the CBIT tax, and new capital exempt.

5
Tax Neutrality and
Capital Cost Recovery:
Depreciation, Inflation,
and Investment Subsidies

One of the points of disagreement between different camps of economists over the Tax Reform Act of 1986 concerned the repeal of an investment subsidy—the investment tax credit (ITC)—in exchange for rate cuts, particularly corporate rate cuts. (The act also provided less generous depreciation, primarily for structures, which is a similar phenomenon.) Supporters of the legislation argued that the investment credit was the cause of economic distortions and that lowering the tax rates and broadening the base would result in a more neutral tax system, and a more efficient allocation of capital. Many of these economists would have preferred even broader reforms, such as corporate tax integration and indexing for inflation. Critics suggested that it was poor policy to exchange a subsidy that applied only to new investment, and thus had the largest "bang for the buck," for a rate cut that provided a windfall to old investment. This group of economists focuses more heavily on the issue of the savings response. They would be less enamored of a rate cut and more interested in providing some sort of subsidy to investment.

This debate over the desirability of investment subsidies is not a new one. Indeed a perusal of the history of the U.S. tax treatment of capital income in the postwar period reveals that much of the change occurring over time has been not through changes in rates but rather through changes in the tax rules regarding the measurement of income and the allowance of various special subsidies. As table 2.1 demonstrates, the corporate statutory tax rate changed very little over a long period of time, but the marginal effective tax rate varied substantially. These changes in marginal effective tax rate as shown in figure 2.1 largely reflected changes restricted to new investments—different rules determining allowances for the depreciation of capital (or capital cost recovery), and changes in explicit tax subsidies to investment in equipment. These burdens also, however, reflected the effects of inflation.

Depreciation, or capital cost recovery—that is, how much of receipts in excess of operating costs is a recovery of original investment—is central to determining the effective tax burden on income from capital and has effects on the composition of the U.S. capital stock. In order to tax the return to capital for an asset that wears out, tax rules must allow the investor to recover his original investment tax free through depreciation deductions, just as the original investment in a bond is excluded from tax when the bond is redeemed.

Depreciation is easy to assess in theory, but difficult in practice. It can also contribute to complexity in the tax law. Indeed one justification for shifting to a consumption or wage tax base is that it is very difficult to measure depreciation correctly and thus very difficult to obtain a truly neutral income tax.

Major changes to provide more rapid tax depreciation were made in 1954, 1962, 1971, and 1981. Restrictions occurred in 1969, 1982, 1986, and 1993. The liberalization of depreciation in the 1960s and 1970s, coupled with the adoption of an ITC in 1962 (with liberalizations in 1964 and 1975), have been accompanied by an erosion in the value of depreciation deductions because of inflation, particularly in the 1960s and 1970s. In the 1980s, while inflation abated, depreciation was further liberalized, giving rise to quite low effective tax rates by historical standards.

The Tax Reform Act of 1986 abandoned the investment tax credit, but retained methods of depreciation that are accelerated by comparison with empirical estimates of economic depreciation. Depreciation continued, however, to be based on historical costs. Although these effects were largely offsetting in many cases, there continued to be substantial variation between tax burdens across assets.

In determining the effects of these policies, as well as assessing the desirability of investment incentives, there are two fundamental questions. First, what rules for allowing capital cost recovery are appropriate to measure income, and are those rules currently used? Second, what type of investment incentives, if any, are desirable?

Based on empirical estimates of economic depreciation, tax rates on business investment would still vary due to the imperfect measurement of income even in the presence of corporate integration. Among structures and equipment outside of oil exploration, as shown in table 3.2, tax rates vary from 14 to 28 percent in the noncorporate sector (with a weighted statutory tax rate of 23 percent). These differences are more pronounced when a broader range of investments is considered, as in table 3.1. And these differentials could easily become magnified through inflation changes or as a result of the restoration of investment incentives, such as the ITC.

Whether explicit investment subsidies likely to be desirable in increasing the efficiency or the equity of the tax system is an unsettled question. The investment credit was repealed in 1986, in part, due to a recognition of its distorting effects across assets. Before this tax change the disparities between different types of assets were much larger, with investments in equipment frequently subject to negligible or even negative effective tax rates. Not only does the ITC cause distortions across assets, it does little to narrow the distortions across investments discussed previously—between corporate and noncorporate investments and between debt and equity finance. These aspects are drawbacks to investment subsidies in general and to the specific one used in the past.

Despite the poor performance of the ITC, given an objective of more even treatment of different types of investments, there is considerable support, both among economists and legislators, for direct subsidies to investment. The most typical form suggested is the one that is most familiar—the ITC. The main rationale for preferring an investment subsidy to a reduction in the tax rate is that it would have a more powerful effect—a greater "bang for the buck." Since a tax break such as the investment credit benefits only new investment, a larger reduction in the effective tax rate can be obtained with a smaller revenue cost. Indeed, this is an argument similar to that which might favor a consumption tax over a wage tax—the consumption tax base is much larger than the wage tax base because it allows an exemption for tax only for new investment.

The investment credit, however, occupies an intermediate position between a wage tax substitution and a consumption tax substitution. This point is not widely understood, and it arises because of depreciation and the concurrent need for replacement capital. When depreciation and replacement of the capital stock are incorporated into the consumption tax analysis, there is no additional tax benefit for replacement investment (depreciation) that can be deducted under either an income or a consumption tax base. The benefit is confined to net investment that increases the capital stock. While an investment credit allows no benefit to the existing capital stock, it does allow benefits to the replacement of that capital stock as it deteriorates. The more it is targeted toward investments that depreciate rapidly, the more it becomes like a wage tax substitution; ironically the very fact that the credit is usually aimed at rapidly depreciating equipment causes it to have less "bang for the buck."

Investment subsidies have also been proposed as countercyclical devices—and in this case the "bang-for-the-buck" argument is much more powerful. Yet, such investment subsidies have been argued to be of limited effectiveness as a countercyclical stimulus. The following sections address these issues. The next section discusses the theory of depreciation as the broader topic of how to measure income correctly and explains how the tax law works. The following section evaluates the case for investment subsidies and discusses the forms they might take. The final section briefly discusses the role of investment subsidies as countercyclical devices.

Measuring Income Correctly

Because the income tax is designed to tax net income, or in the case of investment, the return to capital, depreciation deductions are a necessary and important feature of the tax structure. In particular, for the tax system to operate as implied by the rate structure, depreciation deductions for a given investment must correspond to economic depreciation. Under any system of depreciation (in the absence of inflation) the amount of depreciation deductions taken over the lifetime of an investment will equal the original investment made. Thus depreciation deductions for accounting or tax purposes necessarily sum to the original cost. The timing of these deductions is important, however, and only one pattern over time corresponds to economic depreciation.

Depreciation allowances corresponding to economic depreciation have several important characteristics. First, they permit the investor to recover his original investment tax free, while the tax rate is applied only to the return to that investment. This measurement of return of capital must be made correctly in each period, as the timing of capital cost recovery is crucial; if economic depreciation is allowed for tax purposes, the effective tax rate will equal the statutory tax rate. Second, the amount of depreciation deductions, if reinvested, would permit taxpayers to maintain the real value of their capital stock. Third, economic depreciation captures the expected decline in the real market value of the asset in each period, measured at current prices. (Note that expected depreciation and actual depreciation may diverge because of uncertainty in the market value of assets; this issue is discussed in the section on risk in chapter 3.) If inflation is present, economic depreciation deductions will sum to an amount greater than the historical cost, since depreciation deductions must be restated in current prices.

Measuring Economic Depreciation

With investment in financial assets such as bonds or savings accounts, there is no difficulty in determining what amounts are investment and what amounts are interest. If the bondholder sells his bond for its original cost (as he could do when there is no change in the interest rate), the proceeds of the sale of the bond are the return *of* capital, and the interest he receives on the bond is the return *to* capital and would be taxed. (In the presence of inflation the value of the bond should be increased to reflect current price levels.) Investment in depreciable property, however, involves a wearing away of the asset. When a piece of machinery or equipment is sold, it generally sells for less than it originally cost and may be virtually worthless.

Therefore in an investment in depreciable property the depreciation pattern must be inferred. The investor anticipates a certain stream of revenues or cash flow from his investment, and this stream of revenues determines what depreciation pattern is appropriate ex ante. This point can be illustrated by reference to investment in a bond where the amount of the original investment and the return on the investment can be easily distinguished. Suppose that an investor buys a $1,000 bond that earns a rate of return of 10 percent and that he sells the bond at the end of five years. His stream of revenues or cash flow at the end of each year is

Year				
1	2	3	4	5

Example 1: $100 $100 $100 $100 $1100

The appropriate tax treatment would be to include all of the cash flow in income and allow a deduction for the sale of the bond (equivalent to depreciation) in the fifth year of $1,000.

This type of cash flow pattern is not of course likely to occur with investments in depreciable property, since the stream of revenues is likely to be more even over time and, indeed, to decline. To illustrate this pattern, suppose that the bondholder decides to sell one-fifth of his bonds ($200) in each year. The cash flow pattern would be

Year				
1	2	3	4	5

Example 2: $300 $280 $260 $240 $220

In this case the proper depreciation deduction would be $200 in each period. This form of depreciation is known as *straight-line depreciation*. Note, however, that the cash flow declines in each year.

As another alternative, suppose that the bond holder decides to sell just enough bonds in each period so that he will have an equal cash flow in each year. His stream of cash flow would be

Year				
1	2	3	4	5

Example 3: $263.80 $263.80 $263.80 $263.80 $263.80

To achieve this pattern of cash flow, the investor would have to sell his bonds in increments as follows: $163.80, $180.20, $198.20, $218.20, $239.80. That is, in the first year, he earns interest of $100 and sells $163.80 of his bonds. In the second year he earns interest of $83.62 on his remaining bonds (10 percent of $1,000 minus $163.80) and sells $180.20 of bonds. This pattern of depreciation is slower than straight-line—indeed it is the pattern of principal repayment that occurs in a level payment mortgage. If the pattern of returns were even more concentrated toward the beginning than in example 2, the economic depreciation method would be faster than straight-line.

Unlike the bondholder, the investor in a depreciating asset does not know the return of capital; all he knows is the expected cash flow in each future year. This cash flow is the expected output of the investment times the price minus any operating costs. Sale of an asset for scrap would be included in the last year's cash flow. Therefore the pattern of economic depreciation depends on three characteristics: how long the asset lasts, the pattern of output of the investment over its life (i.e., is it constant or does it decline?), and the scrap value.

The depreciation pattern is inferred from the cash flow pattern through the use of discounted cash flow analysis. The discounted value of an amount to be received in the future (for annual interest) is $A/(1 + r)^t$, where A is the amount, r is the interest rate, and t is the number of years into the future. For example, if $110 is expected in the future and the discount rate is 10 percent, its present value is $100 (that is $110/1.10). $100 invested for a year will grow to $110. If $121 is expected two years from now, its present value is also $100 ($121/(1.10)^2$. $100 invested for two years will grow, with compounding at the end of each year, to $121. Thus the last example can be written as a present value equation:

$$\$1,000 = \frac{\$263.68}{(1+r)^1} + \frac{\$263.68}{(1+r)^2} + \frac{\$263.68}{(1+r)^3} + \frac{\$263.68}{(1+r)^4} + \frac{\$263.68}{(1+r)^5},$$

where r is the rate of return. In this case r is equal to 10 percent (as it would be in all of the other bond sales mentioned above).

After the first year the value of the asset is the discounted value of the remaining four years of receipts, or

$$\$836.20 = \frac{\$263.68}{(1+r)^1} + \frac{\$263.68}{(1+r)^2} + \frac{\$263.68}{(1+r)^3} + \frac{\$263.68}{(1+r)^4},$$

Depreciation therefore is the change in the value of the asset—$1,000 minus $836.20, or $163.80. Depreciation in the next period is the difference between $836.20 and the present value of three years of discounted payments. This example illustrates three principal features of economic depreciation: It sums to original cost; if reinvested constantly, it would maintain the value of the asset; and it is measured by the change in the value of the asset.

Another characteristic of economic depreciation is that it preserves the expected relationship between pre- and post-tax return. For example, in the level payment illustration, if depreciation is allowed based on economic depreciation and the tax rate is 20 percent, the net return on investment will be 8 percent, because the return of 10 percent has been properly measured and taxed. That is, the value of cash flow *after-tax*, if discounted at the 8 percent after-tax rate, will yield the proper present value of $1,000.

Economic Depreciation with Inflation

The percentage of an asset's original cost that should be deducted in each year depends on the projected real output of the asset; that pattern in turn determines the unique pattern of economic depreciation. This depreciation could be measured by observing the change in the value of assets. In the presence of inflation this relationship changes. Indeed it is possible for assets to rise in nominal value because of inflation while actually declining in real value because of depreciation.

Economic depreciation exists, nevertheless, which will result in an effective tax rate equal to the statutory rate but applied only to the real portion of the return. If interest is continually compounded, the real rate is the nominal interest rate minus the inflation rate. Thus, if the nominal interest rate is 10 percent and the inflation rate is 5 percent, the real interest rate is 5 percent. If interest is expressed on an annual basis, the real interest rate is one plus the nominal rate divided by one plus the inflation rate minus one.[1]

Depreciation in the presence of inflation can be computed as the depreciation that would have occurred in the absence of price inflation multiplied by the ratio of the current price level to the price level at the time of acquisition. The price level needed to make this adjustment is the general price level in the economy (e.g., the GNP deflator) and not the change in the price of a new capital asset. If asset prices rise relative to the general price level, the real value of the asset has increased, and the change in value is real appreciation. In fact the proper treatment of this price change would be to include it in income; it would then be proper to increase all future depreciation deductions by the change in relative prices. If, however, the specific asset price is used to adjust depreciation, without including the real change in income at the time it occurs, the effect is to eliminate any realization of real capital gains and losses and compound the error in income measurement.

Empirical Evidence on Economic Depreciation

While economic depreciation can be defined in the abstract, it is difficult to measure in practical terms. Governments are not privy to the investor's expected stream of returns. Rather, investments must be observed as broad aggregates and some general rules defined. There have been several attempts to measure economic depreciation, or at least certain aspects of economic depreciation, some of them made with reference to tax lives used in the past. Tax lives were reduced in 1962 and again in 1971 under the Asset Depreciation Range System. Tax lives are even shorter currently than the 1971 lives. For example, estimates of useful lives indicate that tax lives for equipment averaged 16.1 years (weighted by capital stock) before 1962, were reduced to 11.7 years in 1962, to 9.4 years in 1971, and to 5 years in 1981. The current useful lives are estimated at 6.9, only 60 percent of the 1962 lives.

The Treasury Department (1971) surveyed depreciation lives based on audit information before adopting the 1971 useful life reductions, asking revenue agents and engineers whether most, some, or a few firms were receiving more generous lives than they might otherwise be able to justify. Of the respondents, 42 percent indicated that most firms were receiving shorter tax lives than they could justify, 35 percent indicated some were receiving shorter lives than they could justify, and 24 percent indicated a few firms were receiving shorter lives. These findings suggest that even the 1962 lives may have understated actual useful lives. There was also an interesting laboratory experiment with the 1962 lives, which was never really completed: the use of a reserve ratio test which would test tax lives against actual practice. The reserve ratio test was never invoked because it was likely that most firms would not be able to justify their tax lives.[2] These findings indicated that economic lives for equipment are much longer than current tax lives, probably in excess of 12 years.

Of course, even if the duration of life of an asset could be determined, such information would not be adequate to determine economic depreciation, since the pattern of depreciation over the life would still need to be determined. To assess economic depreciation would require investigation of the prices of new versus used assets, or the pattern of output over time. Other studies have explored these approaches.

A study of depreciation of machine tools by Beidleman (1976) indicated that economic lives were three times as long as the tax lives in force at that time. This study would suggest economic lives longer than 25 years. Beidleman used the method of comparing sales prices of used assets to infer depreciation lives. Taubman and Rasche (1969) examined the pattern of rents for buildings and concluded that tax depreciation substantially exceeded economic depreciation, which was then more generous than it is today.

Probably the most comprehensive study of economic depreciation was undertaken by Hulten and Wykoff (1981). They also used the method of comparing prices of assets of different ages. This used asset price approach is hampered somewhat by the lack of a used asset market for many types of assets. To infer depreciation rates in those markets, they applied a rule of thumb relationship based on the relationship between depreciation rates and economic lives assumed by the Bureau of Economic Analysis. Their numbers are used in calculating effective tax rates above and are also used as the basis for analyzing effects of depreciation in this chapter. It is important, however, to stress that these depreciation rates are imperfect estimates of economic depreciation.

On the whole, empirical research suggests that economic lives are probably a good deal longer than lives allowed for tax purposes and that tax depreciation is considerably accelerated relative to economic depreciation. Of course caution must be exercised in drawing conclusions from these studies, particularly the older ones, as the economic characteristics of capital goods can change. The Treasury Department is currently undertaking studies of depreciation, but the results are limited at this time.

Cost Recovery under the Tax Code

Under the tax code investments are recovered in a variety of ways: depreciation deductions, expensing of costs, deductions of acquisition costs at the time of sale through inventory adjustments, and depletion deductions (for natural resources). The costs of investments in structures and equipment are recovered through tax depreciation. The value of economic depreciation depends on the number of years over which the cost is recovered and how deductions are allocated over time, due to the pattern of production. Similarly tax depreciation depends on the useful life allowed for tax purposes and the rate of deduction allowed by the tax law. All tax depreciation is based on original (historical) cost. That is, depreciation deductions are not indexed for inflation; economic depreciation would be adjusted to reflect inflation.

Under current law depreciable assets are assigned useful lives based partly on the type of asset and partly on the industry. Assets such as computers, office furniture, cars and trucks, and buildings are assigned the same useful lives regardless of the industry. Other assets, such as machine tools, are assigned useful lives based on the industry in which they are used.

The value of tax depreciation depends on the rate at which deductions are allowed. Historically three different types of depreciation methods have been allowed. The straight-line method requires equal deductions in each year and is currently used for buildings. The sum-of-years-digits method was used in the past: Depreciation was the remaining useful life divided by the sum of the digits in the useful life. For example, with a three-year life the sum of digits is 6 (1 + 2 + 3 = 6), and depreciation in the first year would be 3/6, or 50 percent. In the second year depreciation would be 2/6, or one-third, and in the final year 1/6. This method is much more rapid than the straight-line. A third method is declining balance, where a constant rate is applied to the undepreciated balance. For example, in double declining balance, the rate is twice the straight-line rate. Thus an asset with a useful life of 10 years would receive a declining balance rate of 2/10 or 20 percent. Slower declining balance methods are also used for longer-lived equipment assets. A 1.5 declining balance rate, for a 10-year life, would allow a rate of 1.5/10, or 15 percent. Because declining balance methods would never fully depreciate the asset, the taxpayer can switch to a straight-line method (where the remaining undepreciated balance is deducted in equal increments over the remaining useful life). For double declining balance, the optimal time to switch is a midpoint; for slower methods the optimal switch point comes earlier.

Currently, equipment assets are assigned lives of three, five, seven, ten, fifteen, or twenty years. (Equipment is defined by the tax law to include public utility structures.) The first four classes are depreciated under double declining balance methods, and the last two under 150 percent declining balance. Business structures are depreciated at a straight-line rate over 39 years (increased in 1993 from 31.5); residential structures are depreciated at a straight-line rate over 27.5 years.

Investments of course need not be made in the form of purchases of equipment and structures. The purchase of land does not give rise to a depreciation deduction, although the costs of purchasing mineral resources are recovered through depletion. A large fraction of investments are made in the form of inventories, where costs are deducted when the goods are sold. These inventories may include purchase of goods for resale as in the case of wholesale and retail trade or purchases of supplies and materials used in constructing goods for sale. These costs, along with related expenses, are deducted when goods are sold. Although there are a variety of inventory cost methods, two of the most common are FIFO (first-in, first-out) and LIFO (last-in, first-out). In FIFO the costs of inventory are the oldest goods purchased, while in LIFO the costs are the most recent. For an ongoing firm, LIFO has roughly the effect of indexing for inflation (since the last good bought will be valued at current cost), while FIFO does not (since the oldest good bought will be valued at historical cost that is normally below current cost).[3]

A variety of special rules apply to natural resources and agriculture. Some of the costs (e.g., acquisition costs and some exploration costs) of investing in fuel and mineral deposits are deducted through "depletion." Cost depletion, which applies to most fuel producers, is based on the rate at which the mineral reserve is depleted. If the depletion rate is estimated correctly and there is no inflation, this method corresponds to economic depreciation. Independent producers of fuel minerals (up to a limit) and all producers of other minerals are allowed percentage depletion, a deduction for a percentage of output. This method may be much more beneficial than cost depletion. Many costs of finding mineral reserves are, however, expensed. These include intangible drilling and mining costs (labor, supplies, and repairs) and unproductive properties, wells, and mines. Integrated producers (i.e., firms that refine as well as produce) must deduct 30 percent of intangible drilling costs at a straight-line rate over 5 years; a similar provision applies to certain costs of coal and other fuel producers. Many costs of growing timber are expensed, and there is a limited 10 percent credit and seven-year write-off period for reforestation. Most noncorporate farmers can deduct many expenditures that would normally be capitalized (feed, fertilizer, soil conservation costs, and various livestock and crop production costs).

Many investments that produce intangible assets, such as research and development and other forms of technical know-how, and advertising, are expensed even though the returns to such investment are realized over a period of time. The effect of expensing is to create a zero tax rate at the firm level. Organizational costs of setting up a firm are recovered over 5 years.

Certain types of investments should be assigned "negative depreciation" or gains. Gains in the real value of assets, which in theory should be taxed when accrued, are taxed only when assets are sold. A common example is timber; certain types of land may also accrue real gains over time. The gain in value of assets arising from inflation, which should not be included in income, is also subject to capital gains taxes.

Investment Subsidies and Penalties

Obviously an investment subsidy (a reduction in effective tax rate) could arise from allowing depreciation or cost recovery at a faster rate than suggested by economic depreciation. Penalties (increases in effective tax rate) arise from allowing too slow a rate or failing to index depreciation deductions for inflation.

Whether a net subsidy or penalty from these aspects of the tax law exists can be determined by calculating effective tax rates. If the effective tax rate at the firm level falls below (above) the statutory rate, this provision produces a subsidy (penalty). As tables 3.1 and 3.2 (chapter 3) demonstrate, some assets are subsidized and some are penalized. Mining and oil and gas exploration have very low tax rates because of the expensing of most of the costs of these investments. Using the Hulten and Wykoff (1981) estimates of economic depreciation, most equipment investments also receive a subsidy, although these subsidies are frequently relatively small. Structures vary between subsidies and penalties, and inventories tend to be taxed at high rates due to the assumption that some portions are recovered under FIFO accounting.

The Effect of Inflation and Accelerated Methods of Depreciation

Table 5.1 disentangles some of these effects by reporting what tax rates would be with no inflation, and with inflation at twice typical assumed rates (9.6 percent instead of 4.8 percent). The zero inflation rate estimates indicate that tax depreciation is accelerated relative to economic depreciation, especially for certain types of equipment, because all of the tax rates for depreciable assets fall below the statutory rate. The table also indicates that inflation tends to affect effective tax rates more for short-lived assets, which is a standard finding (see Gravelle 1982). For example, the shortest-lived asset class, automobiles, has a 39 percent tax rate at a 4.8 percent inflation rate in the corporate sector. With no inflation, the rate falls to 27 percent, while at 9.6 percent inflation, the rate rises to 46 percent. Corporate industrial structures, by contrast, are subject to a 36 percent effective rate at a 4.8 percent inflation rate. With no inflation rate the effective rate falls to only 31 percent, and with a 9.6 percent inflation, it rises to only 39 percent.

The larger penalties arising from failure to index for inflation for short lived assets occur because these penalties are large relative to the present value of taxes collected. The tax penalty for failing to index for inflation, measured as the present value of the additional taxes paid, rises as assets increase in durability and then falls. (For an asset with infinite durability, e.g., land, there is no penalty at all.) The proportional effects on the tax burden, however, are consistently larger for short-lived assets. The present value of tax payments is smaller for a short-lived asset (which earns income for a shorter period of time) than for a long-lived asset. Even within the range of durabilities when the present value of tax penalties due to failure to index inflation is rising, it does not rise as fast as the present value of taxes paid by the asset. The ratio of the penalty to taxes paid is larger across the entire range of durabilities.

The Design of Investment Subsidies and Neutrality

In general, only a particular type of tax subsidy tends to be neutral across assets.[4] Some subsidies favor short-lived assets, while others favor long-lived assets. The most common subsidy used in the past,

Table 5.1
Marginal effective tax rates: Structures and equipment, varying inflation rates

Asset type	Corporate		Noncorporate	
	No inflation	9.6% inflation	No inflation	9.6% inflation
Equipment				
Autos	27	46	18	36
Office/computing equipment	24	42	15	32
Trucks, buses, and trailers	23	41	15	30
Aircraft	23	40	15	30
Construction machinery	18	34	11	23
Mining/oilfield equipment	23	39	14	29
Service industry equipment	23	39	14	29
Tractors	21	37	13	27
Instruments	22	38	14	28
Other	21	37	13	27
General industrial equipment	20	35	13	25
Metalworking machinery	19	33	11	24
Electric transmission equipment	28	41	18	31
Communications equipment	15	28	9	19
Other electrical equipment	19	33	11	24
Furniture and fixtures	18	32	11	23
Special industrial equipment	17	30	10	21
Agricultural equipment	17	31	10	21
Fabricated metal	24	37	15	27
Engines and turbines	31	43	20	32
Ships and boats	19	33	12	23
Railroad equipment	14	26	8	18
Structures				
Mining/oil and gas	10	12	7	8
Other	33	42	22	31
Industrial	31	39	20	28
Public utility	23	33	14	23
Commercial	28	36	18	25
Farm	22	32	13	22
Rental housing	25	32	15	22
Inventories	34	52	23	41

Note: Based on calculations in appendix B. The calculations do not take into account the 1993 increase in the corporate tax rate from 34 to 35 percent, the increase in individual rates, nor the increase in depreciation write-off periods for nonresidential buildings. These changes had only a small effect.

the investment tax credit, is not a neutral subsidy. It favors short-lived assets. Investment credits are still allowed under current law for certain types of investments although many of these are temporary: incremental R&D expenses of an intangible nature (e.g., costs of labor and supplies), reforestation expenditures (up to a limit), low-income housing, historic preservation, rehabilitation expenditures, and certain energy conservation or alternative energy investments.

A number of different types of investment incentives and their effects on aggregated equipment (which is short lived) and aggregated structures (which are long lived) are shown in table 5.2, weighted by

Table 5.2
Marginal effective tax rates with investment incentives

Investment incentive	Corporate		Noncorporate	
	Equipment	Structures	Equipment	Structures
Statutory tax rate	34	34	23	23
Current law	30	32	21	22
10% investment credit	–12	19	–35	6
With basis adjustment	3	21	–20	8
In excess of depreciation	23	25	13	13
5% investment credit	14	26	0	14
With basis adjustment	19	27	5	15
In excess of depreciation	27	28	17	18
Additional deduction (10% credit equivalent)	–12	19	–10	12
Additional deduction (5% credit equivalent)	14	26	8	17
Depreciating 150% of cost	–55	23	–26	14
Depreciating 125% of cost	4	28	3	18
50% reduction in service life	20	25	13	16
Partial expensing				
25%	24	26	16	17
50%	18	19	12	12
75%	10	10	6	6
100%	0	0	0	0

Note: Based on calculations in appendix B. The calculations do not take into account the increase in the corporate tax rate from 34 to 35 percent, the increase in individual rates, nor the increase in depreciation write-off periods for nonresdiential buildings. These changes had only a small effect.

the shares of capital stock for each type of asset listed in table 5.1. Rates are reported at the firm level for both corporate and noncorporate investment. These tax rates ignore the effects of deduction of interest at the firm level and the effects of personal level taxes on dividends, interest, and capital gains. The advantage of using a firm level tax is that it reveals the effects of investment subsidies most clearly. That is if economic income were measured correctly, the effective tax rate would be the statutory rate.

Under current law both structures and equipment are taxed at rates quite close to the statutory rate. While the corporate statutory rate is 34 percent, corporate equipment is taxed an overall rate of 30 percent and structures at an overall rate of 32 percent. The weighted marginal statutory rate in the noncorporate sector is 23 percent; equipment is taxed at 21 percent and structures at 22 percent, again close to the statutory rate.

Introducing a 10 percent investment credit, which was in effect from 1975 to 1981, produces dramatic variations in effective tax rates. Corporate effective tax rates on structures fall to 19 percent, but effective tax rates on equipment fall to *minus* 12 percent. (A similar pattern appears for the lower 5 percent credit.) In this latter case the offset to the tax burden from the investment subsidy has become so large that there is an *overall* subsidy by the government to the investment. An investment failing to yield an adequate profit in the complete absence of taxes now becomes attractive.

The investment credit strongly favors short-lived assets because the present value of the tax payments is smaller for a short-lived asset (which earns income for a shorter period of time) than for a long-lived asset. A flat rate benefit offsets a larger proportion of this tax for short-lived assets; indeed for the 10 percent credit, the credit is larger than the present value of tax payments. (Another way of thinking about this issue is that short-lived assets are replaced more frequently, so the firm is able to repeat the credit more often.)

A credit has a more powerful effect on noncorporate versus corporate investments, for the same reason. The present value of taxes for noncorporate assets is lower than for corporate assets because the tax rate is lower. The investment credit is the same for both corporate and noncorporate assets and therefore offsets a larger portion of the noncorporate tax paid than the corporate tax paid. This feature limits the value of the investment credit in reducing corporate/noncorporate tax differentials because a credit reduces the tax rate proportionally more for the tax-favored noncorporate investment.

The disparities among assets of different durabilities can be reduced, but not eliminated, by providing for a basis adjustment. With a basis adjustment the amount of the investment that can be depreciated is reduced by the amount of the credit. A basis adjustment was required for the original investment credit adopted in 1964 but was eliminated in 1964. A half basis adjustment applied from 1982 through 1986. Since the present value of depreciation is larger for short-lived assets, this basis adjustment has the effect of making the total credit, net of forgone depreciation, somewhat smaller for short-lived assets than for long-lived ones. Even so, the investment credit with a basis adjustment still favors shorter-lived assets. Of course, in prior law, the ITC had even larger distorting effects on structures vis-à-vis equipment because it was not allowed for structures, other than public utility structures.

A third variation of the investment credit is to allow the credit only for investment in excess of depreciation. This form was originally discussed before the credit was adopted in 1962, and it is a neutral investment incentive. It has a smaller effect in reducing the tax rate because an additional dollar of investment undertaken now will, through the generation of depreciation deductions, reduce credits in the future. That is, when a firm makes an investment, it will receive the credit, but the act of making the investment and its accompanying depreciation will cause credits otherwise available to be lost in the future. Thus a larger credit of this nature would be required to achieve the same average effect, and the credit still reduces noncorporate tax rates proportionally more than corporate ones. But because depreciation is larger for short-lived assets, the credit is neutral across assets (and would result in precisely the same effective tax rates if the beginning system relied on economic depreciation).

The undesirable effects on corporate versus noncorporate investments can be reduced by allowing the incentive in the form of an extra allowance rather than a credit. For example, rather than allowing a 10 percent credit, one could allow an extra deduction of equivalent value ($0.10/u$, where u is the corporate tax rate). This extra allowance produces the same effects on corporate investment as a 10 percent credit.

Its effect on noncorporate investments is moderated because the allowance is valued at the lower noncorporate rate. In effect a uniform credit provides a larger tax-free allowance to low-tax-rate entities than to high-tax-rate ones.

Some investment incentives may be even more distorting across assets of different durabilities than the basic investment credit or investment allowance. One such incentive would be to allow depreciation of more than 100 percent of the asset cost. Such an incentive gives larger up-front tax benefits to shorter-lived assets because the present value of depreciation is greater for these assets. In the illustrations of allowing 150 percent of the cost to be depreciated, the effective tax rate for corporate equipment is minus 55 percent, while the rate for structures is a plus 23 percent.

Another option shown in the table is to reduce tax lives by 50 percent. This option is much more neutral across assets and types of firms than the previous investment incentives because it changes the present value of depreciation more for long-lived assets than for short-lived ones.

The partial expensing options shown at the bottom of the table are relatively neutral, and indeed would be precisely neutral within each sector if they were introduced into a system where tax depreciation was the same as economic depreciation. (The slight differences in tax rates shown within a sector occur because tax depreciation did not correspond exactly to estimated economic depreciation.) These options allow some fraction of the cost of the investment to be deducted when incurred, while the remainder is depreciated. When 100 percent of the investment is expensed, the tax rate is zero. The partial expensing approach is neutral across investments for the same reason that the investment credit in excess of depreciation is neutral: The forgone depreciation for the short-lived asset is greater in present value than for the long-lived asset. Another advantage of partial expensing is that any errors made in measuring economic depreciation become less important as depreciation becomes less important. Of course, short of full expensing, differences would remain between the corporate and noncorporate sectors because of the differing statutory tax rates.

Although these investment incentives can be designed to yield the same overall aggregate reduction in tax rates, they differ not only in how they affect different assets but also in their budgetary patterns.

Investment credits and extra allowances tend to have a relatively even pattern of revenue loss relative to GNP over time. Allowing more than 100 percent of the cost to be depreciated produces small initial costs that rise over time as more new investment falls under the system. Shortening tax lives would cause revenue losses that grow and then decline (as forgone depreciation in the future offsets current revenue losses from new vintages of investments). Partial or full expensing would cause a large revenue cost that declines very rapidly. Gravelle (1993c) illustrates the dramatic differences in these patterns. If an even pattern of revenue loss over time is deemed most desirable, the rough equivalent of partial expensing could be attained by allowing extra deductions that are smaller for short-lived assets than for longer-lived ones.

Evaluating Investment Subsidies: Neutrality versus "Bang for the Buck"

The form of explicit investment subsidy used historically—the investment credit—can be faulted on two grounds, as far as the effects on the allocation of capital are concerned. The investment credit introduces tax distortions where none existed previously—across asset types, and consequently across industries (depending on the mix of assets). The credit also does relatively little to reduce the distortions between corporate and noncorporate capital because of its credit form.

There is a more subtle failing of the equipment credit which has long gone unrecognized. Some of the distortion in the allocation of capital arises because of differential treatment of industries where corporate and noncorporate firms coexist, which is stressed by Gravelle (1989). This misallocation occurs only in those industries where noncorporate firms can effectively compete. Providing a subsidy to manufacturing or utilities does nothing to reduce this distortion, since such industries are dominated by corporate firms. Those industries in which noncorporate firms are more important—agriculture, rental housing, trade, and services—tend to have more assets in structures, inventories, and land.

Investment subsidies can be designed that do not have these faults, such as partial expensing and accelerated depreciation. These criticisms are specific to the investment credit, not all investment subsidies.

Investment subsidies of any type, however, have no effect on the preference for debt, for retentions over dividends, or for distortions in the holding period of corporate stock or other assets. Despite these shortcomings, there is considerable support for investment subsidies, and in particular for the investment credit, among economists and policymakers. One of the main reasons for this support is that investment subsidies are often argued to be more effective than rate cuts in encouraging investment and savings because they do not reduce the tax on the existing capital stock. For a given effect on the cost of capital, the revenue loss will be smaller with a tax subsidy to investment than with a rate reduction. This phenomenon can be understood in the context of the analysis of tax substitutions in chapter 2. Assuming revenues are to be made up with rate increases, the investment subsidy is similar to the replacement of income taxes with a consumption tax base *if there is no depreciation*, while the rate cut replaces capital income taxes with increased wage taxes. This means that like the consumption tax substitution, the investment credit may lead to greater economic efficiency because other taxes can be raised less to offset the smaller revenue cost.

This effectiveness for a given revenue cost does not, however, necessarily imply that the investment subsidy is superior to a rate reduction, for two reasons. First, the same sort of intergenerational distribution that is set in motion by a consumption tax substitution as opposed to a wage tax substitution is also set in motion by investment subsidies. The value of existing assets will fall, causing a loss in wealth (and consumption possibilities) to the old who have already accumulated capital, and a gain to young and future generations. Thus the choice of an investment subsidy over a rate cut must be assessed, in part, in view of its distributional consequences across generations.

The second reason is that assets depreciate, so that much of the investment eligible for the subsidies is replacement investment. Indeed, in the case of equipment, a large fraction is replacement investment. This phenomenon can be illustrated with some simple calculations. For every dollar of initial capital stock, investment is equal to the sum of the depreciation rate and the growth rate; this replacement investment grows (in real terms) with the growth rate of the economy and is discounted at the real rate of return. Thus the present value of all future investment (which will receive the subsidy) is

$$\frac{\text{Depreciation rate} + \text{Growth rate}}{\text{Discount rate} - \text{Growth rate}} \times \text{Capital stock.}$$

As an illustration, the present value of net investment per dollar of initial capital stock, assuming a 7 percent pretax rate of return and a 2.5 percent growth rate would be 0.55. That is, for each dollar of capital there would be 2.5 cents of investment that grows at 2.5 percent and is discounted at 7 percent. An infinite series would sum to $0.025/(0.07 - 0.025)$. The present value of net investment, as a fraction of the sum of the existing capital stock and the present value of net investment, would be 0.36: that is, $0.55/(1 + 0.55)$. In this case granting a subsidy only to net investment would cost only about a third of the cost of a rate cut with the same overall effect on rate of return.

For a subsidy to gross equipment investment, where the depreciation rate averages about 15 percent, the value of net investment per dollar of existing stock would be 3.87. Gross investment would be 15 cents of replacement investment and 2.5 cents of new investment. This amount would also grow at 2.5 percent and be discounted at 7 percent. An infinite series would sum to $(0.15 + 0.025)/(0.07 - 0.025)$. Gross investment, as a fraction of the sum of gross investment and the capital stock, would be 0.80: that is, $3.87/(1 + 3.87)$. In this case the cost of an investment subsidy would be 80 percent of the cost of a rate cut.[5]

Thus the case for choosing an investment subsidy is much less than might initially appear, especially where assets depreciate very rapidly. The investment credit is actually closer to a wage tax substitution than it is to a consumption tax substitution. Indeed, to choose an investment incentive directed at equipment rather than more long-lived assets actually undermines the objective of cost minimizing investment incentives.

The recognition of this "bang for the buck" has, however, led to another kind of proposal, the incremental investment subsidy. This is the approach used for the R&D credit—the credit is allowed only for investment in excess of a base. The base is a fixed amount that is increased with the increase in gross sales of the firm.

Although such an incremental credit approach appears at first to offer the possibility of coming close to the desired goal of eliminating the tax at the margin at a very small cost, a closer examination of such credits reveal some severe limitations and problems. First, as a practical matter, a permanent incremental subsidy is probably impossible to design. In order to maintain a permanent incremental subsidy, the base must move over time. If the base grows with investment, the marginal effect is diluted, since an increase in investment today reduces future credits by increasing the base in the future. The net effect is not very different from a smaller nonincremental credit. Indeed it was for this reason that the R&D credit, which originally had a base that grew with growth in R&D expenditures, was revised in 1989 to have a base that grows with sales.

If the base moves with other economic activity of the firm, the investment subsidy will be diluted less, with the amount depending on the importance of the investment as an input to production of the firm. (An addition to investment will increase output and reduce future credits, though not on a dollar-for-dollar basis.) There is a penalty on other inputs of the firm, which again varies with the relative importance of various inputs. The same effect could be achieved with a regular credit, accompanied by offsetting penalties (negative credits) for labor inputs, intermediate purchases, or other investments.

If the base is moved by growth of investment in the industry as a whole or the economy, most of the marginal effect will be retained, but the base will continually get off track. Fast growing firms will have more of their investment qualify, while slow growing firms will eventually find the base surpassing their investment.

Moreover, even if such a credit could be designed (i.e., if all firms' investments grow at the same rate), an incremental credit will cause (or exacerbate) a decreasing average cost function. The firm must invest up to a certain amount before it becomes eligible for the subsidy. For the marginal investment undertaken by a competitive firm, in equilibrium, the present value of the stream of income equals the cost less the subsidy allowed. The net present value of this investment (outlay plus tax benefit minus present value of return) is zero. But for the investment not eligible for subsidy, the net value is negative. Since a formerly competitive firm will be unable to cover its total costs if it prices in accord with marginal costs, such an incremental credit will tend to drive firms out of the industry, cause firms to be too large and thus produce inefficiently. Gravelle (1993c) provides a mathematical derivation of this effect, showing that an incremental credit is likely to be inferior to a nonincremental one.

In the case of an existing monopoly, these inefficiencies will not occur, and the incremental credit will work at the margin the same way that a regular credit would work. The consequences for oligopoly and monopolistic competition have yet to be explored.

There are also a number of severe administrative difficulties with incremental credits, in particular, determining the base when firms split up or when new firms enter, which make such credits virtually unworkable.

Unfortunately, it is difficult to approach a consumption tax base through these back-door methods of investment subsidies; an explicit consumption tax approach where expensing is substituted for depreciation might be preferable. If investment subsidies are nevertheless contemplated, it would be possible to design investment subsidies that are more efficient than the investment credit by choosing more neutral incentives that apply broadly and using a deduction rather than a credit form.

Investment Incentives as Countercyclical Devices

Investment incentives have been used in the past (and were proposed in 1993) as countercyclical devices to stimulate the economy or to combat inflation. The credit has been frequently suspended, eliminated, or reinstated based on current economic conditions.

Most of the studies of the effectiveness of investment incentives have been either based on models of the short-run demand response, or embedded in short-run macroeconomic models. Hall and Jorgenson (1967, 1972) argued that investment incentives were quite effective in stimulating investment, but this model assumes a fairly large (unitary elastic) short-run investment demand response. This study elicited a variety of criticisms and further studies. Coen (1969) and Eisner (1969), for example, argued that the short-run investment demand response was much smaller, only about a sixth as much. Brannon (1972) also suggested that the interest rate would be driven up.

This notion of demand responsiveness is crucial. If the investment stimulated by a subsidy is larger than the revenue loss—a result that occurs roughly with a demand elasticity in excess of one—the subsidy will be a relatively effective stimulant to demand. If the investment response is much smaller, then spending increases, or transfers to individuals with relatively high short run propensities to consume (e.g., transfer payments) will be more effective. One possible advantage of investment incentives is that temporary incentives (or suspensions) might be more effective than permanent ones, (or a permanent repeal if the objective is to dampen demand). These temporary changes result in a short-term window of opportunity to purchase capital more cheaply.

The debate over the effectiveness of the credit continued in an extensive literature. Bischoff (1971) found that the effects of the investment credit exceed the revenue cost, but Coen (1971) found the incentives were not very effective in relation to revenue forgone. Klein and Taubman (1971), using the Wharton Econometric Model, found investment incentives not very effective; they also found a temporary suspension to have an effect about a third larger than a permanent one. Aaron, Russek, and Singer (1972) also found relatively small effects of the 1969 repeal and the 1971 reinstatement, using the Federal Reserve Board–MIT econometric model. Brimmer and Sinai (1976) found that the investment credit produced only $0.68 in investment for every dollar of revenue loss.

The timing of the effects of an investment subsidy can be important to its power as a countercyclical device. Taubman (1971) argued that the investment credit has limited usefulness because of the slowness of its impact. Gordon and Jorgenson (1975) concurred with this argument, finding about a two-year impact lag associated with the credit. Caton, Eckstein, and Sinai (1977) agreed with this assessment that the credit is a poor stabilizing device.

Other investment studies tended to concur with this view that the effects of investment incentives are modest. Clark (1979), in a time series study, found little evidence that investment is sensitive to price, as did Hendershott and Hu (1981). Auerbach and Hassett (1990) found that the changes in 1986 had little effect on spending on equipment, given the strength of that spending in 1987–89. The same authors, however, suggest in another paper (Auerbach and Hassett 1991) that equipment spending might have grown even faster without TRA. Cummins and Hassett (1992) found a significant response, but Clark (1993) found little evidence of an effect of price on investment.

There are several reasons to expect that tax incentives for investment might have limited usefulness in stimulating investment in the
short run, primarily because of planning lags and because of the lags
in changing the technology of investment. Essentially there are two
reasons that firms may increase investment. First, they may expect
output to increase. This response, called the *accelerator*, is the result of
other forces that increase aggregate demand and simply requires making more of the same type of investment (along with hiring more
workers). The second reason is that the cost of investment has fallen.
Part of this effect may be an output effect—since the overall cost of
investment is smaller, output can be sold for a smaller price and thus
sales would be expected to rise in the future. But part of this effect has
to do with encouraging more use of capital relative to labor.

The accelerator or output effect requires a reaction by the firm to
order more capacity, so there is a lag associated with this effect. The
price effect is subject to this general planning lag, as well as a more
fundamental lag reflecting a change in technology. That is, it is a much
simpler and quicker process to add more production using existing
technology than to change the mode of technology to use a different,
more capital-intensive process.

Moreover, while a temporary investment incentive might encourage firms to purchase capital goods within a brief window, it does not
lead to a new technology of production because of its temporary
nature. On the whole, most of the literature on the investment credit
and other investment subsidies suggests that investment incentives
inherently affect investment with long time lags because of the lengthy
periods involved in business investments projects, making these subsidies ineffective countercyclical devices.

Conclusion

The analysis in this chapter demonstrates the importance of depreciation rules in determining effective tax rates and the sensitivity of those
rules, in value, to the inflation rate. These rules and related subsidies
such as investment credits can greatly affect the overall tax burdens
and differentials in those tax burdens across different types of assets.

There is still a great deal of support for permanent investment
incentives. Providing tax benefits through subsidies to new invest-

ments is a method aimed at implementing a consumption tax approach to reducing the effective tax burden; this approach is, however, not very successful when applied to rapidly depreciating assets such as equipment. Currently these subsidies are quite small in the aggregate. A wide variety of possible ways of designing investment subsidies exist, but many of them are highly distorting across assets. Moreover the use of credits rather than deductions, and the focus of these credits on equipment, mean that investment subsidies in the past have done little to moderate the distortions between corporate and noncorporate investments, or between financial forms of investment.

It is curious, in light of this analysis, that such a flawed vehicle as the investment credit was used for twenty-five years and that there is continued interest in reviving the credit. Part of the explanation for the popularity of the credit in the past is probably simply that its distorting effects have not been well understood. Moreover there is considerable misunderstanding about the consumption nature of the tax substitution.

Support for reinstating an investment credit today may reflect the tendency in the policy debate to dismiss issues of economic efficiency as unimportant. There has also been, as suggested in chapter 3, a tendency to think of investment in equipment as somehow more "productive" than investment in other types of assets because it is associated with developing technology and manufacturing. Although there appears to be no basis for this viewpoint in economic theory, it has a strong hold in the public debate.

Such evidence as we have does not suggest that investment subsidies are very successful as short-term countercyclical devices. At best they are risky choices compared to spending increases or increasing incomes of those individuals with a high short-run marginal propensity to consume.

6   Capital Gains Taxes

Few issues have generated more debate and more changes in tax treatment over time than the capital gains tax. Capital gains taxes have been argued to have a wide range of effects—economic growth, entrepreneurship, risk taking, and a number of allocational issues. But what renders the capital gains tax of particular interest is the "lock-in" effect. Since the tax is paid only when an asset is sold, the tax is delayed by retaining the asset. Moreover, because the heir takes as the cost basis of any inherited assets the market value at the time of death, any gains on assets passed on at death are forgiven entirely. This treatment is referred to as a *step-up in basis*.

Under current law all gains are taxed as ordinary income, although in the past a large fraction of gains (60 percent before passage of the Tax Reform Act of 1986) were excluded. The tax rate on capital gains is currently capped at 28 percent, although marginal tax rates go up to 39.6 percent. Perhaps the most prominent issue in the public debate over capital income taxes in the past few years is whether a capital gains exclusion should be restored.

The consequences of sale can be somewhat different in the case of the sale of depreciable assets because of rules for allowing depreciation on used assets. Indeed, with capital gains exclusions, the lock-in effect can be turned on its head in some cases. The gain on a depreciable asset is the difference between the sales price and the basis. In this case the basis is the original cost less any depreciation allowances already taken. When an asset is sold, however, the purchaser can begin depreciation once more, based on the sales price. The excess of the present value of this depreciation over what would otherwise have occurred offsets the direct burden of the capital gains tax.

In fact taxes can result in an incentive to sell under certain circumstances Hendershott and Ling (1984), Gordon, Hines, and Summers (1988), and Gravelle (1987) discuss the churning incentive. For example, consider the tax law in 1981 which allowed 60 percent of capital gains to be excluded and individuals to take depreciation over fifteen years. For residential property the present value of depreciation was $0.57 (in present value) for each dollar of asset value. If a property was fully depreciated (so that the basis was zero), selling would generate an income for the seller of $0.40 for each dollar of sales price but a deduction for the purchaser of $0.57 for each dollar of sale price. In recognition of this problem, depreciation on equipment (which can be quite large in present value) was recaptured—the portion of capital gain reflecting depreciation already taken was treated as ordinary income. This incentive to sell cannot occur unless there is a capital gains exclusion or a lower capital gains rate, although the changes in depreciation can reduce or magnify the lock-in effect.

Although the lock-in effect has been the primary focus of research into the economic effects of the capital gains tax, a number of other issues arise in the debate, having to do with the cost of the capital gains tax and the effects of the tax on overall savings, on the allocation of capital, and on the distribution of income. The arguments in the public debate (detailed extensively in Hoerner 1992a) appear to focus on different issues than those in the debate in the economics literature. In the recent public debate, four issues have been stressed. The first is the revenue cost (specifically, whether cutting the capital gains tax can actually raise revenue by inducing realizations). The second is the effect of the capital gains tax on progressivity, with one side stressing the concentration of capital gains among high-income individuals and the other arguing that high-income individuals may end up actually paying more tax at lower rates. The third is the possible effect of the capital gains tax on overall savings and investment, and, especially, on entrepreneurship and risk taking. The final issue is the "unfairness" of taxing inflationary gains. Although inflation affects capital income taxes in many ways, nowhere in the public debate has this issue been stressed as much as in the context of the capital gains tax.

A central issue in the economics literature (surveyed by Bailey 1969, Minarik 1983, and Wetzler 1977) is the question of economic efficiency. The tax can affect economic efficiency in several ways. First, the capital gains tax is part of the overall tax burden, as addressed in chapter 2. Thus the capital gains tax is part of the issue of the desirable level of this overall tax. In this respect capital gains taxes are no different from other taxes on capital income—on dividends, interest, and corporate and noncorporate profits.

Second, the capital gains tax plays a role in the allocation between corporate and noncorporate capital (and owner-occupied housing), in the preferences of corporations for debt over equity, and for retaining rather than distributing income, as discussed in chapter 4. Hence the capital gains tax on corporate stock may be viewed in a different light from the capital gains tax on the sale of other assets, most of which occur in the noncorporate sector.

The role of the capital gains tax in risk taking has been a subject of attention. This issue is also discussed in the public debate, often focusing on the effects of the tax on the establishment of new businesses.

A final efficiency issue unique to the capital gains tax (and the related issue of depreciation of used assets) is the lock-in effect itself. Holt and Shelton (1962) explored this issue in a seminal article. The lock-in effect arises from a fundamental shortcoming of the income tax system—the failure to tax real gains (and losses) as they accrue. If accruals of income and depreciation were correctly measured for tax purposes, there would be no tax consequences to the sale of assets and no lock-in effect. But because such accruals are not taxed currently, asset sales create opportunities to tax these unrecognized accruals. As a result the capital gains tax discourages individuals from changing their portfolios, causing them to hold a less preferred set of investments. And, because the tax is forgiven on gains passed on at death, the barriers to sale of assets expected to be used as bequests can be become very large as one ages.

The distributional issues are also a subject for economic analysis, but as is the case with any tax on capital, this distributional effect depends on the behavioral responses of individuals. The debate would proceed in a very different fashion from the rather peculiar distributional arguments that have emerged in the public debate.

One of the missing elements in the public debate is the heterogeneity of the assets that capital gains taxes affects. The economic effects of the capital gains tax cannot be divorced from the underlying nature of the economic activities that give rise to the tax. Thus, even though the capital gains tax is often discussed as a single economic phenomenon, the consequences of the tax depend on the nature of the activity being taxed. Many assets earn their return through a combination of current income and capital gains. Moreover, for depreciable assets, the tax code allows depreciation to be restarted and based on the new sales price, which can affect the cost of trading. What type of capital gain is under discussion determines its contribution to an efficient allocation of capital. As noted above, lowering the capital gains tax on an investment that is heavily taxed, such as corporate stock, may lead to a more efficient allocation of capital. On the other hand, lowering the tax on investments such as real estate, where trades more commonly occur in the noncorporate sector, can cause a less efficient allocation. Thus, before turning to the issues of efficiency and distribution, an overview of the sources of capital gains and how the capital gains tax affects both the tax burden and the lock-in for different types of assets are in order.

Sources of Capital Gains

Capital gains can arise from a variety of sources, and the fundamental issues in capital gains taxation vary depending on the source. These sources include retained earnings of corporations, growth in demand for assets in fixed supply, changes in earning prospects, natural growth (e.g., timber growth and wine storage), mismatching of income and expense, and inflation.

Retained Earnings of Corporations

Capital gains on corporate stock partially reflect the earnings retained by the firm and reinvested (rather than being paid out as dividends). These earnings are just another form of corporate income and reflect the same economic earnings as dividends. In this context capital gains are favorably treated relative to dividends, even if there is no capital gains exclusion, because the payment of tax has been delayed (and, for assets passed on at death, avoided entirely). Yet this income has already been subject to tax at the corporate level. Thus capital gains taxes on corporate stock contribute to the burden of tax on corporate equity capital.

Changes in Earnings Prospects

Capital gains (or losses) also arise from basic supply and demand forces, resulting in a change in earnings prospects over time. They can be anticipated or unanticipated. These shifts in supply and demand may derive from many sources. For example, a gain or loss deriving from supply side sources may occur with investment in a mine that may turn out to be worthless or unexpectedly rich. This type of gain or loss reflects the riskiness of certain activities and is more likely to be pronounced with certain types of assets. A similar sort of supply side effect might occur, for example, if some of an artist's works are destroyed and the remaining works were to rise in value. Another supply side effect might occur when a firm develops a new product or a new production process through investment in research and development.

Gains and losses can also derive from demand side forces. Certain assets are in less than fully elastic supply indefinitely, or over periods of time. (If an asset is in perfectly elastic supply, the supply can be increased without an increase in cost.) These assets include unique works of art and similar collectibles and land in certain locations. As income and the accompanying demand for products and for factors of production grow, these assets rise in value. Some of these changes can be anticipated; others may be unanticipated, arising from an unexpected change in tastes and preferences.

Gains or losses on a fixed-yield asset such as a bond may reflect changes in interest rates (which are really changes in yield). For example, consider a $100 bond that matures in one year for $106 (reflecting a 6 percent interest rate). Suppose that the interest rate drops to 4 percent immediately after purchase so that new bonds will yield only $104. An individual would be willing to pay the owner of the 6 percent bond more than $100, and in fact would be willing to pay $101.92, which would result in the market yield of 4 percent. Therefore the owner of the bond could realize a capital gain. If the interest rate went up rather than down in this example, the owner of the original bond would experience a capital loss.

Gains and losses can also result from tax policy changes. For example, a reduction in the corporate tax rate would likely cause corporate shares to rise in value temporarily and cause capital gains. This effect is similar to an unanticipated change in demand.

In all of these cases the owner has the option of receiving the asset's increase in value by selling and realizing a capital gains or retaining the asset and realizing the increased income in the form of a higher future earnings stream. The only tax treatment that leaves the owner in the same position is to tax capital gains as accrued and the failure to tax capital gains in this way discourages the sale of assets (unless they yield losses).

Natural Growth

Another source of capital gain is natural growth in value, which occurs with timber stands and similar assets. As timber grows, its value increases, and the proper measurement of income would be to subject the real gain to tax as it accrues.

Accelerated Depreciation

Capital gains can also occur because of accelerated depreciation deductions. If tax depreciation exceeds economic depreciation, then a measured capital gain will occur for tax purposes because the basis of the asset will be understated. When capital gains were taxed at preferential tax rates, and depreciation was allowed at full rates, it was possible for the tax law actually to encourage the sale of some assets. To counteract this effect, tax laws frequently required some recapture of depreciation so that some or all of the gain reflecting depreciation would be taxed at ordinary rates. (Under current tax law there is no difference between the tax rates except at the high brackets because the capital gains tax is capped at 28 percent. Depreciation is fully recaptured on tangible property.)

Inflation

Capital gains can occur solely because inflation increases the nominal value of output and therefore the dollar value of the physical capital asset that produces the product. This inflation effect should show up in the value of physical assets, such as real property, and in the value of financial assets that reflect these physical assets, such as corporate stock shares. Note, however, that inflation does not affect bond prices (as long as it is anticipated) but rather shows up in the interest rate.

Unanticipated changes in the inflation rate can affect the interest rate and, in turn, prices of existing bonds. To tax income at the statutory rate, it would be appropriate to correct capital income for the effects of inflation, along with taxing it on an accrual basis.

Contribution of Different Types of Assets to Capital Gains

The major sources of realized capital gains by type of asset are those arising from corporate stock, the sale of buildings, and land. The distribution of gains by asset type is shown in table 6.1, for the latest year for which final statistics are published (1981). About a quarter of net gain arises from the sale of corporate stock and another quarter from the sale of personal residences. Gain from the sale of other financial assets is negligible and, in 1981, actually represented a net loss. Most of the gains from personal residences, although reported, are not taxed (according to preliminary data reported by Holik et al. 1989 for 1985, only 2 percent of capital gains on owner-occupied housing was taxed). The tax code allows for deferral of gains from a residence when a new home is purchased and a once-in-a-lifetime exclusion for individuals over 55. Business and nonbusiness depreciable property primarily reflect sales of real estate, as do most installment sales (sales where the

Table 6.1
Individual capital gains by asset type

Asset type	All gains		Excluding personal residences	
	Gross	Net	Gross	Net
Corporate stock	28.3	24.8	35.6	33.2
Other securities	0.7	–2.1	0.9	–2.8
Commodities	2.4	0.3	3.0	0.4
Capital gains distributions	1.3	1.4	1.6	1.9
Business depreciable property	9.3	11.4	11.7	15.3
Nonbusiness real estate	12.2	14.8	15.3	19.8
Partnership distributions	6.8	6.7	8.6	9.0
Farm land	2.4	2.9	3.0	3.9
Prior year installment sales	6.5	7.8	8.2	10.4
Other	9.3	4.6	11.7	6.2
Personal residences	20.5	25.3		

Source: Calculated from data in Internal Revenue Service, Sales of Capital Assets (1981, 1982) *Statistics of Income Bulletin* (Winter 1985–1986).

gain can be recognized over several years). The category "other," which includes art objects and timber, is relatively small. Capital gains are also received by corporations, but these gains are relatively small, both in comparison to corporate income and in comparison to individual capital gains.

The shares of gains on different types of assets vary from year to year, and the data are reported only on a sporadic basis. For example, corporate stock represents only about 18 percent of gain in 1973 and 17 percent in 1977 because these years represent periods of very little appreciation in the stock values. In 1985, when stocks were appreciating rapidly, the corporate stock share of net gains was about 46 percent (preliminary data reported in Holik et al. 1989). These numbers are roughly in line with historical shares of accruals—outside of owner-occupied housing, accruals in corporate stock gains represent about 42 percent and land about 11 percent of total accruals. These shares illustrate the importance of considering the tax treatment of capital gains on noncorporate assets and on depreciable property, which account for a large fraction of both accrued and realized gains.

Effective Tax Rates on Capital Gains

The effective tax rate on capital gains is affected by several factors: the deferral of gains, the taxation of gains that arise from inflation, and the allowance of depreciation deductions on used assets. The recognition that assets rarely earn their return solely from capital gains is an important consideration when addressing the capital gains tax and the effective tax rate. In measuring the effective tax rate, the level of the real appreciation rate relative to inflation is of crucial importance; the lower this rate relative to inflation, the higher the effective tax rate is. The capital gains tax on the inflationary gain, however, is not spread over the entire asset's return. If the appreciation rate is low simply because most of the return is realized in other forms, such a calculation would provide a misleading impression. (An extreme example of this would be when all income is realized currently and the real appreciation rate is close to zero; in this case even the slightest tax on inflationary gain would be enormous in size relative to the real return.)

Corporate Stock and Other Nondepreciable Assets

Both the effective tax rate and the lock-in effect can be most easily considered in the case of an asset that does not qualify for tax depreciation. The most straightforward case is that of corporate stock. Table 6.2 reports effective tax rates at the personal level on corporate stock at various rates of inflation and with varying assumptions about the dividend rate, for a taxpayer in the 28 percent bracket. All assets are assumed to earn a 7 percent real pretax rate of return (the sum of the dividend rate and the annual rate of appreciation in stock value). Over a long period of time the inflation rate has averaged about 5 percent. As is the case with previous effective tax rates, the tax rates report what statutory rate would have to apply if all real income were taxed as accrued to achieve the same tax burden as the current tax, which is affected by both deferral and application to inflationary gains.

Table 6.2
Effective tax rates on capital gains: Corporate stock

Holding period (years)	No inflation	3% inflation	5% inflation	7% inflation
Dividend rate: 0%				
1	27.3	38.6	46.0	53.2
7	25.9	31.0	35.3	39.2
20	16.9	19.8	21.0	21.8
40	10.9	11.4	11.6	11.7
Until death	0.0	0.0	0.0	0.0
Dividend rate: 4%				
1	27.7	39.2	47.1	54.5
7	26.0	34.5	39.5	43.8
20	23.0	27.3	29.0	30.2
40	20.0	21.3	21.6	21.7
Until death	16.0	16.0	16.0	16.0
Dividend rate: 7%				
1	28.0	39.9	47.6	55.3
7	28.0	37.2	42.6	47.4
20	28.0	33.5	35.8	37.4
40	28.0	30.2	30.8	31.1
Until death	28.0	28.0	28.0	28.0

Note: Based on calculations in appendix B. The calculations assume a 28 percent tax rate and a 7 percent overall real rate of return. Dividend taxes are assumed to be paid currently; the small reduction in tax rate for the capital gain held for one year reflects the benefit of one year's deferral of tax.

The first set of calculations reports effective tax rates on a corporate stock that earns its entire return through appreciation—no dividends are paid. Whether the effective tax rate exceeds or is less than the statutory rate of 28 percent depends on the holding period (which leads to a lower effective tax rate) and the inflation rate (inflation leads to a higher tax rate). These factors interact. Inflation exacts a larger toll when holding periods are short. At the same time the advantage of a longer holding period in lowering the tax rate increases at higher levels of inflation. This latter effect occurs because deferral becomes more valuable at the higher discount rate associated with a high inflation rate. Thus inflation contributes to the lock-in effect.

The second set of calculations reports the tax rates for a typical stock in the steady state. On average, and over a long period of time, corporate stock would be expected to appreciate at a real rate roughly the same as, or perhaps slightly below, the growth rate of the economy. This relationship is confirmed by historical evidence; over the period 1959 to 1989, the real appreciation rate from the New York Stock Exchange index was 3.3 percent, roughly equivalent to the real growth rate of the economy over that period. If firms financed all of their equity investments from reinvested earnings, and if the firm has chosen an optimal debt equity ratio and is engaged in steady state growth, then assets should grow in value at the rate of growth of the economy. If firms financed some growth from share sales, the growth rate might be slightly below the growth rate of the economy. Accordingly the second set of estimates in table 6.2 uses a real appreciation rate for corporate stock approximately the same as has occurred historically in the economy, 3 percent. The dividend rate is therefore 4 percent, for a total return of 7 percent. The final set of calculations is for a firm that earns all of its return in dividends (a 7 percent dividend rate and a zero real appreciation rate). The only effect of the capital gains tax is from the taxation of inflationary gains.

The effective tax rates, in the absence of inflation, fall below the statutory rate, increasingly so as the holding period lengthens. Again this is the advantage of deferral. The effective tax rate is lower, the longer the asset is held and the larger the share of income realized as a gain. For example, with no dividends and no inflation, the tax rate is almost equal to the statutory rate if the asset is held for one year. The tax rate falls to zero if the asset is held until death. Note that small changes in holding periods, assuming gains are realized, do not profoundly affect the tax burden; this is because the advantage of deferral is small at a 3 percent discount rate. While small changes in the holding period in general result in small changes in tax burdens, the burden of selling as the individual approaches death (assuming he wishes to leave a bequest or can borrow against the value of assets) can become quite large.

As the table indicates, inflation can have a pronounced effect on the level of tax and the advantage of holding the asset longer. Inflation causes tax rates to be higher overall because the inflationary gain is subject to tax; it also causes the lock-in effect to be more pronounced because the discount rate becomes larger and the advantage of deferring the tax is greater.

These calculations are also illustrative of the effects of the capital gains tax on certain other types of assets. For example, land may earn its return partially in a current rent and partially in a gain in value over time. The illustration of an asset that earns its return solely through appreciation would also be representative of assets such as art objects. Timber, although it earns a return through appreciation, is subject to lower tax rates because a substantial portion of costs are expensed when incurred. As a result tax rates on timber are lower, and will in fact be negative when held until death.

Depreciating Assets

The effects of the capital gains tax on assets that depreciate are affected by the interaction of depreciation allowances for used assets with the capital gains tax. Effective tax rates for sale of a residential building illustrate this issue.

The capital gain on a depreciating asset is the difference between its sale price and the depreciated basis of the property. The depreciated basis of the property is the original cost less any depreciation deductions taken. Capital gains on depreciating assets arise from two sources. First, inflation can increase the value of an asset in nominal terms, even though its value is declining in real terms. Second, if depreciation is allowed at a rate that is faster than economic depreciation, the sales price will be higher than the tax basis even in the absence of inflation (although both would be below original cost). Like corporate stock the capital gains tax therefore imposes a penalty to trading, particularly when inflation has been high over the holding period. Also, like corporate stock, the effective tax rate would tend to fall with the holding period and rise with the inflation rate.

There is, however, another twist to this effective tax rate calculation because the sale of a depreciating asset triggers a change in depreciation. The purchaser of the building can begin depreciation again, based on the sales price of the asset. The present value of this depreciation can be larger or smaller than the remaining present value of depreciation that would have occurred had the asset not been sold, depending on the sales price of the asset and the number of years over which depreciation is spread. For example, suppose that depreciation is taken on a straight-line basis over ten years and an asset originally cost $1,000, for an annual depreciation deduction of $100. Suppose that the asset is sold after five years and thus has a depreciable basis of $500. In a world with no inflation and a match between economic depreciation and tax depreciation up to this point, no capital gain would be realized. Depreciation would be less valuable, however, since the new purchaser would write off the $500 at $50 a year for the next ten years. Although the same amount would have been written off by the original owner, the depreciation is less valuable for the purchaser because it is now spread over ten years rather than five. At a 10 percent discount rate the present value of depreciation had the asset not been sold is $393, while the present value of depreciation if sold is $316.

Depreciation can, and usually does, act to offset capital gains by being more valuable after sale than before sale. Consider the same example, but one in which the sales price was $1,000 (due to inflation and perhaps to depreciation being allowed to be taken too quickly). In this case there would be a capital gain of $500 (the sales price of $1,000 minus depreciable basis of $500). The purchaser now can deduct depreciation on the $1,000 sales price over the next ten years, for a deduction of $100 for the next ten years. The present value of depreciation in the hands of the purchaser is $632 in this case. When assets are held until death so that there are no capital gains, there can actually be a tax benefit because of the increased value of depreciation.

These relationships can moderate the pattern of effective tax rates with respect to holding period. Moreover, in the presence of a capital gains exclusion, it is possible for sale of assets to actually be encouraged. If the difference between the present value of depreciation in the hands of the seller and the hands of the buyer, times the tax rate, is greater than the capital gains tax, then selling is tax advantaged. Indeed, as noted previously, it was quite easy for such an outcome to occur under the laws passed in 1981, when the write-off period was 15 years, and the exclusion ratio was 60 percent. In this case, if a residential rental property were sold after being fully depreciated, the present value of depreciation was $0.57 for each dollar of sales price, while the income included under the capital gains tax was only $0.40.

Under current law there is always some burden to sale because the present value of depreciation deductions for real estate (depreciation is recaptured for personal property), and there is a relatively small difference in ordinary and capital gains tax rates (and no difference at some income levels). Nevertheless, depreciation plays a role in the pattern of tax burdens by holding period.

Table 6.3 reports effective tax rates on structures, taking into account the capital gains tax along with direct taxes on rents. As with corporate stock we see that the tax rate falls with holding period and rises with inflation when assets are sold and subject to capital gains tax. When assets are held until death, however, it is the assets held for

Table 6.3
Effective tax rates on capital gains: Structures

Holding period (years)	No inflation	3% inflation	5% inflation	7% inflation
Depreciation rate: 2%				
Sold by original owner				
1	27.8	42.9	47.4	54.6
7	27.1	36.7	43.3	48.4
20	24.1	30.1	32.7	34.6
40	20.9	25.7	27.7	29.2
Held until death				
1	20.5	21.6	21.5	21.6
7	18.8	21.8	22.3	23.0
20	17.8	22.2	24.2	25.7
40	18.8	23.7	25.7	27.3
Never sold	19.9	24.5	26.4	29.7

Note: Based on calculations in appendix B. Calculations assume a 28 percent tax rate, an after-tax real return of 5 percent assuming the asset is never sold, and a 2 percent depreciation rate.

the shorter times, in some cases, that experience the lower tax rate. Since no tax is paid at death, the source of variation in tax rate is the change in depreciation treatment, which can be advantageous, particularly at high inflation rates where the value of depreciation based on historical costs can be eroded.

Real estate also benefits from a provision that allows properties to be swapped without current realization through the "like-kind" exchange rules. This provision is of minor importance.

Measuring the Lock-in Effect

The lock-in effect is normally thought of as distorting the preference for trading versus holding an asset. One way to explore this effect is to consider an investment held over a fixed time horizon. In one case, the investor sells his existing asset and purchases a new asset to be held over the specified time horizon. In the other case, the investor retains his existing asset until the end of the time horizon. If both the existing and the new asset earned the same rate of return, the investor would hold on to his existing asset. Therefore one approach is to determine how much higher the rate of return of the new asset has to be compared to the existing asset in order for the investor to be as well off by selling as holding (as suggested by Holt and Shelton 1962).

If the asset is not held until death, the choice of selling now rather than holding involves a speedup in the payment of the capital gains tax. For example, if the time horizon is one year, the tax on appreciation of the old asset will be paid a year earlier under the selling option as compared to the holding option.

Table 6.4 illustrates this lock-in effect for corporate stock under different sets of assumptions, again for a 28 percent tax rate. Down the left-hand column are the number of years the asset has already been held; along the rows are the number of years the new asset is expected to be held (the time horizon). Calculations in this table assume the new asset will also ultimately be sold and a tax paid.

Consider the first set of calculations, with an inflation rate of 5 percent and an asset appreciating at an annual 7 percent rate. If the asset has been held a year, and the new asset is expected to be held for a year, then the new asset must appreciate at a rate 0.4 percentage points greater than the old asset—7.4 percent rather than 7 percent. This

Table 6.4
Increase in return necessary to sale: Corporate stock

Holding period of asset sold	Expected holding period of asset purchased			
	1	7	20	40
A. 5% inflation, 7% growth				
1	0.4	0.3	0.1	0.1
7	2.1	1.5	0.8	0.4
20	3.8	2.5	1.4	0.7
40	4.3	2.8	1.5	0.8
B. 5% inflation, 3% growth, gain in appreciation				
1	0.2	0.1	0.1	0.1
7	1.0	0.8	0.5	0.3
20	2.2	1.7	1.0	0.6
40	2.8	2.1	1.3	0.8
C. 5% inflation, 3% growth, gain in dividend				
1	0.2	0.2	0.2	0.1
7	1.1	0.9	0.7	0.4
20	3.5	1.9	1.3	0.8
40	4.3	2.4	1.7	1.1
D. No inflation, 7% growth				
1	0.1	0.1	0.0	0.0
7	0.8	0.7	0.1	0.0
20	1.8	1.4	1.2	0.6
40	2.4	1.8	1.2	0.7
E. No inflation, 3% growth, gain in appreciation				
1	0.0	0.0	0.0	0.0
7	0.2	0.1	0.1	0.1
20	0.4	0.4	0.3	0.2
40	0.7	0.6	0.5	0.4
F. No inflation, 3% growth, gain in dividend				
1	0.0	0.0	0.0	0.0
7	0.2	0.2	0.1	0.2
20	0.4	0.4	0.4	0.3
40	0.7	0.7	0.7	0.7

Note: Based on calculations in appendix B. Calculations assume a 28 percent tax rate.

increase in required rate of return is small because the short holding period results in a small capital gains tax relative to asset value.

This table indicates that the greatest lock-in effect occurs for assets that have been held for a long period of time. This larger lock-in effect is not surprising because a substantial capital gains tax applies. The required rate of return is also influenced by the expected holding period of the new asset. There are two offsetting effects. If the new asset is expected to be sold soon, there will be a corresponding small speedup in the payment of the tax, but the increased return to offset that early payment of tax will be concentrated in a relatively small time period. A longer expected future holding period means that the tax is paid much earlier, but the offset, in terms of rate of return, will be spread over more years. The former effect is typically larger than the latter so that the largest required rate of return will be necessary if the newly purchased asset is held for a short period of time. This effect is not, however, very pronounced. (This advantage is reduced somewhat if the increased yield is in the form of a higher dividend.)

As expected, the lock-in effect is greater for assets that earn their return primarily in appreciation and is also greater for higher rates of inflation. But the most powerful lock-in effects occur when investments are expected to be held until death. In this case, choosing to sell rather than hold involves payment of tax on the appreciation of the currently held asset that would not otherwise have been paid. These calculations are shown in table 6.5, and the required rate of return can be very large. Compare the calculations for asset already held for forty years and a one year time horizon. In table 6.4 the required increase in return for a typical case of 5 percent inflation and a gain in appreciation (panel B) is 2.8 percentage points. In table 6.5, where the asset is expected to be held until death, the increase is 31.3 percentage points!

Thus the most severe cases of lock-in occur less from the capital gains tax per se than from the failure to tax capital gains at death. With a large amount of accumulated gain, sale prior to death requires the tax to be paid when it would otherwise have been escaped rather than delayed. These effects are most pronounced when the new asset will be held for a short period of time, as the increased return must cover a short period of time, but must make up for the large accumulated capital gains tax.

Table 6.5
Increase in return necessary to sale: Corporate stock, held until death

Holding period of asset sold	Expected holding period of asset purchased			
	1	7	20	40
A. 5% inflation, 7% growth				
1	3.2	0.5	0.2	0.1
7	17.3	2.5	0.9	0.4
20	29.4	4.2	1.5	0.7
40	32.5	4.6	1.6	0.8
B. 5% inflation, 3% growth, gain in appreciation				
1	2.2	0.3	0.1	0.1
7	12.8	1.8	0.5	0.3
20	25.3	3.6	1.3	0.6
40	31.3	4.5	1.6	0.8
C. 5% inflation, 3% growth, gain in dividend				
1	3.0	0.4	0.2	0.1
7	17.8	2.5	0.9	0.4
20	35.1	5.0	1.8	0.9
40	43.4	6.2	2.2	1.1
D. No inflation, 7% growth				
1	1.9	0.3	0.1	0.0
7	11.5	1.6	0.6	0.3
20	23.7	3.4	1.2	0.6
40	30.5	4.4	1.5	0.8
E. No inflation, 3% growth, gain in appreciation				
1	0.8	0.1	0.0	0.0
7	5.4	0.8	0.3	0.1
20	13.5	1.9	0.7	0.3
40	21.8	3.1	1.1	0.5
F. No inflation, 3 % growth, gain in dividend				
1	1.2	0.2	0.1	0.0
7	7.5	1.1	0.4	0.2
20	18.8	2.7	0.9	0.5
40	30.2	4.3	1.5	0.8

Note: Based on calculations in appendix B. Calculations assume a 28 percent tax rate.

Table 6.6 shows similar calculations for the sale of a structure. These effects show some minor anomalies, due to the effects of tax depreciation and its relationship to economic decline. Again the most pronounced effects are in the case of assets expected to be held until death.

The analysis of the effects of the capital gains tax—and its interaction with depreciation on used assets—reveals certain important aspects of the tax consequences on the sale of assets. First, the effective tax rate may exceed or be less than the statutory rate, depending on the holding period and the inflation rate. When assets are held until death, the tax rate usually falls below the statutory rate. Second, the lock-in effect is increased the longer the holding period of the existing asset, is greater in the presence of inflation, but is most powerfully affected by the failure to tax capital gains at death.

Table 6.6
Increase in return necessary to sale: Structures

Holding period of asset sold	Expected holding period of asset purchased			
	1	7	20	40
A. 5% inflation, new asset sold				
1	0.2	0.2	0.2	0.2
7	1.5	1.3	1.1	0.9
20	3.2	2.8	2.2	1.8
40	3.8	3.1	2.3	1.9
B. No inflation, new asset sold				
1	0.0	0.0	0.1	0.1
7	0.2	0.3	0.4	0.4
20	1.2	1.4	1.4	1.1
40	1.9	1.8	1.6	1.3
C. 5% inflation, held until death				
1	2.6	0.4	0.2	0.2
7	15.7	2.5	1.2	0.9
20	33.6	5.4	2.3	1.8
40	38.9	5.7	2.5	1.9
D. No inflation, held until death				
1	0.7	0.1	0.1	0.1
7	5.9	1.2	0.8	0.4
20	24.5	4.9	1.7	1.2
40	38.8	5.5	2.0	1.3

Note: Based on calculations in appendix B; assumes 5 percent real after-tax return and 27.5-year life.

The Capital Gains Tax and Economic Efficiency

General Issues of Savings and Allocation of Investments

The capital gains tax can affect the overall burden of taxes and the allocation of capital to different types of investments. Despite the considerable attention paid to the capital gains tax, it accounts for only a small portion of the overall tax on capital income. Many assets are never sold or are held until death. The federal capital gains tax is responsible for less than 10 percent of the overall federal capital income tax burden. But the case for altering the tax on the grounds of overall tax burden is subject to all of the uncertainties and ambiguities discussed in chapter 2, which suggest that there is not a particularly strong case for altering the tax.

Thus, in general, claims that a capital gains tax reduction is important for economic growth or for efficient allocation between consumption and savings appear unsupported by the evidence. The efficiency gains are probably small and a more direct approach of decreasing the government deficit would be more likely to succeed in increasing savings.

The capital gains tax also plays a role in the allocation of resources. In this case, however, there is only one revision to the capital gains tax that is unambiguously likely to gain in allocative efficiency—indexation of corporate stock for inflation. Such a measure would improve the allocation between corporate and noncorporate uses and reduce the distortion caused by favoring debt over equity capital. At the same time indexation would not distort the choice between paying out earnings in dividends versus capital gains because the inflationary gain would be taxed in either case, assuming that the firm does not wish to distribute more than its real profits. (If a firm distributes some of the inflationary gain, it will in effect be distributing part of the amount necessary to replace its capital stock or will be required to sell assets to do so, since retaining the inflation premium simply maintains its real capital stock intact. Therefore one would normally view the trade-off to be the shares of real profit retained or paid out.) Even though the direction of the welfare benefits is clear for indexing capital gains for inflation, using the revenue forgone to reduce the corporate tax rate would result in greater efficiency gains because it would simultaneously reduce the tax burden on equity and increase it on debt. It would also reduce any persisting tax burden differences across sectors.

A capital gains rate cut for corporate stock, such as an exclusion, would accomplish the goal of reducing the tax burden on corporate capital and on corporate equity but would exacerbate the preference for retention. Allowing capital gains tax reductions to all noncorporate capital would only spread benefits to the noncorporate sector, which is favored by the tax system in the first place. Indeed a general capital gains cut might exacerbate the differences between corporate and noncorporate tax burdens. Thus a general capital gains rate cut appears uncertain to achieve any allocative efficiency gains.

Another efficiency issue associated, particularly in the public debate, with the capital gains tax, is the issue of entrepreneurship and risk taking. Yet the argument that capital gains taxes discourage risk taking is less than clear. Recall that a tax can actually encourage risk taking because, while it reduces the expected return, it also reduces the variation in return. Indeed taxes can encourage investment in risky assets by making the government a partner in risk taking. Moreover encouraging risk taking, relative to that which the market would undertake on its own, has yet to be established as desirable.

The main caveat to this risk-taking analysis is that there are statutory limits ($3,000 currently) on the amount of capital losses that can be offset in any one year against ordinary income. (Losses can be carried forward indefinitely, however.) Without such limits, individuals would be free to realize their losses and never pay any taxes on gains. Indeed this characteristic could result in negative tax collections from capital gains, as individuals realize and offset losses against ordinary income, yielding tax benefits that exceed payments on gains.

Although much attention has been focused on the effects of restrictions on loss offsets, there are nevertheless substantial risk-reducing effects of the capital gains tax. Variations in return manifested as smaller or larger gains are subject to the full risk-reducing effects of the tax. Moreover individuals with sufficiently heterogeneous assets or relatively small portfolios enjoy the full risk-offsetting effects of the tax for losses as well. Hence the case for cutting the capital gains tax to increase risk taking is suspect. Nor is there evidence that the burden of individual capital gains taxes is suppressing the availability of venture capital; quite the contrary—Poterba (1989) found that 90 percent of venture capital funds were supplied by investors not subject to personal taxes (tax exempt, foreign, and corporate investors).

Efficiency Costs of the Lock-in Effect

The primary argument for reducing the capital gains tax lies in the lock-in effect. If this effect is powerful, there is a strong case for taking measures to reduce it. Indeed, if it is large enough, not only would tax reduction yield large welfare gains relative to the magnitude of the revenues collected, but it is also conceivable that lowering the tax would actually raise revenues through increased realizations.

Individuals realize capital gains for two reasons: to consume or to exchange one asset for another. In the case of the former motivation, sale would be unnecessary in a riskless world with perfect financial institutions because individuals could borrow against the value of assets to finance consumption. Financial markets are not perfect, and risk is present. Individuals may therefore prefer financing consumption by selling assets rather than borrowing, in order to maintain the desired degree of risk and return. In the case of the exchange motivation individuals might sell assets to purchase others for one of two reasons: because they wish to achieve a more desirable investment portfolio (i.e., one that is more diversified or more appropriate to the desire for risk versus return) or because their expectations about future returns differ from those of the market. (If all individuals had identical expectations, there would be no need to sell because changes in relative returns would be capitalized into asset values.) Of course individuals may wish to sell assets such as an operating business if they wish to retire or engage in a different economic activity. Owner-occupied housing might be sold because of a change in consumption tastes, because of retirement or job relocations, or because of changed financial circumstances.

Despite these general notions of the theory of lock-in effects, the underlying model of capital gains realizations has never been fully developed. Kiefer (1990) and Burman (1991) have proposed models based on differing expectations of rates of return. Econometric studies of the realizations response have, however, been based on "reduced form" estimates that simply assume some negative relationship between tax rates and realizations without basing the form of this relationship on a formal model.

Research that attempts to measure the effects of lock-in has been going on for many years. What is most apparent is that investors do respond to a temporary tax rate reduction or to changes in tax rates when the adjustment made is relatively modest (a small change in holding period). The first effect was forcefully demonstrated in 1986 when a cut in the capital gains tax was announced but did not take effect immediately, resulting in an enormous surge in realizations toward the end of that year.

Some research focused on the differential between short-term and long-term gains and the willingness to make minor changes in holding period to avoid the tax. During periods when tax relief was granted to capital gains, typically in the form of an exclusion, only gains held for a certain time, usually six months or a year, were eligible for special treatment. Fredland, Gray, and Sunley (1968) found evidence that investors do postpone realizations in order to qualify for special treatment. The evidence on the lock-in effect after a gain has become long term was inconclusive based on early studies (Seltzer 1951; Hinrichs 1963; Brannon 1974). Seltzer and Brannon looked at changes in realizations over time; Hinrichs observed a higher ratio of short-term to long-term gains in the lower-income brackets. In all of these early studies, however, there were problems with the lack of an explicit model of the decision to sell, and of controls for other factors, as well as a failure to quantify the lock-in effect.

The responsiveness of realizations is usually couched in the form of a measure of the elasticity—the percentage change in realizations divided by the percentage change in the tax rate. This elasticity would not necessarily be constant at all tax levels—in general, one might expect that it would be higher at higher tax rates. On average, if the elasticity is close to one, a small cut in the tax would increase revenues. The welfare cost of the tax is related to the elasticity—the higher the elasticity, the greater the distorting effect of the tax.

The publication of a study by Feldstein, Slemrod, and Yitzhaki (1978) ushered in a new era of extensive and increasingly sophisticated econometric studies. This study by Feldstein et al. was the first use of extensive cross-sectional data (observations across many taxpayers in a single year) to estimate statistically the response to a capital gains tax cut, and it found a very large responsiveness to the level of the capital gains tax. Their results not only indicated that the welfare cost of the tax was large (an elasticity of about 4, evaluated at the mean tax rate in their study) but also that cutting the tax would raise revenues.

This seminal study was vulnerable, however, to a number of criticisms. It focused on high-income taxpayers and solely on corporate stock. Moreover the very large response it found was difficult to square with the record of realizations over time because the model predicted that a relatively small increase in the tax rate would cause realizations virtually to disappear.

In a subsequent article Minarik (1981) found that the results were greatly affected by how observations were weighted, and found, with similar data and a different weighting scheme, a much smaller elasticity (well under 1). The debate on the proper weighting method was never fully resolved.

Another weakness of the single cross-sectional approach was the possibility that individuals with low tax rates who realized significant gains may have been doing so in response to a temporary rather than a permanent drop in their tax rate. There is a much greater benefit to realizing gain when the tax rate is low, and individuals with temporarily low tax rates would have a incentive to realize gains in one year that they otherwise would have spread over many years. Auten and Clotfelter (1982) explored this effect with panel data (data that extends for each taxpayer over several years). They constructed a permanent rate by averaging tax rates over three years and then tested for the differential response to the permanent rate and to a deviations of the current tax rate from that permanent rate (the transitory component). Their results suggested a powerful and significant response to a temporary drop in taxes, but a smaller and uncertain response to a permanent change. With some specifications Auten and Clotfelter were not able to obtain a statistically significant relationship between realizations and permanent tax rates (i.e., any relationship found could not be confidently shown to be other than the result of a random relationship). The Auten and Clotfelter results suggest that it is very important to take some account of transitory effects.

Another study published in that same year by Auten (1982) used a mix of time series and aggregated income classes, and it found an elasticity of around one. A later study of a similar nature was done by

Lindsey (1987). Such mixed studies are very difficult to evaluate. Both cross-sectional and time series studies suffer from weaknesses (detailed below), and a mixed study makes it even more difficult to sort out the possible biases.

A Treasury (1985) study included another estimate based on panel data, similar to the approach used by Auten and Clotfelter (1982). This 1985 study also reported elasticity estimates based on time series—how aggregate realizations of capital gains varied over time with the overall tax rate. The time series study tended to show a lower response than the cross-sectional study (the first was slightly under one, and the second slightly over one). The reverse should have been true, for time series studies may be picking up, in part, the short-run response to a tax change. This problem was particularly serious given the fact that tax rates had been cut toward the end of the time period under study. When taxes are cut, there is a possibility of a large initial response (as existing portfolios are unlocked) followed by a more modest effect. This temporary response would overstate the elasticity as compared to the true long-run response. This pattern was later documented in an explicit trading model by Kiefer (1990).

More time series studies (Congressional Budget Office 1986; Congressional Budget Office 1988; Darby, Gillingham, and Greenlees 1988; Auerbach 1989a; Jones 1989) simply indicated that time series estimates could vary depending on the time period covered and the specification used, but by and large, they revealed elasticities below one. Two cross-sectional studies (one using panel data) in 1989 (Auten, Burman, and Randolph, and Gillingham, Greenlees, and Zeischang) found large responses similar to those found by Feldstein et al., although the study by Gillingham et al. was flawed by not being able to deal with transitory tax effects because they did not have a panel. Moreover it is clear from the Auten, Burman, and Randolph study and in a later comment by Burman (1990) that the authors were uncertain as to the meaning of their results for estimating the effects of a permanent reduction the capital gains tax rate.

The public debate over the revenue costs of a capital gains tax cut became, in part, a debate over the reliability of various econometric approaches. This critical debate is outlined in several papers (Congressional Budget Office 1988; Auten, Burman and Randolph 1989; Auerbach 1989a; Burman 1990; Gravelle 1990; Slemrod and Shobe 1990, Gravelle 1991d; Burman 1991; Auten and Cordes 1991).

There have been numerous criticisms of cross-sectional, or panel data. These studies cannot effectively distinguish between transitory and permanent effects (even the techniques of averaging tax rates were imperfect in this respect because the average tax rate over a few years is not necessarily the permanent tax rate). Other problems include the presence of unmeasured individual specific effects, endogeneity in the tax rate (in a progressive system increased realizations can cause higher tax rates), correlation between tax rate and income and wealth variables in a progressive tax system that make the separation of income and price effects difficult, and lack of a wealth measure or, more important, a measure of accrued unrealized gains. At least some critics (Auerbach 1989a; Gravelle 1990) suggested that these problems are sufficiently disabling that micro-data studies could not tell us anything about the responsiveness.

Critics of aggregate time series studies have pointed to the lack of consideration of dynamic transition effects, limited number of observations and limited variation in the tax rate, and imperfect aggregation of tax rates. Many of the problems present in the cross-sectional or panel data studies are also present in time series, although they may be less disabling. The correlation between income and tax rate and endogeneity of the tax rate is much less important given the variation arising from statutory tax changes. Wealth and accrued gains can be measured, although not very precisely (particularly in the case of accruals). Indeed, despite the importance of the accrued gains measure, only the Congressional Budget Office (1988) in one specification included it: In this case the elasticity was quite low and not statistically significant. Moreover changes such as the increased trading that typically accompanies a rising market and changes in brokerage fees are often not incorporated in these studies. Some of these problems tend to make time series estimates too high, some too low, and some just lead to questions about reliability. Both types of studies can be criticized because the reduced form relationships (the relationship between realizations and gains) are not carefully built on a theoretical foundation.

Beginning in 1990, a heated debate on the realization response to capital gains tax cuts and the consequences for revenue costs occurred, fueled in part because the Joint Committee on Taxation (JCT) assumed a smaller response than did the Treasury's Office of Tax Analysis

(OTA). The JCT used a 0.7 elasticity at a 20 percent tax rate and a 0.875 elasticity at a 25 percent tax rate.

OTA used a 0.9 elasticity at a 20 percent rate and a 1.125 elasticity at a 25 percent tax rate. (The form of the estimating function is such that the elasticity rises with the tax rate.) OTA's elasticity, coupled with some other aspects of a capital gains tax cut proposed at that time, resulted in a revenue gain while the JCT's elasticity resulted in a revenue loss.[1] Despite the acrimonious debate that ensued, the range in the two assumptions was far less than the range of response estimated in the econometric literature, which varied from a failure to identify any significant response to a response of 4 to 5.

The importance of the realizations response, both for measuring revenue consequences and for measuring welfare changes, is illustrated in table 6.7. In order to measure welfare, these calculations are based on the assumption that the individual is indifferent to selling or holding at the margin. In that case the gain in welfare from selling is equal to the tax to be paid. This assumption holds true strictly only for assets that would otherwise be held until death so that holding involves paying no tax. Most of the unrealized gains do reflect assets that are never sold, but this assumption does overstate the welfare gain somewhat. (The tax paid on increased realizations deriving from selling assets more frequently results in a reduction in deferral rather than a forgiveness of tax.)[2] With this assumption, and an estimate of the relationship between realizations and tax rates, it is possible to calculate a welfare gain from cutting the capital gains tax consistent with each elasticity assumption. (The details are given in appendix B).

The projected percentage of revenue loss offset (if the offset is more than 100 percent, the tax cut would gain revenue), the welfare gain as a percentage of output, and the welfare gain as a percentage of forgone revenue are shown for three policies: elimination of the tax, a 50 percent exclusion, and a 30 percent exclusion. Five different elasticities are shown: a lower elasticity of 0.25, the elasticities of 0.7 and 0.9 used by the JCT and the OTA, respectively, a somewhat higher elasticity of 1.20, and an elasticity of 4, is similar to the higher elasticities estimated in several cross-sectional studies.

The results in table 6.7 suggest that if the capital gains response is quite large, then there is a powerful case for eliminating the tax altogether and certainly a case for providing an exclusion (although, as discussed below, a better option might be taxation of gains held until death). For example, with an elasticity at 1.2, there would be a small revenue gain to reducing the tax by 50 percent (the offset is 111 percent of the original revenue loss), and welfare would be improved by 0.8 percent of GNP. For a relatively small tax, this is a very large welfare gain.

The higher elasticities in the table should almost certainly be ruled out, however. For example, if the elasticity of 4 were assumed, repealing the capital gains tax would have been estimated to increase realizations (beginning with a baseline of about $200 billion) to $3 trillion—over 60 percent of GNP in 1988! Even a 30 percent exclusion would have been predicted to increase realizations to $900 billion, a

Table 6.7
Revenue effects and welfare gains from capital gains tax cuts

Elasticity	Revenue offset (percent)	Welfare gain as percentage of	
		GNP	Revenue loss[a]
A. No capital gains tax			
0.25	0.0	0.17	17.0
0.70	0.0	0.60	59.9
0.90	0.0	0.85	84.9
1.20	0.0	1.32	132.1
4.00	0.0	28.48	1,848.3
B. 50% exclusion			
0.25	16.9	0.13	30.2
0.70	54.9	0.40	178.0
0.90	75.5	0.54	448.0
1.20	111.7	0.80	*
4.00	1,118.2	7.32	*
C. 30% exclusion			
0.25	22.9	0.08	36.0
0.70	70.0	0.25	281.7
0.90	93.7	0.34	1,778.8
1.20	132.6	0.48	*
4.00	812.4	2.83	*

Note: Based on calculations in appendix B. Assumes a 25 percent tax rate, elasticities valued at a 20 percent rate, and a semilog function.

a. The asterisks indicate that the revenue is not lost but gained. Note that these calculations do not follow the rule that the welfare loss rises with the square of the tax rate because the behavioral relationship is far from linear.

number that is far outside of any historical experience. It is these unrealistic elasticities that in turn give rise to unrealistic measures of the welfare cost of the capital gains tax—28 percent of GNP in the case of the elasticity of 4.

Indeed, it is in some respects extraordinary that although the Bush administration never used such a large elasticity in calculating revenue estimates (the results arising from such a choice would have strained credulity), administration officials "justified" their own choice of elasticities by reference to the large estimates derived in the two cross-sectional studies prepared in 1989. These studies yielded enormous elasticities. The officials in fact asserted that the cross-sectional techniques were superior to the time series studies relied upon by the JCT.

Of course an argument might be made that the short run elasticity could be much larger, but the historical record suggests that such large effects are untenable in either the short run or the long run. Moreover the cross-sectional studies that yielded these high elasticities should have, in theory, been measuring a long run effect.

At what point, however, does the elasticity become reasonable? The next steps taken in assessing the potential magnitude of the behavioral consequences to lock-in proceeded, from such "reality checks." Auerbach (1989) suggested that there was nothing in the historical record of capital gains relative to accruals to justify even an elasticity of one. Gravelle (1991d) formalized this notion by setting up a simulation model that sought to find the upper limit to this realizations response. This limit was based on the axiomatic recognition that a permanent response could never be so large as to result in realizations larger than accruals (if every asset were sold every year, realizations would roughly equal accruals). She employed the most common functional form of the realizations elasticity and found that the maximum upper limit was an elasticity of 0.5. This maximum upper limit assumes that in the absence of any costs of trading, all assets would be sold each year. This is an unreasonable assumption. Even without trading costs, assets would be held for longer periods and passed on at death simply because they continue to be desirable assets in some cases. (Individuals keep assets in savings accounts and other forms not subject to costs of trading for long periods and pass these assets on at death. Moreover some assets tend to have intrinsic value in the hands of the owner, such as controlling shares of corporate stock or family businesses. Even for other assets there are nonmonetary costs of trading such as the time spent arranging transactions.) Thus, if the functional form assumed is reasonable, the true elasticity would be below—and perhaps well below—0.5.

Using a slightly different simulation model, Burman (1991) found a similar magnitude of effects. Moreover a recent cross-sectional econometric study by Burman and Randolph (1992), which relied on variation in taxes across states, found an elasticity of about 0.3. Relying on the variation in state tax rates deals with some of the fundamental problems of cross-sectional analysis, since these tax rates are exogenous. Along with Gravelle's (1991d) research, these more recent assessments suggest that the lock-in effects may not be very large, and the case for reducing the capital gains tax due to this effect is much less compelling. If the elasticity is at the lower number included in table 6.7 (0.25), then the efficiency gains from reducing the tax, as well as the revenue response, are not very large, and the case for reducing the tax on efficiency grounds, particularly for noncorporate investments, is not made.

Equity Issues

The original tax benefits for capital gains granted in 1921 responded to an equity problem—bunching of income in a progressive tax system. Individuals who earned income over many periods might report a large gain and be subject to high taxes simply because their income in that year was very large. This issue involves fairness across taxpayers. The individual who earns his income in a more even fashion is benefited relative to the individual who earns his return in a more sporadic form.

This equity issue has largely disappeared from the debate. Income averaging provisions provided relief from bunching; this offset was supplanted by the flattening of the tax rate structure in 1986. In addition the tax advantages of deferral of income were recognized as offsetting the tax burdens on individuals who held an asset for a long period of time.

A new issue, which appears to relate to horizontal equity, is the argument that individuals are taxed on gains that arise from inflation and that this result is unfair. Indeed this view has caused some individuals to support indexation of capital gains for inflation, while rejecting a more explicit exclusion of the same overall worth. While this argument about fairness has a strong emotional appeal, it is flawed from an economic standpoint. If the taxation of inflationary gains is expected, then relative returns adjust to provide the same after-tax yield, net of risk, as that earned on other assets. That is, by imposing a heavier tax on capital gains due to the taxation of inflationary gains, the pretax return required by investors is driven up (and, with a fixed savings rate, drives down pretax returns elsewhere). As long as capital markets are reasonably efficient, the equal treatment of different kinds of capital income is probably not very important from an equity standpoint (although it may be quite important from an efficiency standpoint). Without question, the taxation of inflationary gains does raise the overall tax burden, although that effect is offset by the deferral advantage and the failure to tax capital gains at death. The real equity issue is that of vertical equity. Like any capital income tax, the capital gains tax tends to burden high-income individuals. In the case of the capital gains tax, capital gains are particularly concentrated at the high end of the income scale.

The issue of how to interpret the consequences of the capital gains tax for vertical equity has become quite complex (an overview of these issues can be found in Davis 1991). Some of the arguments in the public policy debate have strayed far from the distributional analysis of the tax as suggested by economic theory. A straightforward distributional study of the capital gains tax suggests that for the 30 percent exclusion proposed by the Bush administration in 1990, two-thirds of the tax reduction would go to individuals with incomes over $200,000, approximately those individuals in the top 1 percent of returns. (The data discussed here can be found in Hoerner 1992, 293–95.) Over 83 percent would go to those with incomes over $100,000. The administration countered with several arguments. First, it argued that a large fraction of those who would receive benefits have incomes of less than $50,000. Using the JCT numbers, about half of those with capital gains fall into this class. This argument is just a misleading use of statistics— changing the subject from the dollar benefits received to the number doing the receiving. Because the vast majority of taxpayers have incomes of less than $50,000, recipients of virtually any type of tax benefit would be dominated by these individuals.

The administration's second argument was that many of the individuals who receive capital gains may only be in the high-income classes because of a large one-time gain. While this argument was valid to some extent, the proposed solution—to exclude capital gains when measuring income—is untenable. (When capital gains are excluded from the measure of income for classification purposes, 26 percent of the benefits would be received by individuals above $200,000 and 39 percent by individuals with incomes above $100,000.) Most individuals who receive capital gains do so frequently. When incomes were classified based on a five-year average of income, the JCT found that 54 percent of tax benefits from a cut would be received by those with incomes over $200,000 and 74 percent received by those with incomes over $100,000. Thus, while correcting for infrequent realization of gains had some effect, it was not of a great magnitude.

The final argument made was that high-income individuals would not benefit from the tax because they would end up actually paying more tax due to higher realizations. Even if one believed, however, that such an outcome would occur, such an approach to measuring the distributional benefits is clearly inappropriate. Taxpayers who have their rates cut would clearly be better off, even if they paid more taxes, because they have an unmistakable welfare gain.

As an illustration, consider the case of a taxpayer in the 28 percent bracket, and the consequence of introducing a 30 percent exclusion. For each dollar of original capital gains realizations, the taxpayer is actually paying a tax of 28 cents; assuming no behavioral response, his tax reduction is 8.4 cents for each original dollar (30 percent of 28 cents). At an elasticity of 0.25, this individual has a tax benefit of 6.2 cents for each original dollar—his 8.4 cents reduction is offset by the additional taxes paid on induced realizations. At an elasticity of 0.9, he would be subject to a 0.6 cent *increase* in taxes.

He is clearly, however, not worse off. If we were to sum the tax reduction and the change in welfare, his gain would be greater than measured by static numbers—8.9 cents for a 0.25 elasticity and 10.2 cents for a 0.9 elasticity. These gains include the direct cash effects plus the welfare gain (the method of calculation is shown in appendix B). For example, with the 0.25 elasticity his direct tax payment falls by 6.2 cents for each dollar of original realization, but his welfare gain from a more favorable portfolio of investments is valued at 2.7 cents for each original dollar of realizations.

Of course the true burden of the tax was greater in the first place (prior to the 30 percent exclusion) if one adds both the direct tax paid and the cost of the distortion from the lock-in effect—34 cents rather than 28 cents at the 0.25 elasticity and 56 cents at the 0.9 elasticity. The burden is larger at the larger elasticity because the cost of the distortion is greater. It would be appropriate to take these extra burdens into account in measuring the initial burden of the tax for distributional purposes.

A full-blown utility based analysis of the effect of the capital gains tax would take into account welfare gains from reduced lock-in, as well the any tax driven changes in relative pretax rates of return to assets. Such an analysis would, however, still result in the burden of the capital gains tax (and any benefit from reducing it) concentrated among high-income taxpayers.

Policy Options

Indexing versus Exclusions

Reducing the capital gains tax has been proposed via either a flat exclusion or indexing for inflation. A comparison of these alternatives was also done by the Congressional Budget Office (1990); also see Halperin and Steuerle (1988) for a discussion of inflation indexing in general. Both approaches would lower tax burdens and would reduce lock in, but they would have somewhat different effects depending on the holding period. As far as affecting the overall effective tax rate, inflation indexing tends to be more beneficial, given the same real appreciation rate, for assets held a short period of time compared to assets held a long period of time. Since the tax burden is heaviest for assets held for a short period of time, the inflation indexing approach would lead to more even tax rates across assets that vary by holding period. Inflation indexing would also result in larger exclusion equivalents for assets that appreciate at a slower rate (i.e., corporate stock that pays large dividends). From this perspective, inflation indexing leads to more even tax rates across different assets, held for the same period of time.

Indexing for inflation would not, however, necessarily accomplish more to reduce the lock-in effect. Assets that face the more serious barriers to sales are assets that have been held a long time and that would be held until death. Inflation indexing would be relatively less beneficial to these assets than an exclusion of equal cost because long-lived assets receive a relatively smaller exclusion from inflation. This effect is demonstrated in table 6.8, which reports the lock-in effect under an exclusion equivalent to indexing for a seven-year asset. For assets held until death the barriers to sale are reduced proportionally more for an exclusion than for inflation indexing if held for a long period of time. For example, the required increase in appreciation in the new asset (to be held for seven years) when selling an asset (held for forty years) is 4.5 percent under current law (panel B, table 6.5), 3.1 percent with indexing (panel E, table 6.5), and 1.8 percent with an exclusion equivalent (panel B, table 6.8). When the asset is expected to be sold in the future in any case, there is a tendency for indexation to be slightly more beneficial than the exclusion, but the differences are quite small.

Indexing does seem superior for reducing risk taking, were it not for limits on the deduction of losses, since a source of variation in return (uncertain inflation) would be eliminated. Moreover, with a fixed inflation rate, reducing the rate will increase the variation in real return, while inflation indexing will maintain the full tax rate—and full sharing of risk with the government—on variations in real return.

Table 6.8
Increase in appreciation necessary to sale: Corporate stock, exclusion equivalent to indexing a seven-year asset

Holding period of asset sold	Expected holding period of asset purchased			
	1	7	20	40
A. 5% inflation, 3% growth, sold				
1	0.1	0.1	0.0	0.0
7	0.4	0.3	0.2	0.1
20	0.8	0.7	0.4	0.2
40	1.0	0.8	0.3	0.3
B. 5% inflation, 3% growth, held until death				
1	0.1	0.1	0.0	0.0
7	5.4	0.8	0.3	0.1
20	10.4	1.5	0.5	0.3
40	12.6	1.8	0.6	0.3

Note: Based on calculations in appendix B. Calculations assume a 28 percent tax rate.

In practice, however, the loss restriction would apply more frequently in such a world. Currently many assets with real losses actually generate nominal gains because of inflation; with indexing, these assets would produce losses. Indeed indexing proposals generally include some further restrictions on losses, such as preventing indexation from turning a nominal gain into a nominal loss. The need for these restrictions arises from a concern that individuals could simply realize their losses and hold to their gains. Indeed this stricture was applied on a strict transaction-by-transaction basis by the House passed indexing proposal in 1992 (H.R. 4210). This restriction would be undesirable for the purposes of minimizing risk.

Prospective Relief

Some capital gains reduction plans would apply only on a prospective basis. Either indexing or an exclusion could be made to apply only to newly purchased assets (H.R. 4210 as passed by the House in 1992 contained a prospective indexing scheme). Some assets, as a result, would not be affected by the reduced lock-in effects for a long period of time. In other cases there would be an incentive to dispose of assets more quickly in order to qualify. (To prevent wasteful transactions, such a plan could allow "mark to market" where gains are reported and tax paid without the asset being sold; this approach would not work well with assets without established market price, e.g., real estate.) Prospective tax cuts would delay any efficiency gain but would result in less cost in the short run.

Taxing Gains at Death

Even if the lock-in effect is deemed important, allowing reductions in the capital gains tax through an exclusion or inflation indexing are not the only options that might be considered. As shown in tables 6.4 through 6.6, the most serious barriers to sale occur because capital gains are not taxed until death. There at least two possible solutions to this problem. One solution would be to constructively realize capital gains at death so that the tax would be paid at that time. There are, however, some problems with this option. Assets must be valued at death because of the estate tax for individuals who are subject to the tax, but the estate tax only applies to large estates. (Transfers between spouses have special exemptions, but constructive realization could be delayed until the death of the spouse.) In addition, if assets are not to be sold, there may be problems with accumulating the cash needed to pay the tax. The estate tax is sometimes criticized because it can result in the forced sale of properties, and this effect would be increased by imposing a capital gains tax. Such problems might be reduced with flat exemptions. Another option is carryover of basis. The reason that capital gains escape taxes at death entirely is that the heir takes the market value at death as the new basis. If, instead, the original basis were assigned to the heir, the tax could only be postponed, not forgiven, producing lock-in effects similar to those in table 6.4 or the upper portion of table 6.6. Carryover of basis at death would also eliminate any problems of forced sale.

Both constructive realization at death and carryover basis confront the administrative problem that the heirs may not know the original basis. One could simply assign a zero basis (which would provide incentives for individuals to provide such information to their heirs) or some safe harbor minimum basis as a share of value. (Existing owners of inherited assets that have never been sold could continue with their current basis.)

Accrual Equivalent Taxation

Another more general revision of the capital gains tax would be to charge interest on deferrals or, as a more straightforward approach, to calculate an exclusion equivalent that will provide the same results as accrual taxation. These types of schemes have been explored by a number of authors (Vickrey 1939; Brinner and Munnell 1974; Auerbach 1991a). Under the simplest method, setting an exclusion rate that is the equivalent of accrual taxation, it would be necessary to determine the nominal and real appreciation, rate and then calculate what the value of an asset earning an after-tax real rate would be. The difference between these two values would be the tax, and the exclusion rate would be the difference divided by the tax times the gain. This approach would lead to an inclusion rate higher than one for long lived assets but would of course never exceed the sales price of the asset. It would, however, have to be coupled with carryover basis or constructive realization at death. While such an approach is mathematically complicated, and would be precise only with a constant rate of real appreciation, tables prescribing exclusion/inclusion rates for a matrix of the ratio of sales prices to basis, and holding periods, could be easily prescribed.

Problems with Depreciable Assets

All schemes for changing the capital gains tax could produce difficulties in the case of depreciable assets. The basic problem is the possibility that the lock-in effect would be reversed by allowing a low rate on gains but increasing depreciation deductions. This problem is especially important when depreciation is very rapid. One approach is to require recapture—the part of the gain that reflects depreciation deductions could be taxed at ordinary rates.

Indexing capital gains leads to difficult issues in modifying the changes for depreciable assets. The most straightforward approach would be to index the undepreciated basis and then take the difference between the sales price and that basis as the gain. This scheme would have no effect on gains on assets that are held for the full period of tax depreciation. It would be better to combine the indexing of capital gains with indexing of depreciation and slower depreciation. The undepreciated basis would be indexed and would correspond more closely to market value, reducing any capital gain that arises. This approach could not of course be applied to owner-occupied housing, where no depreciation is allowed.

Revenue Neutral Changes

If revenue losses are not desirable, it would be possible to make some changes in the capital gains taxes that both raise and lower revenue. One possibility is to combine capital gains relief for corporate stock with either constructive realization or carryover basis at death. This approach would reduce the lock-in effect considerably and also benefit those assets that are more heavily taxed for other reasons. In addition adoption of certain types of corporate tax integration schemes would provide relief for capital gains on corporate stock.

Summary

Evaluation of the capital gains tax and how it affects the efficiency and equity of the tax system hinges on several issues. A central one in the economics literature has been the lock-in effect—an effect that has been the subject of much disagreement. Some econometric studies have suggested that this effect is very powerful; more recent work in both simulation approaches and revised econometric studies indicate that the response may be modest. If the lock-in effect is not so large, the case for cutting capital gains taxes is much weaker, either on the welfare grounds that economists would stress or on the revenue grounds (especially the possibility of losing virtually no revenue) that figured prominently in the public debate.

Indeed, given the uncertainty about behavioral responses, it is not clear that an overall cut in capital gains taxes (if made up by other tax increases) would improve economic efficiency. Much of capital gain arises from noncorporate capital that is already favored relative to corporation capital. And, while cutting the capital gains tax would reduce the favoritism toward debt in the corporate sector, it would increase the incentive to retain earnings.

The capital gains tax burden is concentrated toward higher-income individuals, and any reduction in the tax would in turn benefit these individuals. It is this distributional issue that has been a major argument against cutting the capital gains tax. The analysis does suggest that a cut in the tax on corporate stock would be more likely to contribute to a more efficient tax system than an across-the-board cut; if combined with taxation of capital gains at death to make up revenues, such a policy does appear likely to improve welfare, without incurring large distributional effects. Whether such relief should take the form of indexing the basis or an exclusion is uncertain.

7 The Corporate Alternative Minimum Tax and the Passive Loss Restriction

Although the corporate alternative minimum tax (AMT) and the passive loss restriction are mechanically very different, they are similar in that they are designed to increase tax burdens on taxpayers who "use tax preferences too much." These provisions impose a different set of tax rules under certain circumstances. These circumstances can depend on the overall business and investment activities of the taxpayers, linking different investments together in a way not dictated by the technology of production or the preferences of the taxpayer. They can alter the tax burdens faced on the same investments by different firms and taxpayers that would otherwise be identical, as well as the relative tax burdens on different investments for a single firm or individual. They are more likely to affect taxpayers in times of recession. They can change the relative tax burdens as a function of the amount of debt. And their goal, to reach taxpayers who are taking advantage of generally available tax deductions, is difficult to justify on standard grounds of economic efficiency and simplicity.

They are considered together in this chapter because the fundamental question is whether such tax rules are likely to contribute to the broad goals of tax policy—efficiency, equity, and administrative simplicity. The analysis presented here suggests that they are unlikely to do so, or that other revisions in the tax code would achieve the objectives more effectively. The most important such structural revision would be to measure income more precisely through indexation of interest payments and deductions for depreciation (combined with some offset for the corporate double tax), accompanied by matching tax depreciation more closely to economic depreciation.

The corporate AMT was estimated by Dworin (1987a) to affect 20 percent of corporations initially. A subsequent study by Gerardi, Milner, and Silverstein (1992) for tax years 1987–1990 showed that while only a small fraction of corporations paid the AMT, a significant fraction of large corporations were subject to this minimum tax. In the largest size classification ($500 million or more in assets), about 20 to 25 percent of firms paid the AMT rather than the regular tax. According to a recent release by Arthur Anderson (1992), 60 percent of major corporations in their survey are currently subject to the AMT.

Indeed it might seem that the AMT is as important a focus of attention as the regular corporate tax in evaluating the overall effects of tax policy. The high rate of coverage in the Arthur Anderson study may, however, reflect a selective sample of firms. Moreover current high coverage rates may result from both the recession and the natural growth in coverage given the number of years that have elapsed since the minimum tax was enacted. It seems likely that the frequency of firms falling under the AMT will decline in the future, and the tax will become relatively unimportant, except for some industries. The passive loss restriction is likely to have more permanent effects, with its importance varying with changes in economic activity and inflation rates.

The corporate alternative minimum tax and the passive loss restriction were added by the Tax Reform Act of 1986 (TRA), although the corporate alternative minimum tax replaced a different, and less important, add-on corporate minimum tax. The alternative minimum tax for individuals was already in existence, but it actually became much less important when the capital gains exclusion was eliminated. In this chapter the individual AMT is not discussed because of its unimportance. In any case many of the arguments discussed here apply as well to the individual AMT.

How the AMT and Passive Loss Restriction Work

The AMT applies if the calculated tax burden under the AMT is larger than the burden under the regular tax. The AMT base is broader, but the rate is lower (20 percent, rather than the regular tax rate of 35 percent). There is a set of less generous depreciation rules—depreciation is figured using longer lives (set at the midpoint of tax lives under the pre-1981 asset depreciation range system), and the method for equipment is restricted to 150 percent declining balance depreciation. These differences in depreciation are only applied to assets acquired after the TRA. The AMT base also includes other tax provisions, including intangible drilling costs and certain accounting differentials.

In addition the AMT base includes 75 percent of the excess of the AMT taxable income over another alternative tax base called *adjusted current earnings* (ACE). ACE is in turn based on a concept of earnings and profits (E&P). The E&P base disallows some additional deductions, by requiring the capitalization of intangible drilling costs and disallowing the typically more generous LIFO (last-in, first-out) inventory accounting.

To sum up, there are three potential taxes that the firm might calculate: the regular tax rate (0.35, for a large corporation) times the regular base, the minimum tax rate (0.20) times the minimum tax base, or the minimum tax rate (0.20) times a base that is weighted one-quarter by the AMT base and three-quarters by the ACE base. The highest tax will be paid. The third calculation will be larger than the second if the ACE base is larger than the AMT base.

Additional taxes paid under the minimum tax can be carried over indefinitely and used as credits against regular tax liability. This carryover is very important for firms, since the differences between the tax bases include timing differences. If there were no carryover, then a firm beginning on the AMT with its slower depreciation could end up not being able to deduct the full costs of its assets, and tax rates could become very high.

The passive loss restriction disallows certain deductions in part by disallowing losses on certain types of investments deemed to be passive in nature (investments in which the taxpayer does not materially participate). Property rental, including real estate rental, is automatically defined as a passive activity. There is an exception, however, for real estate investments of taxpayers with adjusted gross incomes of $100,000 or less who actively participate in the management of property; these individuals are allowed to deduct losses up to $25,000. (This $25,000 is phased out for adjusted gross incomes between $100,000 and $150,000.) In 1993 an exception was also added for real estate for certain individuals who are materially involved in real estate (the exceptions requires a minimum of 750 hours of participation and half of business income to be derived from real estate).

If tax deductions exceed rent, the excess deductions are not allowed to be taken against other income (e.g., wages and portfolio income in the form of interest and dividends). These restrictions were phased in over several years but are now fully effective. If unused losses remain when the property is sold, they are deductible in full at that time. Thus the taking of deductions is deferred, rather than disallowed, if property is sold.

Roots of the AMT and Passive Loss Restriction

The notion of imposing some sort of minimum tax dates back to the 1960s. Graetz and Sunley (1988) discuss the precursor of an alternative tax suggested by Senator Russell Long of Louisiana in the early 1960s. The first minimum tax provisions were placed into law in 1969, in part, due to a study by the outgoing (Johnson) administration that showed many high-income taxpayers paying no tax. This minimum tax was an add-on tax. Certain tax deductions deemed to be preferences were subject to an separate tax, which was paid in addition to the regular tax. This add-on tax was shifted to an alternative tax—a lower rate on a broader base—for individuals in 1978. That change was in response to criticisms that the individual add-on tax could create relatively high tax rates on capital gains. For corporations the add-on tax tended to be relatively modest in its effects for corporations.

The first notion of some sort of loss restriction came in a proposal in 1973 for a limitation on artificial accounting losses. This proposal, which was never enacted, was similar in concept to the notion of an alternative minimum tax—individuals would compute income under a different set of accounting rules and the differences in deductions would be disallowed.

The revisions in the corporate minimum tax and the introduction of the passive loss restriction in 1986 were, in large part, reaction to two phenomena that had received a great deal of attention in the early 1980s. First, many large and profitable corporations were reporting extremely small tax burdens which arose in turn from factors that were largely temporary—the recession, the enactment of accelerated depreciation in 1981, and safe harbor leasing provisions. Accelerated depreciation naturally causes tax burdens to fall, particularly after a few years, because cumulated depreciation swells and then declines.

This pattern occurs because accelerated depreciation is a deferral of tax, operating like an interest free loan. Depreciation is pushed toward the present, causing taxes to fall. As investments under the new system age, the depreciation deductions associated with these investments become smaller than they otherwise would have been (i.e., the loan is repaid). While taxes will not rise to their previous level, in the long run they will more closely approach their previous level. Thus the large deductions and low taxes arising from accelerated depreciation were a temporary phenomenon.

Safe harbor leasing provided an opportunity for firms that could not fully use accelerated depreciation because of lack of sufficient tax liability to effectively "sell" these tax benefits to other firms, by selling and then leasing back equipment. The lessors could benefit from the tax breaks, passing these benefits back, in part, to the lessee through lower lease payments than would be the case without the tax subsidies. Safe harbor leasing was well received by many economists because it overcame a problem in the tax law. In order to use tax benefits, a firm had to have sufficient tax liability to use them. New firms and firms in difficulty, with low incomes, were not able to benefit from the new accelerated depreciation. One of the consequences of safe harbor leasing was that profitable lessors reduced—and, in some cases, virtually eliminated—their tax liability. While such a phenomenon should have been expected (and while these tax savings should be largely passed back to lessees), a furor arose over the appearance of profitable firms paying no taxes. For this reason, and to raise revenues, safe harbor leasing was repealed in 1982. The deductions associated with prior leases, however, continued to produce low tax rates for many firms even after repeal of the safe harbor provisions.

The low tax rates resulting from the swell in depreciation deductions and safe harbor leases in place attracted attention and criticism during the years immediately prior to 1986. The AMT was a response to that criticism; indeed the original AMT was designed (through a "book preference") to prevent a firm from reporting profits but paying no corporate income tax.

The other phenomenon that attracted attention was the explosive growth in tax shelters—particularly in large syndicated operations with passive investors. Tax shelter operations and their growth are discussed in Cordes and Galper (1985), Nelson (1985), and Dworin

(1986). These shelters had been growing rapidly even before the changes in 1981; shelters in real estate may have been spurred on by the much more rapid depreciation enacted in 1981. The number of limited partners doubled between 1981 and 1987 (Nelson and Petska 1990). It is also likely that these shelters were encouraged by more readily available financing from technically insolvent, inexperienced, and/or high-flying thrift institutions. There was a growing belief that these tax shelters allowed individuals to invest solely for the tax benefits—and indeed many of them operated as a way of selling tax benefits to investors who had sufficient income from other sources to use the deductions in full.

The 1986 passive loss restriction, which disallowed the deduction of losses on certain investments and by certain taxpayers, was at least in part a reaction to the growth of these tax shelters.[1] Yet, like the AMT, other forces should already have been moving to slow down the growth of these shelters. In 1986 depreciation for real estate was made considerably less generous. Moreover the reduction in inflation rates would have reduced a tendency for large losses to occur. Interest deductions relative to rents tend to be high in the early years of an investment when inflation is high, since the interest payment must include a premium for inflation. Indeed, from the perspective of 1986, the investments most likely to be affected by the passive loss restriction were existing tax shelters. The natural contraction in the growth of shelter activity was apparently delayed because of the excesses in real estate financing that continued to occur during the remainder of the 1980s. These excesses led to the substantial over building of structures, particularly commercial structures.

As enacted, the passive loss restriction was different from its predecessor proposal for the limit on artificial accounting losses in 1973. Rather than identifying losses that were deemed to be "artificial" due to too generous tax treatment, all losses were simply disallowed. Thus the passive loss restriction can prevent the deduction of real economic losses as well as those losses generated from tax deductions.

Although there was strong support in some quarters for a "backup" tax system to prevent excessive use of tax deductions, they have not received an enthusiastic reception from economists. Analysis and discussion of the passive loss restriction is, however, almost nonexistent among economists. And analysis of the corporate minimum tax has been limited. Some economists have been critical of the minimum tax; even those who favored it did so with reservations.

Efficiency Issues

The Alternative Minimum Tax

The AMT originated in the House Ways and Means Committee and was included in the final 1986 act, but there was little discussion of the economic effects until after the provision was incorporated into law. In initial discussions of the tax while it was being considered or shortly thereafter, Harter (1986), Lucke, Eisenach, and Dildine (1986), and Dworin (1986a, 1986b) focused on the circumstances that might cause a firm to fall under the AMT. The likelihood of a firm becoming subject to the tax depends on the kinds of assets the firm holds, which would affect the relative size of the larger minimum tax base. As a general principle, firms with a concentration of depreciable assets would be more likely to fall under the AMT because a large part of the differential base stemmed from differences in depreciation allowances. Firms with higher debt shares would also be more likely to fall under the minimum tax. Since the minimum tax rate is 20 percent and the regular rate 35 percent, firms will fall under the minimum tax when the ratio of the two tax basis (minimum to regular) is 35/20. Interest deductions lower both taxable bases by absolute amounts, making it more likely that the minimum tax will apply. And rapidly growing firms will be more likely to be subject to the AMT because the differences in depreciation will be larger relative to income. Finally, economic cycles could affect exposure to the tax—if income fell substantially the differences in depreciation and other deductions between the two tax bases would loom larger.

Several issues relating to economic efficiency were raised in initial analysis of the AMT. An obvious effect of the minimum tax is that it could encourage firms to combine in ways that would reduce exposure to the tax, or that the tax could encourage certain types of equipment leasing and perhaps discourage other types (Dildine 1987; Bernheim 1989). Graetz and Sunley (1988) note that the AMT would artificially influence the mix of a firm's activities.

Subsequent studies considered some of the potential efficiency effects from the minimum tax. These effects are mixed. Sunley and

Graetz (1988) and Gravelle (1988) discuss differentials in the tax burden on new investment that occur across firms. Indeed, even though
the minimum tax applies only if it is in excess of the regular tax, the
marginal tax burden on new investment for firms subject to the AMT
is frequently smaller than the marginal burden on new investment for
regular tax firms, because the value of the lower tax rate outweighs the
loss from the restricted deductions. This differential across firms introduces distortions in the allocation of investment—a minimum tax firm
would find investments profitable that a regular tax firm would not.

Bernheim (1989) subsequently argued that even if the minimum tax
produced distortions between different firms making the same investments, it could reduce the distortions across different investment within a single firm. He also noted that the minimum tax makes debt
finance less attractive because of the lower tax rate used to deduct
interest.

These differentials across firms, assets, and debt ratios are illustrated in table 7.1, reflecting the recent tax law changes enacted in 1993,
that increased regular tax burdens (a slightly higher tax rate and
longer depreciation periods for buildings). The first column shows the
marginal effective tax rates across different assets for firms under the
regular tax. The next three columns show the marginal effective tax
rates (relative to the regular firm's discount rate, i.e., the spread
between pretax return and discount rate divided by pretax return) for
three assumptions of debt share.

For the typical case of one-third debt finance, the marginal tax burden is usually lower under the minimum tax. The marginal tax burden
under the minimum tax rises as the debt share increases because the
firm's value of deducting interest is smaller than the value for the firm
under the regular tax.

Assuming a typical debt share of one-third, the minimum tax
results in a smaller marginal tax burden for most investments. The differences are small in most cases for equipment, where the slower
depreciation for the minimum tax is more important in present value
terms, and thus, more fully offsets the lower rate. For structures the
effects are more pronounced; they are quite large for buildings (other,
commercial, and industrial). This large difference occurs because the
current 39-year depreciation period for buildings (enacted in 1993) is
almost as long as the assumed minimum tax life (40 years) and the

Table 7.1
Marginal effective tax rates: Regular and minimum tax

Asset type	Regular tax	Minimum tax No debt	1/3 debt	2/3 debt
Equipment				
Autos	40	18	24	29
Office/computing equipment	36	26	31	35
Trucks, buses, and trailers	35	22	27	32
Aircraft	35	29	34	38
Construction machinery	28	19	25	30
Mining/oilfield equipment	34	27	33	37
Service industry equipment	34	24	30	34
Tractors	32	24	29	34
Instruments	33	27	32	37
Other	32	25	31	35
General industrial equipment	30	24	30	34
Metalworking machinery	28	21	27	32
Electric transmission equipment	38	28	33	37
Communications equipment	23	21	27	32
Other electrical equipment	29	23	28	33
Furniture and fixtures	28	21	26	31
Special industrial equipment	26	22	27	32
Agricultural equipment	26	19	25	30
Fabricated metal	33	25	30	35
Engines and turbines	40	26	31	36
Ships and boats	28	23	29	33
Railroad equipment	22	18	24	29
Structures				
Mining/oil and gas	12	10	17	23
Other	42	25	31	35
Industrial	39	25	29	34
Public utility	31	20	26	31
Commercial	36	21	27	32
Farm	30	18	24	30
Land	35	20	26	31
Inventories	43	26	31	36

Note: Based on calculations in appendix B, with a 6 percent real discount rate, a 5 percent inflation rate, and a 10 percent nominal interest rate. These calculations incorporate a 35 percent corporate tax rate and the new longer write-off period for nonresidential buildings. The calculations do not include the effects of ACE. If ACE applied, the effective tax rates would be 12, 19, and 25 percent for oil and gas (for no debt, 1/3 debt, and 2/3 debt, respectively). They would be 31, 36, and 40 percent for inventories.

methods are the same. Thus there is no depreciation benefit to offset the higher regular tax rates. The effects are also large for inventories, where is there is no difference in recovery periods.

The marginal minimum tax burden (relative to the marginal regular tax burden) rises substantially with more leverage. The tax rate rises by around five percentage points when leverage is doubled from one-third to two-thirds; it falls by a similar amount when leverage is eliminated entirely.

The variations across investments within a firm occur under both taxes, but the minimum tax appears to produce smaller variations. For example, the regular tax produces variations (excluding the outlying case of oil and gas structures) ranging from 22 to 43 percent; the minimum tax, at a one-third debt finance assumption, produces rates ranging from 24 to 31 percent.

Recall that there is also an addition to the base of the minimum tax for part of the difference between the AMT base and the adjusted current earnings (ACE). The ACE adjustment for the minimum tax would not always apply. When ACE applies, it has no effect on property other than inventories and oil and gas structures because the depreciation differential was eliminated. (Rates when ACE applies are discussed in the table notes.) In general, oil and gas investments are taxed at somewhat higher rates under the AMT if there is debt finance, and these rates are increased if ACE rules apply. The ACE rules narrow the differences between tax burdens under the regular and minimum tax when they apply. ACE raises the tax rate on oil and gas because intangible drilling costs must be recovered under cost depletion, a slower method than that allowed for the AMT. When investments in inventories are affected by ACE, the tax burden rises because all inventories are subject to less generous FIFO accounting (the regular and AMT taxes assume firms use one half LIFO and one-half FIFO).

These calculations provide a mixed picture of the efficiency effects, which would depend on the substitutability of investments across and within firms and the substitutability of debt for equity. An additional dimension to this argument was added by Lyon in several papers (1990, 1991, 1992a, 1992b). He points out that the marginal tax burden on new investment could vary dramatically because firms can switch between the tax bases. For example, a firm may have a higher marginal tax burden on the regular tax than it would if it were permanently on the AMT, but its marginal tax burden may be highest if the investment is made when a firm is first subject to the AMT and, in later years, to the regular tax. In this case the firm is denied the full benefit of accelerated depreciation deductions, but the income in the later years of the investment will be taxed at the higher rate. Of course the opposite would be true of a firm that switches from the regular tax to the AMT. Lyon argues that these considerations make it less likely that a firm will experience smaller differences across assets because of the minimum tax.

Moreover, since it is difficult for many firms to predict whether they will be on the regular or minimum tax, the marginal tax burdens on new investments are subject to uncertainty, thereby creating an additional riskiness in the returns on investment. Since this risk must be compensated for, it causes an additional burden on firms that move between the different tax bases.

Any of these potential efficiency gains could be obtained by other methods, without incurring the losses associated with the minimum tax. More precise depreciation schedules, for example, could reduce variations among assets; in any case those variations are relatively small except for the heavy taxation of inventories (which could be reduced by indexation of inventory costs). Similarly the differences between debt and equity finance could be reduced by indexing of interest payments and deductions, perhaps accompanied by a small corporate rate reduction to offset the revenue gain. On the whole, on efficiency grounds the minimum tax does not appear to perform very well. Even if the gains offset the losses, the AMT is a second-best solution.

The minimum tax would be unlikely to apply to most firms in the long run. Gravelle (1988) looked at major industry classifications and found that in the long run regular tax payments would typically be considerably higher than the payments under the AMT. The closest approaches of the minimum to the regular tax were in oil and gas extraction when run as a separate business, and transportation where almost all assets are depreciable ones.

Some of the current criticism of the AMT is occurring because so many firms are subject to the AMT. This effect should not be surprising, because the maximum coverage of the AMT could have been predicted to occur approximately seven years after the passage of the 1986

Act—or around 1993. This peak occurs because most investment falls into a seven-year depreciation class, and the maximum differences in cumulated depreciation deductions between the regular and AMT bases would occur at the end of the regular depreciation cycle. The current widespread coverage of the tax in 1992 was also likely to be magnified by the recession, which lowers profits relative to tax deductions.

This long-run steady state could, however, take many years to achieve, and some firms would be more likely than others to be subject to the minimum tax. Moreover the presence of three different tax accounting systems—the regular system, AMT, and ACE, as well as the firm's book depreciation, leads to a considerable amount of additional complication in accounting (although this accounting was simplified by the 1993 revisions). Firms have to compute these alternative methods, even if they are not ultimately subject to the minimum tax.

Passive Loss Restriction

The passive loss restriction has received relatively less attention than the minimum tax in the academic literature. Although the restriction would mainly affect high income individuals, the average marginal tax rate of most owners of rental housing was typical of other investments—about 23 percent. Even in the case of high-income (and high tax-rate) investors, Gravelle (1987a) and Burman, Neubig, and Wilson (1987) concluded that the passive loss restriction would have relatively small effects on investments in real estate under ordinary conditions. This view was recently echoed by the real estate industry. Hoerner (1992b) quotes Jeffrey DeBoer of the National Realty committee as stating (p. 15): "The passive loss rules prevent people from deducting real economic losses—They don't really bite until you have real losses."

Under normal conditions of profitability, tax losses appear for two reasons: borrowing, and a mismatch between tax and economic depreciation. The effects from the former occur because nominal interest payments are deducted and because the pattern of interest payments over time is quite different from the pattern of rents. Rent payments rise over time, assuming inflation is larger than depreciation. Interest payments decline over time; inflation causes these payments to be larger initially. Thus, in the initial years of the property's operation, interest payments can be quite large relative to the rents and returns, especially if there is a lot of inflation.

Gravelle (1987b) further explored the sensitivity of the effects of the passive loss restriction to various assumptions for the top 1 percent of taxpayers, those most likely to be adversely affected by the restriction (see table 7.2). The percentage changes in required rents necessary to hold the after-tax return constant after the changes in the Tax Reform Act of 1986 were calculated. The base-case assumptions—typical of a tax shelter model—were that 80 percent of the cost of the investment was borrowed. Gravelle found that TRA would increase required rents by 10 percent without the passive loss restriction, but by 11.6 percent with the restriction—for a net effect of only 1.6 percent. Only in the first two years would the property yield tax losses.[2]

The likelihood of being affected by the restriction depends very much on borrowing. Increasing the debt ratio to 90 percent results in a

Table 7.2
Effect of the tax reform act of 1986 on rents: Tax shelter model

| | Percentage increase in rent | | |
	Without loss restriction	With loss restriction	Number of loss years
Base case	10.0	11.6	2.0
90% leveraging	16.7	30.1	6.5
70% leveraging	4.8	4.8	0.0
10% equity return	11.4	16.5	4.3
15% equity return	8.7	8.7	0.0
0% depreciation rate	13.5	20.0	4.4
3% depreciation rate	7.2	7.2	0.0
2% inflation rate	7.3	7.3	0.0
6% inflation rate	12.3	18.0	3.8
27.5-year holding period	8.2	10.0	2.0
10% land cost	12.2	16.5	3.4
30% land cost	7.9	7.9	0.0

Note: The base case assumptions leverage the rate at 80 percent, the holding period at 10 years, the real return to equity at 12.5 percent, the depreciation rate at 1.5 percent, the nominal interest rate at 10 percent, the inflation rate at 4 percent, and the share of cost allocated to land at 20 percent. In all cases the mortgage term was thirty years, and the tax rate fell from 45.3 percent to 28.9 percent, an estimate of the marginal tax rate changes for the top 1 percent of the income distribution provided by the Congressional Budget Office. The nominal interest rate was assumed to move point for point with inflation.

higher rents due to the passive loss restriction of over 13 percent. This effect of leveraging on tax losses occurs because of the pattern of interest deductions relative to rents over time. Rents grow with the rate of inflation and decline with the rate of depreciation; using the assumptions of a 1.5 percent depreciation rate and a 4 percent inflation rate, they would grow at 2.5 percent per year. Interest payments in a level-payment mortgage, however, decline over time. Thus initially interest payments will be relatively large compared to rent. The upshot is that the likelihood of a tax loss is powerfully affected by borrowing. Indeed, when the leveraging rate is reduced to 70 percent, the passive loss restriction has no effect. Thus the passive loss restriction may be seen as an indirect penalty on borrowing. As such it may be viewed as indirectly increasing efficiency by offsetting the tax favoritism to borrowing by high tax rate investors.

Tax losses are also affected by the equity return—the higher the return, the less likely a loss because more of the rent will reflect that return. In the illustrative tax shelter model the passive loss restriction becomes somewhat more important with an equity return of only 10 percent, but it disappears entirely with a return of 15 percent.

Table 7.2 also illustrates the importance of depreciation. The higher the economic depreciation rate, the larger is the required rent and the less likely is a tax loss. Initially the tax depreciation rate is about 3 percent, and when economic depreciation is at approximately the same rate, there is no effect of the passive loss restriction. If the asset does not depreciate, however, the restrictions become more important.

The passive loss restriction also has greater effects during higher inflations because of the relationship between interest deductions and rents over the life of the investment. Finally, the passive loss restriction is less likely to be binding when land costs are larger because of the relationship between tax and economic depreciation. These calculated effects of the passive loss restriction exaggerate the effects of the limit because they assume the taxpayer has no other properties. Of course, if the taxpayer has investments in other real estate yielding a positive taxable return, losses can be offset against this income as well.

This analysis indicates that the passive loss restriction is easily avoided by reducing the borrowing rate, and this effect might be viewed as desirable given the tax advantages to borrowing by high tax rate individuals. This view of the passive loss restriction, however, holds only if economic conditions are "normal." If the property turns out to yield a smaller return than expected, either because of general economic conditions or because of the specifics of the investment, the passive loss restriction is more likely to have an effect even if the investor anticipated no effect. The restriction therefore interferes with the risk reduction effects of the tax system—when times are good the full return is taxed, but when times are bad the losses may not be fully deductible.

This effect has been made clear by the current depression in real estate markets, when many properties are operating at an economic loss due to excessive over building. Under these circumstances the passive loss restriction is probably going beyond disallowing tax-generated losses and is instead disallowing true economic losses.

Because of the economic environment, it is difficult to assess the effects of the passive loss restrictions. Petska (1992) reports that partnership losses, after declining in 1987, rose in 1988 and 1989. These losses may, however, reflect general economic conditions and losses might have otherwise declined had the industry not been in a depressed state.

Equity Issues

Both the AMT and the passive loss restriction were motivated in large part by notions of equity. In particular, there was a concern that corporations and individuals earning high profits or incomes should not be able to avoid paying tax, and that this state of affairs was unfair.

Yet this equity case appears to be largely without merit in the case of the AMT. Economic theory indicates that individuals require equal after-tax rates of return after tax from different investments. Firms that were paying low taxes may have been doing so because of the mix of investments they had or because of other circumstances that would have been capitalized in the value of stocks. There is no reason to believe that imposition of the minimum tax would have increased equity across taxpayers, particularly since the owners of the firm tend to change constantly. For corporations differential taxes involve issues of efficiency, not equity.

Of course, to the extent that the minimum tax raised tax burdens on capital income, it may have increased the progressivity of the tax system. But that effect would hold for any tax increase on capital income.

The case for horizontal equity is not justified in the case of the passive loss restriction. Again after-tax returns should adjust to reflect tax differentials across high-income individuals. Thus the low tax rates observed by individuals in these investments should have reflected, to some extent, lower pretax returns. There may, however, be a case for vertical equity. High tax rate individuals were able to take advantage of other aspects of the tax law, in particular the ability to deduct the inflation portion of interest payments at a high tax rate. This feature of the law would make the tax system less progressive and the passive loss restriction, either by applying directly or by constraining the use of interest deductions, might bring the system into closer accord with the progressivity intended by the tax rate structure.

The passive loss restriction (along with the full taxation of capital gains and the repeal of individual retirement accounts for high-income individuals) was a trade off for the lower tax rates imposed by the Tax Reform Act of 1986, which aimed for both revenue and distributional neutrality. At the same time the passive loss restriction, like the minimum tax, was likely to raise more revenue in the short run than in the long run, thus largely acting as lump sum taxes on existing owners of capital (see Gravelle 1992a).

One strong political justification offered for the minimum tax is the need to provide some appearance of fairness by preventing those instances in which firms with profits had no tax liability. Certainly an appearance of fairness is important in an income tax system that relies, in part, on self-assessment by individuals. The major difficulty with this argument is that these instances, largely generated by the 1981 tax changes, would have disappeared in any case due to the natural decline of large depreciation deductions with the passage of time and the enactment of other provisions (e.g., the repeal of safe harbor leasing).

Policy Options

Despite different mechanisms the AMT and the passive loss restriction share many common effects. They offset the favoritism toward debt finance, which contributes to efficiency. At the same time they contribute to unnecessary riskiness in investments. They also differentiate across investments in a variety of ways that may not be consistent with economic efficiency, and the case for adopting them on equity grounds is weak.

The minimum tax, in particular, scores poorly on both efficiency and equity grounds. Moreover, because of the time path of depreciation, it will wane in importance over time in both revenue impact and coverage of firms, while nevertheless continuing to complicate the tax law.

The advantageous effects of these provisions could be achieved by more straightforward methods. One obvious approach would be the indexation of interest payments, which would eliminate the favoritism toward debt on a more consistent basis.[3]

The minimum tax can be altered in several ways whether or not more direct reforms are undertaken. One is to simply leave the system intact, recognizing that the importance of the AMT will fade considerably in the future. Yet another option is to wait a few years until the importance of the tax begins to fade and then eliminate it as a simplification measure. Another option is to drop the ACE adjustment, which would simplify tax compliance considerably.

It is somewhat difficult simply to abandon the AMT, since there are accumulated credits that firms now have the right to carry over. To allow a smooth transition, another option is to conform AMT accounting to regular tax accounting for future investments (dropping the ACE requirements), which will prospectively bring the two bases back into harmony.

The response in the political arena to the passive loss restriction has been peculiar. Most of the pressure to revise the passive loss restriction was directed at lifting the restriction for certain individuals directly involved in other real estate activities, such as developing and managing properties. Lipton (1992) argues for this revision. Such an exception was enacted in 1993.

The passive loss restriction is applied to losses incurred in a trade or business when the taxpayer does not materially participate. It was never intended to restrict losses for ordinary business operations. All rental activity is considered passive in nature. There was, however, a "carve out" in the rental area allowing individuals with less than $150,000 in income to take a full or partial deduction, if the taxpayer materially participates in the activity. The proposals for providing relief to certain real estate operators claim that real estate should be "treated like any other business" by allowing deductions for active participants. In some proposals these active participants were limited to those managing and developing real estate; in others participation was extended to brokerage, financial, and appraisal activities. The exclusion finally adopted involved a broad definition of the industry but required a substantial fraction of income and amount of time be devoted to the activity.

This type of solution is a second-best solution to the problems arising from the passive loss restriction. It simply defines a new set of individuals who will be eligible for full-loss offset; there seems no special merit to the activities of these individuals compared to others who may rent property but be engaged in other activities. Its advancement of equity or of efficiency is not at all clear.

The passive loss restriction may be reformed in a several ways, which could minimize its negative effects. It could of course be eliminated altogether, or eliminated for new investments (the latter approach would reduce the revenue cost). An approach that would eliminate the worse cases of disallowing economic losses would be to allow in full deductions for operating costs and property taxes. Another approach would be to identify those items that are to be disallowed (e.g., accelerated depreciation or a portion of interest deductions reflecting inflation).

The indexation of interest payments and deductions (combined with corporate rate relief) would be a move toward greater efficiency in the tax system. In the presence of such a change, the passive loss restriction would probably become insignificant.

8

Tax Treatment of Retirement Savings: Pensions, IRAs, and Other Tax-Deferred Savings

The tax code provides benefits for retirement savings through pensions and through certain other savings vehicles. Although this treatment originates in part from administrative difficulties in assigning pension rights for tax purposes, the common justification given for tax benefits for retirement savings is the need to encourage savings and retirement income.

There are three different ways in which savings for retirement receive tax benefits: through employer-sponsored pension plans (including plans for the self-employed), through individual retirement accounts (IRAs), and through deferral of tax on the increase in the value of life insurance policies and annuities. By far the largest of these benefits is for employer-sponsored pensions plans—forgone revenues because of these plans is estimated at over $50 billion, or over 10 percent of the total individual income taxes. Munnell (1991) has also estimated that the cost of excluding contributions from the social security tax base is $39 billion. Keogh plans, for the self-employed, cost slightly over $2 billion, IRAs cost about $7 billion, and deferral of tax on earnings of life insurance investments is over $8 billion. Thus by almost any standard, the benefits provided are large.

Pension plans have accounted for increasing shares of wealth. According to the U.S. Department of Labor (1989), pension holdings rose from 13 percent of corporate bonds in 1950 to 39 percent in 1987. Pension holdings rose from a negligible share of corporate stock in 1950 to 24 percent by 1987. According to the balance sheets issued by the Board of Governors of the Federal Reserve System, pension fund wealth rose from 2.7 percent of total wealth in 1953 to 17.4 percent in

1991, for a 1991 total of $3.2 trillion in pension assets. About 2.2 percent of wealth (about $400 billion), according to these balance sheets, is in life insurance companies, down from 5.4 percent in 1953. While there are no direct estimates of funds in IRAs, $172 billion was deposited in these accounts during their period of universal availability (1982–86). By the end of 1991, $685 billion of IRA and Keoghs (tax preferred pension plans for the self-employed) were held in financial institutions (Employee Benefit Notes, Employee Benefit Research Institute, July 1992). The tax benefits provided for these plans can amount to very generous tax treatment of the return provided, extending to highly negative tax burdens (i.e., the provision of actual tax subsidies) for many types of investments.

The economic issues associated with these tax provisions include standard efficiency and equity issues. Conventional economic theory, however, suggests that these tax benefits are unlikely to contribute to the efficiency of the tax system, in part, because so many of them do not affect marginal savings decisions. Moreover the tax benefits tend to be distributed to higher-income individuals, not only because high-income individuals are more likely to own capital but also because employer pension plans disproportionately benefit high-income individuals. Finally, in the case of employer pension plans, there are considerations of horizontal equity that are not typically very meaningful for other capital income tax provisions. Only individuals whose employers provide plans are eligible for the benefits; these plans tend to be more common in certain industries such as manufacturing and mining, more common among larger firms, and more common in firms that are unionized.

In some cases the public debate surrounding tax benefits for retirement plans has been quite different from traditional economic questions. In the case of pensions there has been very little interest in the broad economic consequences of tax benefits, other than the presumed effects of increased savings and retirement income. Virtually no discussion of taxing the returns to these investments, either through assigning income to individuals or taxing the returns of the trusts, has occurred. Instead, most of the policy debate as been concerned with potential abuses of the tax benefits—ensuring that these plans are not used as a shelter for income of highly paid "key" personnel, that the tax provisions are not abused through excessive contributions or used as a corporate tax avoidance device, and that the plans are made financially secure. Hence over the years there have been numerous legislative changes aimed at regulating these plans in various ways. There has, however, been little attention paid to the economic effects of these regulations, in particular, those affecting vesting.

There has been a heated debate over the desirability of individual retirement accounts (IRAs), following the restrictions of these plans for higher-income individuals not covered by an employer plan in the 1986 Tax Reform Act. This debate has focused on two primary issues: the effects, if any, on savings and the distributional effects across incomes. The policy debate over IRAs more closely parallels the traditional issues of economic efficiency and savings than does the debate over pension plans. The policy debate over life insurance has been primarily directed at tightening the use of life insurance annuities as a tax sheltering device, although this option is generally open to most individuals provided some purchase of life insurance is involved.

The tax treatment of pensions and the nature of pension plans are complex. Nevertheless, understanding how these plans work is crucial to understanding the economic issues involved. The following section provides an overview of the different types of pension plans, as well as the treatment of IRAs, along with discussions of the consequences of effective tax rates. Information on the relative magnitudes of these plans is also discussed. The issues of efficiency, equity, and possible revisions are then considered in turn.

An Overview of How Retirement Plans Work

Employer Pension Plans

Through most of this century there was a continual rise in the use of employer-provided pension plans. Bloom and Freeman (1992) suggest that this increase was due to rising real incomes coupled with the tax advantages, along with the Supreme Court's 1949 Inland Steel decision, making pensions a mandatory negotiating subject in collective bargaining. They also report that this trend has reversed in recent years: From 1980 to 1990 contributions, as a percentage of compensation, declined from 5.8 percent to 3.9 percent. Part of the decline, they suggest, was due to rising real rates of return that required fewer assets to meet pension obligations. Another factor was the decline in pension coverage, primarily of males. This decline has not been fully explained. Of course the decline in the use of pension plans could also have reflected lower marginal tax rates.

Employer pension plans fall into two major categories: defined-benefit plans and defined-contribution plans. Defined-benefit plans dominate employee coverage, although their share has been declining. According to Chang (1991), between 1977 and 1985 the proportion of employees covered in defined-benefit plans declined from 84 to 71 percent of the total. She suggests that the reasons for the decline are the increased regulation of defined-benefit plans and the employment shift from the manufacturing sector to the service sector, defined-benefit plans being more common in the former.

Antidiscrimination rules prevent the plans from being restricted to key, highly compensated employees. Coverage can be integrated with social security: Benefits and contributions under social security can be taken into account in determining whether the plan discriminates. Because of this integration the plans tend, on the whole, to benefit higher paid employees disproportionately.

Pension plans are also subject to rules and regulations regarding vesting—the circumstances under which individuals receive a nonforfeitable right to benefits. Vesting may be "cliff" vesting (employees are fully vested in the plan's benefits at one point in time), which now must occur after five years. Vesting may also be proportional; such proportional vesting must begin after three years and be completed after seven years. Some industries are characterized by multiemployer plans, where individuals who move from one firm to another can take their benefits with them. These plans are subject to funding limits.

Defined-Benefit Plans

A defined-benefit plan specifies the benefit to be received by the employee. Typically the level of benefits on retirement are related to previous salary and depend on some combination of age and years of service. Employees may be able to retire early and take reduced benefits. Because the benefits of the plans are not directly tied to contributions, many regulations on funding apply. In addition most benefits are insured by the Pension Benefit Guarantee Corporation (PBGC), a publicly chartered and backed corporation.

One of the difficult problems with defined-benefit plans is setting the desired level of funding vis-à-vis benefits. If funding is inadequate, employees' benefits may not be fully protected. If plans are overfunded, however, firms can use the pension trusts as a vehicle for sheltering income. Some critics (Ippolito 1991) have suggested that the limits regarding the amount of funding (relative to benefits promised) adopted in 1987 are too strict.[1] A Treasury (1991) report on this subject suggested that the effects would not be very great, however.

In the absence of inflation, defined-benefit plans tend to insure employees against variations in returns; such would not be the case in defined contribution plans. Defined-benefit plans, while related to recent earnings, are not indexed for inflation during the payout period (although employers frequently make ad hoc adjustments). Moreover workers who leave an employer before retirement age frequently have benefits related to their wages at that point. As a result workers can experience considerable variation in real retirement income from these plans.

Defined-Contribution Plans
Defined-contribution plans are those where benefits are based on contributions made by the employees or on their behalf by employers. There are several types of defined-contribution plans.

Money-purchase plans typically allow a fixed percent of wages to be paid to pension trust. The employee then receives an annuity at retirement. In assessing nondiscrimination, these plans can also be integrated with social security.

Profit-sharing plans are, as the name implies, tied to the profitability of the firms. Unlike other plans, these funds can be withdrawn by the employee prior to retirement (although they are then subject to tax). Another variation is a stock-bonus plan provided in the form of stock.

Thrift and salary-reduction plans allow employees to decide how much to contribute these plans, but only salary-reduction plans benefit from a tax exclusion. These plans are sometimes referred to by Internal Revenue Code Sections—401(k) plans for the profit sector, section 457 plans for state and local government employees, and 403(b) plans for nonprofit institutions. These salary-reduction plans were allowed in 1978 to the profit sector and to state and local governments (they have

already been available in the nonprofit sector). In 1983 these contributions were required to be included in the taxable base for the social
security payroll tax. In 1986 salary-reduction plans were extended to
federal government employees. In that same year the dollar limit on
annual contributions to all salary-reduction plans (except 403(b) plans)
was reduced from $30,000 to $7,000, to be indexed for inflation. (The
limit for contributions to nonprofit plans was temporarily frozen at
$9,500, and it will begin to rise when the indexed limit in other plans
reaches the same amount; the previous limit was $8,728.)

Employee stock ownership plans (ESOPs) provide for retirement
benefits through ownership of stock of the company by employees.

Simplified employer plans (SEPs) are personal accounts, much like
individual retirement accounts but with the amounts established by
employers. Contributions are proportional to wages, and plans can be
integrated with social security.

Keogh Plans

Keogh (H.R. 10) plans allow self-employed individuals to establish
pension plans. The restrictions on these plans are similar to those on
employer plans.

Individual Retirement Plans (IRAs)

There are two types of individual retirement plans. Deductible IRAs
are treated the same as employer plans—contributions are deductible,
current income is not taxed, but benefits are taxed when withdrawn.
These IRAs are available to all individuals not covered by an employer
plan and to individuals below certain income limits even if covered by
an employer plan. Eligibility for the deduction is phased out between
$40,000 and $50,000 of adjusted gross income for married couples.
Individuals above those income limits, and not covered by an employer plan, can contribute to an IRA without deducting the contributions;
earnings are not taxed until received.

The annual contribution limit is $2,000 (up to 100 percent of earn-
ings); there is also a small ($250) contribution allowed for a nonwork-
ing spouse. If funds are withdrawn prematurely, they are subject to a
15 percent penalty for early withdrawal. Withdrawals can begin at age
59 and 1/2 without penalty.

Tax Treatment of Returns on Life Insurance and Deferred Annuities

Earnings of life insurance plans are not subject to tax as earned; rather, taxes are deferred and are not subject to tax until paid at retirement (usually as an annuity). Death benefits are not subject to tax, however. This deferral is also accorded to those annuities that essentially have no life contingency. These tax deferrals are effectively available to anyone who wishes to invest in them.

Effects of Tax Treatment on Marginal Effective Tax Rates

If social security is disregarded, the marginal effective tax rate on pension plan earnings is equivalent to no tax at all at the individual level, provided statutory marginal tax rates are identical in the contribution and retirement years. A simple example, with an asset held one year until retirement, illustrates this effect. Suppose that the tax rate is 50 percent. An individual who receives a $100 in wages will receive $50 in net income, which he then invests in a bond with earns a return of 10 percent, subject to tax. His income available for retirement is $52.50. Suppose that the $100 is instead placed into a retirement trust, earning $110 after a year and then paid out. The $110 is subject to a 50 percent tax, for a retirement income of $55. This outcome is identical to allowing the $50 of after-tax income to earn a 10 percent yield that is not subject to tax.

   If the employee's statutory marginal tax rate is lower at retirement, the marginal effective tax rate is actually negative. If the statutory marginal tax rate is higher during retirement, there is a positive marginal effective tax rate. Moreover if the individual is subject to social security taxes, then the contribution will not be subject to social security. An additional social security tax constitutes a true burden if the yield on the social security payments (in future benefits) is less than a market return, an outcome typical of most recipients of pension benefits. Thus avoiding social security taxes provides a subsidy for pension plans.

   Contributions to IRAs, for individuals below a certain income level or for those not covered by an employer plan, are allowed to be deducted from income. Like employer-sponsored pensions the earnings are not subject to tax until received as benefits. This treatment is the same as that of pension benefits, although unlike pension contributions, there is no possibility of forgoing social security taxes. The marginal effective tax rate is zero if statutory marginal tax rates are the same in retirement as during the contribution years. If the marginal statutory tax rate is higher (lower) in retirement, the marginal effective tax rate is positive (negative).

Earnings on life insurance reserves paid as death benefits are subject to no tax, because the earnings are not taxed. Nondeductible IRAs (for those above the threshold covered by an employer plan) and earnings from life insurance reserves that are eventually taxed as annuities are subject to a effective positive tax, but this tax is deferred and may be applied at the lower rates that occur during retirement. If the deferral is for a long period of time, effective tax rates are very low.

In various cases these treatments amount to a net tax subsidy at the individual level (the returns to pension benefits are actually supplemented with government payments through forgiveness of social security and/or lower tax rates at retirement), no tax at all (pensions that would not be covered by social security and deductible individual retirement accounts, assuming tax rates are constant, along with accrued earnings on life insurance received as a death benefit), or taxed, but at an effective rate lower than the statutory rate (nondeductible IRAs and earning on life insurance received as an annuity). In the case of either subsidized or taxed investments, the effective tax subsidy or burden depends upon the expected holding period.

Pension and life insurance earnings can be invested in debt instruments, corporate equities, or noncorporate investment of a passive nature (e.g., real estate). The latter is relatively uncommon. Since debt is subject to a negative effective tax rate at the firm level (due to the deduction of the inflation portion of interest), these investments will be subject to a negative tax overall even if there is no tax at the individual level. Equity investments in corporate stock are subjected to the corporate-level tax, and thus incur a positive overall tax. Direct equity investments in assets are subject to individual's tax rate, which is zero if tax rates are constant.

Efficiency Issues

Pension and other retirement benefits are occasionally defended as an indirect way of moving toward a consumption tax base, and are also argued to be a means of promoting retirement income. Yet a conventional efficiency analysis suggests that these plans are not very successful in obtaining a less distorting tax system. This conventional analysis will be addressed first, and then the various arguments offered in defense of pension tax benefits will be considered.

A Conventional Efficiency Analysis

Consider first the most common type of pension tax benefit—one that involves belonging to an employer pension plan where the individual employee has no direct control over the amounts contributed to pensions on his behalf. Such a plan cannot reduce the marginal tax rate on savings, which is the source of tax distortions, because the employee has no direct control over the amount invested. (Although the employee may have some input, for example, through voting in a union, or can vary his employment to choose a plan according to his retirement objectives, these choices are not about marginal contributions.) If the pension benefits fall short of his savings objectives, he still faces the tax on capital for any additional increment to savings. Such a plan does nothing to affect the tax consequences of this decision. If, on the other hand, the benefits exceed his desired objectives, he is forced to save beyond his preferences, an outcome that would reduce his welfare directly.

Pension-related tax benefits could have effects on wages. Here there are two cases. First, contributions may be established at some dollar limit fixed by law. If contributions are fixed regardless of income, the tax changes have no effect on work effort or on reducing the distortion between labor and leisure. In this case the pension benefit must be viewed as a fixed wage grant that would influence his willingness to choose between a job with and without pension coverage. Obviously this effect is a distorting one: It alters capital/labor ratios and output between firms with and without pensions (Atrostic and Burman 1990). Moreover distortions are magnified if lost revenues must be made up by increased taxes elsewhere.

A pension benefit could reduce distortions if additional work effort results in more pensions and more tax benefits. In this case the pension tax benefit acts as a tax reduction on wages. If, however, the pension plan results in forced savings beyond the employee's preferences, that benefit is offset by the induced distortion. Moreover pension benefits may be subject to considerable uncertainty, introducing an unnecessary source of risk. Even if the pension benefit acts as an offset to wage taxation, it is likely that a straightforward reduction in wages would be more efficient. Regardless of which combination of affairs occurs, as long as the revenue must be made up elsewhere, it seems likely that tax benefits to pensions act to magnify tax distortions and contribute to inefficiency in the tax system.

When the individual can control the amount of savings, as in certain types of defined contribution plans, the distortion arising from taxing savings is reduced, although the form of the receipt (in pension benefits that may not be readily available) may not be optimal. When the employee is contributing at a maximum dollar ceiling, however, and would save in excess of that amount absent the tax benefit, there will be no marginal effects on savings. And, in both cases, there continues to be a tax induced distortion in one's choice of employer.

For IRAs, which are not associated with a specific employer, the effects on reducing distortions will be nonexistent for those individuals whose contributions are already at the maximum and who would have saved in excess of that amount absent the tax benefit. Such a benefit is in the nature of a lump sum-offset to taxes, and increased taxes of other types needed to offset revenues will introduce additional distortions. Even when individuals are contributing below the dollar maximum, the lack of liquidity of IRAs (they can be cashed in only with payment of a significant penalty) detracts from the overall marginal benefits. Similarly tax benefits received through deferral of income in life insurance policies are diluted by the restrictions on the form and the lack of liquidity.

In addition to these direct questions about the effects of tax benefits for retirement plans, there are some special issues surrounding employer plans. To address these, it is necessary to ask what function pension plans serve, tax benefits aside. After all, pensions predated the introduction of income taxes.

One of the reasons frequently argued for the development of employer defined-benefit pension plans arises from a basic problem of human capital formation. Employers invest in their employees. Employees are less productive initially (and may even impose a net cost); if employees leave after this training has occurred, the employer does not earn a return on his investment, in terms of higher productivity. For a variety of reasons it may not be possible to set wages at true training wages (due to minimum wages, the need for some sort of subsistence wage, or practical difficulties with setting negative wages). One alternative is to induce individuals to stay with the firm for a long period of time by offering pension benefits that are received in full or in part after a certain period of time (Becker 1962).

In this case defined-benefit pension plans may be serving a useful purpose in the market because in their absence employers would be less willing to invest in productive on-the-job training. In order for pensions to serve this purpose, however, it may be desirable to allow vesting after only many years of service so that the employer can obtain his full return. That is, employees may initially receive wages above their marginal productivity, and then receive wages below their marginal productivity. They will be willing to stay on the job even when earning a wage below what they could earn elsewhere if they will ultimately accrue some benefit in the form of a pension, albeit only after a relatively long period of employment. In this case the early vesting rules enforced by tax regulations would subvert the economic purpose served by pensions. Similarly the employer may not wish to offer the same pension plan to all employees, but rather restrict it to those where on-the-job training is important. Again antidiscrimination rules may lead to less efficient investment in training because they constrain the way in which the plans may operate.

As long as tax benefits are provided, there is some need for these types of rules to prevent the benefits from being used simply to shelter income of a narrow class of employees. But the rules aimed at restricting abuse will likely introduce inefficiencies.

Pension plans may serve other purposes as well. For example, defined-benefit pension plans may be an easy way to separate older workers, a method less damaging to morale than firing. Both defined-benefit and defined-contribution plans may also reflect the advantages of pooling resources to obtain better investment yields, as well as allowing some insurance elements (by allowing disability-related benefits). In union-negotiated plans they may reflect the dominance of more senior workers in union. These functions could of course be performed absent tax benefits, and it is not clear what effect tax benefits have on serving these purposes.

This conventional analysis of pension and related benefits suggest that the provisions are likely to contribute to greater inefficiency in the economy.

Other Justifications: Administrative Concerns, Effects on Savings, and Retirement Incomes

There are several arguments frequently cited as justification for generous pension benefits in the tax code. These include administrative problems of attributing income, effects on overall savings, and the need to provide for retirement income. The following discussion reviews both the conceptual arguments and the empirical literature on the effects of pensions and IRAs.

Administrative Issues

Perhaps the most compelling of these arguments is also one of the oldest—the issue of attribution of income. In the case of defined benefit plans, assigning income to individuals for purposes of taxation is difficult and complicated. Before an individual is vested, there is no clear claim on pension benefits even though contributions are made on behalf of that individual. The assignment of such income would be difficult to justify on legal grounds.

This argument played a role in the development of pension tax benefits many years ago, and it remains a barrier to taxing income of pension contributions to individual employees. It does not preclude some partial offsets, however. Given today's relatively flat tax rates and the concentration of benefits among higher-income individuals, it would be possible to tax pension income by taxing the income of the pension trusts themselves. Even a partial tax at the 15 percent rate would free up revenues that could be used for lowering capital income taxes generally and yet would be unlikely to exceed in the vast majority of cases the taxes that would have been imposed if pension income could be attributed. Thus while the administrative issue may preclude the complete elimination of tax benefits for pensions, it would not preclude at least a moderation of those benefits.

Effects on Savings

As discussed in chapter 2, it is not clear that the government should be intervening to increase private savings or that it can be successful in doing so. The consequences of pension plans on savings are, however, also unclear. In most cases individuals are not affected at the margin; thus there is no price effect to encourage further savings. (There may be an effect on the labor supply, however.) The sole effect of the pension benefits in this case would be an income effect.

In the case of pension plans, however, where taxes are deferred, the implications of the income effect for savings are uncertain. This uncertainty occurs because the contributions are deductible up front but taxable when received. Individuals must take into account the future taxation of their pensions and save accordingly in order to pay the future tax. The total effect on saving will be the sum of the normal decrease in savings (due to the income effect which would unambiguously decrease savings if the pension tax benefit were simply offered in the form of an direct exemption of the tax on earnings) plus the offsetting savings of the initial revenue cost to the government. With relatively long time horizons, the overall effect is likely to decrease savings of those who receive the pension benefit. This result occurs because the advantages of compounding of interest at the pretax rate on existing savings outweighs the future tax to be paid.

Although the income effect is likely to decrease savings, some individuals may be subject to forced savings if pension contributions exceed otherwise desired savings levels. Moreover pension plans may encourage early retirement, and thus increase savings, but at the cost of course of reducing overall income through reduced labor supply.

The consequences also depend on how the government finances the revenue loss. If the government increases the deficit, national savings should unambiguously decrease in those cases where there is no price effect. If taxes are raised elsewhere, the consequences depend strongly on the extent to which individuals anticipate the time path of revenue changes. If all individuals were identical and they all could perfectly anticipate taxes, the effect on savings would be zero, unless the tax rate on capital increased. In this latter case there would be a price effect which discourages savings, and savings would decrease.

Is there evidence that pension plans have actually increased savings? The Congressional Budget Office (1987b) concluded that the evidence does not support such a view. A number of studies have compared the wealth of pension holders with those of nonpension holders with otherwise identical characteristics; Munnell (1987) reviews these studies. While initial studies by Cagan (1965) and Katona (1965) found that workers with pensions saved more in other forms than those without pensions, later studies (Munnell 1974; Munnell 1976; Diamond and Hausman 1984; Avery, Elliehausan, and Gustafson 1985) found substantial offsets. The results have varied, but the latest study found an offset of about 68 cents of reduced nonpension saving for pension savings. These recent results would, however, seem to suggest that pensions have increased saving if those with and without pensions were otherwise identical—otherwise the total assets of those with and without pensions would have been the same.

These studies cannot, however, control for two important factors. First, assume the government makes up the revenue with other taxes. These increased revenues will alter the savings behavior of individuals in the economy in general. A comparison of pension holders with those without pensions will provide no means of calculating this general effect, since the increased taxes could have depressed the nonpension savings of both those with and without pensions. A second factor, noted by the Congressional Budget Office (1987b), is the likelihood that those with a greater preference for savings would have chosen to work in firms with pension plans. Thus these types of studies cannot really establish a positive overall effect of pensions on savings; such a finding would be consistent with an increase, a decrease, or no change. There remains, however, a possibility that some individuals with pensions have been forced to save more than their preferences.

The other piece of evidence that raises questions about the effects of pensions on overall savings is the fact that the overall savings rate has not increased over a long period of time, even as pensions grew dramatically. For example, according to the General Accounting Office (1992), pension benefits as a percentage of employee compensation increased from 2 to 3.9 percent from 1950 through 1980. Despite this rapid growth, there was no general increase in the savings rate over that time period. Of course this type of evidence is also limited. The growth in social security might have been expected to reduce saving, and the maintenance of the saving rate over this time period in the face of social security program growth might reflect a positive effect of private pensions. At the same time there are factors that would have increased savings. For example, the increase in the life span, and hence the period of retirement, might have been expected to increase private saving. Thus these observations of the savings rate over time cannot establish an increase in the savings rate as a result of pension tax benefits.

There has also been a flurry of empirical research on individual retirement accounts. IRAs were generally available to all individuals, including the higher income individuals who tended to use them, for a brief period from 1982 through 1986. The question of the effect of IRAs on savings has been the subject of a lively debate. This debate is summarized below, but more detailed overviews of the issue, with varying viewpoints expressed, can be found in Burman, Cordes, and Ozanne (1991), Gravelle (1991c), Venti and Wise (1992), and Skinner (1992).

Unlike pensions, investing in IRAs is up to individual discretion. A relatively small fraction of individuals chose to invest in IRAs, particularly in lower and moderate income brackets. Most of those who did invest in IRAs invested the maximum amount allowed.

The debate about the effect on IRAs is unusual in that some of the argument has proceeded outside the familiar economist's framework of individuals making choices about consuming over time periods. Consider first, however, what the theory underlying this conventional framework of analysis would suggest about IRAs. This analysis is the same as that suggested above for pensions. Income effects are ambiguous: The income effect could increase or decrease private savings depending on the time horizon, but the increase in initial savings would be less than the government revenue loss from the initial up-front deduction. The aggregate effect depends on how the government finances the revenue loss and how well individuals anticipate these changes. (The tax reductions in the 1980s, however, were accompanied by a deficit.)

The effectiveness of IRAs in increasing savings can be considered in a bit more straightforward fashion by means of a thought experiment where in one case the government provides for IRAs and the tax savings increase the deficit, and in the other case where the government does nothing. After all, if there were ways to cut spending on public consumption or increase taxes in general in order to increase government savings and the national savings rate, such opportunities could be taken advantage of without introducing IRAs. In such a framework the effect of IRAs on national savings can be addressed by considering the question of whether IRAs increased private savings by more than the tax savings, or the equivalent, whether IRAs reduced consumption of individuals who contributed to them.

According to conventional theory these income effects would unambiguously increase consumption and reduce national savings, while price effects would increase national savings. From the standpoint of conventional theory, IRAs appear unlikely to succeed in increasing savings. The evidence that price effects outweigh income effects (reviewed in chapter 2) is weak. Moreover about three-quarters of contributions were made by taxpayers who contributed the maximum amounts according to Galper and Byce (1986). If an individual would have saved the maximum amount in any case, there is no price effect at the margin and thus no increase in savings through a substitution effect. Some of these taxpayers could, however, have had smaller savings in the absence of IRAs. In most cases, according to the empirical research discussed below, taxpayers with IRAs also had other savings. Thus from the standpoint of conventional economic analysis, IRAs appeared unlikely to increase savings because IRA savings, like pension savings, were largely inframarginal.

The conventional theory thus suggests that IRAs did not increase savings but rather substituted for private savings or were financed out of the initial tax reduction. Why, then, has there been such a controversy about the effects of IRAs on savings? The reason for this controversy is, in part, that some empirical studies (themselves the subject of controversy) have concluded that IRAs did increase savings.

These empirical results have in turn been justified on theoretical grounds by arguments that individuals do not make savings decisions in the fashion suggested by conventional economic theory. Rather, individuals might have been strongly influenced by the heavy advertising that accompanied the sale of IRAs by banks or the prospect of an initial up-front tax savings. Or individuals might tend to save more if their savings could be tied up in a fairly inaccessible fashion. This theory is related to the notion of "mental accounts" (Thaler 1990)—that individuals compartmentalize their savings and may actually seek out less liquid ways of savings to discipline themselves to save. In this theory the penalty for withdrawing funds from IRAs becomes an attractive, rather than an undesirable, characteristic of IRAs that makes them different from other, more accessible, savings accounts.

What sort of empirical evidence might be found on the issue of IRAs and savings? Those who view savings from the conventional perspective point not only to the general empirical literature but also to what happened to savings rates in the 1980s. The period of universal IRA availability was also a period when savings rates *fell* rather than rose. IRAs constituted a large fraction of personal savings (about 30 percent) and an even larger fraction of nonpension personal savings. Bosworth (1989), for example, points out that if we are to believe that IRAs were new savings, we would also believe that personal nonretirement saving fell from 6 percent in the mid-1970s to virtually zero during the period 1981 to 1986. It is of course possible that savings rates would have been even lower were it not for IRAs, but these simple observations make it more difficult to believe that IRA contributions were net new savings.[2]

Most of the empirical research about IRAs focuses on cross-sectional studies—examining the behavior of different individuals during the period of IRA availability.

But these studies have not been in a traditional framework of measuring the effect of tax rates and other variables on savings, which has largely been rejected for studying savings behavior.

The first point made about IRAs was similar to the studies of pension savings—individuals who tended to be savers in general were also likely to save in IRAs (Hubbard 1984; Feenberg and Skinner 1989). For example, Feenberg and Skinner stressed in their study that individuals who had IRAs on average had increased their other assets during the period of the study. Although this relationship is sometimes cited as evidence that IRAs increased savings, such a finding does not really support this conclusion. As in the case of comparisons between those with and without pensions, these relationships may mean little except perhaps that those who tend to save, tend to save through both vehicles. Indeed this correlation would be likely to be more powerful than in the case of pensions, for having a pension is only one attribute of work while investing in IRAs is entirely discretionary. Individuals who were planning to save would be expected to use the tax-favored IRA vehicle.

The study that is perhaps most frequently cited as evidence that IRAs increased savings is one done by Venti and Wise (1990), who suggested that IRAs came almost entirely from the tax savings plus consumption and did not substitute for other savings. The findings in this study support the notion that IRAs had a strong effect on savings.

The Venti and Wise model was actually set forth in what appears to be a conventional analysis (as opposed to a model that emphasizes advertising, response to an immediate tax benefit, and mental accounts). Venti and Wise set out to discover a substitution elasticity between savings invested via IRAs and savings invested in other forms. Their study relies heavily on the fact that a lot of individuals save but not through IRAs. They reasoned that if IRAs and non-IRA savings were perfect substitutes, one would not observe cases where individuals did not use IRAs; the fact that there are many such observations is evidence that IRAs are not close substitutes for other savings. If so, IRAs are more likely to represent net additions to savings, particularly since Venti and Wise treated savings, rather than future consumption, as a commodity (i.e., they treated an IRA as if it were an entirely different and new commodity rather than a price reduction in an existing commodity—consumption in retirement).

The Venti and Wise model was subject to criticism based on the fundamental modeling in the conventional vein (Gravelle 1991c; Burman, Cordes, and Ozanne 1990; Kotlikoff 1990). Their line of reasoning fails to take into account an important factor—some saving is done for the short term or for precautionary reasons. In such circumstances IRAs are undesirable savings vehicles because there is a penalty on early withdrawals. The absence of saving through IRAs may have simply reflected that fact that many individuals wished to save for short term objectives. That is, there is a perfectly reasonable explanation of the behavior they observed within the framework of a conventional savings model. Moreover the model Venti and Wise used is inconsistent with a general theoretical model of savings (i.e., the relationships they used cannot be derived from a general analysis of consumption choice over time). Thus it is incorrect to draw conclusions about the effect of IRAs on total savings from their observations if one relies on conventional economic theory. Nor is their model capable of distinguishing between the conventional theory and the alternative theories, since their data set is incapable of distinguishing between savings undertaken for retirement and savings undertaken for precautionary reasons.

A study by Gale and Scholz (1990) took a different approach to the same data. They observed that some individuals contributed at the maximum level, while others did not. This limit might become binding simply because high-income individuals are likely to have higher savings objectives and reach the limit, while lower income individuals would not. They tried to predict a general overall savings function and then to test, by examining the pattern of non-IRA saving, whether there appeared to be an offset for the IRA savings. (They allowed individuals that did not contribute to IRAs to be treated differently from those who did contribute—their study focuses on the differences between those who contributed at the maximum and those who contributed less than the maximum.) The approach taken by Gale and Scholz is interesting but fraught with difficulties, especially in trying to estimate the overall savings patterns. In any case their conclusions were that IRAs had negligible effects on savings.

An interesting, and different, approach to the issue was undertaken by Manegold and Joines (1991). They noted that some individuals were eligible for IRAs before 1982, and they simply compared the change in the savings rate for those previously contributing to IRAs and those newly contributing. If IRAs increased savings, these new contributors should have had an increase in savings rates relative to those who were previously eligible. They found no difference, which would suggest that IRA saving was substituting for other saving. (This finding suggested that individuals did not even save the tax benefit.) More sophisticated statistical studies yielded mixed results.[3]

The conclusions that can be drawn about the effects of these retirement benefits on savings are not definitive. Conventional economic theory does not suggest that these plans would have a very pronounced effect on savings, and there seems no clear empirical evidence that tax favored pensions or IRAs increased savings in contravention of that theory.

It is always possible of course that individuals do not make the precise sorts of calculations posed by the theory. Perhaps the most reasonable conclusion to draw from this analysis is that relying on these plans to increase savings is chancy—increasing the government savings rate through reduced deficits might be a more certain route to increased savings.

Effects on Retirement Incomes
The remaining argument typically made about pensions is that they increase retirement income. A conventional analysis would indeed suggest that pensions increase retirement incomes; even though savings may not increase, retirement incomes should, simply because pensions tax benefits have an income effect. Again, in order to make up the revenue cost of the pension tax benefits, taxes elsewhere must be larger for an equal revenue yield. Thus the retirement incomes of those not covered by pensions would be expected to fall. That is, the government may be successful in increasing the retirement incomes of some individuals, but the cost will be in reducing the retirement incomes of others.

This argument also raises the general question of why the government should have, as its objective, the raising of retirement incomes. There is an argument for insuring a minimum retirement income, particularly if society is pledged in any case to provide subsistence for those in poverty in their retirement years. By mandating such a system, the problem of the improvident becoming free riders would be overcome. But such an objective should be aimed at minimum benefits, not at increasing benefits for higher-income individuals who tend to benefit most from pensions in the first place. Indeed such a system of insuring minimum retirement—social security—is already in place.[4]

Equity Issues

Tax benefits to pensions and other forms of retirement have been criticized on the grounds that they primarily benefit high-income individuals and that they have very uneven coverage.

Vertical Equity

Benefits to pension funds are concentrated among higher income individuals. According to Munnell (1991) only 30 percent of nonagricultural wage and salary workers were covered by plans in 1988, but 73 percent with annual earnings over $50,000 were covered. She presents data indicating that pensions provide only 2.5 percent of retirement income in the lowest quintile, 6.2 percent in the next, 13.7 percent in the next, and about 20 percent in the top 40 percent.

Although pension benefits are concentrated among higher-income individuals, the Congressional Budget Office (1987b) suggests that there may be some tendency, because of antidiscrimination rules, for higher-income individuals to subsidize lower-income individuals to induce them to participate. This, however, appears a minor, and difficult to quantify, offset to the general lack of coverage of lower-income individuals.

IRAs are more focused on middle-income class individuals because of the dollar ceilings and the income limits. They do not, however, tend to benefit lower-income individuals who have little tax liability and little savings.

Horizontal Equity

According to Munnell (1991) about half of full-time workers are covered by pension plans; according to the General Accounting Office (1992) about 40 percent of households with retirees receive pension income. The Congressional Budget Office (1987a) indicates that pension participation is more common for older workers, for certain industries (participation is high in manufacturing, communication, public utilities, and the public sector and low in agriculture, construction, retail trade, and services), for large firms, and for unionized firms.

In many cases horizontal equity is not a particularly important issue for evaluating taxation of capital income because pretax rates of return adjust to tax differentials. This viewpoint is not valid in the case of pension tax benefits because these benefits do not generally affect the margin. Nor are workers very free to change jobs to qualify, since there are many other job attributes that determine employment choice. Even if they were, the size of the benefit received in defined benefit plans is strongly affected by the length of time a person works for only one employer. Qualifying for tax benefits is, to some extent, random—depending on whether one's employment is in certain industries, in large or small firms, or spread among one or more firms. The uneven coverage of pension plans in this case raises some legitimate concern about fairness to taxpayers who otherwise have similar incomes. The allowance of IRAs to individuals without pension plans may increase horizontal equity by expanding tax benefits.

Possible Revisions in Tax Treatment

Despite the frequent assumption in the public debate that tax benefits for pensions are desirable, neither the equity nor the efficiency arguments paint them in a very favorable light. Nevertheless, it is extremely difficult, for administrative reasons, to contemplate taxing distributions and income to individuals under defined-benefit plans. While, on average, most contributions will accrue to someone, there is some uncertainty for a given individual. Vesting is not immediate, and the value of the future pension, particularly given the tendency not to index explicitly for inflation, is uncertain.

Another problem with explicitly attributing contributions to individuals would be the transition. Retired individuals now receiving a pension would be beneficiaries of a windfall if contributions and income were taxed but payments were not. To introduce transitional rules to move to such a system would be extremely complex, although a one time assessment against assets might be feasible.

As alluded to above, an alternative approach would be simply to tax the earnings of the pension funds themselves. If all individuals had the same tax rate, this treatment would be the same as taxing contributions and earnings but excluding payments. No rate would be precisely right, but given the concentration of benefits to high-income individuals, a 15 percent rate would probably be only a partial tax. It would also be relatively easy to impose a payroll tax on contributions, although it would then be appropriate to assign these incomes to individuals for purposes of computing benefits. Also it is unclear whether there would be some constitutional barrier to taxing funds maintained by state and local governments.

There are two possible ways not yet mentioned that tax benefits for pensions might be restricted. One approach is to gradually reduce the limits on contributions. This approach seems decidedly second best, if pension plans serve generally useful economic purposes. All of the complications contained in present tax law will remain. A result might be to downscale pensions beyond the optimal size for other purposes. Firms might also offer both limited tax-benefited plans and plans without tax benefit (nonqualified plans where contributions are not deductible to the firm).

Another way to tax pensions would be via some other mechanism that would, while not explicitly taxing pensions, serve the same purposes. One such approach is to index interest payments for deduction from and inclusion in income. This approach would increase the tax burden on firms, with an offsetting reduction for taxable recipients but not nontaxable ones. Various approaches to integration, such as imputation/credit methods that do not provide refundable credits, would cut taxes only for taxable investors. The Treasury integration study (1992) includes a proposal to provide a single tax on business (i.e., no deduction of interest, no taxation of interest, and no dividends or capital gains taxation) that would clearly raise the tax burden on pensions by disallowing interest deductibility. Indeed one of the advantages of this proposal, aside from its gains from altering various distortions introduced by the corporate tax, is that it would lower tax burdens at the margin by imposing them on inframarginal investments. Taxing income from IRAs and life insurance products does not involve the serious administrative difficulties that occur in the case of pensions, and this could be achieved through disallowing tax benefits for IRAs and including inside buildup of life insurance plans in income.

9 A Potpourri of Capital Income Tax Issues

The previous chapters have addressed broadly applicable provisions of the tax code—the fundamental rate structure and rules regarding the measurement of income for broad categories of investment. This chapter surveys a variety of special issues in the taxation of capital income. It is by no means comprehensive, for there are a plethora of minor deviations from neutral tax treatment, many of which are documented in the annual tax expenditure budget of the government. The objective is to provide a general overview of the issues associated with these provisions and to refer the reader to the literature on the subject. The topics addressed include housing and consumer interest deductibility, the tax treatment of intangible investments (including research and development), special tax treatment of the extractive industries, exemption of interest on tax exempt bonds, problems in the tax treatment of certain organizational forms (financial institutions, cooperatives, and nonprofit enterprises), tax incentives for small businesses, and tax incentives for geographic location. The final segment is a listing of some remaining items not addressed elsewhere.

Housing and the Deductibility of Consumer Interest

The treatment of owner-occupied housing relative to other assets has been touched upon in several other chapters in this book. This section briefly discusses some of the literature specifically associated with the housing issue and some of the special provisions in the tax law that benefit housing.

Housing is an important part of the capital stock; owner-occupied housing alone is responsible for about 30 percent of the capital stock.

Owner-occupied housing (along with other consumer durables) has been historically favored by the tax law, as demonstrated in figure 2.2 of chapter 2; tax rates on average are typically around zero. The major benefit for owner-occupied housing is the failure to tax imputed rent. As discussed in chapter 3, the effective tax burdens vary across tax-payers and forms of investment. Those who itemize deductions are allowed to deduct property taxes; this magnifies the tax benefit, producing a net subsidy rather than a tax (a negative tax rate). Taxpayers who do not itemize and who rely on debt finance are subject to a tax that may be substantial if there is significant debt finance. Based on average leveraging rates and rates at which taxpayers itemize, the overall tax rate is typically close to zero.

As suggested in chapter 3, justifications for the exclusion of imput-ed income for owner-occupied housing have included possible spillover effects from homeownership, an offset for the local property tax, and administrative difficulties of taxing this income. As suggested in that chapter, the spillover argument seems doubtful. Property taxes also apply to rental housing and other real property (and in some cases personal property); moreover the property tax may act in part as a benefit tax. The exclusion may, however, be justified by the adminis-trative difficulties of taxing imputed income.

Even though taxing imputed rent would be quite difficult adminis-tratively, restrictions on the deductibility of mortgage interest and property taxes is relatively simple. Indeed an elimination of these pro-visions entirely would simplify the tax law by substantially reducing the number of taxpayers that itemize deductions.

Deductibility of property taxes has been supported on the grounds that disallowing a deduction would interfere with the tax structures of local governments by favoring income taxes (which are deductible); of course deduction of sales taxes is already disallowed, so the validity of this argument is not clear. The property tax may also be viewed as an way to subsidize local governments and the major activity of local governments—education. A more direct subsidy mechanism would seem appropriate, particularly as the property tax deduction benefit benefits wealthier taxpayers who tend to own houses and tend to itemize deductions—and also benefits wealthier jurisdictions. (One could also criticize the deductibility of other state and local sales taxes on similar grounds.)

As indicated in chapter 3, it is appropriate to deduct interest payments in an income tax system. Currently only mortgage interest is deductible; other forms of consumer interests (e.g., on car loans or credit cards) are disallowed. The ability to deduct mortgage interest only affects the decisions of individuals who itemize. The major justification for disallowing the deductibility of interest is that it is an indirect way of taxing imputed rental income. Of course disallowing interest deductibility will result in a preference for equity rather than debt finance of housing.

The estimated welfare cost of the favorable treatment of owner-occupied housing has varied in the literature. Total excess burdens of differential capital taxes in large-scale general equilibrium models capture the distortions from the favorable treatment of owner-occupied housing as part of an overall estimate. In chapter 4 the estimates from Gravelle (1989) indicated that most of the welfare gain of 0.9 percent would be achieved by taxing corporations at the same rate as noncorporate business; the remaining loss due to beneficial treatment of owner-occupied housing would be about 0.1 percent of consumption. (The gain would probably be larger with disaggregation of taxpayers into income classes, since the tax advantage varies considerably.)

Jorgenson and Yun (1988) find that preferential treatment of housing accounts for about half of distortions from misallocation of capital. (The discussion associated with owner-occupied housing is probably around 1 percent of income; Jorgenson and Yun only report estimates in present value dollar terms.) The gain in general equilibrium models would probably be larger if the preferential provisions were removed while maintaining corporate taxes.

A number of studies that have focused particularly on housing have tended to find excess burdens that range from about 0.1 percent of output to about 1 percent of output (Laidler 1969; Rosen 1979; Berkovec and Fullerton 1992). The latter study employed a portfolio model to determine investment choice and produced an efficiency cost of about 1 percent of output. Gains from disallowing property tax deductions would be about 0.2 percent of output, while gains from disallowing mortgage interest deductions would be about 0.1 percent of output.

The benefits of this treatment tend to accrue to higher-income individuals who are more likely to itemize deductions. According to

Poterba (1990), 60 percent of individuals in the lowest income decile are renters, while only 15 percent of individuals in the top decile are. According to distributional data provided by the Joint Committee on Taxation, almost 85 percent of the tax benefits of the mortgage interest deduction go to the top fifth of taxpayers.

There are also some more specialized tax provisions associated with housing. Capital gains on home sales are deferred if another primary residence is purchased within two years. Moreover taxpayers over 55 are allowed a one-time exclusion for $125,000 of gain on their residence. The tax law also allows state and local governments to issue tax exempt bonds to finance home mortgages and construction of rental housing. There is a very generous tax credit for low-income rental housing. This low-income housing credit was originally enacted as a temporary provision and has been extended many times. In 1993 it was made permanent. Burman (1992) and the Joint Committee on Taxation (1992) discuss the low-income housing tax credit.

As a practical and political matter, there has been virtually no interest in taxing imputed income from owner occupied housing. Moreover the major itemized deductions associated with homeownership—the deduction of mortgage interest and property taxes—are regarded as so popular that outright repeal would appear doubtful. There is currently a ceiling on the mortgage interest deduction so that interest associated with mortgages above $1 million is not eligible; lowering this ceiling might be a possible revision.

Intangible Capital

Most analyses of the current tax system incorporate the tax treatment of tangible capital goods—structures, equipment, inventories, and land. But investment—in the sense of forgoing resources in the present to obtain them in the future—extends beyond these more concrete investments. These intangible investments are diverse. They include expenditures on research and development to produce new innovations, expenditures on job training to increase the productivity of the work force, and expenditures on advertising to increase the market for the final product. Indeed recent controversies about the tax treatment of purchased intangibles have suggested an even broader array of potential intangible assets—from the accumulated data files of newspapers to the value of a broadcasting frequency (Mundstock 1990; General Accounting Office 1991).

Assessing the magnitude of these investments is extremely difficult. In the case of research and development expenditures and advertising, some of these costs can be separated out; in the case of other expenditures there is not even a series of expenditures. Translating an historical series of expenditures into a stock of capital is problematic because it depends on the depreciation rate. How quickly does an expenditure on advertising and the increased patronage it creates deteriorate? How rapidly does a new innovation lose its value?

Lyon and Fullerton (1988) have used historical series and an assumed depreciation rate to calculate that the stock of intangible assets created by advertising is 4 percent of the overall capital stock, while the stock of assets created by R&D is 7 percent. These assets are not large as a fraction of the capital stock in the aggregate, but they are not insignificant. Moreover in some industries they are quite important. For example, Lyon and Fullerton found that advertising accounted for 28 percent of the capital stock in the finance and insurance industries and 18 percent of the capital stock in food and tobacco manufacture. Other industries where advertising was slightly more important than average were trade, services, and the manufacture of chemicals, rubber, textiles, apparel, and leather. In many industries of course advertising is of virtually no importance (e.g., mineral extraction). In the case of R&D, the stock of R&D was largest as a fraction of total capital in the manufacture of transportation equipment (56 percent), motor vehicles (30 percent), metals and machinery including electronics (20 percent), and chemicals and rubber (17 percent). There is virtually no R&D outside manufacturing, and many types of manufacturing involve little R&D.

These numbers should be interpreted cautiously. Some types of intangible investments (e.g., those for job training) are not captured in these measures. Moreover it is difficult to establish the depreciation rate of the assets. In addition these assets are fundamentally different in the productive process from physical capital—they may enhance the productivity of capital, labor, or both inputs. But they are suggestive of the importance of these investments in some industries.

Due in part to the necessities of tax administration, these intangible investments are typically effectively subject to no tax on their return.

The costs of expenditures on salaries and rents for research and development, on training programs to increase worker productivity, and on advertising are deducted as current expenses. The effect of expensing is to create a zero tax rate at the firm level. To capitalize these expenditures involves considerable uncertainty as to useful life. Thus it would be possible to capitalize some of these costs and depreciate them but difficult to do so accurately. For other types of investments in intangibles, even the measurement of costs would be virtually impossible. How might one separate the expenditure on wages for a new employee into costs of training versus payment for current labor services?

In addition to being expensed, investment in research and development is eligible for a tax credit. Gravelle (1985), the Joint Economic Committee (1985), Altschuler (1988), Cordes and Watson (1987), Cordes (1989), the General Accounting Office (1989b), and Hall (1993) discuss the economic issues surrounding the credit. The combination of a credit plus expensing results in a net subsidy at the level of the firm for that investment. The research and experimentation (R&E) tax credit was adopted in 1981. This credit is primarily used by large corporations—corporations with $250 million or more in assets claimed 80 percent of the credit (General Accounting Office 1989b).

The R&D credit was structured as an incremental credit by being allowed only in excess of the average expenditure over the previous three years. Although the intent of this original design was to increase the incentive per dollar of revenue loss, various analyses (Gravelle 1985; Charles Rivers Associates 1985) showed that such an approach reduced the incentive as well as the cost. This effect occurred because an increase in spending currently would increase the base for figuring future credits. In effect the credit would be received in the current period and paid back over the next three years. Moreover, depending on the expected growth pattern of expenditures and other characteristics of the firm, it was possible for the credit to actually discourage investment (if it increased the future base without generating current credits), causing the credit to be worth only about 4 percent rather than 20 percent (General Accounting Office 1989b). In 1989 the growth of the base was uncoupled from actual expenditures, restoring the marginal effect.

In addition the issue of expensing of intangibles and the credit, there is the issue of how taxes encourage or discourage the sale of businesses with intangible assets. The capital gains tax applies to the sale of intangible assets, just as it does to other assets of the firm. Essentially any value of the firm in excess of the value of its physical assets is considered an intangible asset. There are, however, some disputes on how to treat these assets for purposes of cost recovery, which has led to considerable administrative difficulties. As in the case of depreciable assets the nature of the cost recovery can act to offset the burden of the capital gains tax (Gravelle and Taylor 1992) and affect both investment and lock-in effects.[1] The complexities in the tax law led to the adoption of a uniform write-off period for all purchased intangibles (of 15 years) in 1993.

Intangible assets are treated very generously, with tax rates of zero at the firm level for non-R&D investments and negative tax rates, or subsidies, for investments in R&D. These beneficial treatments contribute to a departure of the tax system from neutrality. Nevertheless, it is not clear that these treatments are necessarily counter to economic efficiency. In certain types of expenditures, such as the creation of technical know how of the firm and on-the-job training, the identification of expenditures and the policing of those expenditures by the government is virtually impossible.

In addition a subsidy may well be justified for some of these expenditures. Job training to produce general skills is typically underprovided in a market economy; absent slavery the firm cannot ensure that it will receive the returns from its investment in the human capital of its workers. (As noted earlier, pensions may be a way of dealing with this market failure, but the government might actually be interfering in this options.)

Another important area of intangible investment is the investment in R&D. Again this is an investment that is typically underprovided in a market economy. Most evidence indicates that the social return to R&D is considerably higher than the private return. This research is surveyed in Congressional Budget Office (1984), Bernstein and Nadiri (1984, 1988), and Kiley (1993). Mansfield (1977) has estimated that the average social return on R&D is 56 percent, which would justify a very large subsidy.

Even if R&D is underprovided, it is not clear that a tax subsidy is the best alternative because spillover effects vary from one project to the next. The optimal intervention may be through patent laws, direct subsidies, or direct research by the government. Nor is it clear that the incremental format of the credit does not have adverse effects on market structure or result in unfair discrimination across firms. In practice, however, it may be difficult for the government to identify research projects that have large spillovers, and direct spending may not be superior to a generally available tax subsidy.

Some critics have charged that tax subsidies are not effective, citing the low estimated response of R&D expenditures to changes in price. Earlier studies have found elasticities to be in the range of 0.2 to 0.5 (Bernstein and Nadiri 1989; Nadiri 1980), although Baily and Lawrence (1987, 1992) and Hall (1993) report estimates as high as 1. The literature on this issue is reviewed by Cordes (1989). Gravelle (1985) suggests, however, that is difficult to calculate these effects given lack of information on the economic depreciation rates of these investments. Nevertheless, if the social return is very high, a subsidy would be justified even if the response were small.

While there is some justification for the generous treatment of certain intangibles, there seems to be less of a case for the treatment of advertising costs. The economic role of advertising is complex. The economics literature on industrial organization suggests that while advertising may be manipulative, it may also serve a useful economic purpose by informing individuals and enhancing competition and variety. Free markets can devote either too little or too much of their resources to advertising (see Krouse 1990). At least one important theory of advertising—establishing brand name—relies on the notion of a capital investment to yield a stream of future returns. A firm is signaling its intention to provide quality goods by making an up-front expenditure. In expensing such investments, a firm derives a tax benefit that may be inefficient. Providing some capitalization of advertising costs might be desirable, particularly if the revenues raised could be used to reduce other distortions in the tax system.

Tax Treatment of the Extractive Indu

Tax treatment for the extraction of minerals, particularly oil and gas, has been very generous through most of history. For many years percentage depletion—allowing a deduction of a certain fraction of gross output—was allowed, which resulted in the deduction of certain costs of exploring for the resource and of acquiring mineral rights many times in excess of the original costs. Percentage depletion was first allowed only for oil and gas industry, with various hard minerals added over a period of time. The percentage depletion allowance for oil and gas was eliminated when oil prices rose dramatically in the mid-1970s, but the provision for hard minerals (and a small amount allowed for independent oil and gas producers) is still in place.

Even without percentage depletion, oil and gas extraction is treated very generously. All of the costs of acquiring tracts and drilling holes are allowed to be expensed when abandoned, even though these costs represent part of the costs of finding productive properties. Moreover most of the intangible costs of drilling producing wells (supplies, repairs, etc.) are also expensed. Recent tax legislation has, however, required corporate producers to write off 30 percent of these costs over five years. Abandoned properties and intangible development costs can also be deducted for hard minerals. These provisions are not as important for many hard minerals because a larger fraction of the cost of the extraction is in depreciable machinery.

There is a voluminous debate that has occurred over the years on the issue of the desirability of providing tax benefits for oil and gas extraction. McDonald (1963), Brannon (1974), and the General Accounting Office (1990) provide overviews of this issue. Many of these issues would apply to the treatment of hard minerals as well.

Historically the arguments made for percentage depletion were that oil and gas exploration were very risky and that a strong domestic capacity was needed for national defense. The first argument has been evoked to justify many types of tax subsidies. Yet risk arguments do not clarify why risk should be encouraged, nor do they take into account the natural risk reduction mechanisms of the tax (it reduces variability in return as it reduces risk and thus could actually encourage risk taking). The national defense argument has also been used to justify a wide range of subsidies. While there may be some need to prepare for minimum supplies needed to finance warfare, encouraging greater production (and eventual depletion) of domestic reserves hardly seems optimal—provision of a strategic reserve would seem the solution in this case.

The existence of externalities or spillover effects in the oil and gas industry are not clear since there are both negative and positive externalities (Peterson 1975). Exploration may be undersupplied because the exploration of one party provides information on the location of deposits to other parties—in this case, as with R&D, the firm may not be able to capture the full social benefit to exploration. At the same time, given a fixed amount of potentially discoverable resources of a given quality, there is an incentive to find these reserves before someone else does, which may cause too rapid a rate of discovery. Of course in addition to these offsetting externalities suggested by Peterson are possible negative spillover effects from environmental concerns.

Tax-Exempt Bonds

Interest on bonds issued by state and local governments are not subject to tax, with some restrictions on private activity bonds. This treatment has been the subject of extensive economic analysis (Ott and Meltzer 1963; Zimmerman 1991a). Excluding the interest on these bonds from taxation causes the interest rate on state and local bonds to be lower; for securities of equal risk the interest rate on these bonds would be equal to the after tax interest rate on taxable bonds. This treatment causes the cost of state and local capital expenditures to be less than it would otherwise be.[2] It is important in assessing these issues to distinguish between the types of bonds under consideration: public goods, publicly owned commercial facilities, private bonds, and arbitrage bonds.

Perhaps the most common type of bond issued is to finance traditional public goods or quasi-public goods such as schools and highways. These commodities are ones that are difficult for the private market to produce in optimal quantities because of difficulty in pricing or because of large spillover effects. If these spillover effects are confined to the local or state community that financed the expenditure, and the state and local community provides the optimal level of spending, there is no justification for federal support. If, however, there are spillover effects or underprovision of goods, then participation in financing by the federal government may be justified. In that case the failure to tax interest on state and local bonds may be a reasonable part of an optimal tax policy.

There are, however, several difficulties with this argument. First, the tax subsidy is a general one that does not distinguish among projects and therefore cannot match the subsidy to the spillover effect or to the degree of under provision. While there may be some justification for proving support to highways used by nonresidents or to education in general, there is less, or perhaps no, reason to subsidize local police and fire protection. A more efficient approach would allow the targeting of benefits to specific uses through grants or subsidies for specified projects.

Second, it is not clear that capital expenditures should be subsidized relative to current inputs, at least for many types of expenditures. If there is a spillover effect to public education, the spillover warrants subsidizing teacher's salaries as well as classroom construction. Only if there is a bias against capital spending, would such a subsidy be justified.[3]

A second category of projects are those that are financed with state and local bonds and owned by state and local governments but that are perfectly capable of being carried out as private enterprises (e.g., are publicly owned power plants and state liquor stores). There is no justification for subsidizing these facilities by allowing tax-exempt bond financing. There are restrictions on using tax-exempt bond financing to purchase existing electric and natural gas utilities, but there is no restriction on using bonds to construct new facilities. And there are exceptions to this rule.

A third category of projects are private-activity bonds, where the state or local government issues tax-exempt bonds whose proceeds are in turn lent to private businesses. The economic issues surrounding these bonds are reviewed in Zimmerman (1991a). The rapid growth of these private-activity bonds led to restrictions on the tax-exempt privilege so that only categories of bonds for certain purposes and for small issues are eligible.[4] There is also a volume cap, based on a per capita limit (with a minimum value), that restrains the size of these types of projects.

Despite these restrictions private-activity bonds remain important, accounting for one-third of new issues in 1990 (Kenyon 1991), or over $40 billion. The subsidy for private-activity bonds is nothing more or less than a direct subsidy to business, through a somewhat circuitous route. It should therefore be evaluated on the same grounds—spillover effects—as other tax subsidies to private investments are evaluated. Justifying most of the specific uses for the private-activity bonds would be difficult to do, particularly given the option of alternative approaches to correcting spillovers.

A final category of bonds issued are arbitrage bonds. A state or local government could issue tax-exempt bonds and invest the proceeds of the issues in taxable bonds, thereby yielding a net payment. This arbitrage opportunity is, absent other constraints, a virtually unlimited opportunity to receive federal government payments. A whole variety of rules have been put into place to limit diverting the proceeds from issuing of bonds to investments in higher yield taxable bonds.[5] These rules do not always work perfectly; in any case the arbitrage restrictions can only be applied on direct basis. There is nothing to prevent indirect arbitrage. For example, states and localities that would normally use tax finance for some portion of investment projects would use these projects as an opportunity to engage in arbitrage. Metcalf (1990) presents some evidence that state holding of financial assets were responsive to the yield differential between taxable and tax-exempt bonds, which would tend to support indirect arbitrage.

Most of the issues described above are efficiency issues, having to do with the misallocation of resources brought about by the subsidy (an exception being arbitrage bonds, which involve an abuse of the intention of the benefit). There is, however, another issue that was important in the past when tax rates were graduated. The relative yield on taxable versus tax-exempt bonds reflects an implicit tax, which in turn should be equal to the tax rate of the marginal investor. Investors with tax rates above that of this marginal investor receive higher returns because of the tax subsidy. Another way of saying this is that the government could provide the same benefit in terms of an interest subsidy at a smaller revenue cost, since an interest subsidy would not accrue extra benefits to high tax rate investors. Indeed in the economic literature on tax-exempt bonds this phenomenon is known as *transfer efficiency*, referring to the cost of delivering the subsidy (as opposed to the optimal allocation of resources as efficiency is more commonly used). With the flatter tax system in place, this transfer efficiency cost has become relatively unimportant (Auten and Trautman 1992). This issue could return, however, were adoption of more rate brackets to take place in the future.

The economic justifications for tax-exempt bond interest seem weak. Essentially the subsidy seems simultaneously not targeted (it is not based on spillover effects) and wrongly targeted (it singles out capital over current expenditures). Providing aid to state and local governments could probably be achieved in a more efficient fashion. Nevertheless, it is politically very difficult to contemplate such a change given the fierce opposition of state and local governments.

Special Types of Businesses

While the tax law differentiates across investments and between corporate and noncorporate enterprises, certain types of businesses have been subject to special rules. These businesses include firms engaged in providing financial and investment services (banks and insurance companies), cooperatives, and nonprofit organizations.

Financial Firms and Insurance Companies

Banks and insurance companies have historically enjoyed partial or complete exemption from federal income tax, arising largely from the difficulties in measuring reserves and because many of these firms are mutuals. When firms are mutuals, the patrons play a dual role of customer and investor, and it is difficult to isolate these roles.

Another problem was that commercial banks were allowed to hold tax exempt bonds, while still deducting interest paid to depositors, without any of the constraints applied to other firms.

Until 1951 thrift institutions were exempt from tax, and even when they became taxable, extremely generous deductions for bad debt reserves resulted in extremely low tax rates. Commercial banks were already subject to tax but were also allowed very generous bad debt reserves. Legislation over time has gradually eliminated these excess bad debt reserves (some small benefits are allowed for certain small commercial banks and certain thrifts). The 1986 act also restricted the ability of commercial banks to deduct interest paid on deposits used to hold tax-exempt bonds. Credit unions, however, are exempt from tax. This treatment stems from their mutual nature and the notion that they are organized as cooperative or nonprofit enterprises for the benefits of their members. Credit unions, however, currently provide the same financial services as commercial banks and thrifts, and there seems little justification for exempting them (see Bickley 1990 for a review of the arguments). The effect of tax exemption for credit unions is to favor their capital investments relative to those of other industries.

Life insurance companies present two difficult problems of taxation. The first is that they must have reserves to meet their obligations to policyholders in order to measure underwriting income, and it is by no means straightforward to determine the appropriate level of these reserves. Second, many life insurance companies are organized as mutuals. These companies were subject to a separate set of tax rules; recent legislative changes have attempted to match the treatment of these companies to those of other corporations by prescribing market interest rates to compute reserves and by allocating income to mutuals based on the earnings of stock companies. There has been some debate about how successful these changes have been (Department of the Treasury 1988; General Accounting Office 1989a).

Similar problems of measuring reserves and the presence of mutual firms have also plagued the property and casualty insurance companies. Many of these problems were addressed in 1986, particularly the rules that allowed these firms to add to reserves, without discounting, losses incurred that would not be paid until some future date. Special benefits remain, however, for small property and casualty firms: The smallest firms are exempt from tax; other small firms may elect to be taxed only on their investment income. There are also some special rules effectively exempting Blue Cross and Blue Shield from tax.

Cooperatives

Businesses organized as cooperatives are either directly exempt from tax (telephone and electric cooperatives) or effectively exempt from tax by allowing the deduction of "patronage dividends." These are payments to customer-owners, and their deductibility is defended on the grounds that they are in the nature of price reductions. These dividends can, however, be deducted even if they are not paid in cash, but merely allocated to the patron, as long as 20 percent is paid in cash. Business customers must include them in income. There are cooperatives in many different industries, but the most important ones are agriculture and consumer cooperatives. Caplin (1969) and Shrader and Goldberg (1975) discuss agricultural cooperatives.

Nonprofit Enterprises

There are many organizations that, though organized in the same fashion as corporations, are nonprofit enterprises. These enterprises rely
on a combination of fee charges, government support, and donations.
Clotfelter (1991) indicates that the largest groups of nonprofit organizations are in the health field, followed by the education field. These
organizations, which include hospitals, nursing homes, and private
educational institutions, receive the majority of their income from
charges to customers, just as do normally taxable firms. They also rely
on government payments and donations as well. The next largest nonprofit organizations are religious and rely on donations. There are also
a variety of social service and legal organizations that rely largely on
government funds.

   Although income taxes to not apply to these organizations, there is
a tax imposed on unrelated business income. This unrelated business
income tax does not, however, apply to insurance companies owned
by nonprofit organizations such as fraternal societies and employee
associations. There is also negligble tax on investment income of private foundations (which are also subject to a number of restrictions).
In addition there are government-owned enterprises that perform
functions quite similar to commercial businesses (e.g., the Government
Printing Office and municipal power facilities), as well as some examples of privately owned government sponsored enterprises, such as
the Federal Home Loan Bank.

   According to Weisbrod (1988) nonprofit enterprises own 1.8 percent
of the nation's assets (compared to the federal government that owns
3.9 percent and state and local governments that own 8.5 percent).
While this share is small, these firms are important in some industries,
particularly in the rapidly growing health care industry.

   In assessing the issue of taxing nonprofit enterprises, it is important
to consider why they exist, particularly in the case of commercial nonprofits that seem virtually identical to profit-motivated enterprises. In
theory, it would seem that many of their functions could be performed
by either the government or by private businesses. Hansmann (1991)
reviews several of the economic theories that have been advanced to
explain these organizations. He classifies nonprofit enterprises into
those that are donative (relying on contributions) and commercial

(relying on fees). He also classifies each type as mutual (run by the patrons) or entrepreneurial (run by a self-perpetuating board). As an illustration, a donative mutual would be an organization like Common Cause, a donative entrepreneurial would be an organization like the March of Dimes, a commercial mutual would be an organization like the American Automobile Association, and a commercial entrepreneurial would be a nonprofit hospital.

A theory suggested by Weisbrod (1974) is that certain functions that are in the nature of public goods functions (e.g., medical research) may be performed by the private sector because a consensus cannot be reached among voters. Those individuals who prefer these goods but do not constitute a majority might band together voluntarily to do so.

This theory could explain certain types of nonprofit enterprises but not others. In particular, it does not explain the existence of nonprofit enterprises in areas where services are easily provided by normal business operations. A theory that could explain these commercial nonprofit enterprises, suggested originally by Nelson and Krashinsky (1973) and since elaborated on by several economists, is the *contract failure theory*. This theory suggests that consumers are reluctant to purchase certain goods from firms that are motivated by profits and might take advantage of customers. This problem would be particularly likely to occur when there is information asymmetry (e.g., in a hospital where the customer's information about the need for the service is limited relative to the firm's information) or where the service is purchased on behalf of someone who cannot properly evaluate the product (e.g., child care or a nursing home for an elderly relative.) By purchasing the service in this way, the benefits of the efficient provision motivated by profit considerations are traded for insurance against possible exploitation.

Another theory discussed by Hansmann and invoked to explain organizations such as exclusive social clubs, is the consumer control theory. Here there are no information problems as would occur with the contract failure theory; rather the appeal of such a club is the association with other members. This argument suggests that the nonprofit approach is simply used to establish control over the enterprise by the patrons and prevent a profit-making owner from earning monopoly profits.

There are two types of potential justifications for providing tax benefits to nonprofit enterprises. One justification is that they are engaged in the social function of support for the poor. The other justification is that these firms are engaged in producing some commodity that is otherwise undersupplied.

While some nonprofit enterprises are engaged in redistribution, many others are less beneficial to the poor than one might think. Clotfelter (1991) in his overview indicates that nonprofit hospitals do not serve the poor any more than do the for-profits; this function is generally left to public hospitals. Clients of nonprofit nursing homes appear to be more affluent than clients of either for-profit or government facilities. Private educational institutions (they are virtually all nonprofit) also tend to serve higher income individuals than do the public institutions. Nonprofit activities directed at the arts (art museums, the ballet) also benefit the wealthy. Nonprofit organizations engaged in social services (e.g., drug abuse and mental health facilities) do, however, tend to benefit the poor. Religious organizations engage in relatively little redistribution (most of their expenditures are for club goods that benefit the congregation, although some expenditures are for the poor). Given the relative importance of these different functions, nonprofit organizations on the whole do not appear to be involved in providing substantial benefits for the poor.

Indeed Odendahl (1990) suggests that the philanthropic elite primarily support the types of goods they themselves consume—a lot of philanthropy goes to support the institutions of the rich such as art museums, the ballet, and prestigious schools. A similar point is made by Zimmerman (1991b), who notes that some nonprofit activity is philanthropic paternalism—the wealthy determine what types of organizations will be funded and may directly benefit from the expenditure (front row seats at performances or an entree into a prestigious school for children).

Of the three motivations for nonprofit enterprises—public goods provision, contract failure theory, and consumer control—only the first would appear to justify tax relief on efficiency grounds. Even in those cases, the potential private benefits received by the donors make the case for tax relief less than clear. In the case of enterprises that deliver essentially the same services as for-profits where there are no spillover effects, the consequences of tax benefits are to misallocate resources.

Tax Incentives for Small Businesses

Although chapter 4 stressed the favorable treatment that the current tax system provides to unincorporated businesses, that tend to be small, there are in fact some specific tax benefits that are targeted to small businesses. These include a provision allowing $17,500 of property to be expensed (with the amount phased out so that firms with $200,000 or more do not qualify). These special benefits, which have been in the tax law since 1959, were recently increased in 1993. A second provision, enacted in 1993, allows exclusion of half of the gain of original issue stock by small business corporations if held for five years. A provision in the tax law also allows losses on small business stock to be deducted as ordinary rather than capital losses. In addition the tax law has long contained graduated tax rates for corporations. Since small corporations are nevertheless likely to be owned by high income individuals, the normal rationale for progressive tax rates does not apply. Indeed these lower tax rates probably mostly serve as a way of sheltering income of higher-income individuals who may be able to divert some earnings into lower corporate tax brackets. This treatment can be beneficial if such earnings are retained in the firm.

The tax law also contains a provision that allows small corporations (less than 35 shareholders) to elect to be taxed as partners (these businesses are termed *Subchapter S corporations*). This provision does not provide a special subsidy; rather, it allows these businesses to avoid the additional corporate tax.

The recent expansion of small business tax benefits was largely argued on the grounds that small businesses tend to create the great majority of jobs. This argument can be disputed on factual grounds. Also it is not so much that small businesses create jobs but rather that new businesses create jobs and new businesses tend to be small—and tend to fail. In addition some of the growth may reflect sectoral growth in industries that tend to be composed of smaller businesses. Brown, Hamilton, and Medoff (1990) discuss these patterns of job growth.

Even if small businesses are responsible for more job growth, this observation would not create an argument for a capital subsidy for two reasons. First, if there were indeed a legitimate objective to increase the amount of jobs in small businesses, a capital subsidy would be inappropriate and could even decrease the demand for labor by encouraging the substitution of capital. More important, there is nothing in economic theory to suggest a subsidy to labor simply because its use is growing in a given area.

Another argument that is sometimes made for small business subsidies are that small businesses are more innovative. Some studies have indicated that within an industry there are more innovations per employee. Brown, Hamilton, and Medoff (1990) examine this literature. These studies are difficult to do, but in any case providing an incentive for all small business is a very inefficient way to target benefits, since most small businesses operate in industries where innovation is not likely to be important. For example, more than half of equipment in small corporations and unincorporated businesses (that would be eligible for expensing) is used in the service sector and only 5 percent in manufacturing, based on distribution of equipment investments (Gravelle 1990). Similarly more than half of the assets of smaller businesses that would likely be eligible for the capital gains preference are in trade and services.

It is possible to defend the expensing provisions on the grounds that it simplifies tax accounting for small businesses, although this argument does not explain why benefits are limited to equipment. The other provisions seem difficult to justify on equity, efficiency, or simplicity grounds.

Geographically Targeted Tax Incentives: Enterprise Zones

Although states and localities have long used tax incentives, which were often in the nature of property tax relief, to encourage firms to locate in certain regions, the U.S. tax system has generally not included such provisions. There were a series of tax benefits aimed at the U.S. territories (discussed in chapter 10), but these territories did not enjoy the full benefits of federal government programs.

Interest in establishing federal "enterprise zones" where businesses would be eligible for tax benefits blossomed following the 1992 riots in Los Angeles. Legislation was included in tax bills passed by the Congress, but not signed by the president (for other reasons) in 1992. The 1993 legislation provided some tax incentives for a limited number (nine) of "empowerment zones" that would receive a wage sub-

sidy for employing residents of the zone and a capital subsidy in the
form of the ability to expense $20,000 of investments equipment and
expanded ability to use tax exempt bonds. There were a larger number
(95) zones that were eligible for tax exempt bond financing. In most
cases these benefits will be available for ten years.

The rationale for enterprise zones was to aid depressed areas, and
the individuals in those areas, by encouraging firms to move into these
areas and to residents. Some suggestions have been made that the
existence of depressed areas may represent a market failure; others
argue that the failure of businesses to locate in certain areas reflect economic costs of doing business.

Enterprise zones have been criticized on the grounds that they are
ineffective and inefficient means of stimulating economic activity,
either because tax considerations are not important enough or capable
of influencing activity in areas that are seriously depressed or because
most of any increase in business activity will be relocation from another area. This relocation might be of considerable concern if it comes
from a neighboring area that is also poor. Moreover, in general, there
is some question as to the desirability of targeting aid to poor individuals based only on where they live. Papke (1993) reviews the literature
and issues surrounding enterprise zones.

If the objective of the targeting provision is to aid poor residents of
the zone, capital subsidies would appear to be questionable. Subsidies
to capital make the use of capital more attractive than the use of labor,
and it is possible for such subsidies to make residents of the zone
worse off by reducing the demand for labor.

Miscellaneous Provisions

The details of how the tax law treats different kinds of specific assets
could fill volumes. For example, there is an extensive set of issues that
has to do with fundamental accounting rules—the proper matching of
income and expense in order to properly measure income. Among the
issues here are how to treat a future negative cost (e.g., decommission-
ing of nuclear plants and mining reclamation costs), how to account
for various income and costs accrued but not paid (including long-
term contracts, installment sales, and accounting for inventory), and
how treat interest payments that involve original issue discount.[6]

Many of these issues were dealt with in legislation in the 1980s, and there are attempts in most cases to construct accounting rules that measure income correctly. Of course one of the most fundamental issues—the failure to correct income for inflation—causes a mismatch of income and expense in many areas of the tax code dealing with depreciation, inventory accounting, and the measurement of interest.

There are also a complex set of rules that govern corporate reorganization (acquisition, merger, division, and liquidation) and that determine whether gain will be recognized and taxed when corporations are reorganized in various ways. There are still ways in which corporate reorganizations can take place to preclude the recognition of gain. In 1986, however, the ability of corporations to distribute property without paying tax was curtailed (this change was referred to as the repeal of *General Utilities* after a court case establishing some of the regulatory framework that allowed avoidance of taxes).

In addition there are a series of differential tax benefits for different investments, in many cases deliberately enacted to further some social goal or because of some sort of historical development. Some of these provisions have a time limitation and will lapse unless extended. Brief explanations of many of these provisions, and their revenue costs, can be found in the tax expenditure budget published in the annual budget documents. More detailed information on background, motive, and economic effects can be found in the Senate Budget Committee Tax Expenditure Compendium (1992).

There are a series of tax benefits for certain types of investments particularly in energy, natural resources, and agriculture, either to encourage these activities or to simplify accounting. Many of these provisions involve allowing investment credits, and allowing costs to be expensed (deducted immediately) rather than being capitalized. These include a 10 percent credit for investment in solar and geothermal energy facilities, expensing of many of the costs of timber growing that would otherwise be capitalized, a 10 percent tax credit plus seven-year amortization for up to $10,000 invested in land clearing and planting trees, and expensing of capital outlays such as feed, fertilizer, soil and water conservation, and a variety of other costs that would normally be capitalized. There are also provisions allowing capital gains tax treatment for incomes that would not normally be treated as capital gains: royalties on coal and iron ore, and unharvested crops.

There are a range of other special provisions. These include a 20 percent investment credit for historic preservation, a 10 percent investment credit for rehabilitation of certain older structures, deferral of taxes by shipping companies under the U.S. flag, credits and expensing provisions for expenditures on disabled access, a credit for testing of orphan drugs and provisions that allow deferral and exclusions for interest on savings bonds. There are also some provisions that reflect a desire to obtain equitable treatment, including provisions as narrow as a longer loss carryover for Alaskan Native corporations and income tax forgiveness on loans forgiven for insolvent farmers.

Most of these provisions are not motivated by equity concerns but rather for allocational reasons. It is difficult, however, to justify these special provisions on efficiency grounds in most cases, since few of these activities seem to provide spillover effects, and in none of them have such effects which have been measured and tax benefits tailored to the results. In addition some of the original rationales (e.g., administrative simplicity for farmers) cannot be justified in the current environment, where farmers are more sophisticated, and certainly as sophisticated as small business managers in other industries.

10   Capital Income Taxation in
         an International Economy

Many analyses of capital income taxation do not take into account the possibility of international trade or the flow of international capital from one country to another. There is a good reason for first considering tax policy without such concerns. The analysis of capital income taxation is much more complex in an open economy. It is, however, easier to explore the consequences of participation in an international economy once the general nature of the domestic tax system and the analysis of that system in a closed economy are considered.

International trade and "international competitiveness" are popular objects of concern in the political arena. For example, the Ways and Means Committee held hearings on "Factors Affecting International Competitiveness of the United States" in June and July of 1991. Yet the popular debate can stray far from the analysis of capital income taxation as found in the pages of economics journals and textbooks. The popular focus can be most easily seen in arguments that the United States should replace the corporate income tax with a value-added tax, because corporate taxes add to the cost of the product while the value-added taxes will be rebated on exports.

Perhaps in no other area is it as necessary to first dispense with the myths that surround the debate on domestic tax policy than when dealing with the issues surrounding the performance of the economy in an environment of international commerce. Three of these myths seems to be (1) exports are "good" and imports are "bad," (2) "international competitiveness" is a term that has meaning and can be judged by some measure, typically the trade balance or market share, and (3) the ability of U.S. firms to obtain market share is hampered by the tax burdens arising from capital income taxation.

These arguments can be contrasted with the questions brought to bear on the issue by economic theory, namely what tax policies are likely to enhance the standard of living, or welfare, of the United States and of the whole world. These questions are difficult to answer, in large part because of the lack of worldwide coordination in domestic tax policies regarding capital income taxation. They also are uncertain because the maximization of U.S. welfare is not be identical with the maximization of worldwide welfare.

In the following section the questions that crop up in the political debate—and the frequent fallacies in reasoning those questions reflect—are discussed. The second section explores the issues of efficient domestic tax policies in an international context, and how well the U.S. tax system conforms to an efficient system.

The Myth of "International Competitiveness"

If economists tend to agree on anything, it is probably the desirability of free trade, largely unhampered by tariff barriers and other trade restrictions. Although there are theories of optimal tariffs and subsidies that suggest the possibility of one country unilaterally bettering itself, few economists would propose such strategies as a guide to U.S. policy given the uncertainties, information requirements, possibilities of retaliation, and general distaste with such "beggar-thy-neighbor" policies carried out by one of the most economically advanced countries.

The object of unfettered trade is to allow a country to sell goods that it has a comparative advantage in producing, in exchange for other goods. Comparative advantage means that a country can produce its exported goods at a cheaper price relative to its cost of producing goods it imports, not that it can produce exports more cheaply on an absolute basis. Exports and imports are not good or bad; rather, the exchange of goods can make everyone better off. Tariffs and barriers to trade interfere with this free exchange.

International competitiveness—as it is often popularly understood—as increasing market share is a pointless objective. The United States cannot increase its market share in all markets, nor should it wish to do so, since it is the value of goods consumed (not goods sold) that contributes to welfare.

The misunderstanding of the role of capital income taxation can be most easily understood with a simple balance-of-payments example and the corporate income tax. Suppose that there is a single export good sold and a single good imported. Set aside for the moment the possibility of flows of investment. Foreigners must sell their currency to buy dollars to purchase the export; U.S. importers must sell dollars to buy foreign currency to pay for imports. Since the supply and demand for each currency must be equated, the dollars received by foreigners for goods imported from them must exactly equal the dollars paid for exports. Suppose now that a corporate tax is imposed, and it raises the price of the export good by 5 percent. The amount of currency necessary to purchase the export rises by 5 percent as well. Foreigners do not have enough dollars gained from the sale of their imports to purchase the old supply, nor do they wish to buy as much as the new higher price. Their demand for dollars will fall, driving down the value of the dollar. The value of the dollar will fall by the original increase in price, restoring the original equilibrium exactly.

From any one firm's point of view, it may appear that the increased costs occasioned by the tax are making it less competitive. But as long as all exports are subject to the increased cost, changes in the exchange rate will exactly offset that price effect. Of course, if there are many goods, a corporate tax will raise the price of some goods more than others, while the exchange rate will fall by only the average price. Some firms will lose market share and others will gain—this same phenomenon appears domestically, and it is a consequence of uneven taxation in the domestic economy. Uneven taxation distorts price and output for foreign as well as domestic demanders. Gravelle (1986) shows that these price effects are actually quite small in any case. The efficiency solution to this problem does not require the elimination of taxes but rather the imposition of uniform taxes.

Consideration of an open economy becomes important in the formulation of domestic tax policy not because of this type of cost analysis but because of the possibility of flows of investment around the world. It is this issue that is the subject of a voluminous economics literature, and it is addressed in the remainder of this chapter.

Issues of International Taxation

As in domestic taxation there are issues of both efficiency and of distribution, which are considered in turn. These efficiency and equity issues have been considered in a variety of books and articles (Richman 1963; Krause and Dam 1964; Musgrave 1975; Slemrod 1988).

Because it is necessary to explain certain concepts, the first section considers the efficient allocation of capital, given that a capital income tax is in place. The second section considers the distributional issues. How these concepts relate to the U.S. tax system are considered in the following section. In the final section the issue of the desirability of capital income taxes is revisited by assessing how such a question might be modified an open economy environment.

Efficient Capital Income Taxation in an International Economy

Efficient taxation is, in a domestic economy, equated with optimal taxation; in the absence of external effects it is also a neutral system that taxes all capital in the same fashion. These concepts need to be modified in an international environment, to take into account the possibility of many tax regimes and the fact that one country has the possibility of increasing its welfare at the expense of others. Two objectives are considered: the maximization of worldwide welfare and the maximization of national welfare.

Maximizing World Welfare
In the absence of taxes on capital (and tariffs), goods and investments will flow around the world to produce efficient production and consumption, absent external effects. Some countries may export capital to others, depending on the opportunities for productive investment and the differences in savings rates across different countries. Goods will be produced efficiently and traded efficiently. The equation of neutral, efficient, and optimal taxation remains in this framework.

If all capital were subject to a uniform rate, this condition of allocative efficiency would still obtain (although, as in the analysis of domestic taxation, such taxes could alter consumption patterns over time). Whatever capital is generated by savings would be devoted to its most productive uses.

Countries may, however, wish for a variety of reasons to choose different rates of tax or to tax on a different basis. Moreover countries have the power to tax their own capital wherever deployed around the world and/or all capital deployed within their borders regardless of origin. If all countries choose to tax all forms of income within their grasp, then capital exported from one country and employed in another would be subject to double taxation. In practice countries have eschewed this type of treatment.

To explain the consequences of different taxation schemes, first consider two simple choices. Countries could, in theory, choose between two taxing schemes: tax on the basis of residence of the owner (a country will tax worldwide income of its citizens), or tax on the basis of location of the capital (a country will tax all income earned in its borders). These systems are referred to as *residence-based taxation* and *territorial* (or *source-based*) *taxation*.

If all countries chose residence-based taxation, each country would tax its residents on their capital income whether derived from domestic or foreign investment. This system results in *capital export neutrality*. This system is illustrated in the upper panel 1 of table 10.1 for an initial rate of return before tax of 10 percent. Country A has a tax of 50 percent and country B a tax of 25 percent. Capital export neutrality will not alter the location of capital (although taxation itself could alter the overall size of the capital stock). Residents of country A will earn the

Table 10.1
After-tax rates of return, assuming 10 percent pretax return, with high-tax (50 percent) country A and low-tax (25 percent) country B

Country of residence	Country of use	
	A	B
Panel 1: Residence taxation (capital export neutrality)		
A	5.0	5.0
B	7.5	7.5
Panel 2: Territorial taxation ("capital import neutrality")		
A	5.0	7.5
B	5.0	7.5
Panel 3: Country A uses credit method, country B territorial		
A	5.0	5.0
B	5.0	7.5
Panel 4: Country A uses territorial, country B uses credit method		
A	5.0	7.5
B	5.0	7.5

same rate of return (5 percent) in either location and will have no incentive to alter their investments. Residents of country B will also earn the same rate of return in each location and have no incentive to move, although their rate of return will be higher—7.5 percent. The fact that capital within a country is taxed differently does not lead to differences in required pretax returns because different after-tax returns are earned. Capital export neutrality will therefore not change the allocation of capital, and it will be efficient assuming that capital is efficiently allocated in the absence of taxes.[1]

Suppose, instead, that all countries choose a territorial method—only taxing capital invested within its borders, as shown in panel 2 of table 10.1. Note now that residents of both A and B will earn a higher rate of return when capital is invested in country B. This approach will cause capital to flow from country A to country B, raising the rate of return in A and lowering it in B, until after tax returns are equated somewhere between 5 percent and 7.5 percent. This system is referred to as *capital import neutrality* because the same rates are applied to investment in a given country. This term is a misnomer. Although there is a superficial appearance of neutrality in the application of equal rates in a location, this system is not neutral in the sense of not altering the location of investment. It produces an inefficient allocation of capital because capital in country B is less productive (earns a lower rate of return before tax).

The distribution of tax payments is also altered. Under a residence-based tax, A will collect tax on its own capital wherever deployed. With a territorial tax, A will collect its tax on capital invested in A, regardless of ownership. Whether its taxes are higher or lower depend on whether it is a net importer or exporter of capital and on how the changes in capital flows alter incomes.

Countries do not tax on the residence basis—rather, they claim the first right of taxation to any investment in their own countries. Some countries practice pure territorial taxation (e.g., France and the Netherlands) at least with respect to direct investment. Other countries, such as the United States, England, Canada, and Japan practice a mixed system which can result, but does not necessarily result, in capital export neutrality. This system is a credit imputation system—the country imposes taxes on investment in its territories, taxes investment of its residents earned abroad, but allows a credit against tax for foreign taxes paid on capital invested abroad by its residents. This credit is given in order to avoid double taxation. Because this credit system does not refund foreign taxes in excess of the domestic tax rate, the system of capital export neutrality is not pure. (The refund is limited in order to avoid giving other countries carte blanche to raid the U.S. Treasury.) The United States also practices deferral of income of controlled foreign corporations. Income is not taxed until repatriated to the United States as a dividend, which is a movement toward territorial taxation.

These cases are illustrated in the remaining two panels of table 10.1. In panel 3 the high tax rate country (A) uses the credit method and the low tax rate country the territorial method. Note that the residents of country A would earn the same return as in residence-based taxation but that country B collects part of the tax. Residents of country B prefer to invest domestically where their taxes are lower. This system can conceivably yield an efficient outcome (assuming capital is perfectly substitutable). Residents of country B will begin to withdraw their capital to its site of higher yield. Residents of country A will then withdraw their capital into domestic uses as well. One possible outcome is that all of country B's capital will be invested in B, while A may have some investment in A and some in B. There will be no change in the rate of return, simply a substitution of ownership. There is also a possible inefficient outcome, where so much capital flows into B that the net rate of return between A and B is equated for B's investments despite the differential tax. In this case all of country A's assets will be invested in A, and the allocation of capital will be the same as when both countries use the territorial method.

An identical solution is reached if both A and B are credit method countries. The low tax country will be effectively forced to a territorial method—it will collect no tax on its exported capital because credits will wipe out the tax.

Panel 4 of table 10.1 illustrates the case when A is a territorial taxer and B uses the credit methods. Since B has a lower tax rate, the incentive effects are identical to the case where everybody taxes on a territorial basis, since B's credit system will not affect the tax burden of its citizens' investments in A.

These two country examples indicate that one country can achieve efficient allocation if it is both a high tax rate country and a heavy exporter of capital. The real world is of course much more complicated than this two-country example, since there are many countries, since investments are not perfect substitutes, and since there are many other complexities of taxation (e.g., debt vs. equity capital). These examples do illustrate, however, why there is more likelihood for efficient worldwide allocation of capital when countries choose a credit method.

These choices can, however, affect tax revenues. A country that is a capital exporter collects more revenue under a residence based system than a territorial based system. The effects in a mixed world are difficult to determine. In panel 4 of table 10.1, for example, country A collects tax on all domestic investment plus a partial tax on foreign investment; thus it is likely to collect more taxes under this system if it is an exporter of capital. A capital importer will probably collect more tax using a territorial basis.

Note, however, that the importance of these tax differentials depends on how mobile capital is across international boundaries. The less mobile capital is, the less deleterious for worldwide economic efficiency departures from residence based taxation are. Feldstein and Horioka (1980) suggests that capital is not very mobile: They find that increases in a country's savings were closely associated with increases in investments. Similar results were found by Feldstein and Bacchetta (1989). Hartman (1984), Boskin and Gale (1987), Young (1988), Jun (1990), and Slemrod (1990) have studied the relationship between rates of return and direct investment (both outbound and inbound). Although the results have varied, there is a tendency to find some influence of relative rates of return on investment flows. Nevertheless, these relationships fall short of perfect international capital mobility.

Maximizing National Welfare
The preceding analysis suggests that a country appears most likely to contribute to worldwide efficiency if it uses residence-based taxation or a system reasonably close to a residence system. There have, however, been other objectives proposed for tax choices. One of these would be to set taxes so as to maximize the welfare of the home country. These notions have given rise to another concept known as *national neutrality*. National neutrality has been used with reference to outbound investment, and it proposes that foreign taxes be allowed not as

a credit against U.S. taxes but as a deduction. The argument for this system is that the social (pretax) return *accruing to the country* on investments made at home and abroad be equated. In terms of the numbers used earlier, if country A were using national neutrality and country B territorial taxation, country A would only allow a deduction for country B's taxes. The rate of return after tax would be 3.75 percent (50 percent of the after country B's taxes return of 7.5 percent). This system would induce the withdrawal of capital owned by A from country B until the rate of return rose sufficiently to equate after tax returns. This system would also equate the total return received by A on its capital, whether via taxes or profits, regardless of where used.

Actually a country would have to go through some more complex calculus to actually optimize taxation. A decision would also have to be made regarding the treatment of capital imported from other countries. In general, countries benefit from the importation of capital from other countries because they receive the excess of the inframarginal return over the marginal return that is actually paid. To achieve an optimal tax rate, a tax even larger than that implied by national neutrality would be required, as discussed by Feldstein and Hartman (1979), even when the reaction of the host country is taken into account. Setting of the tax rate on inbound investment would involve a trade-off between receiving the benefits of foreign investment and collection of taxes—it would depend on the elasticity of the supply of capital with respect to changes in rate of return. Brumbaugh (1992) shows that the optimal tax is one divided by the sum of one plus the elasticity of supply of the foreign capital with respect to U.S. rate of return. If the elasticity is very large, the tax will be close to zero, while if the elasticity is very small, the optimal tax will be very large. Brumbaugh reports that the literature focusing on outbound and inbound direct investments suggests elasticities that probably in the range of 1 to 4, suggesting an optimal tax rate of 20 to 50 percent. The Feldstein and Horioka (1980) research that suggested more limited mobility would imply high tax rates, however. Of course the tax rate would also depend on the tax treatment by the country of origin—if that country imposes a tax and a foreign tax credit, the tax rate would need to be set to at least collect tax at the foreign country's rate.

There are numerous difficulties in adopting and implementing a system that is designed to maximize national welfare. Although there were arguments in the past to at least move toward such a system by allowing foreign taxes to be deductions from income rather than credits against tax, such a system is currently not being considered. Determining the appropriate tax rates would be extremely difficult. Moreover the reactions of other countries to such a regime should be taken into account. Such reactions could undo the original purpose of the system and make all countries worse off. Gordon (1992) outlines some of the complexities that would be confronted in assessing how countries aimed toward an optimal tax might behave. Finally, there is a fundamental question as to the desirability of choosing a system whose objective is "beggar thy neighbor."

The choice of tax policy in an international economy is an enormously complex one given the role that other countries and their policies play. Nevertheless, there is much to be said for striving to meet the standards of capital export neutrality within the constraints of that international system.

Distributional Considerations

Residence-based taxation not only has different consequences for efficiency from territorial taxation; it also has consequences for distribution. As noted above, a capital-exporting country will collect more revenue from a pure residence-based tax than it will from a pure territorial based tax. A territory-based tax system will provide larger revenues to capital importers than a residence based system. For revenue purposes the mixed systems using a foreign tax credit are more like territorial taxation because the first right of taxation is allowed by the country of location of investment rather than the country of ownership.

The choice of residence versus territory-based tax systems can also affect the incidence of a tax through the induced flows of capital and can result in indirect distributional effects. For example, in a closed economy with capital inelastically supplied, the burden of a tax on capital income does in fact fall on the owners of capital. With a uniform rate on capital income, the corporate tax is also likely to fall on capital (Gravelle and Kotlikoff 1993). Such a tax imposed in a country engaged in international trade would have identical effects if all taxes were imposed on a residence basis. There is no incentive to move capital, and the after-tax return to capital falls regardless of the location of investment.

The consequences can be quite different, however, if a territorial system is used. If a country imposes or increases a tax unilaterally in such a system, capital invested within the country is reduced as the rate of return falls. The country imposing the tax will be left with a smaller capital stock and smaller domestic output. Under certain extreme conditions the effect of such a system would be to impose the burden on labor, the immobile domestic factor. Gravelle (1994) points out, however, that this conclusion only holds if capital is perfectly mobile and if domestic and imported goods are perfect substitutes. (In this case the pretax rate of return to capital must rise, the price of the product must remain fixed, and therefore the wage rate must fall by the amount that the capital return rises.) Once domestic and imported goods are treated as imperfect substitutes, it is possible for the price to rise and for part of the tax to be exported to foreign capital. Labor may in fact be unaffected by the tax.

These kinds of consequences make it clear that the incidence of tax in a world that largely or partially follows the precepts of territorial taxation is uncertain, but it is possible for a country to impose part of its tax burden on others given a territorial tax system.

Implications of the Analysis for the U.S. Tax System

International tax issues are less important if capital is not very mobile—that is, if investors view foreign and domestic investments as highly imperfect substitutes. The evidence on this issue is mixed, although all of it suggests that capital in different locations are not perfect substitutes. Reaching conclusions about the implications of international trade and capital flows for evaluating the U.S. tax structure is, however, uncertain even if capital is mobile because the United States cannot act alone. As suggested earlier, however, capital export neutrality has much to recommend itself. What changes might be considered to conform the U.S. system as closely as possible to capital export neutrality?

There are a variety of aspects of the U.S. tax system that are related directly or indirectly to evaluation of the system in an international environment. The following discussion is divided into the three issues:

fundamental explicit departures from capital export neutrality, problems of administration and coordination in the measurement of the tax base, and the interplay of the domestic tax distortions with international capital allocation.

Explicit Departures from Capital Export Neutrality
The option of pure residence-based taxation is not feasible given the normal practice of countries claiming the right to tax returns to investment located within their borders. This effect is not universal. Some countries do grant tax sparing or tax holidays in order to attract foreign investment. Moreover many countries have tax treaties with the United States that result in a largely residence based system at the personal level on dividends, interest, and capital gains.

Countries tend, however, to tax corporate source income generated within their borders. Given such a system, in some ways the tax credit system is a reasonable way to operate to move in the general direction of capital export neutrality. Under such a system foreign investment owned by domestic firms is taxed under the U.S. tax law, but a credit is granted to prevent double taxation. This system conforms with the first right of taxation granted to the country of location. This system also imposes a tax on foreign investment located in the United States. If the foreign tax rate is lower than the U.S. rate, capital export neutrality is achieved with respect to U.S. outbound investment, but the other country does not obtain capital export neutrality with respect to its investor's choice between domestic investment and investment in the United States. If the U.S. tax is lower than the foreign tax rate, outbound investment is discouraged, but this effect is no worse than the case where the United States employs a territorial system. If the foreign country employs a credit method, its investors will be indifferent between domestic and U.S. taxation; if the foreign country employs territorial taxation, inbound investment into the United States is encouraged. On the whole, short of movement to a true residence-based tax system, the best opportunities for efficient taxation are achieved when countries practice the credit approach.

There are, however, several respects in which the current system departs from capital export neutrality, which could be altered. (The provisions discussed below are addressed in much greater detail in Joint Committee on Taxation 1991.)

First, corporations may organize their foreign activities in subsidiaries incorporated under foreign laws, and in general, income of these foreign corporations, even though U.S. owned and controlled, are not subject to tax until income is repatriated in the form of dividends to the U.S. parent. (When dividends are paid, they are grossed up by the amount of foreign tax, U.S. corporate tax is imposed, and a foreign tax credit is allowed.) This deferral of tax moves toward a territory-based tax system and, of course is advantageous when the foreign taxing jurisdiction has low or nonexistent tax rates.[2]

Because this provision was used to avoid U.S. tax by shifting income into corporations in low tax jurisdictions, certain types of income earned by controlled foreign corporations (CFCs) that are more than 50 percent owned by U.S. corporations are currently taxed under Subpart F of the tax code. Most of this income is income of a passive nature that is easily moved, relating to sales, insurance, transportation, and similar activities. It would, however, be feasible to tax all such income and eliminate deferral entirely, moving closer to a system of capital export neutrality. Existing deferral rules are currently estimated to cause a revenue loss in excess of a $1 billion per year, according to estimates by the Joint Committee on Taxation.

Second, while the foreign tax credit is limited is to the U.S. tax rate, it does not apply separately to each investment in each country. There have been some rules limiting the averaging of the credit across certain broad categories of income, but these rules do not apply separately to each country. Thus excess unused credits from investments in a high-tax country can be used to offset U.S. tax otherwise due on investments in a low-tax country.

Third, the foreign tax credit applies against all taxes deemed to be income taxes, including subnational taxes, while taxes imposed by U.S. states and localities are only deductible. This differential treatment means that there may still be an incentive to invest abroad because of the additional domestic tax due at the state and local level. This effect is relatively small, since domestic subnational corporate tax rates are not large and are deductible from income.

Fourth, the foreign tax credit is limited to 90 percent of tax liability when the company falls under the minimum tax. While this rule prevents a company with some worldwide income from escaping U.S. tax liability altogether, it discourages outbound investment by allowing less than a full foreign tax credit.

Fifth, the United States provides some tax deferral to the domestic use of capital to produce goods for exports, thus allows some tax benefits for foreign sales corporations.[3]

Finally, there is a possessions tax credit for businesses operating in the U.S. possessions, and it effectively eliminates any U.S. tax on these operations. This provision is deliberately provided as a direct benefit to firms investing in the possessions. The provision's largest impact is on Puerto Rico. (This provision was recently restricted in a manner that converts it, in part, into a wage subsidy, which may target it more efficiently to helping individual workers in Puerto Rico. See the discussion of enterprise zones in chapter 9 for further examples of domestic incentives for geographic location.)

Even if all of these aspects were corrected, there would still be a failure of capital export neutrality because excess credits would still exist. Refunding excess credits would open the U.S. Treasury to foreign countries who could impose high taxes that would nevertheless be refunded by the United States. In addition individuals and firms could make portfolio investments (invest in stock of true foreign corporations) and capital export neutrality would be impossible to obtain.

Measurement of Income
Another practical difficulty in achieving efficient taxation, given that countries do not use residence-based taxation, is the fundamental difficulty of measuring the source of income. A U.S. corporation that operates abroad has income that accrues to capital invested in both places. It is often difficult to divide the income between the two locations. The two operations buy and sell goods from and to each other, but in many cases of relatively unique products there is no observed market price to determine the correct price. Moreover the domestic parent corporation may develop new technology, and it is difficult to measure the proper price charged to an affiliate for use of this technology if the technology is not otherwise licensed for use by unrelated firms. Additional funds for investment may be borrowed by either the parent company or the affiliate.

These problems have become extremely complex, since there is an incentive to locate taxable income in the jurisdiction that will yield the lowest overall taxes paid. In the case of a foreign subsidiary where foreign tax rates are low, there is an incentive to locate income in the foreign affiliate if some or all of the foreign affiliates profits are retained abroad (and thus not subject to current higher U.S. taxes). There are a variety of ways to achieve this purpose for a multinational corporation. Goods can be sold to the foreign affiliate at a low price, and goods can be purchased at a high price. If one company develops a new technology, the use of the technology can be licensed to the affiliate at a rate above or below the royalty rate that would be charged to an unrelated party. Borrowing could be restricted to the affiliate in the high-tax country.

The basic rules governing the allocation of income—through transfer pricing rules and through allocation of deductions—are in sections 482 and 861 of the Internal Revenue Code. These rules have been the source of many difficulties and taxpayer disputes—and the subject of numerous papers and studies (Duerr 1972; Treasury 1988; Frisch 1989). A detailed description of these rules can be found in Joint Tax Committee (1991).

Another problem with sourcing rules is the possibility of differences between the U.S. and foreign jurisdictions. Such differences can lead to double taxation of income if the foreign jurisdiction allocates more income to the foreign operation than the U.S. taxing authorities. Then income can become subject to foreign taxes without the benefit of a tax credit if the foreign tax authority's tax rate is high enough to generate unused credits. This problem arises in cases where the income is from a branch or with repatriated dividends; it is most severe in the case of high-tax jurisdictions.

In some ways sourcing problems seem insoluble. The most recent proposed regulations in this area by the United States would try to identify similar businesses and measure the typical rates of return earned. Another approach would be to use an allocation formula based on capital, labor, sales, or some combination of these.

It is clear, however, that deferral of foreign source income aggravates this problem. Some of the most notorious cases of battles fought out between the Internal Revenue Service and the taxpayer in the courts are cases where operation of the subsidiary is in a foreign low-tax jurisdiction where profits are not currently taxed to the U.S. parent. Taxing such income on a current basis would eliminate the incentive to shift income to these subsidiaries. It would not of course solve the general problem of disputes between national tax jurisdictions, although there are mechanisms for negotiating such agreements.

Relationship of Domestic Tax Distortions to International Taxation
Flaws in the taxation of income in the domestic tax system can also
have implications for the treatment of outbound and inbound investment. The changes in the Tax Reform Act of 1986 settled some of these
issues. For example, the previous investment credit was restricted to
domestic investment, causing a disincentive for outbound investment
that was not eligible for the credit.

One of the most serious problems with failure to measure income
properly is in the tax treatment of interest income. Because the inflation portion of interest is allowed to be deducted by corporations the
tax rate at the firm level is negative. As a result the effective tax rate on
debt-financed inbound investment in the United States is negative,
and the rules for efficient taxation are not satisfied. If other countries
follow the same practices, the departure from efficient taxation will be
a function of the different rates of inflation as well as the tax rates—
both corporate and personal. To achieve efficient taxation, not only
would income have to be taxed on a residence basis, but income
should be corrected for inflation both in its deduction at the firm level
and its inclusion at the individual level.

There are of course a variety of differentials in the taxation of different types of investment—corporate and noncorporate, different types
of assets, and industries. In general, the best approach would appear
to be to strive for a neutral domestic tax system, as it seems unlikely
that differentials in taxation that prove to be inefficient in a closed
economy would contribute to efficiency in an open economy.

Possible Revisions in International Tax Treatment
If the objective is to move in the direction of conforming the U.S. tax
more closely to capital export neutrality, certain revisions that would
move in that direction would be appropriate. These revisions include
current taxation of earnings of controlled foreign corporations, application of the foreign tax credit on a per country basis, and revision of
various special rules that depart from neutral taxation such as foreign
sales corporations and the possessions credit. Efforts could also be
made to further develop regulations that lead to correct allocations of
profit.

The international environment also complicates the issue of reform
of the corporate tax system. The recent Treasury study (1992) on this

issue devotes considerable attention to how to treat the foreign tax credit and inbound investment in the case of an integration system. If firms are effectively taxed on a partnership basis, capital export neutrality might now be violated in many instances because outbound investment would be taxed at a higher tax rate than inbound investment. To some extent these problems make alternative approaches, such as the elimination of tax on interest and dividends or the approach of a single level of tax at the corporate level on both interest and dividends, more attractive.

The Desirability of Capital Income Taxes: Revisiting the Issue in an Open Economy

We return in this section to the issue addressed in chapter 2. While the previous sections have addressed structural features of a capital income tax and how those features cause an inefficient allocation of capital, this section returns to a focus on the domestic tax system and whether the desirability of capital income tax is increased or decreased by consideration of an open economy.

Consider first the behavioral response to a decrease in capital income taxes in a closed economy. The tax shift may or may not increase savings, depending on the type of tax substitution. Suppose, however, that it does increase domestic savings and also increases welfare. The increased capital stock will eventually drive down the pretax rate of return on capital and thereby dampen the savings response. Assuming that labor supply is either constant or reduced, the wage rate will then rise. One can then, at least in theory, measure the welfare gain of individuals in the domestic economy in order to evaluate the desirability of the tax shift—that welfare gain depends on the ability of firms to substitute capital for labor, the intertemporal substitution elasticity that determines the power of the savings response, and the labor supply elasticity (willingness to substitute between consumption and leisure). As indicated in chapter 2, there is not any clear evidence on the magnitude or even the direction of this effect.

To consider the consequences in an open economy, one must consider whether the capital income tax is a residence-based tax or a source-based tax. For a residence-based tax savings will increase as before, but some of the savings will be exported (invested abroad). How much is exported depends on the mobility of capital across national boundaries and the size of the country relative to the world. Because the capital stock rises less, the rate of return is driven down less, the savings response is diluted less, and the wage rate rises less. The distribution of welfare in the domestic economy will be different; the efficiency gains would likely be larger. At the same time, however, individuals in the rest of the world will be affected, and a decision must be made as to whether to consider the welfare effects for these individuals.

Consider now a territorial or source-based tax where the tax reduction will apply to both domestic and foreign suppliers of capital actually employed in the domestic economy. The reduction in tax will increase the rate of return earned by investing in the domestic economy by both domestic and foreign suppliers. Capital will flow into the country, driving down the rate of return. This effect will tend to reduce domestic savings and dampen any behavioral response to the tax via increased savings. Welfare gains of domestic individuals will likely be smaller than in the closed economy case. The flow of capital into the domestic economy will, however, increase the rate of return in the rest of the world and increase the savings of foreigners (assuming that savings response is positive).

The outcome is even more complex for the mixed systems that are in place in many countries. Other countries that employ a credit imputation system may simply collect more taxes on their investments in the United States without changing the rate of return earned by these countries. U.S. firms investing abroad will receive no greater rate of return abroad. In that case the savings response in the United States will be closer to that of a closed economy, although some of that savings may still flow abroad.

These illustrations indicate that the desirability of lowering capital income taxes and the attendant efficiency gains depend on what type of tax is being altered and what systems of taxation are being used by other countries. It also depends on whose efficiency is being considered. Moreover, depending on the type of tax change being contemplated and the surrounding tax environment, lowering taxes may or may not cause a misallocation of capital across countries.

This brief sketch suggests that the desirability of capital income taxation is even more complicated an issue to consider in an open economy environment. Slemrod (1988) addresses these and other issues in more detail. A crucial concern is the mobility of capital: If capital is not very mobile, then the closed economy results will obtain in large part. As noted earlier, the degree of capital mobility is in considerable doubt.

Unfortunately, the uncertainties surrounding the analysis of taxation in an open economy provide little guidance to the question of the desirable overall level of capital income taxation. As suggested in the overall review of capital income taxation in this book, economic theory and analysis has more to say about how a capital income tax should be designed than how large it should be.

11 Economic Analysis of Capital Income Taxation and Tax Policy

Tax revision involves trade-offs between administrative, distributional, revenue, and efficiency considerations. Nor is the economist's ideal solution always politically feasible. But, as suggested throughout this book, one is struck by the gulf between the arguments that dominate the public debate over tax policy and the arguments that economists would address.

This final chapter contains two parts. The first part is an overview of what type of tax revisions, as suggested by the analysis in this book, lead to a more efficient tax system. Many of these revisions are also identified by Steuerle (1991). The second part contrasts these changes with those revisions that have been at the forefront of the public debate, and explores some of the reasons for the differences in focus. This second section discusses some of the processes of making tax policy that might be refined to facilitate a focus on economic analysis.

Moving toward a More Efficient Tax System

The preceding analysis has identified some fundamental provisions, and some minor provisions, that cause the tax system to be less efficient. The one fundamental aspect of the tax law that appears to cause the greatest tax distortions is the double tax on corporate income. Integration of corporate and individual income taxes, or even a partial alleviation of the double taxation problem, would probably contribute the most, per dollar of revenue lost, to increasing allocative efficiency.

Mismeasurement of capital income due to inflation can also affect the neutrality of the tax system. There are several ways in which inflation causes the mismeasurement of income: It causes interest payments and receipts to be overstated, it causes the value of FIFO inventory deductions to be understated, it causes depreciation to be understated, and it causes capital gains to be overstated in real terms. But, aside from the inventory correction, indexation of capital income by itself may not be the most attractive option.

Indexation could exacerbate certain distortions, since in many cases, the effects of inflation may be offsetting other provisions. For example, while inflation causes debt finance in the corporate sector to be heavily favored over equity, this same provision also benefits corporate investment relative to noncorporate investment. Indexation of interest payments would be, however, clearly desirable if accompanied by relief for the corporate double tax on equity taxes. Similarly indexing depreciation for inflation would create distortions across short-lived and long-lived assets where none currently exist and would benefit these assets relative to inventories (whether indexed or not). A combination of appropriate lengthening of lives and indexation of depreciation for inflation could, however, lead to a more efficient system.

Finally, indexing capital gains might not be as efficient as an exclusion of equal cost in reducing the lock-in effects of the capital gains tax. The exclusion is relatively less beneficial to assets held for a long period of time that are more affected by lock-in.

Another distorting aspect of the current tax system is the beneficial treatment of owner-occupied housing. It would probably not be feasible politically or from an administrative standpoint to tax imputed rent on owner-occupied housing, however. A second-best, and perhaps more modest, revision might be to limit the amount of mortgage interest that can be deducted (or to disallow interest deductions entirely). Even this solution has the drawback of favoring equity over debt finance, however.

To achieve major revisions could cost revenues. One way of alleviating this revenue loss would be to increase the taxation of returns on pension funds. The analysis of pension funds indicates that these investments are not likely to be marginal, so taxes could be increased on them without affecting economic efficiency.

For broad structural revisions of this nature, the proposal outlined by Treasury (1992) for a comprehensive business income tax (CBIT) is interesting. Under their proposal the personal level tax on corporate income (dividends and capital gains) would be eliminated. In addition interest deductions would be disallowed, but such interest would not be taxable to the recipient.

The Treasury suggested that the same tax rate be applied to unincorporated businesses. The uniform tax rate approach might be difficult to implement, for it would require separating capital from labor income of unincorporated businesses. But much of the current distortion would still be eliminated even if unincorporated businesses continued to have the individual rates apply. The proposition would, in a fairly simple fashion, accomplish most of the desired structural revisions. It would maintain the current corporate tax on pensions and also impose that tax on interest income, by taxing at the firm level.

CBIT would lose very little revenue (and indeed could raise revenue if the higher corporate rate were applied to noncorporate businesses), allowing a somewhat lower corporate rate. It could be extended to mortgage interest as well. Alternatively, mortgage interest could still be deducted but be taxed to the recipient. To avoid the holding of mortgages by tax exempts such as pension funds, such direct mortgage interest could be subject to a tax (at the corporate rate) when received by pensions and other tax-exempt holders. (Mortgages channeled through corporate intermediaries would be taxed at that point.)

This approach would largely eliminate the distortion between corporate and noncorporate investment. It would completely eliminate corporate financial distortions, eliminate the lock-in effect on corporate stock, and reduce the favoritism toward owner-occupied housing. At the same time it would avoid many of the complexities inherent in full corporate integration and in direct inflation indexing.

There are a number of more specific revisions to capital income taxes that would also appear to improve the efficiency of the tax system; some of them might raise revenues to finance other improvements. Indexation of inventories and depreciation has already been mentioned. While the current combination of accelerated depreciation and failure to index roughly offset each other, this tenuous balance depends on inflation rates being around 4 or 5 percent. At much higher or much lower inflation rates, these effective tax rates could change substantially, especially for short-lived assets. Moreover providing a pattern of capital cost recovery that more closely corresponds to economic depreciation would put new firms on a more even footing with existing businesses, since new businesses do not initially earn enough income to use all of the accelerated depreciation deductions. Allowing this indexed basis in figuring capital gains would also reduce the lock-in effect for the sale of real property, since gain would not be exaggerated due to accelerated depreciation or overstated due to inflation.

The minimum tax and the passive loss restriction appear to lack much justification. Moreover an indexation of interest or, as proposed by Treasury, a disallowance of interest deductions, combined with a better match between tax and economic depreciation, would render these provisions largely redundant in the long run.

There are a number of minor revisions to the tax law that could be considered. There seems to be little justification for the generous benefits applied to intangible drilling costs and mining development costs. Indeed these activities would continue to receive benefits because of loss deductions for unproductive properties, even if drilling and development costs were capitalized. Percentage depletion also seems to have little justification on efficiency grounds. Other possible revisions, if revenue needs to be raised, are to capitalize advertising expenditures, to tax credit unions and cooperatives the same as other businesses, and to restrict further or eliminate the tax exemption for state and local bond interest. The latter revision might be offset with some other, less distorting, benefits to the states and localities (e.g., grants).

Taxation in an international environment would probably best approximate efficient tax policy by moving more closely to capital export neutrality. This approach might justify current taxation of earnings of foreign subsidiaries, imposing a per country foreign tax credit limit, and repealing the foreign sales corporation provisions. The possessions credit also interferes with capital export neutrality, although it might be desirable to provide some other form of aid to Puerto Rico. The comprehensive business income tax outlined by the Treasury Department would mesh nicely with the foreign tax credit mechanism. The enforcement of sourcing of income rules would be facilitated by these changes as well, since firms would have less incentive to allocate income to low-tax foreign jurisdictions.

The analysis in chapter 5 also suggests some directions in which tax policy should *not* move if the aim is an efficient tax system. Investment subsidies may be desirable, but they can easily be designed in a fashion that is inefficient—such as an equipment investment credit. Partial expensing is an efficient approach.

Investment subsidies are, however, simply a movement toward consumption taxation. If they are considered desirable, they might be more effectively done simply by replacing depreciation with expensing. The advantage of debt finance could be eliminated by disallowing interest deductions (and not including interest payment in income). Perhaps the most serious problem with this approach is the occasional purchase of investment properties by individuals and new start up firms that would not have the cash flow to absorb the initial investment costs. One possible way around this problem is to continue to deduct interest but to include net borrowing in income.

Such a system might be resisted by declining firms that would no longer receive depreciation deductions, and would not be making any new investments. (This effect would also occur with a switch to a consumption tax base, such as a value-added tax.) To ameliorate this problem, expensing could be allowed for investments in excess of a fixed base that sums to current depreciation deductions. For a firm growing at a normal rate, this approach would be no different from disallowing depreciation deductions; declining firms would still be able to continue depreciation.

Such tax subsidies to investment move the tax system toward a consumption tax base. In chapter 2 the question was posed as to whether a capital income tax had an appropriate place in an efficient tax system. The answer to that question, even on pure efficiency grounds, was not clear. Nevertheless, one alternative might be an explicit shift to a system that does not tax capital.

Options include a wage tax base and a consumption tax base. Most proposals by those who do not favor an income tax system have been to move in the direction of a consumption tax base, in part, because a wage tax already exists in the form of a payroll tax and, in part, because the consumption tax will, in theory, yield a larger tax base. It is useful to explore the possibility of an explicit consumption tax approach.

Although a consumption tax approach is theoretically straightforward, there are some serious obstacles to overcome. Two widely disparate approaches are frequently discussed—a shift to an indirect tax such as a value-added tax (VAT) or a sales tax and a direct consumption tax approach that would be collected much as the current income tax is collected.

Imposing an indirect consumption tax would be quite straightforward. One could use a VAT so that a firm pays a tax on its gross income and receives a credit for taxes paid by its suppliers. There would be no direct tax on individuals. The same approach, often referred to as a *business transfer tax,* is really a subtraction method VAT. Using such an approach, businesses would simply subtract all purchases (of intermediate products and of capital acquisitions) from its receipts. This tax base would be quite different from the current business income tax since no deductions for wages or interest paid would be allowed. Another approach would be to tax all goods at final sale through a national sales tax.

There are, nevertheless, some very serious drawbacks to VATs and sales taxes on distributional and administrative grounds (Treasury Department 1984; Congressional Budget Office 1992b; Gravelle 1992b). There are administrative problems with this tax base, particularly in the receipt of income from consumer durables such as owner-occupied housing. Moreover there would be pressures to rebate the tax on government purchases (including state and local purchases), that would erode the tax base.

The most serious problem with this indirect tax approach is that it would substitute a regressive tax for the current progressive income tax. It would involve a shift in the distribution of tax burdens across incomes—and of course, as indicated in chapter 2, some shift across generations. It would also require a one-time increase in prices if a fall in the nominal wage and possible short-run contractionary effects are to be avoided.

The problem of abandoning a progressive tax could be dealt with in part by choosing instead a direct tax mechanism. In this case income would be taxed to individuals and corporations, but savings would be deducted and borrowing included. Progressivity could be maintained with respect to this consumption base. This direct tax approach was considered by the Treasury Department in its Blueprints for Basic Tax Reform (1977).

Although academic studies have frequently focused on this direct tax approach, there would be some surprising and unfamiliar aspects to taxpayers. Such a system, for example, would require individuals to include borrowed funds in their tax base. (Since the return from owner-occupied housing is already exempt from tax, purchases of housing and mortgage borrowing could be excluded from the system.) Moreover taxpayers would be required to keep records of their financial transactions. Although such a consumed income tax has been discussed in the economics literature, in practice it is very difficult to envision such a system.

One possibility is a hybrid system, such as that proposed by Hall and Rabushka (1986) or Bradford's X-tax (1986). These systems involve carving out the wage portion of the consumption tax base and taxing it to individuals, just as in the current income tax system. Although Hall and Rabushka proposed a flat rate tax, it is simple enough to make the wage tax at the individual level progressive (as suggested by Bradford). Thus businesses would subtract wages paid and purchases of both supplies and capital goods from income. Individuals would be taxed only on their wages, unless they run a business. Noncorporate businesses would compute the tax base in the same manner as corporations; partners would include their share in income. Like the expensing-in-place-of-depreciation alternatives mentioned above, however, such a system could create problems for start-up firms and occasional large investments by individuals. This type of approach is not radically different from a proposal to replace depreciation with expensing. Indeed, were the Treasury's comprehensive business tax proposal to be combined with the substitution of expensing for depreciation, we would in fact obtain the same general base as the Hall-Rabushka or X-tax approach. There would be no capital income to tax to individuals except through their direct ownership of business assets, and such a tax would not be a tax on new investment but rather a lump-sum tax on old capital.

Whether consumption taxation is achieved through some explicit mechanism, or through modifications of the income tax base to allow full or partial expensing, the issues of distribution across generations and uncertainties with respect to efficiency gain emerge. Such uncertainties seem less problematic with fundamental income tax revisions, such as the integration of the corporate income tax. Corporate tax

integration remains the clearest candidate for revision in moving the
income tax to a more efficient system.

The Tax Policy-making Process

In the popular debate we see no surge of interest in corporate tax integration. Although there is agitation about the minimum tax and the
passive loss restriction on the part of the business and real estate lob-
bying groups, there is no move afoot to make serious changes in these
provisions. Indeed much of the agenda suggested by the efficiency
analysis is absent from the public debate.

Consider the two provisions that have dominated the debate over
capital income taxation in the past few years—cutting the capital
gains tax and restoring individual retirement accounts for high
income individuals. Using standard economic analysis of where to
cut capital income taxes as discussed in this book, the case for restoring IRAs seems weak. If these investments are largely inframarginal,
they cannot contribute to a more efficient tax system; indeed, they use
up revenues that could be devoted to other areas. They add to the
complexity of the tax system and benefit a narrow and well off class
of individuals (only about 15 percent of taxpayers contributed to IRAs
and only the top third of the income distribution would benefit from
this restoration).

Capital gains tax cuts may contribute to economic efficiency. They
would probably not top the list of provisions most likely to produce
welfare gains, although a good case can be made for capital gains
relief to corporate stock. Among some groups, indexation of capital
gains for inflation has proved particularly appealing. Also proposals
for prospective capital gains benefits have received considerable support.

As noted earlier, many provisions that appear to score high on efficiency grounds receive scant attention in the political process. Despite
the interest in corporate tax integration expressed by many economists and many Treasury Departments over the years, corporate tax
integration has never made much headway. A proposal for a dividend deduction and indexation of interest made by the Treasury in its
original tax proposal in 1984 was diluted and eventually eliminated
entirely from the tax reform bill as it moved through the White House
and the Congress.

Why have particular provisions appeared so persistently in the tax debate, and why are others absent from the debate? The agenda before the public at any one time relates to in part to the preferences of important individuals in the tax policy process. Moreover some changes are popular with certain constituencies. Both IRAs and capital gains taxes have constituencies who see an immediate economic benefit. The state of affairs is considerably different from that surrounding corporate tax integration. While one might expect corporations to be advocates of corporate tax integration, such a change may actually be viewed with disdain by corporate managers who fear increased pressures to pay out dividends to stockholders. Most proposals envision the corporation as the point to either apply the tax or to withhold taxes of shareholders, so corporations do not see an immediate effect on the bottom line as they would with provisions such as investment credits and accelerated depreciation.

There are also other reasons for the popularity of the certain provisions in the public debate and the lack of popularity of others that are disturbing for the formulation of optimal tax policy. These reasons include short-run revenue requirements, misperceptions about the effects of tax benefits on savings and economic growth, and misperceptions about fairness and equity.

Revenue Considerations

Certainly one reason for the attention to certain proposals is the constraints of the budget process. Under the current budget rules a revenue loss from a tax cut has to be made up from some other source over a five-year budget horizon. Capital gains tax cuts were argued by the Bush administration to actually gain revenue because of the large assumed behavioral responses. Much of the debate over the capital gains tax has been over the revenue consequences of these provisions. Given the wide disparity in econometric estimates of this response, it has been possible to argue that cutting the capital gains tax is a "free lunch" from a budgetary standpoint, even in the wake of a growing disenchantment with "supply side economics."

Indeed some proposals have also been made to make capital gains tax cuts (especially indexing gains for inflation) prospective—only on newly acquired assets. This approach can in fact lead to a short-run *gain* as individuals cash in some assets in order to qualify for future tax relief. This type of indexing can cost a great deal in the long run but may cost very little or even gain revenue over the budget horizon.

A similar revenue issue emerged in some versions of IRAs. Certain proposals have been made to allow so-called back-loaded IRAs. The original IRA allowed an up-front deduction for contributions when made and taxation upon receipt, the same treatment as that applied to pensions. The back-loaded IRA would not allow the initial deduction but would also not tax receipts—just is like a tax exempt bond. These two alternatives are the same in economic terms (they produce zero effective tax rates on the returns to investment), but they have vastly different budgetary effects over time. Because of the annual dollar limits on contributions, the revenue cost of the back loaded IRAs (which reflect forgone taxes on interest earned on the total accumulation of tax favored assets) grows rapidly and reaches a higher steady state peak that front-loaded IRAs. Thus the back-loaded plans have a very small cost in the budget horizon compared to the traditional forms. Indeed some plans even proposed to allow individuals to shift funds from traditional to back-loaded IRAs without paying the full tax on withdrawals. These plans create an incentive to roll over contributions, pay tax, and, like prospective capital gains relief, raise some money in the short run to offset or more than offset the small initial revenue loss. Even though the budget process has probably kept the deficit from being larger than it is, having the acceptability of tax policies hinge so heavily on short-run versus long-run revenue consequences seems unlikely to contribute to the making of optimal tax policy.

Understanding Effects on Savings and Economic Growth

An argument that was often advanced in support of both IRAs and capital gains cuts was the effect on savings and economic growth. Yet these provisions would probably be low on the list of ways to increase savings. First, the most direct route to increase savings would be to reduce the deficit, given the uncertainty about the effects of tax changes on savings. Second, both of these provisions seem poor candidates even among tax incentives for increasing savings. IRAs involve inframarginal investments that in theory ought not to increase savings. Moreover, as discussed in chapter 8, despite one econometric study that found a savings response, there is little evidence in the literature as a whole and in critiques of that study that IRAs increased savings. This evidence is, in any case, a slender reed on which to base a savings policy.

Capital gains tax cuts also don't rate very high as savings incentives, since they benefit existing capital. A capital gains cut is like a shift to wage taxation and thus is less likely to increase savings than a consumption-type cut.

If capital income tax cuts are financed through increased deficits, then the effect on savings is much more likely to be negative. Another way of stating this policy conclusion is that if some program can be cut or if some additional revenue source becomes feasible to tap, the best way to translate such increases in revenue into savings is for the government to save that increase directly through reductions in the deficit.

The assumption that reducing capital income taxes will have positive and significant effects on the savings rate is surely one the most important myths that governs tax policy-making, and one that needs to be dispelled if we are to achieve a more efficient tax system.

Understanding Fairness

The concept of fairness is often evoked in the debate over taxes and yet so often misapplied. For example, many individuals might willingly approve tax benefits to unincorporated or small businesses while disapproving of any corporate tax reduction, although the owners of these businesses might, on average, be more wealthier than the typical corporate stockholder. Indexing capital gains for inflation may be acceptable to many individuals who would not accept an exclusion, because the former is "fair" and the exclusion is just another tax break for the wealthy. This different viewpoint may persist, even if the two proposals have equal effects over all of the taxation of capital gains.

In introducing "fairness" into the tax policy debate, the major problem is the failure to recognize behavioral responses and tax incidence. Although there are some disputes about the incidence of the corporate tax, there is no dispute at all about the fact that someone—

stockholders, capital owners in general, labor, or consumers—must pay the tax.

Careful thought about tax incidence would also reveal the fallacy in seeing most tax provisions regarding capital income as having any effect on equity aside from distributional effects across income class-es. (Tax breaks for pensions, which are inframarginal, are an excep-tion and do have horizontal equity implications.) If a particular type of income is granted preferential treatment, then there should be behavioral responses that tend to equate after-tax returns—and it is in differences in after-tax returns that horizontal equity is violated. Differentiating across individuals with respect to the investments they hold—which can be easily altered—is a completely different proposition from distinguishing among individuals with respect to how may family members they support or what extraordinary med-ical bills they are paying—which cannot be easily altered.

One of the most dramatic instances of inappropriately appealing to fairness was in the case of the minimum tax on corporations, which assumed that it was "unfair" for some corporations to pay relatively little tax. Rather either pretax returns or asset values should have already adjusted to reflect any tax differentials. The minimum tax was not needed to ensure fairness; its role in enhancing efficiency, as dis-cussed in chapter 7, is somewhat suspect.

Another peculiar viewpoint that reflects this misunderstanding of equity is the apparent acceptability of inflation indexing of capital gains by those who would find an explicit exclusion unattractive. For many reasons—efficiency reasons having to do with a lock-in effect, the relative effects on the corporate and noncorporate sectors, and administrative reasons that are quite compelling—a reduction in capi-tal gains tax rates might actually be preferred. If some assets benefit relatively more than others, so will the demand for these assets, with the expected result of choosing one approach over another a change in pretax rate of return. This is an efficiency issue, not an issue of equity.

Possible Revisions in the Policy-making Process

There is no way to focus tax policy on those provisions whose revi-sion might yield the greatest efficiency gains or to straighten out understanding of the fundamental equity and efficiency issues involved, other than by intellectual argument. There are, however, procedural revisions that might make the system work somewhat better in introducing economic analysis into the debate.

Most of the changes would involve changes in the official documents that are produced when a tax change is proposed. Such documents, produced by the administration and by the Joint Committee on Taxation, typically include revenue estimates and distributional tables. (The Joint Committee on Taxation discusses the reasons for many of the decisions they make on these issues in a document published in 1993.)

The revenue estimates provided currently extend over a brief time horizon—typically no more than five years. For many provisions this period of time is insufficient to reveal the true cost of the provisions. The argument for limiting the time horizon for revenue estimates is typically that the magnitudes become more uncertain the farther into the future they go.

This argument should be reconsidered, however. The need for revenue estimates is not so much to predict dollar magnitudes of revenue costs but to illustrate the general pattern of the cost. Part of the need is to prevent tax policies from being chosen simply because they look cheap in the short run. Thus the fundamental questions are whether a tax provision will remain relative constant as a percentage of GNP and whether it will grow rapidly (or decline rapidly) in the future. One does not need precise, or even imprecise, dollar forecasts of the economy to answer this question. Indeed what one typically needs is a reasonably simple model of the activity under question and some simple assumptions involving growth rates over time.

Given that the establishment of general patterns is possible without a precise forecast of the economy, one option would be to adopt a revenue estimating system that would conform uneven revenue patterns to even ones of the same value (Gravelle 1993a). Proposals that are economically identical would also be identical in the revenue cost process. This result could be accomplished by taking the present value of tax losses and converting losses to a constant-relative-to-GNP annuity. Tax rate changes, investment credits, and all other provisions that already have a constant pattern of loss relative to output would not be affected, but a whole variety of provisions that have costs that are large in the short term or in the long term would be put on a consistent cost basis. Failing that approach, a second-best approach would be to accompany each revenue estimate with a steady state estimate—that is, an estimate of what the cost of the provision would be had it been in place a long time. Such steady state estimates are not consistent as is the present value/annuity approach discussed above, but they would at least alert policymakers when unusual revenue patterns are involved.

A second innovation that would be desirable would be to allocate corporate income taxes to individuals in distributional tables. Even though there is some dispute about the proper allocation, such an approach would reinforce the notion that the corporate tax is a tax on individuals, and it would make the assessment of tax packages including corporate and noncorporate changes more consistent.

Distributional tables should also be provided that include measures that economists find meaningful for understanding distributional consequences. For example, distributional data are often provided with only dollar amounts of tax change across the income classes, or occasionally with percentage changes in tax liability. The common measure economists would use is percentage changes in after-tax income. Gravelle (1992a) illustrates how enormously different a distributional picture is painted by these different conventions. Since perceptions can so important in the policy debate, such a consistent reporting of distributional consequences, if not the only distributional measure provided, certainly should be *one* of the measures provided. (Indeed official statistics often don't even include enough data to calculate these measures.)

These innovations in the process of analyzing tax legislative proposals are fairly straightforward and could become part of a standard analysis applied to each tax program considered. Others may be somewhat more visionary but are well worth consideration. One is to provide distributional effects by generation. Kotlikoff (1992) provides a detailed discussion of generational accounting and Gravelle (1992a) investigates the generational effects of the Tax Reform Act of 1986. Another is to provide distributional tables that reflect effects on individuals with different lifetime earnings.

Yet another innovation is to provide more analysis of efficiency effects of competing policies, and analysis of how particular provisions alter effective tax rates on different forms of investment. The efficiency analysis has primarily been left to a hit or miss process of individual researchers studying the issue; the Treasury Corporate Tax Integration Study (1992) was an exception that specifically focused on the issue.

Some of these suggestions are to prevent a major misunderstanding of the effects of specific policies or to avoid "smoke and mirrors" games with the budget process. To achieve a more efficient tax system requires a more focused policy-making process.

Steuerle (1991) suggested that the 1990 Budget Act suffered from a lack of direction. If one views the 1986 Tax Reform Act as one of the most successful in recent history in achieving a more efficient and equitable revision of the tax code, then the lessons learned are that the process began with some sort of vision on the part of the Reagan administration based on economic principles of efficiency, equity, and simplicity (part of that vision was a more neutral income tax system) and that the specifics of a legislative reform program were spelled out and eventually proposed by the administration. There are occasions where visions but no action occurred. One such occasion is the Treasury Integration Study (1992). There are also, sadly, many occasions of action without vision. To return to the theological metaphor with which the book begins: The state in which we find the tax system is due to both sins of omission and sins of commission.

Appendix A:
History of Capital
Income Taxation in the
United States

This appendix provides a history of the major provisions of the U.S. tax code affecting the taxation of capital income. The history is organized by topic. Topics include—in order—tax rates, depreciation policy, the investment tax credit, inventory accounting, capital gains taxes, minimum taxes, retirement income (pensions, individual retirement accounts, taxation of life insurance reserves etc.), housing and consumer interest, the research and experimentation tax credit, tax treatment of the extractive industries, tax-exempt bonds, special taxation of certain businesses (financial institutions, insurance companies, cooperatives, and nonprofits), and international tax rules. A list of major tax legislation is appended, along with the sources used to compile this history.

Tax Rates

Tax rates were initially quite low in the income tax for both corporations and individuals. The 1909 corporate tax was set at 1 percent. The rate was raised to 2 percent in 1916 and 6 percent in 1917. Between 1918 and 1935 the rate hovered around 12 and 13 percent (12 percent in 1918, 10 percent in 1919–21, 12.5 percent in 1922–24, 13 percent in 1925, 13.5 percent in 1926–27, 12 percent in 1928, 11 percent in 1929, 12 percent in 1930–31, and 13.5 percent in 1932–35)

During this period flat exemptions were allowed at various times. A $5,000 exemption was allowed in 1909, but the exemption was eliminated in 1913. A $2,000 exemption prevailed in 1918–27, a $3,000 exemption in 1928–31, and no exemption in 1932–35.

In 1936–37 the rates of tax were differentiated on retained and distributed earnings and graduated. All earnings were subject to a tax ranging from 8 to 15 percent, with the top rate applying to income over $40,000. Undistributed profits were subject to a surtax ranging from 7 to 27 percent. This split rate system was eliminated in 1938, when taxes ranged from 12.5 to 16 percent on the first $25,000 and 19 percent on amounts over $25,000.

In 1940 a rather peculiar rate structure was adopted, with rates rising and then falling. On the first $25,000, rates ranged from 14.85 to 18.7 percent; then rates went up to 38.3 percent, then to 36.9 percent for income over $31,964, then back to 24 percent for incomes over $38,565. In 1941 rates ranged from 21 to 25 percent on the first $25,000, 44 percent until income reached $38,461, than 31 percent thereafter. From 1942 to 1949 rates were applied to the first $25,000 (25 to 29 present in 1942–1945 and 25–29 present in 1946–49), the second $25,000 (53 percent), and amounts over $50,000 (40 percent in 1942–45 and 38 percent in 1946–49). This notch rate system, which targeted an overall effective tax rate, proved a source of some contention.

From 1950 through 1974 a lower corporate rate applied only on the first $25,000. This lower rate was 23 percent in 1950, 28.75 percent in 1951, 30 percent in 1952–63, and 22 percent in 1964–74. The rate on income above $25,000 was 42 percent in 1950, 50.75 percent in 1951, 52 percent from 1952–63, 50 percent in 1964, and 48 percent from 1965–74. Also a 10 percent surcharge applied to all rates in 1968–69, and a 2.5 percent surcharge applied to rates in 1970.

Beginning in 1975, a graduated rate structure was adopted. From 1975 to 1978 rates were 20 percent on the first $25,000, 22 percent on the next $25,000, and 48 percent on income above $50,000. For 1979–87, different rates were applied to the first four $25,000 increments of income: These rates were 17, 20, 30, and 40 percent in 1979–81. The first two rates were 16 and 19 percent for 1981 and 15 and 18 percent for 1983–86. For 1987 they were 15, 16.5, 27.5, and 37 percent. The top rate was 46 percent for 1979–86, but a notch rate of 51 percent was in place in 1984–86 on income between $1,000,000 and $1,405,500. In 1987 the rate was 42.5 for $100,000 to $335,000, 40 percent for $335,000 to $1,000,000, 42.5 percent for $1,000,000 to $1,405,000, and 40 percent on income over $1,405,000. In 1988 rates were 15 percent on the first $50,000, 25 percent for $50,000 to $75,000, and 34 percent afterward with a notch rate of 39 percent on income between $100,000 and $335,000.

In 1993 the corporate tax rate was increased to 35 percent for taxable income in excess of $10 million. The benefit of the 34 percent rate was phased out at 3 percent of the excess when the firm reaches an income of $15 million, leading to another notch rate of 38 percent between $15,000,000 and $18,333,333.33.

The individual rate structure is too detailed to present here. Initially income tax rates were very low, ranging from 1 to 7 percent, with large exemptions relative to income. The early income tax covered only a small portion of the population initially. The top rate was quite high in the 1917–21 period, dropped over the 1920s, rose again to relatively high levels through 1981 (where at times the rate was as high as 94 percent). Generally, the period 1942–63 was characterized by the highest top rates; top rates dropped until they reached 70 percent in 1971, 50 percent in 1982, and 28 percent (with a notch rate of 33 percent) by 1988. The top rate was increased to 31 percent in 1990, when the notch was eliminated. In 1993 the top rate was increased to 39.6 percent. The coverage of the tax increased over time, and prior to 1986 covered even individuals defined as living in poverty; exemptions were increased in the 1986 law to eliminate poverty-level families from coverage of the tax.

Depreciation Policy

Much of the development of depreciation policy is through the regulatory rather than the statutory process. Indeed for much of the history of the tax, the tax code itself merely made an allowance for depreciation with specifics left to the taxpayers or Treasury regulations.

The Civil War income tax of 1861–72 made no mention of depreciation, but the 1894 law explicitly allowed it, and this legislative reference to depreciation continued when the modern corporate income tax began in 1909 and the overall income tax in 1913. Regulations indicated that this provision included an accounting for obsolescence as well as wear and tear and exhaustion. For purposes of the current income tax, dating from 1913, depreciation policy can be divided into phases: 1913 to 1934, 1934 to 1954, 1954 to 1962, 1962 to 1970, 1971 to 1980, 1981 to 1986, and 1987 to present. Depreciation has always been based on historical cost.

1913 to 1934: Depreciation at the Taxpayer's Discretion

Extraordinary as it may seem today, for the first twenty-one years of the income tax law, the determination of depreciable lives was left to the taxpayer. The then Bureau of Internal Revenue rarely challenged the taxpayer's choice. A straight line method, familiar in accounting, was also used for tax accounting. Indeed the first Bulletin F issued in 1920 indicated that it was impractical to prescribe lives. This document also indicated that the Bureau approved only the straight line method (or unit of production method generally used in natural resources). In 1931 the Bureau issued another version of Bulletin F. This time Bulletin F was accompanied by a pamphlet listing the probable useful lives of 2,700 industrial assets. It is perhaps not surprising that this singular freedom on the part of taxpayers to determine their tax liability could not persist.

1934 to 1954: The IRS Prescribes Useful Life

An era in depreciation policy ended in 1934 by shifting the burden of proof as to the reasonableness of the deduction to the taxpayer. This change was stimulated by a report of a House Ways and Means Committee subcommittee on December 3, 1933 (Prevention of Tax Avoidance), which revealed a substantial increase in depreciation deductions and showed that in 1931 corporate depreciation deductions were larger than corporate taxable income.

The report recommended a reduction of 25 percent in depreciation deductions in the following three years, in view of the revenue needs at a time of depression and what was considered an alarming increase in these deductions. The secretary of the treasury, in a statement before the subcommittee, proposed that such reduction could be accomplished more equitably by shifting the burden of proof as to the reasonableness of the deduction to the taxpayer. The Ways and Means Committee agreed, and the 25 percent statutory deduction was not included in the bill.

Treasury Decision 4422, published in 1934, required the taxpayer to furnish facts regarding his deductions and laid the burden of proof of showing reasonableness of the deduction on the taxpayers. Thereafter most taxpayers tended to follow the useful lives prescribed in Bulletin F. A third and last edition of this document was issued in 1942, providing the average useful life of about 5,000 assets and longer lives (and thus lower deductions) for a substantial number of assets. In 1946 the IRS approved the use of the 150 percent declining balance method of depreciation.

The change in the depreciation regime produced many controversies between the IRAs and taxpayers. As a result the IRS indicated in a revenue ruling (Revenue Ruling 90 in 1953) that the Service would generally not disturb depreciation deductions and that adjustments would only be proposed where there was a clear and convincing reason.

1954 to 1962: Accelerated Depreciation Methods

The Internal Revenue Code of 1954 recodified the tax law, writing in the 1953 regulations and providing statutory allowance of accelerated depreciation methods including sum-of-years digits, declining balance, and any method that would not result in larger depreciation deductions during the first two-thirds of the life that exceeded amounts allowed under double-declining balance. The reasons for accelerated depreciation methods included both a more accurate reflection of depreciation (particularly obsolescence) and stimulation of business investment. The notion of a safe harbor depreciation range where taxpayers would not be challenged on lives if the difference was less than 10 percent of IRS lives was discussed, but was not incorporated into law.

Taxpayers were relatively slow to adopt the new accelerated methods, and a substantial portion of depreciation was still claimed under the straight-line method. Small businesses were also allowed an additional first-year allowance for 20 percent of the cost up to a dollar limit. Legislation in 1959 allowed businesses to deduct 20 percent of the first $10,000 of depreciation ($20,000 for a joint return) for tangible property.

1962 to 1971: Industrywide Lives

The use of so many different asset lives proved unwieldy. In addition, in late 1961, a Treasury survey of depreciation methods indicated a need for simplifying the guidelines and shortening lives. Revenue Procedure 62–21 substituted 75 industrywide class lives for the 5,000 or so Bulletin F lives. It also shortened lives by 30 to 40 percent. The procedure also instituted a reserve ratio test, which required taxpayers to compare their actual replacement experience with the guidelines and to adjust their lives accordingly. Taxpayers had a three-year grace period in which they could use the lives without applying the test.

Also in 1962, as part of the enactment of the investment credit, the basis for depreciation was reduced by the amount of any investment credits taken. This basis adjustment was eliminated in 1964. In addition, in 1962, rules were enacted requiring the recapture of depreciation on equipment when sold (i.e., the gain that reflected that any depreciation taken would be treated as ordinary income rather than capital gain). In 1964 recapture was also enacted for buildings, in varying amounts, depending on how long the building was held, but only for depreciation in excess of straight line. (These recapture rules were phased in.)

As in the case of the 1954 accelerated methods, the shorter lives were justified on the basis of economic stimulus and recognition of obsolescence. In addition the objectives of offsetting the effects of inflation on increased replacement costs of assets was mentioned. In 1965 the reserve ratio test was modified, and the moratorium on using it extended, since it seemed likely that many taxpayers could not pass the test. In 1969 depreciation methods for nonresidential real estate and used property were restricted to 150 percent declining balance (used nonresidential real estate was restricted to straight line and used residential property with a useful life of 20 years or more was restricted to 125 percent declining balance). The 1969 revision also required recapture of all depreciation in excess of straight line for nonresidential real property (again with transition rules).

1972 to 1980: The Asset Depreciation Range

The year 1971 saw yet another era in depreciation policy. Early in January the Treasury Department announced the introduction of a new depreciation policy. Proposed regulations were written and hearings were held, with the regulations adopted in June. The new system, the asset depreciation range (ADR) system, made two major changes. First, it allowed taxpayers to vary class lives up to 20 percent—in effect shortening tax lives. Second, it repealed the reserve ratio test.

The Treasury indicated two major considerations in adopting the new policy. First, the ADR system was expected to simplify the administration of depreciation and reduce controversies between the taxpayers and IRS. The reserve ratio test was felt to have a number of defects—it was complex, created numerous administrative problems, and was a major source of taxpayer disputes. In addition it reflected historical experiences of the taxpayer, argued to be a poor guide to future depreciation in an era of rapid technological change. The taxpayer could fail the test if he kept overage equipment on a standby basis, which encouraged premature retirement. Second, the ADR system, according to the Treasury, was an attempt to recognize obsolescence because of technological change, pollution control requirements, foreign competition, and the high rate of capital formation since 1962.

Besides these reasons the ADR system was expected to have a beneficial economic impact by reducing unemployment, stimulating investment in modern equipment, and increasing productivity. The ADR system was included with minor modifications in the Revenue Act of 1971. In 1976 recapture of depreciation in excess was straight line was applied to residential real property, with some exceptions for low-income rental housing.

1981 to 1986: A Break with Economic Depreciation

The Economic Recovery Tax Act of 1981 abandoned any attempt to relate depreciation policy to actual useful life. Equipment assets were assigned a flat five year life except for automobiles, which were assigned a life of three years. In addition, since all equipment assets were given a half-year depreciation in the year placed in service, but with depreciation completed in five (or three) calendar years, the effective write-off periods were actually 4.5 or 2.5 years. Specific write-off amounts in each period were legislated. Eventually this pattern was designed to correspond roughly with a double-declining-balance method. To limit the revenue loss, however, the percentages were initially set at 150 percent declining balance with a phase-in to the full double-declining-balance equivalents. All structures were assigned a life of fifteen years, and given a 175 percent declining balance method.

The depreciation system was part of the overall tax reduction enacted in 1981 and the major motivation was to stimulate investment. It was also argued, however, that this system would greatly simplify tax accounting. In 1981 all depreciation for nonresidential real property was to be recaptured, unless the taxpayer elected original use of the straight line method, in which case no depreciation was recaptured. The 1981 legislation also substituted first-year expensing (in the amount of $5,000) for the provision that allowed a 20 percent first-year write-off for $20,000; this amount was to be gradually increased to $10,000.

In 1982, responding to both revenue needs and the recognition that the combination of depreciation and investment credits was so large as to create negative tax rates for equipment, the phase-in of faster depreciation methods was abolished, and the basis for depreciation was reduced by one-half the investment tax credit. In 1984 the tax life for structures was increased to 18 years; it was subsequently increased to 19 years in 1985.

1986 to Present: A Return to Relating Depreciation to Economic Life

The Tax Reform Act of 1986 revised depreciation once more. Equipment assets were placed in six categories: 3, 5, 7, 10, 15, and 20 years. The first four classes were depreciated under double-declining balance, and the last two under 150 percent declining balance. The assignment to class was based on the categories in the ADR system. Nonresidential structures were depreciated over 31.5 years and residential structures over 27.5 years, both using the straight-line method. Depreciation recapture rules were maintained but became moot as the capital gains exclusion was eliminated, until the 1990 Act limited the top tax rate on capital gains to 28 percent.

The Tax Reform Act was intended to even up the tax rates and equate effective and statutory tax rates. Although depreciation was still accelerated, the benefit was roughly offset by the use of historical cost depreciation at current interest rates. In 1993 the depreciation period for nonresidential buildings was increased to 39 years, as a trade-off for relaxing the passive loss restrictions. In that same legislation the amount of investment in tangible property eligible for expensing in the first year was increased to $17,500.

Investment Tax Credit

The investment tax credit was originally adopted in 1962, at a rate of 7 percent for equipment. The rate was allowed at 3 percent for public utility property, and because of regulations this eligible property included assets such as power plants that are defined as structures in the National Income Accounts. The purpose of the investment credit was to stimulate investment in assets.

The original investment credit required the basis for depreciation to be reduced by the amount of the credit; this basis adjustment was removed in 1964 in order to increase the incentive effect and simplify the credit. Although the credit was originally viewed as a permanent part of the tax code, it then entered a period of suspension and restoration. In 1966 President Lyndon Johnson proposed that the credit be suspended as an anti-inflationary measure. The credit was originally to be suspended from October 10, 1966, through December 31, 1967. In March 1967, however, the President proposed the immediate restoration of the credit, and it was restored on March 10, 1967.

In 1969 the credit was repealed, again because of arguments that the credit had contributed to inflation. It was decided to repeal rather than to suspend the credit to prevent it from becoming a deterrent to investment and to simplify administrative problems The credit was reenacted at a 7 percent rate in 1971 (4 percent for public utilities), again as a means of stimulating economic growth.

In 1975 the investment credit was temporarily increased to 10 percent (including public utility property). This increase was extended in 1976 and 1977 and finally made permanent in 1978. The purpose of these temporary increases was short-term stimulus; the credit was extended because investment in equipment continued to lag.

In 1982 the basis for depreciation was reduced by half the investment credit. The investment tax credit was repealed by the Tax Reform Act of 1986, again as part of the movement toward evening up the tax treatment of different assets and equating effective and statutory tax rates.

Inventory Accounting

Inventory accounting was always fundamental to measuring income and was a part of established accounting methods. The 1918 tax law stated that the secretary of treasury had the authority to require taxpayers to account for inventory. Very early in the history of the tax law, however, farmers were permitted to use the cash method (deducting costs when incurred) and in most cases they continue to do so today for most individual farms and some small farm corporations.

Normally the cost of inventory is not deducted until goods are sold, and historically the method used was first-in, first-out (FIFO), which assumed that the item sold is the oldest in inventory. In 1938 the Congress allowed the use of a last-in, last-out (LIFO) method for two industries—nonferrous metals and hide and leather tanners. LIFO is advantageous when costs, are rising in that the last items acquired will have a higher cost, and thus LIFO will result in larger deductions.

In 1939, in response to strong pressure from business, all industries were made eligible for LIFO. LIFO could only be used, however, if the same system were used for financial accounting. Since LIFO resulted in the reporting of smaller profits, many firms have never adopted this inventory-accounting method.

Much of the history of the inventory accounting issue is to be found in regulations rather than tax law. For example, in 1960 regulations allowing for dollar value LIFO, which allowed goods of a similar nature to be pooled, were adopted. One important regulation adopted in 1973 required "full absorption" inventory accounting which required indirect costs to be included in inventories as well as the direct costs of materials and labor. The Tax Reform Act of 1986 included a broader array of costs, including overhead costs, in the costs that must be assigned to inventories.

Capital Gains Taxes

Capital gains were treated as income when realized under the original 1913 income tax. While gains were taxable regardless of how they were earned, the deduction of losses was limited to losses connected with the taxpayer's trade or business.

Revision of the tax treatment began almost immediately. The Revenue Act of 1916 allowed a deduction for losses from transactions entered into for profit to the extent of gains, and the Revenue Act of 1918 allowed a full deduction of these losses.

The first major revision was in 1921. This law defined capital assets as property acquired for profit or investment, held for two years or more. This definition excluded property acquired for personal consumption, stock in trade, and inventory. An alternative tax of 12.5 percent was allowed on the gains from the sale of capital assets for individuals. The prior treatment of losses was retained. The major reason given for this special tax treatment was the bunching problem—the possibility that gains accrued over many years would be realized in a lump sum and could be subject to heavy taxation with progressive tax rates.

In 1924 property acquired for personal use was added to the definition of capital assets, and long-term losses for individuals were limited to a reduction of tax equal to 13.5 percent of the loss. Major revisions of the capital gains tax treatment were made in 1934. For individuals, a sliding scale was substituted for the alternative tax, which allowed the inclusion of gains and losses depending on the holding period. One hundred percent was included if the asset was held for a year or less, 80 percent if held for one year but not more than two, 60 percent if held for more than two but not over five years, 40 percent if held for more than five but not more than ten years, and 30 percent if held for ten years or more. While loss deductions were limited to the same percentage as the income inclusions, deductions of losses against ordinary income were limited to $2,000 for both corporations and individuals. Capital assets were defined as all property held by the taxpayer except for stock in trade, inventory, or property held for sale to customers.

The 1938 revenue act again made major revisions in the taxation of capital gains for individuals. Gains from assets held 18 months or less were considered short-term and all the gain was included in income. Gains on assets held more than 18 months were long-term gains. Two-thirds of long-term gain on property held less than 24 months (but not more than 18 months) was included in income, while one-half of long-term gain on property held 24 months or longer was included. Individuals could also elect to be taxed at a rate of 30 percent on the included portion of the long-term gain. Losses were included to the same extent as gains, or the taxpayer could take a credit of 30 percent of the included loss, whichever yielded the greater tax. The $2,000 limit for deducting capital losses from ordinary income was removed for individuals, but short-term losses could only be deducted from short-term gains, with a one-year carryover. Another major revision was the exclusion of depreciable business property from the definition of capital assets, allowing the losses on this property to be deducted in full by both individuals and corporations. The $2,000 limitation on capital loss deductions from ordinary income for corporations was retained.

The Revenue Act of 1939 made changes in the treatment of capital losses for corporations. The act distinguished between short-term losses on capital assets held less than 18 months and long-term losses on assets held 18 months or more. Long-term capital losses were fully deductible; short-term losses were only deductible from short-gains with a one-year carryover.

A new system of tax treatment of capital gains and losses was instituted by the 1942 Revenue Act. For both individuals and corporations, gains held for six months or less were considered short-term and taxed in full, while gains held for more than six months were considered long-term. Individuals could exclude one-half of long-term gains or could elect an alternative tax of 25 percent on all long-term gain. Corporations, while they included all gain in income, could elect a 25 percent tax on long-term gains. Individual capital losses were determined by combining short-term gains and losses with long-term losses or included gains (which allowed a two-for-one offset of long-term gains by short-term losses). Individuals were limited to a deduction of $1,000 against ordinary income and were allowed to carry over capital losses for five years to deduct from capital gains and $1,000 of ordinary income. Capital losses, both long and short term, could not be deducted from ordinary income by corporations but could be carried over to be deducted from either type of gain. Capital assets were defined to exclude real as well as depreciable property used in the trade or business. However, although losses on the sales of this property were treated as ordinary losses, gains were treated as capital gains.

The Revenue Act of 1951 provided for the computation of individual gains and losses separately to prevent the two-for-one offset of long-term gains by short-term losses. An unlimited loss carryover for individuals was provided by the 1964 Revenue Act. The Tax Reform Act of 1969 repealed the 25 percent alternative tax for individuals, in stages, for all but the first $50,000 of gains and increased the alternative rate for corporations to 30 percent. A three-year carryback on capital losses for corporations was added and only one-half of net long-term capital losses (in excess of net short-term capital gains) for individuals could be deducted from ordinary income, with the $1,000 limit on offsetting ordinary income still applying.

The effective rate on some capital gains was increased by the minimum tax provisions of the 1969 Act, which included capital gains as a preference item; this tax could add another 10 percent tax on the excluded portion. The 1969 Act also added a maximum tax of 50 percent on earned income; this provision could increase the tax rate on capital gains because the amount of income eligible for the maximum rate was reduced by the amount of preference income (which included excluded gains). The 1976 Tax Reform Act increased the holding period to one year (with a transitional period of nine months), increased the minimum tax rate to 15 percent, and increased the amount of ordinary income offset by capital losses to $3,000 (with a transition of $2,000).

Capital gains tax issues were central in the Revenue Act of 1978, when it was argued that the combined effects of the minimum tax and maximum rate on earned income produced very high marginal tax rates. (For the top rate with the minimum tax applicable, the rate could be 42.5 percent—35 percent for the regular tax and another 7.5 percent for the minimum tax. The earned income tax limit could raise the tax to a theoretical maximum of 48.125 percent). That act substituted an alternative minimum tax for the add on tax, eliminated the effects of the maximum tax on earned income, and allowed an exclusion of 60 percent of capital gains rather than 50 percent. As a result the maximum capital gains tax rate was 28 percent. The 1978 Act also repealed the 25 percent alternative tax on capital gains.

The 1981 legislation reduced the maximum individual tax rate to 50 percent, thus reducing the maximum rate on capital gains to 20 percent with a 60 percent exclusion. The 1986 Tax Reform Act eliminated the capital gains exclusion so that the top rate could be as high as 33 percent (the notch rate). In 1990, when the notch was eliminated and a 31 percent rate added, the maximum rate on capital gains was set at 28 percent.

In addition to these statutory rules, there are a number of special treatments of capital gains. Gains passed on at death receive a basis in the hands of the heirs at market value. Thus these gains are never taxed (although they are subject to an estate tax). The Tax Reform Act of 1976 introduced carryover basis (the heir would take as basis the original basis of the decedent), but this provision was never allowed to take effect and was repealed in 1980.

Until 1986 taxpayers were allowed to report gains on the installment basis—that is, when payments for property were made on an installment basis, gain would not be recognized until installments were received. Purchasers of depreciable property could, however, take depreciation on the full basis when purchased.

Gains from the sale of personal residences largely escapes tax. In 1951 a provision was introduced that allowed the deferral of capital gains tax on the sale of a home if another residence were purchased within a specified period. In 1964 a provision was introduced that allowed a very limited exclusion of gain on the sale of a home for individuals 65 and over (the exclusion applied in full only when the sales price, did not exceed $20,000). For homes sold at higher prices, only a portion could be excluded. In 1976 the ceiling was increased to $35,000. The 1978 act allowed a one-time exclusion of $100,000 of gain and extended it to all taxpayers 55 and over; the exclusion was increased to $125,000 in 1981.

Certain income not normally considered capital gains was made eligible for capital gains treatment: income from cutting timber (1943), income from coal royalties (1951) and from iron ore royalties (1964). The argument for including timber cutting was in part to equalize the treatment of sales of timber as a stand and the cutting of timber. In addition there has been varying treatment over the years for installment sales, where payments for a property are spread over a number of years.

In 1993 a provision was adopted that allowed a 50 percent exclusion for gains on stock of small corporations (with less than $50 million in gross assets). Stock must be original issue and held for five years to qualify.

Minimum Tax

Sunley and Graetz (1988) trace the roots of the minimum tax to a proposal by Senator Russell Long, in the 1960s, for an optional simplified tax that would have allowed a lower tax rate on an expanded base.

In 1968 the Nixon administration recommended such an alternative tax, but the taxpayer would have been required to pay the higher of the two taxes. The expanded base would be regular taxable income increased by certain preferences (tax-exempt income or deductions): tax-exempt interest, excluded capital gains, appreciation on donated property, and the excess of percentage depletion after cost was fully recovered. The alternative tax rate would have been half the regular tax rate. Itemized deductions would have been allocated proportionally to taxable and tax-exempt income. Graetz and Sunley indicated that the main objective of this tax was a back-door method of increasing the capital gains tax.

In 1969 the administration proposed a limit on preferences and an allocation of itemized deductions between preference and nonpreference income; this approach was adopted by the House. The objective of these provisions was to focus on high income individuals who paid little or no tax, and a similar tax on corporations was not envisioned.

The Senate, however, adopted a different approach—an add-on minimum tax, which applied low rates (5 percent was proposed by the Senate Finance Committee, but the rate was increased to 10 percent on the Senate floor) to preference items. This tax was paid in addition to the regular tax, was applied to corporations as well as individuals, and allowed deductions of regular tax liability plus $30,000.

In 1970 provision was made for carrying over unused regular tax deductions. In 1971 the list of preferences was expanded. The Tax Reform Act of 1976 increased the rate to 15 percent, reduced the flat rate exemption to $10,000, and allowed only half of regular tax liability to be deducted. (Corporations could still deduct full regular tax liability.) The Tax Reduction and Simplification Act of 1977 modified the definition of tax preferences subject to the minimum tax.

The Revenue Act of 1978 first introduced an alternative minimum tax for individuals; this tax was payable if liability exceed the regular tax plus add–on minimum tax. Rates were graduated up to 25 percent. The 1981 act lowered the rate to 20 percent and altered some of the preferences. The 1982 act eliminated the add-on minimum tax.

In 1986 the add-on minimum tax for corporations was replaced by the alternative minimum tax at a 20 percent rate. The alternative minimum tax base included a broader definition of income (with less generous depreciation methods and longer lives, among other differences), along with other provisions regarding natural resources, inventories, and so forth. The minimum tax base also included one-half of the excess of book income over the minimum tax base (if it was larger). This book income base was to be converted to an alternative base termed adjusted current earnings (ACE) which specified certain rules for calculating depreciation and other deductions rather than leaving it to book income determination; also 75 percent of the difference was to be included in income. Unlike the regular AMT base, which included differential depreciation only for assets acquired after 1986, the ACE base covered all depreciation. Any additional taxes paid under the minimum tax could be carried over and credited against regular tax liability in the future. In 1993 the depreciation difference between ACE and the regular AMT base was eliminated.

Tax Treatment of Retirement Savings

Employer pensions developed well before the income tax and certainly before the income tax was important. The first income tax law made no provision for the tax treatment of these pensions, but regulations issued in 1914 (Treasury Decision 2090) ruled that pensions paid to employees were deductible. Later regulations allowed pension contributions to be deductible, and they were taxable to various entities (employers, pension trusts, or employees). Trust earnings were taxable.

The Revenue Act of 1921 exempted earnings of stock-bonus or profit-sharing plans from tax; the Revenue Act of 1926 extended this treatment to pension trusts. Firms could deduct contributions to cover accruing liabilities but not past service accruals. Many firms began accumulating taxable reserves for these past service accruals, and the Revenue Act of 1928 allowed reasonable contributions for these reserves. There were no coverage or vesting requirements, minimum funding rules, or limits on benefits.

Like many provisions added early in the history of the income tax, the original rationale of this treatment is not clear, although it seems likely that these rules may have been developed to resolve technical problems of assigning trust income. The 1921 change was introduced in the Senate Finance Committee and the 1926 change added on the Senate floor, with no debate in either case.

Many employer plans did not survive the depression, and in many cases benefits were revoked. As plans revived in the late 1930s, concern developed about the use of these plans on tax evasion. The 1938 Revenue Act required that employer contributions to a tax-exempt trust could not be withdrawn until all liabilities were paid. This provision prevented firms from making contributions in profitable years and withdrawing them in loss years.

The Revenue Act of 1942 was a signal year for the treatment of pensions. It required that plans could not discriminate in favor of management or highly paid employees. The plan had to cover at least 70 percent of employees, or a fair cross section, and could not provide proportionally higher benefits for higher paid workers. The rules allowed, however, an integration with Social Security so that benefits to earnings ratios could be higher for wages above the social security earnings base. It also introduced rules to prevent overfunding. After the war, nontax regulations were applied to collectively bargained multi-employer plans (the Taft-Hartley Act, in 1947). The Welfare and Pensions Plans Disclosure Act of 1958 provided for regulations, reporting, and disclosure. In 1962 the Self-employed Individuals Retirement Act allowed self-employed individuals to establish pension plans, known as Keogh (H.R. 10) plans.

The Employee Retirement Income Security Act of 1974 (ERISA) was a major piece of legislation directed at concerns that workers could not count on benefits. This act provided, minimum standards for participation, vesting, funding, and plan asset management. It also created the Pension Benefit Guaranty Corporation (PBGC) to insure benefits against plan termination.

This act provided a minimum age for coverage (25), a minimum service requirement of one year, and minimum vesting standards, one of which was full vesting at ten years. Limits on the annual benefit were established: Under a defined benefit plan the maximum was the lesser of $75,000 (subject to cost-of-living adjustments) or 100 percent of the employee's highest three-year average. Under a defined contribution plan the maximum was the lesser of $25,000 (subject to cost-of-living adjustments) or 25 percent of pay. Self-employed individuals were allowed to deduct the lesser of 15 percent of earned income or $7,500 a year. The 1974 Act also established individual retirement accounts (IRAs) for individuals not covered by an employer plan, subject to a maximum limit of 15 percent of compensation but no more than $1,500.

The Tax Reduction Act of 1975 provided a tax credit for employee stock ownership plans (ESOPS), as an add-on to the investment tax credit. This approach essentially caused the government to purchase and donate the stock. The ESOP credit was scheduled to expire several times but was extended until it was repealed by the Tax Reform Act of 1986.

The Revenue Act of 1978 provided for some new types of vehicles. One was the allowance of tax deferred savings, or 401(k) plans, which operated like IRAs—contributions could be excluded in income until withdrawn. The act also allowed "cafeteria" plans, whereby employees could select the type of fringe benefit, which included 401(k) savings vehicles. The 1978 Act also created a simplified employer plan (SEP) which allowed employer contributions to IRAs, with a limit of $7,000. The 1980 legislation (Multiemployer Pension Plan Amendments Act) attempted to preserve these plans, which were in financial difficulty, by requiring stricter funding rules.

The Economic Recovery Tax Act of 1981 (ERTA) extended IRAs to all employees, increased the limit to $2,000 and added a $250 deduction for unemployed spouses. Employees could also make voluntary contributions, within limits, to tax-sheltered annuities and qualified plans. ERTA also raised the limits for Keoghs, SEPs, and defined-contribution plans of subchapter S corporations to $15,000.

The Tax Equity and Fiscal Responsibility Act of 1982 reduced the maximum funding and contribution limits, which at that time, after indexation, had risen to $136,425 and $44,475, from $90,000 and $30,000. These higher limits were extended to SEPs. The Act also introduced restrictions on "top-heavy" plans where more than 60 percent of benefits were to key employees. These provisions required that such plans limit the amount of compensation considered, provide for more rapid vesting of other participants, provide minimum contributions and benefits for other employees, and reduce the aggregate limit on contributions and benefits for certain employees. The 1983 Social Security Amendments required that amounts in 401(k) and other salary reduction plans be included as compensation for payroll tax purposes.

The 1984 Deficit Reduction Act froze funding and contribution limits for two more years and made some minor changes in various plans. The

Retirement Equity Act of 1984 required that joint and survivor annuities be provided able only be waived by the spouse, as well as coverage for a spouse if the employee died before retirement. The age of participation was lowered, and breaks in service liberalized.

The Tax Reform Act of 1986 disallowed full IRAs for individuals covered by an employer plan at higher-income levels. These individuals could make nondeductible contributions and escape tax on the earnings until withdrawn, a treatment that was less generous than the IRA provision. Also the 1986 Act froze maximum contributions to defined-contribution plans until they fell from one-third to one-fourth of the maximum defined benefit, which would then be indexed starting in 1988. Contributions to elective deferrals for most salary reduction plans were limited to $7,000.

Tests for broadness of coverage (antidiscrimination rules) among employees were made more stringent and maximum vesting was shortened from ten to five years. The extent to which social security benefits could offset pension benefits was reduced. A 10 percent excise tax was applied to funds taken out of plans (reversions) arising from overfunding.

The Pension Protection Act, included in the Omnibus Budget Reconciliation Act of 1987 (OBRA), introduced some rules to prevent underfunding and excessive overfunding of pensions—by setting funding limits between 100 percent and 150 percent of current benefit liabilities (all liabilities currently owed if the plan was terminated)—along with some other technical changes. The Revenue Reconciliation Act of 1989, included in the Omnibus Budget Reconciliation Act of 1989, modified the special tax treatment for ESOPs and made some technical changes in pension rules. The Revenue Reconciliation Act of 1990, included in the Omnibus Reconciliation Act of 1990 increased the tax on reversions from 15 percent to 20 percent and set up rules allowing the transfer of assets to retiree health plans.

Life insurance death benefits were excluded from income in the original 1913 income tax law, possibly because they were viewed as similar to bequests. Failure to tax accruals of income is based on the principle of constructive receipt, that is, that an individual cannot be taxed on income until it is received or is readily available to him. The Deficit Reduction Act of 1984 placed some limits on what investments can be characterized as life insurance.

Housing and Consumer Interest

Imputed items are not generally included in income unless there is a specific provisions. The deductions for mortgage interest and property taxes date to the original 1913 income tax law; that law did not distinguish between interest and taxes associated with business versus consumer use. These provisions became less important when the standard deduction was introduced.

In 1986 the consumer interest deduction was restricted to mortgage interest. Limits were placed on the amount of debt secured by a mortgage to restrict it to the purchase price plus improvements (debt to finance certain medical and educational costs secured by the mortgage were also allowed). The dollar ceiling was placed on mortgages in 1987. In 1990 a provision was adopted requiring the phase out of itemized deductions for high adjusted gross incomes (over $100,000 for married individuals). This phase-out is temporary and will last through 1995.

The low-income housing credit was adopted in 1986. It replaced a number of other provisions in the law that favored such housing construction and that were repealed by the 1986 legislation. The credit was extended numerous times and made permanent in 1993.

Research and Experimentation Tax Credit

The tax credit for research and development was enacted in 1981 as a temporary credit (expiring at the end of 1985) for 25 percent of eligible expenditures in excess of the average over a three-year base period. There was also a minimum base of 50 percent of expenditures. Eligible expenditures included intangible expenses for R&D and 65 percent of contract research. It excluded R&D related to social sciences and the humanities.

The credit was extended (retroactively to the beginning of 1986) by the Tax Reform Act of 1986. The rate was reduced to 20 percent. A special separate credit for university research was also included, with a separate base period. The base was narrowed somewhat and payments for leasing personal property were eliminated. The credit was again extended only on a temporary basis, through the end of 1988.

The credit was extended, a year at a time, by the Technical and Miscellaneous Revenue Act of 1988 (TAMRA), the Omnibus Reconciliation Act of 1989, and the Omnibus Reconciliation Act of 1990. The Tax Extension Act of 1991 extended it through June of 1992. The 1988 legislation reduced research expenditures to be expensed by one-half the credit. The 1989 legislation changed the base to allow it to grow independently of actual expenditures; the base instead grew at the rate of growth of sales. The 1989 legislation also allowed the credit to apply to R&D associated with a prospective as well as current line of business and reduced the amounts eligible to be expensed by the full amount of the credit. The latest retroactive reinstatement and extension of the credit occurred in 1993, when it was extended through June 30, 1995.

Tax Treatment of Mineral Extraction

The original 1913 act provided a general allowance for the exhaustion, wear and tear, including recovery of expenditures on mineral extraction not to exceed 5 percent value of output. Under general rules allowing for deduction of losses, dry tracts, dry holes, and unproductive mines have always been eligible for deduction, even though such unsuccessful ventures are part of the cost of locating productive properties. In 1916 a deduction for depletion was specifically mentioned, not to exceed the market value of product mined and not to exceed capital originally invested (or the March 1913 fair market value). This latter date was due to a decision not to tax appreciation occurring before the income tax was imposed.

In 1918 discovery value depletion was enacted to keep more recent discoveries that contributed to war effort from being less favorably treated than earlier properties; this provision allowed the taxpayer to use as a depletable basis the value at discovery or within thirty days. In 1921 Congress, concerned with size of these allowances, limited them to 100 percent of net income; in 1954 depletion allowances were further restricted to 50 percent of net income.

Percentage depletion for oil and gas was enacted in 1926, largely to cope with administrative problems associated with discovery value depletion, including lags and delays, discrimination among properties, and general problems with estimating prices and discount rates. The percentage depletion rate, based on a compromise between the two houses, was set at 27.5 percent of gross income from property, limited to 50 percent of net income. Percentage depletion was designed to approximate the value of discovery value depletion.

In 1932 percentage depletion was extended to coal (5 percent), metals (15 percent), and sulphur (23 percent). There were further extensions of percentage depletion in 1942 to clay, asphalt, and flurospar. The 1951 act provided for a 10 percent rate for coal, and the 1954 act allowed a 15 percent rate for all minerals unless otherwise specified. Some minerals were provided a rate of 23 percent, some 10 percent (including coal), some 7.5 percent, and some 5 percent.

In 1969 percentage depletion rates were lowered to 22 percent for oil and gas and rates on other minerals that were set at 23 and 15 percent were reduced to 22 and 14 percent. In 1975 percentage depletion on oil and gas was repealed except specified flat exemptions from the repeal for independent producers. The eventual level of exemption was 1,000 barrels a day, and the eventual rate was 15 percent. In a general cutback of preferences, the excess of percentage depletion deductions over original cost basis was reduced by 15 percent in 1982 and 20 percent in 1984 (the increase to 20 percent did not apply to coal and iron ore).

Intangible drilling costs (IDCs), which included expenses such as labor, supplies, and repairs with no salvage value, were allowed to be expensed through regulation in 1917. In 1954 this option was incorporated in the statute. Exploration expenditures (which would otherwise be depletable costs) other than oil and gas were allowed to be expensed a flat amount of $75,000 in 1951. In 1954 this amount was raised to $100,000. Firms could deduct without limit if they recaptured these costs after production began. The 1969 act made all such exploration expenditures subject to recapture.

In 1918 development expenditures for mines in the preproduction period were capitalized and after production were expensed. In 1951 all development expenditures were allowed to be expensed. The 1982 act cut back on these expensing provisions slightly by requiring that 15 percent of IDCs of integrated corporations be capitalized over a three-year period and that 15 percent of mining exploration and development costs be expensed over five years. In 1984 these amounts were increased to 20 percent; in 1986 the amounts were increased to 30 percent and the period was extended to five years for IDCs.

Tax-Exempt Bonds

The evolution of the exclusion of interest on tax-exempt bonds might be argued to begin with historical court decisions, since for many years an argument was made that the Constitution might prohibit the taxation of this interest. The first such court decision was *McCulloch* v. *Maryland* in 1819, which prohibited state taxation of an instrumentality of the federal government—in this case the Bank of the United States. This decision was probably not directly applicable to the issue of federal taxation of interest on state and local bonds but is the first such decision that might have some relevance to the issue. The next case was *Collector* v. *Day* in 1871, which disallowed a tax on salaries of state and local officials under the Civil War income tax.

In 1895 *Pollock* v. *Farmers Loan and Trust Co.* (better known for finding the income tax of that period unconstitutional) indicated that the federal government could not tax interest of state and local entities. During the discussion of the Sixteenth Amendment, which allows a direct income tax, this issue was considered and assurances were given that state and local interest income would not be taxed. The 1913 income tax act specifically excluded this interest.

Andrew Mellon proposed taxation of state and local bond interest in 1921; the Roosevelt administration made the same proposal in 1935. The Supreme Court in *Helvering* v. *Gerhardt* (1938) found that state and local salaries were taxable. Despite proposals by the Harding, Coolidge, Hoover, and Roosevelt administrations to tax state and local bond interest in these early years of the income tax, such legislation was never passed by Congress, leaving the legal issues not entirely settled.

Action on the taxation of state and local bond interest did not begin until the growth of industrial development bonds (IDSBs) The first such bonds were issued in 1936 by Mississippi. In 1954 an amendment was agreed to that eliminated the use of bonds to build factories or other facilities that could be leased to private firms, but an enormous outcry caused a reversal of this policy.

The Revenue and Expenditure Control Act of 1968 began limiting private activity bonds. This act disallowed bonds that were IDBs (at least 25 percent of proceeds used for private purposes and 25 percent of debt service secured by private property). There were numerous exemptions to this restrictions—for example, for sewage, pollution control, airports, wharves and docks, and mass transit, and for small issues. Changes in definitions of excluded issues occurred on several occasions (1971, 1976, 1978, 1980 [Windfall Profits Tax Act], 1981, 1982, 1984,1986, 1987, 1988, 1989). In 1980 volume caps on these issues were introduced (Mortgage Subsidy Bond Act of 1980); these volume caps were extended in 1984 and broadened in 1986. Also, in 1986, the 25 percent test was reduced to 10 percent. The 1987 act limited the use of tax-exempt bonds outside the volume cap to purchase existing power plant facilities unless needed to meet increased demand or annexation. There were also restrictions on arbitrage bonds, beginning in 1969, limiting the amount of bond proceeds to be invested in financial assets. These rules were revised on numerous occasions—in 1976, 1978, 1980, 1982, 1984, 1986 (this change denied advance refunding to most private activity bonds and allowed it to occur only once for other bonds), 1988, 1989, and 1993. The issue of the constitutionality of taxation was settled in *South Carolina* v. *Baker* (1988), which firmly established the right to tax interest on state and local bonds.

Taxation of Special Forms of Business

Financial Institutions

Financial institutions (banks and life insurance companies) have historically been subject to relatively low, or no, taxation for a variety of reasons. In part, this relief reflected the fact that many of these institutions were organized in mutual form. In other cases there were difficult problems of measuring income because of the need for special reserves.

Credit unions are not currently subject to tax, largely on the grounds that they are organizations formed for the mutual benefit of members. State chartered credit unions were always exempt. In 1934 federal credit unions were authorized and in 193, exempted from tax.

For similar reasons thrift institutions were long exempted from tax. When these institutions were first taxed in 1951, they nevertheless retained effective exemption because of generous allowances for bad debt reserves (which were allowed as a percentage of outstanding loans). These liberal bad debt allowances allowed complete exclusion from the tax until Revenue Act of 1962. That act restricted the bad debt reserves to 60 percent of taxable income, gradually to be reduced to 40 percent. These benefits were allowed if a certain fraction of loans were in qualified loans (primarily residential mortgages). In 1987 the limit was reduced to 8 percent.

Commercial banks were subject to tax but were allowed relatively generous bad debt reserves (at 2.4 percent of loans) in 1947. In 1969 these bad debt reserves were gradually reduced to 1.2 percent, and in 1981 they were phased out, so reserves now have to reflect experience.

Life insurance companies have been taxed in a variety of ways. Beginning in 1921, they were taxed only on investment income not needed to fund obligations to policyholders ("free" investment income"). Underwriting income (premiums less benefits) was not taxed.

The Life Insurance Tax Act of 1959 set up a complex system of taxation. There were three different tax bases. The first was free investment income. The second was gain from operations (the excess of premiums and investment income not needed to fund obligations). In calculating this latter base, reserve additions were allowed for future obligations, generally reflecting the additions required by state regulators. Limited deductions were allowed for policyholder dividends and other special deductions. The company was taxed on the smaller base. In figuring the second base, however, policyholder and special deductions were limited to $250,000 plus the excess of the income from the second base (before the deductions) over the income from the first base. This limited the ability of the special deductions to allow the second base to be reduced by more than $250,000 less than the second base. If the company's gain from operations was more than its free investment income base, it would be taxed on half the excess. The untaxed portion of the second base was added to a deferred tax account and taxed only when distributed.

These different tax bases meant that some companies would not be taxed on additional investment income, while others would not be taxed on additional underwriting income. Companies entered into "modified co-insurance" arrangements with each other that effectively allowed firms to transform taxable investment income into untaxed underwriting income, and vice versa.

The 1982 Act eliminated the provisions that caused the modified coinsurance arrangements. The 1982 act also allowed, on a temporary basis, a flat deduction for policyholder dividends (85 percent for stock companies and 77.5 percent for mutual companies). The special taxation of life insurance income came under considerable criticism, and there were attempts to conform the treatment of life insurance firms to other corporations. There are, however, some departures from the rules that would apply to corporations.

First, there was a special deduction equal to 20 percent of taxable income. There was also a small life insurance company deduction for 60 percent of the first $3 million of taxable income. This deduction is phased out between $3 million and $15 million; it applies only to firms with assets of less than $500 million. Second, the calculation of reserve additions was based on federally prescribed rules regarding discount rates and mortality/morbidity tables used by regulators in the majority of states. The discount rate was based on the greater of the prevailing ftate rate or the five year average of the federal midterm rate. Third, mutual firms' deductions of policyholder dividends was reduced by a typical rate of return on equity based on the experience of stock companies. In 1986, when corporate tax rates were lowered, the 20 percent special deduction was eliminated.

Cooperatives

Certain cooperatives were historically tax-exempt, based on rulings in the early 1920s that viewed them as mutual organizations. These cooperatives were originally largely farm cooperatives, but they also include telephone and consumer cooperatives. All cooperatives can deduct patronage dividends paid to patrons on the grounds that they are reductions in prices. These patronage dividends were deductible even if not actually paid out but just allocated to patrons. The 1962 tax legislation stipulated that earnings cannot be deducted unless 20 percent of the allocation is in cash. This allocation must be treated as income to the business customer (but not to consumers).

Nonprofit Businesses

The evolution of the taxation of nonprofit businesses, which were generally not subject to tax, can be found in the restrictions placed on them. In the late 1940s the Mueller's macaroni firm was donated to New York University, stimulating legislation in 1950 to tax business income unrelated to the charitable or other purpose. The tax on unrelated business income applied to all tax-exempt organizations except governments.

In 1969 investment income of private foundations was subjected to a 4 percent tax; this tax was lowered to 2 percent in 1978 and 1 percent in 1985. The 1969 act also placed a number of restrictions on foundations, including limits on self dealing and on stockholdings.

International Tax Issues

Foreign Tax Credit and Deferral

The initial corporate income tax, as enacted in 1909, provided that domestic corporations be taxed on income from all sources and foreign corporations on income from business transacted and capital invested in the United States. The jurisdictional claim to all worldwide income have been essentially unchanged, and like many early provisions resulted in very little debate. Income from foreign corporations earned abroad would not be subject to tax even if these corporations were owned by U.S. corporations, except as income was repatriated, under these general rules.

Under this and the 1913 income tax, foreign taxes were deductible from income. In 1918 a foreign tax credit was allowed that rebated the amount of income, war profits, and excess profits taxes paid to foreigners. This credit was addressed to the problem of double taxation. In 1921 a foreign tax credit limit provided that credits granted could not exceed the U.S. tax due on the foreign source income. This credit limit was on an overall basis, so excess taxes in one country could be offset by making investments in low-tax countries. In 1921 attempts were made to eliminate the taxation of foreign source income entirely, which would have produced a territorial system. Such a provision was passed by the house. It failed in the Senate in part due to the opposition of Senator Robert LaFollette. In 1928 provisions regarding the allocation of income under section 482 were adopted.

Between 1932 and 1954 both the per country and the overall limit on the foreign tax credit were imposed, with credits allowed based on the smaller amount. From 1954 to 1960 a per country limit was enforced, from 1960 to 1975 the taxpayer could make a choice, and since 1976 an overall limit has been mandatory. In 1942 the credit was allowed for taxes paid in lieu of income taxes. Also in 1942 a Supreme Court decision (*American Chicle Company v. U.S.*) interpreted the foreign tax credit as applying to actual dividends paid (not the dividends plus associated foreign taxes paid).

In the early 1950s regulations that were first private, and then public (Revenue Ruling 55-296) allowed per barrel taxes paid to Saudi Arabia and other petroleum-exporting countries to qualify as creditable tax. This treatment was apparently motivated by foreign policy considerations, but it caused considerable debate over many years. These payments were fundamentally no different from royalties that would normally be deductible. These taxes/royalties were eventually imposed at very high rates and were very important when the overall limit on the foreign tax credit was used, since the excess credits generated in the oil-producing countries could be used to offset U.S. tax on distribution and refining operations in other countries. This issue continued to be contentious for many years, fading from the scene when many of the countries took over ownership of the properties directly.

In 1958 provisions were added allowing the carry-back and carry-forward of foreign tax credits. In 1962 dividends received from foreign corporations were required to be grossed up (the amount of foreign tax paid added back) before applying the credit, which increased the tax rate. Although this approach was recognized as generally correct, gross-up was not applied to corporations of less developed countries.

In 1976 gross-up of dividends was also required for less developed country corporations. In addition a foreign loss recapture rule was imposed to prevent situations where a company deducted a loss (reducing U.S. tax liability) and then in subsequent years took foreign tax credits against income. The 1986 act provided for further restrictions on the foreign tax credit by providing for separate "baskets" for certain types of income to which the foreign tax credit limitation would separately apply.

In the late 1950s and early 1960s, there was an enormous growth in tax havens in low tax countries, with income funneled into these locations. In 1961 the Kennedy administration proposed to tax income of controlled foreign corporations on a current basis. While full taxation was not adopted, in 1962 certain income of controlled foreign corporations, primarily passive income and sales and service income, were taxed on a current basis. This provision was directed at tax havens and at the kinds of income that could be easily relocated from one jurisdiction to another. These deferral provisions were strengthened in various ways in 1975, 1976, 1982, 1984, and 1993. Regulations regarding the allocation of income were also tightened in the 1960s in response to these problems of tax havens.

Other Provisions

In 1942 a special deduction was allowed for Western Hemisphere Trade Corporations, which reduced the effective tax rate by 14 percentage points. The original purpose was to exempt certain corporations engaged in operations in the Western Hemisphere but outside the United States from the high wartime surtaxes. The provision was continued after the war and finally repealed in 1976.

Special deductions that could wipe out taxes entirely were allowed to China Trade Act Corporations as part of the China Trade Act of 1922. These provisions became relatively unimportant after the communist occupation of mainland China in 1949 and were restricted to a few companies operating in Hong Kong or Formosa. This provision was finally repealed in 1976.

Income earned in the U.S. possessions was exempted from tax in 1921 for possessions corporations (domestic corporations deriving 80 percent of gross income from a possession and 50 percent of gross income from the active conduct of a trade or business in a possession). The original purpose was to promote U.S. trade and commercial relationships with the possessions, and there was particular concern at that time with the status of firms in the Philippines, then a U.S. possession. Under these rules a parent corporation could not deduct dividends received from a parent corporation; thus tax free repatriation could only occur when subsidiaries were liquidated. The tax benefits could, however, apply to income invested outside the possessions. Beginning in 1939, Puerto Rico engaged in an economic development program that included tax forgiveness and depended heavily on the U.S. tax-exemption.

In 1976 the provision was revised, as a result of two problems. The first was that all of the possessions corporation income was benefited, not just that amount that was earned in the possession. Second, there was an incentive to reinvest proceeds outside of the possessions corporations. The 1976 act restricted the tax benefit to possessions income and allowed tax free repatriation. Exemption was accomplished by imposing a corporate tax and simultaneously allowing a credit for the tax (it is referred to as the *Section 936 credit*). In 1982 there was some tightening of the provision including an increase in the fraction of active income required to qualify to 65 percent. In 1993 limits were imposed on the credit, with the taxpayer choosing which limit to apply. Under the first limit, the credit could not exceed an economic activity base that included 60 percent of qualified labor compensation, 15 percent of depreciation deductions for short-lived property, 40 percent of depreciation deductions for medium-life equipment, and 65 percent of depreciation deductions for long-lived equipment. Under the second, the credit would be limited to a fraction of that which would otherwise be allowed, beginning at 60 percent in 1994 and phasing down to 40 percent in 1998 and after.

The predecessor of Foreign Sales Corporations was the Domestic International Sales Corporation provision adopted in 1971, which effectively allowed the deferral of tax on half of income intended for export. This provision was originally developed during an era of fixed exchange rates and part of the objective was to increase exports. There was also some argument that this provision offset the advantages of deferral in locating operations abroad. Restrictions on DISC benefits for natural resource products and scarce products were adopted in 1975. A provision making DISC incremental, which substantially reduced its value, was adopted in 1976. The FSC provisions were substituted for DISC in 1984 in order to conform the provision with GATT regulations, since some countries had argued that DISC provisions were in violation of these rules. The tax benefits of FSC and DISC were approximately of the same magnitude.

Table A.1
Major tax legislation and common acronyms

Corporation Excise Tax of 1909
Revenue Acts of: 1913, 1916, 1918, 1921, 1926, 1928, 1934, 1938, 1939, 1942, 1951
Internal Revenue Code of 1954
Revenue Act of 1962
Self Employed Individuals Retirement Act of 1962
Revenue Act Of 1964
Tax Reform Act of 1969
Excise, Estate and Gift Tax Adjustment Act of 1970
Revenue Act of 1971
Employee Retirement Income Security Act of 1974 (ERISA)
Tax Reduction Act of 1975
Tax Reform Act of 1976
Tax Reduction and Simplification Act of 1977
Energy Tax Act of 1978
Revenue Act of 1978
Crude Oil Windfall Profit Tax Act of 1980
Economic Recovery Tax Act of 1981 (ERTA)
Tax Equity and Fiscal Responsibility Act of 1982 (TEFRA)
Deficit Reduction Act of 1984 (DEFRA)
Tax Reform Act of 1986
Omnibus Budget Reconciliation Act of 1987 (OBRA 87)
Technical and Miscellaneous Revenue Act of 1988 (TAMRA)
Omnibus Budget Reconciliation Act of 1989 (OBRA 89)
Omnibus Budget Reconciliation Act of 1990 (OBRA 90)
Omnibus Budget Reconciliation Act of 1993 (OBRA 93)

Bibliographic Notes

In preparing this historical summary, I relied on a number of very useful sources that provide histories in more detail:

• A detailed history of tax rates, including corporate rates, and the bottom and top individual tax rates is contained in Joseph Pechman's *Federal Tax Policy* (1987).

• Much of the description the development of depreciation policy and the investment credit is taken from Gravelle (1979).

• Graetz and Sunley (1988) include a summary of the origins, predecessors and history of the minimum tax.

• An extensive history of the development of pension plans in general and of the evolution of the tax treatment of these plans is contained in Congressional Budget Office (1987a).

• Dennis Zimmerman's book (1991) on tax-exempt bonds contains several segments on the history of these bonds, including the development of municipal bonds themselves, the legal framework (including court cases as well as legislation), and a detailed history of legislation between 1968 and 1989.

• Agria (1969) includes a detailed description of the tax treatment to mineral extraction.

• *Tax Expenditures: Compendium of Background Material on Individual Provisions* (Senate Budget Committee 1992) contains histories and original rationales of over 100 different provisions of the tax law.

• Information on the origin of the foreign tax credits for oil payments imposed by the certain Middle Eastern governments is based on Davidson (1978–79).

In addition to these specific histories and the tax law itself, the various committee reports accompanying tax legislation along with the general explanations prepared by the Joint Committee on Taxation were used to determine the rationales of various revisions.

Appendix B:
Methods of Calculation
and Data Sources

This technical appendix provides information and formulas underlying several of the calculations in the book. The first section provides information on the effective tax rates that appear in chapters 2, 3, 4, 5, and 7. The second section provides the data for calculating the lock-in effects of the capital gains tax in chapter 6. The next section provides the formulas for calculating excess burden in chapter 6. The final section provides information on data sources.

Marginal Effective Tax Rates

A marginal effective tax rate is determined by a discounted cash flow analysis, where the internal rate of return with and without taxes is compared. This type of measure can take into account the timing effects that are crucial features of certain tax preferences, including accelerated depreciation and deferral of taxes on capital gains until realization.

Illustrations of Effective Tax Rate Calculations

The following numerical examples show how effective tax rates are affected by an investment credit, accelerated depreciation, and failure to index depreciation, using a simple example where an investment earns a return over two periods. Calculating tax rates requires the use of the concept of present value, which is simply a method of determining how much investment today at a given interest rate would be necessary to earn a future amount. For example, at a 10 percent interest rate, $100 invested today will be worth $110 a year from now—$100 times $1 + i$, where i is the interest rate), or $100 times 1.10. If a payment of $110 a year from now is to be expressed as a present value, it would be divided by $1 + i$; that is the present value of $110 a year from now discounted at 10 percent is $100/1.10, or $100. Similarly, if $100 were to be invested for two years at a 10 percent rate, compounded annually, the future payment would be $100 times $(1.10)^2$, or $121. The present value of $121 earned two years from now, discounted at 10 percent, will be $121/(1.10)^2$, or

$100. Using present value is necessary to differentiating between the greater value of money earned closer to the present and the lesser value of money earned further in the future.

Now consider an investment of $100 that yields a payoff after one year of $60 dollars and a payoff after two years of $55, thereafter becoming worthless. The rate of return on this investment is 10% and by discounting each of the payments by this rate of return, we see that the present value if $100. That is, the sum of $60 divided by 1.10 and $55 divided by $(1.10)^2$ is $100.

Suppose that there is a tax of 50 percent, so the rate of return is 5 percent. Since this investment is depreciating in value, taxation must allow for a deduction for the recovery of the original cost of $100. The correct depreciation for this particular investment is $50 in the first year and $50 in the second year. The correctness of this figure can be checked by discounting the after-tax cash payments at the after-tax rate of return and making sure that they sum up to $100. In this case the taxable income in the first period is the total payment ($60) minus depreciation ($50), for a taxable income of $10 and a tax payment of $5. The after-tax cash flow is $55—$60 less tax paid of $5. In the second period, taxable income is $5 ($55 minus $50), tax paid is $2.50, and after-tax cash flow is $52.50 ($55 less tax paid of $2.50). The discounted sum of these two payments is $55/1.05 plus $52.50/$(1.05)^2$, or $100.

Suppose now that an investment credit is allowed for 5 percent of the cost with no adjustment for depreciation. (Such a credit existed in the past; on some occasions, however, the cost [or basis] of depreciation was reduced by the amount of the credit. With a full basis adjustment depreciation would apply only to the $95 of actual cost rather than the $100.) The after-tax cash flows for this investment remain the same. The taxpayer's investment, however, has fallen—he pays only $95 after receiving the investment credit of $5. To determine the true after-tax rate of return on this investment, it is necessary to search for the rate of return r that will cause the payments to sum to $95. That is, what value of r will result in $55/(1 + r)$ plus $52.50/(1 + r)^2$ adding to $95. This value of r turns out to be 0.087237. The effective tax rate in turn is 12.8 percent, since this fraction of the pretax return of 10 percent is paid out in taxes. That is, $(0.10 - 0.087237)/0.10$ is 0.128. Even though the statutory marginal tax rate is 50 percent, the effective rate is only 12.8 percent when the credit is allowed.

A second illustration is of accelerated depreciation. Suppose that, instead of allowing $50 of depreciation to be deducted in each period, we allow $75 in the first period and $25 in the second period. In the first period, a tax savings is realized, since $60 less $75 yields a negative taxable income of $15 and a tax refund of $7.50. After-tax cash flow in the first period is $67.50. In the second period, taxable income is $30 ($55 minus $25), and a tax of $15 is paid. Thus cash flow in the second period is $40 ($55 minus $15). Note that the total overall payment is the same as in the case where correct economic depreciation is allowed ($107.50), but some of the earnings are moved from the second period to the first. It is necessary to find the rate of return r that will discount these two payments to $100; that is, $67.50/(1 + r)$ plus $40/(1 + r)^2$ equals $100. That return is 0.05437. The effective tax rate in turn is 45.6 percent (0.10 − 0.05437)/0.10. By allowing $25 of depreciation to be moved from the second to the first period, the effective tax rate falls from 50 to 45.6 percent.

The final, and most complicated, illustration is the effect of inflation. When inflation occurs, the nominal value of payments in the future rises with the inflation rate. Also the nominal rate of return must rise to reflect inflation. For example, if the inflation rate is 5 percent, to earn a real return of 10 percent, $100 invested for a single year must grow to $115.50. This is necessary because $110 in real purchasing power has risen by 5 percent—$110 times 1.05 is $115.50. In the investment illustration, if inflation is 5 percent, the $60 value in the first period will rise by 5 percent, to $63 ($60 times 1.05). Similarly the $55 value in the second period will rise even more proportionally, to $60.64 ($55 times 1.05^2). To measure real income correctly, one could increase the depreciation allowances to reflect higher price levels, but indexing depreciation deductions for inflation has never been allowed. When depreciation remains fixed, cash flow in the first period is $56.50 ($63 minus 50 percent of taxable income, which is measured as $63 minus $50). Cash flow in the second period is $55.32 ($60.64 minus 50 percent of taxable income, which is measured as $60.64 minus $50). The rate of return that discounts these amounts to $100 is 0.0781; that is, $56.60/1.0771 plus $55.32/(1 + 0.0781)^2$ is $100. This 7.81 percent return is, however, a nominal return. To convert it to a real return requires dividing 1 plus the nominal return by 1 plus the inflation rate, and subtracting 1, or 1.0881/1.05 − 1. This exercise yields a real rate of return of 2.67 percent, and an effective tax rate of 73.2 percent; that is, (0.1 − 0.0267)/0.1 = 0.732.

Effective Tax Rate Formulas

The formulas used to calculate effective marginal tax rates are continuous time methods; taxes are assumed to be paid continuously and interest rates are continuously compounded. This result is an approximation of the actual payment of taxes.

In the case of a depreciating asset, the relationship between pretax return and after tax return in the corporate sector is determined by the rental price formula of Hall and Jorgenson (1967):

$$r_p = \frac{(r_f + \delta)(1 - t_f z(1 - mk)) - k}{1 - kt_f} - \delta, \tag{1}$$

where r_p is the pretax real return, r_f is the after-tax discount rate of the firm, δ is the economic depreciation rate, t_f is the statutory tax rate of the firm (equal to the corporate tax rate for corporate production and equal to the individual tax rate for noncorporate production), z is the present value of depreciation deductions for tax purposes, k is the investment tax credit rate, and m is the fraction of k that reduces the basis for depreciation purposes. The value of depreciation is discounted at the nominal discount rate, $r_f + \pi$, where π is the rate of inflation. This formula applies to investments in equipment and structures subject to depreciation.

The value of z depends on the useful life for tax purposes, the discount rate, and the method of depreciation. For straight-line depreciation equal amounts are taken over the life of the investment. For a five-year property, this fraction is $1/5$. Under straight-line depreciation the formula for z is

$$z = \frac{1 - e^{-(r_f + \pi)T}}{(r_f + \pi)}, \tag{2}$$

where T is the useful life. Note that depreciation is discounted at the nominal rate of discount—the real rate plus the inflation rate. If depreciation were indexed it would be discounted at the real rate.

A second method, which was used in the past but not currently, is the sum of years digits method. In this method depreciation in each year is the number of years of remaining life divided by the sum of the years in the life. Thus for a five-year property the sum of digits is $1 + 2 + 3 + 4 + 5$ or 15, and depreciation is $5/15$, $4/15$, $3/15$, $2/15$, and $1/15$ in each of the five years. The formula for this type of depreciation is

$$z = \left(\frac{z}{(r_f + \pi)}\right)\left[1 - \left[\frac{1}{(r_f + \pi)T}\right]\left[1 - e^{-(r_f + \pi)T}\right]\right]. \tag{3}$$

A final method is the declining-balance method. In the declining-balance method, a rate that is a multiple of the straight-line rate is applied to the depreciated balance. For example, for the five-year property, a double-declining-balance method would allow a deduction of $2/5$ in the first years. In the second year the deduction would be $2/5$ times $(1 - 2/5)$. If the method were 150 percent declining balance, the rate would be $1.5/5$. Under this method the cost would not be fully depreciated; thus declining-balance methods allow the taxpayer to switch to the straight-line method at any time. The optimal time to switch is when the declining balance rate is equal to the straight-line rate. For example, if T^* represents the point at which the method is switched, the optimal time is when $x/T = 1/(T - T^*)$, where x is the multiple of the straight-line rate. Solving this equation, the optimal value of T^* is at $(x - 1)/x$ times T. Thus, when x is 2, the optimal time to switch is when $T^* = T/2$, when x is 1.5, the optimal time is when $T^* = 1/3$. In this case, the formula for declining balance is

$$z = \frac{x\left[1 - e^{-(r_f + \pi + x/T)T^*}\right]}{(r_f + \pi)T + x} + e^{-(r_f + \pi + x/T)T^*}\left[\frac{1 - e^{-(r_f + \pi)(T - T^*)}}{(r_f + \pi)T + x}\right]. \tag{4}$$

Investments in inventories simply produce all of their output at a time in the future. In this case, assuming that the returns are not indexed

$$e^{(r_f + \pi)T} = e^{(r_p + \pi)T}(1 - t_f) + t_f, \tag{5}$$

where T is the holding period. This type of calculation applies to inventories at the level of the firm, when FIFO (first-in, first-out) accounting is used. When LIFO (last-in, first-out) accounting is used, π is set to zero in equation (5). This formula simply expresses the mathematical relationship between pretax and after-tax return when income is taxed on a realization basis. This approach treats inventories as goods under construction whose accrued value is not taxed until the product is sold; this deferral aspect is relatively unimportant in the case of inventories where holding periods are very short.

Discount rates will differ between the corporate and noncorporate sector. For the noncorporate firm, the discount rate is the overall net after-tax return r. In the case of the corporate sector, however, there is another layer of tax imposed, so r_f for the corporate firm is different from than r. Corporations are allowed to deduct interest at their higher statutory tax rate, including the inflation premium, and this interest is subject to individual tax at the personal level. In addition the equity return to capital is subject to tax as dividends and capital gains.

The discount rate of the corporations is equal to a weighted average of debt and equity:

$$r_f = f(i(1 - t_f) - \pi) + (1 - f)E, \tag{6}$$

where f is the fraction financed by debt, i is the nominal interest rate, t_f is the corporate statutory rate, and E is the return required by stockholders prior to personal level taxes. The discount of the noncorporate firm and of individual investors in general is

$$r_f = f(i(1 - t_f) - \pi) + (1 - f)E(1 - v), \tag{7}$$

where t_f is the individual tax rate and v is the effective tax rate on corporate equity at the personal level. This formula simply says that the overall net after-tax return is a weighted average of the after-tax return to debt and the after-tax return to equity, assuming individuals must earn the same return on their equity investments in the noncorporate sector as in the corporate sector. The value of v is determined by the formula

$$E(1 - v) = s_d E(1 - t_f) + \left\{ \frac{ln\left[e^{(E(1-s_d) + \pi)T} (1 - t_g) + t_g \right]}{T} - \pi \right\}, \tag{8}$$

where s_d is the share of the real return paid out as dividends, t_f in this equation is the individual statutory tax rate, T is the capital gains holding period, and t_g is the capital gains tax rate. The first part of this equation is the after-tax return on dividends; the second part is the after-tax return on capital gains, derived from a formula of the same functional form as (5).

The tax rate on owner-occupied housing is calculated by determining a cost of capital, which is

$$r_p = f(i(1 - nt_f) - \pi) + (1 - f)E^* - nt_g, \tag{9}$$

where n is the fraction of interest and property taxes deducted by homeowners and g is property taxes as a percent of asset value. The effective tax rate is raised by the inability to deduct interest payments in full and lowered by the ability to deduct property taxes in part. Effective tax rates are measured as $(r_p - r)/r_p$.

Measuring the Capital Gains Tax Rate and the Lock-in Effect

The capital gains tax on structures is based on the formula

$$r_p = \frac{(r+\delta)(1 - tz - e^{-(r+\delta)T})}{(1-t)\left[1 - e^{-(r+\delta)T}\right]} - \delta, \tag{10}$$

If the asset is sold before depreciation is completed (assuming straight-line depreciation),

$$z = \frac{1 - e^{-(r+\pi)T}}{(r+\pi)+T} + \frac{(T-T')}{Te^{-(r+\pi)T'}}, \tag{11}$$

where T' is the holding period and T is the depreciation period.

The increase in yield necessary to sell an asset (nondepreciating) is determined by the formula

$$e^{(g+\pi)(T_1+T_2)}(1-t)+t = \left[e^{(g+\pi)T_1}(1-t)+t\right]\left[e^{(g+g^*+\pi)T_2}(1-t^*)+t^*\right], \tag{12}$$

where T_1 is the period of time the asset has already been held and T_2 is the period of time the new asset is to be held. If the new asset is to be taxed, then t^* is set equal to t, the individual's tax rate; if the new asset is to be held until death, then t^* is set at zero. The value of g^* is the increase in appreciation rate of the new asset; if the increase in return derives from increased divides, then g^* is equal to $D^*(1 - t)$, where D^* is the increased rate of dividends.

For a depreciating asset (structure) the formula that determines the increase in rent (R) necessary to trade assets is

$$tz\,(T) = R(1-t)\left[\frac{e^{-(r+\delta)T_1} - e^{-(r+\delta)T}}{r+\delta} + tz\,(T_1) + tz\,(T_2)\left[\,e^{-(r+\delta)T}\,\right]\right], \tag{13}$$

In this equation $z(T)$ is calculated based on equation (11).

Excess Burden and Revenue Yield for Capital Gains Taxes

The relationship between realizations and accruals is based on the formula

$$G = Ae^{-bt}, \tag{14}$$

where G is gains realized, A is a constant, b is a constant (the realizations coefficient), and t is the tax rate. The elasticity is bt. Revenue is equal to tG. The excess burden of the capital gains tax relative to a new rate is obtained by measuring the area under the realizations curve:

$$EB = A \left[\frac{e^{-bt^*} - e^{-bt}}{b} - (t - t^*)e^{-tb} \right], \tag{15}$$

where t^* is the new tax rate and t is the current tax rate.

Data Sources

Table 2.1

The historical individual tax rate series is derived from data supplied by Peek and Wilcox (1986) and data supplied by the Department of Treasury. Inflation rates from 1979 to 1989 are based on the Drexel-Burnham-Lambert Decision Makers poll of January 16, 1990. Inflation rates in earlier years are based on the adaptive expectations model of Hendershott and Hu (1981). This method uses a geometric weight of the previous seven quarters. The inflation rates are based on the GNP deflator and are taken from various issues of the Economic Report of the President. Nominal interest rates are Baa bond rates taken from table B-71 of the Economic Report of the President 1991.

Figure 2.1

Effective tax rates in figure 2.2 are calculated based on the appropriate formulas, using the data in table 2.1. These effective tax rates are shown in table B.1. The after-tax return to corporate equity, $E(1 - v)$, is set equal to the real after-tax rate of return plus a fixed risk premium of 4 percent. This risk premium is chosen to obtain realistic levels of the return to corporate stock (Hendershott and Hu 1981).

The depreciation rates for equipment and structures used to construct tax rates and elsewhere in the model are taken from Hulten and Wykoff (1981); rates for rental housing and owner-occupied housing are set at 1 percent (Leigh 1990). The holding period for inventories is set at four months, based the ratio of inventories to sales, and half of inventories are assumed to be FIFO. Data on the average holding period of corporate stock indicate a holding period of seven years. A substantial fraction of gains, however, are held until death. Based on historical realizations to accruals ratios, about half of capital gains are held until death (Gravelle 1991). Based on data from tax returns, about half of property taxes and interest on owner-occupied housing are deducted; property taxes are estimated to be 1.4 percent of asset value.

The value of f (fraction borrowed) is set at one-third, consistent with historical averages from the Board of Governors of the Federal Reserve Board Balance Sheets for the U.S. Economy. Based on historical averages, two-thirds of the real return on corporate equities is paid out as dividends.

Table B.1
Estimated marginal effective tax rates

Year	Corporate	Noncorporate	Owner occupied	Total
1953	70	37	-1	58
1954	57	23	-1	43
1955	58	24	-1	44
1956	60	25	-1	46
1957	61	27	-1	48
1958	61	26	1	47
1959	58	25	1	45
1960	55	23	1	42
1961	55	22	1	42
1962	48	17	1	35
1963	47	16	1	34
1964	44	14	0	31
1965	42	13	1	29
1966	42	14	1	30
1967	45	17	1	33
1968	50	20	3	37
1969	58	28	5	45
1970	54	26	5	42
1971	50	21	5	38
1972	51	21	5	38
1973	51	21	5	38
1974	55	25	7	42
1975	56	27	11	44
1976	53	23	7	40
1977	49	23	6	40
1978	58	26	10	46
1979	57	29	11	45
1980	60	33	15	48
1981	48	24	12	38
1982	43	22	9	35
1983	46	20	8	34
1984	44	20	7	33
1985	44	20	7	33
1986	45	19	6	33
1987	44	22	4	33
1988	43	22	4	33
1989	43	22	4	33

Asset lives, investment credits and depreciation rates and methods are reported in tables B.2 through B.5. When aggregating capital to construct tax rates, capital stock shares are weighted by pretax returns. Capital stock shares for types of assets within equipment and structures are given in table B.4; allocations across industries and asset types within firms are in table B.6. Capital stock shares by asset type are based on cumulating historical investment over time and applying depreciation weights to obtain capital stocks for 28 different business assets. These assets are allocated to industry using the capital flows tables. For further detail on the construction of assets as well as the measurement of tax lives and investment credits, see Gravelle (1982, 1983). The stock of land and allocations of land among industries are taken from Eisner (1980). Allocations of inventories are taken from tax return data. Corporate shares of output are based on Gravelle (1989).

Figure 2.2

The after-tax rate of return series in figure 2.2 is based on the formula in equation (7), using data from table 2.1. The after-tax rate of return for equity is equal to the real after-tax interest rate plus a 4 percent risk premium.

Data used to construct the savings rate are taken from the Economic Report of the President 1991 for 1953–58 and the Economic Report of the President 1993 for 1959–89. The savings rate is calculated by dividing net private savings by disposable income. Net savings is gross private savings minus capital consumption allowances (tables B-28 and B-22, respectively, of the 1991 Economic Report and tables B-26 and B-20 of the 1993 Economic Report). Disposable income is gross national product (table B-1 of the 1991 Economic Report and B-20 of the 1993 Economic Report) minus capital consumption allowances (table B-22 of the 1991 Economic Report and table B-20 of the 1993 Economic Report) minus total government receipts (table B-79 of the 1991 Economic Report and table B-77 of the 1993 Economic Report). The actual data represented in figure 2.3 are shown in table B.7.

Remaining Effective Tax Rate Tables

For comparative calculations in chapters 3, 4, 5, and 7, the inflation rate is set at 4.8 percent (based on recent measures) and an assumed 6 percent after-tax return for corporations and a 5 percent after-tax rate of return for noncorporate firms, based on historical averages. The remaining adjustments depend on the particular comparisons being made and are discussed in the text.

Table B.2
Asset lives: Equipment and structures

Asset type	1954–61	1962–70	1971–80	1981–86	1987[a]
Equipment					
Autos	4.2	3.0	3.0	2.5	5.0
Office/computing equipment	9.8	7.0	7.0	4.5	5.0
Trucks, buses, and trailers	9.8	7.0	5.0	4.5	5.0
Aircraft	16.1	11.5	9.2	4.5	6.8
Construction machinery	9.8	7.0	5.0	4.5	5.0
Mining/oilfield equipment	16.1	11.5	9.2	4.5	7.0
Service industry equipment	17.3	12.4	9.9	4.5	7.0
Tractors	12.4	8.9	7.1	4.5	6.4
Instruments	18.0	12.9	10.3	5.1	[b]
Other	15.4	11.0	8.8	4.5	7.0
General industrial equipment	17.3	12.4	9.9	4.9	[c]
Metalworking machinery	13.6	9.8	7.8	4.2	6.7
Electric transmission equipment	22.4	17.3	13.8	7.3	[d]
Communications equipment	18.7	14.4	11.5	4.5	5.0
Other electrical equipment	15.7	11.3	9.0	4.5	7.0
Furniture and fixtures	14.0	10.0	8.0	4.5	7.0
Special industrial equipment	16.1	11.5	9.2	4.5	6.5
Agricultural equipment	14.0	10.0	8.0	4.5	7.0
Fabricated metal	24.8	17.8	14.2	6.6	[e]
Engines and turbines	29.4	22.6	18.1	10.8	[f]
Ships and boats	28.0	20.0	16.0	4.5	10.0
Railroad equipment	26.3	18.8	15.0	9.5	7.0
Structures					
Other	40.0	40.0	31.0	[g]	31.5
Industrial	40.0	40.0	36.0	[g]	31.5
Public utility	32.0	28.0	22.0	12.9	[f]
Commercial	40.0	40.0	37.0	[g]	31.5
Farm	40.0	40.0	20.0	[g]	20.0
Residential	40.0	40.0	31.0	[g]	27.5

a. In 1993 the depreciable life for nonresidential structures (other, industrial, and commercial) was increased to thirty-nine years.
b. Twelve percent at 5, 81 percent at 7, 7 percent at 20.
c. Four percent at 3, 14 percent at 5, 73 percent at 7, 9 percent at 20.
d. Five percent at 5, 53 percent at 7, 42 percent at 20.
e. Eighteen percent at 5, 40 percent at 7, 42 percent at 20.
f. Twenty-five percent at 15, 75 percent at 2.
g. Fifteen years 1981, eighteen years 1982–83, nineteen years 1984–86.

Table B.3
Investment credit rates: Equipment and structures

Asset type	1962–68	1971–74	1974–80	1981–86
Equipment				
Autos	2.3	2.3	3.3	6.0
Office/computing equipment	7.0	7.0	10.0	10.0
Trucks, buses, and trailers	4.6	4.6	6.6	10.0
Aircraft	7.0	7.0	7.0	10.0
Construction machinery	4.6	4.6	6.6	10.0
Mining/oilfield equipment	7.0	7.0	10.0	10.0
Service industry equipment	7.0	7.0	10.0	10.0
Tractors	6.0	6.0	9.0	10.0
Instruments	7.0	7.0	10.0	10.0
Other	7.0	7.0	10.0	10.0
General industrial equipment	6.4	6.4	9.1	9.6
Metalworking machinery	6.0	6.0	8.6	9.4
Electric transmission equipment	4.8	5.7	10.0	10.0
Communications equipment	4.6	5.2	10.0	10.0
Other electrical equipment	7.0	7.0	10.0	10.0
Furniture and fixtures	7.0	7.0	10.0	10.0
Special industrial equipment	7.0	7.0	10.0	10.0
Agricultural equipment	7.0	7.0	10.0	10.0
Fabricated metal	7.0	7.0	10.0	10.0
Engines and turbines	5.1	5.6	10.0	10.0
Ships and boats	7.0	7.0	10.0	10.0
Railroad equipment	7.0	7.0	10.0	10.0
Structures				
Public Utility	3.0	4.0	10.0	10.0

Note: A full basis adjustment is applied to 1962 and 1963, and a half basis adjustment is applied to 1982–86.

Table B.4
Cost recovery rules and capital gains exclusions

Asset type	Year	Depreciation method or exclusion
Equipment (including public utility structures)		
	1953	Straight line
	1954–80	Sum-of-years digits
	1981	Double-declining balance
	1982–86	150% declining balance
	1986–present	Assets in 3-, 5-, 7-, or 10-year class; double-declining balance. Assets in 15- or 20-year class 150% declining balance
Structures		
	1953	Straight line
	1954–69	Sum-of-year digits
	1969–80	Nonresidential structures— 150% declining balance; residential structures— sum-of-years digits
	1981–86	175% declining balance
	1987–present	Straight line
Treatment of oil and gas[a]		
	1953–69	27.5% depletion
	1970–74	22% depletion
	1982–83	7.8% recovered over 3 years
	1984–86	7.8% recovered at 5 years
	1987–present	12% recovered at 5 years
Capital gains		
	1953–78	50% exclusion
	1979–86	60% exclusion
	1987–present	No exclusion

a. Nine percent of costs is covered by depletion unless percentage depletion applies; the remainder of cost is expensed. For minimum tax calculations, 39 percent is recovered over 10 years under the minimum tax, and 39 percent through cost depletion under ACE.

Table B.5
Economic depreciation, minimum tax lives, and asset shares

Asset type	Economic depreciation	Alternative minimum tax lives	Share of category
Equipment			
Autos	0.3333	3.0	4.6
Office/computing equipment	0.2729	7.0	5.0
Trucks, buses, and trailers	0.2537	7.0	8.3
Aircraft	0.1818	11.5	1.9
Construction machinery	0.1722	6.0	3.4
Mining/oilfield equipment	0.1650	11.5	1.7
Service industry equipment	0.1650	9.0	3.2
Tractors	0.1633	8.9	2.9
Instruments	0.1473	12.9	6.5
Other	0.1473	11.0	2.7
General industrial equipment	0.1225	12.2	6.8
Metalworking machinery	0.1225	9.6	6.7
Electric transmission equipment	0.1179	17.3	5.4
Communications equipment	0.1179	10.0	10.5
Other electrical equipment	0.1179	11.3	1.8
Furniture and fixtures	0.1100	10.0	5.8
Special industrial equipment	0.1031	11.5	6.6
Agricultural equipment	0.0971	10.0	4.9
Fabricated metal	0.0917	17.1	3.3
Engines and turbines	0.0786	22.6	2.0
Ships and boats	0.0750	18.0	2.3
Railroad equipment	0.0660	11.9	4.4
Structures			
Mining/oil	0.0663		7.6
Other	0.0454	40.0	1.3
Industrial	0.0330	40.0	16.7
Public utility	0.0316	27.5	27.8
Commercial	0.0230	40.0	40.6
Farm	0.0237	40.0	6.1

Source: Depreciation rates are based on Hulten and Wykoff (1981).

Table B.6
Distribution of capital stock by industry, sector, and broad asset type

Industry	Share of total	Corporate share	Asset composition of industry			
			Inven- tories	Struc- tures	Equip- ment	Land
Rental housing	12.7	7.1	0.00	0.73	0.00	0.27
Agriculture	4.5	22.8	0.10	0.12	0.11	0.67
Oil and gas	4.3	82.7	0.05	0.78	0.09	0.08
Mining	0.7	82.8	0.03	0.52	0.37	0.08
Construction	2.1	70.2	0.05	0.19	0.68	0.08
Transportation	2.2	91.3	0.02	0.46	0.43	0.09
Trade	15.4	78.5	0.36	0.45	0.14	0.05
Services	10.3	63.5	0.03	0.47	0.42	0.08
Manufacturing	11.9	100.0	0.30	0.33	0.31	0.06
Utilities	7.2	100.0	0.04	0.64	0.24	0.08
Owner-occupied housing	28.8	0.0	0.0	0.73	0.0	0.27
Total	100.0	47.2	0.11	0.56	0.15	0.18

Source: Gravelle (1989).

Table B.7
Savings rates and estimated rates of return

Year	Savings rate	Rate of return
1953	11.0	1.93
1954	10.5	3.57
1955	11.4	3.27
1956	12.1	2.95
1957	11.9	2.82
1958	11.5	3.02
1959	11.7	3.70
1960	10.6	4.42
1961	11.6	4.65
1962	12.5	5.03
1963	12.2	5.21
1964	13.5	4.98
1965	14.3	5.10
1966	14.0	5.21
1967	14.7	5.63
1968	12.9	3.62
1969	11.5	3.29
1970	12.3	4.63
1971	13.7	4.07
1972	12.8	3.89
1973	15.0	4.00
1974	13.1	3.43
1975	14.6	2.60
1976	13.1	3.74
1977	12.6	3.69
1978	13.2	2.64
1979	12.4	2.94
1980	11.7	2.98
1981	12.7	5.18
1982	12.0	6.66
1983	11.1	5.46
1984	13.8	6.52
1985	11.8	5.97
1986	9.7	4.76
1987	8.7	5.64
1988	9.3	6.00
1989	7.8	5.73

Source: Savings rates from the Economic Report of the President (1953–89).

Notes

Chapter 2

1. The case for consumption taxation stretches back to the seventeenth-century political philosopher Thomas Hobbes and continues with such luminaries as John Stuart Mill, Irving Fisher, and Nicholas Kaldor. The debate over the merits of income as opposed to consumption taxation continues today; further discussion and historical perspective may be found in Bradford (1980), Brazer (1973), Goode (1980), Kahn (1973), and McLure (1988).

2. It is important to distinguish between these two bases. For example, Gordon and Slemrod (1988) and Shoven (1991) suggest that capital income taxes do not collect much revenue, by contrasting the taxes collected under the current system with those collected under a consumption tax approach. This finding does not indicate that capital income taxes are not collected but rather that net investment is small relative to capital income. To determine whether taxes are collected on capital income requires a comparison to a shift to wage taxes. Moreover in any given year income taxes can be unusually low because of recent accelerations of depreciation or downswings in the economy, one or both of which were the case in these studies.

3. The calculations refer only to federal income taxes and they employ the traditional view of dividends, as discussed in chapter 4. They also do not account for a number of minor features of the tax law.

4. Fullerton, Gillette, and Mackie (1987) also reach this conclusion when using the traditional view of dividends, although their overall tax rate is higher (38 percent) due to the incorporation of state and local income and property taxes. Jorgenson and Yun (1990), however, find effective tax rates have increased as a result of the 1986 Act— seven percentage points for corporate investment, four percentage points for noncorporate investment, and less than a percentage point for owner-occupied housing at a 6 percent inflation rate.

5. These studies include those of Wright (1969), Heien (1972), Weber (1975), Springer (1975), Taylor (1971) and Gylfason (1981), and Makin and Couch (1989). Heien, Taylor, and Gylfason found positive interest elasticities but did not correct for inflation or taxes. Weber and Springer corrected for inflation, but not taxes, and found a negative interest elasticity. Wright corrected for taxes but not inflation; his estimate was of a

pure substitution effect, which he found to be quite small; the interest elasticity could easily be negative. Makin and Couch corrected for inflation, but not taxes, and found a significant results for some time periods but not for others. Feldstein (1970b) suggested that failure to correct for inflation biases the results and could lead to a coefficient of different sign. Carlino (1982) also addresses the effects of failure to correct for inflation and taxes.

6. A recent exception was a series of studies focused on the effect of individual retirement accounts, which were generally available, subject to a dollar ceiling, between 1982 and 1986. The contributions to this topic reached varying conclusions as to the effects of IRAs on savings; a detailed review is deferred until chapter 8.

7. Changes in private savings could offset changes in government savings. Some economists have in fact theorized that changing the deficit (or government savings) will have no effect on overall savings in the economy. Under this theory, referred to as Ricardian equivalence, individuals will recognize that with an increase in the deficit, the future tax burdens are placed on themselves or their descendants and will increase their own savings as a result. Similarly a decrease in the deficit will cause an offsetting decrease in private savings as individuals recognize the reduction in future tax burdens.

The full effects of Ricardian equivalence require some strong assumptions—among them that individuals are altruistically linked, that they recognize the future consequences of current deficits, and that capital markets work perfectly. These assumptions are in doubt. For example, Altonji, Hayashi, and Kotlikoff (1992) suggest that if families were altruistically linked in this fashion, consumption of family members would be independent of their share of family resources, which the evidence does not support. There appears to be substantial evidence that many individuals are liquidity constrained (cannot borrow freely from future lifetime resources to consume in the present). There is, however, considerable dispute about the empirical evidence on the degree to which private savings might respond to a change in government savings. See Bernheim (1987) and Seaton (1993) for a review of the literature and for different perspectives on this issue. Note, however, that Ricardian equivalence does not appear consistent with events in the 1980s—the private savings rate fell as deficits, and government debt increased substantially.

8. As with most statements of economic effect, there are some exceptions. One possible exception occurs with risky investments, where the welfare of individuals may be improved when the government shares in the risk via taxation. This welfare improvement might occur if the government is less risk averse than individuals. Another is that taxes used to correct existing market distortions (e.g., pollution taxes) actually increase efficiency.

9. The discussion in this section refers to the effects of a permanent shift from one tax base to the other in a closed economy. Researchers have also studied the effect of temporary shifts and of whether or not the shift is announced in advance. See Judd (1987) and Auerbach and Kotlikoff (1987) for further exploration of these issues. A discussion of how these models would be altered in an open economy is deferred until chapter 10.

10. Although these models are attractive because they are simpler to compute, obviously society is not composed of infinitely lived individuals and no new additions to the population. Such models would nevertheless be justified if Ricardian equivalence, discussed at the end of the section on savings, were valid.

11. Fullerton and Rogers (1993) examine the removal of different types of taxes and replacement with a uniform consumption tax; their measures of efficiency cost include other types of distortions (e.g., differential tax treatment of capital income from different sources). Most of their welfare effects are, however, still small.

12. An investment credit or similar subsidy for new investment should cause the prices of existing assets to fall, acting in part as a consumption tax would, by burdening existing holders of assets. The investment credit also, however, allows a credit for replacement of the capital stock, hence its intermediate position between a consumption tax and a wage tax. This point will be explained in more detail in chapter 5 under the discussion of "bang for the buck."

13. Auerbach and Kotlikoff (1987) used the same tax rates for wages and capital income —15 percent. This rate is probably reasonable for wage income but too low for capital income. The effect of using this capital income tax rate on welfare is ambiguous—it causes the distortion from capital income taxes to be too low but also causes a larger offsetting increase in the leisure/consumption distortion to be too low as well. Results reported by Gravelle (1991b) suggest that welfare gains would be slightly larger with a 30 percent tax rate but would still be quite small.

Chapter 3

1. When relative prices are not changing and firms are at least maintaining inventories, income is correctly stated for inventories under the last-in, first-out (LIFO) method of inventory accounting, where the last item sold is treated as the last item purchased. For accounting under the first in, first-out (FIFO) inventory method where the last item sold is treated as the oldest in inventory, there is an understatement of cost of inventories and an overtaxation of inventory profits.

2. For further discussion of this issue, see Baumol and Oates (1975).

3. Although conventional growth theory clearly demonstrates that there is no relationship between the level or allocation of capital and the growth rate, a recent study by De Long and Summers (1991) reported a positive relationship between growth rates and investment in equipment. It seems likely that the relationship they found is the result of a few observations in a very small sample. Indeed Auerbach, Hassett, and Oliner (1993) found that the relationship disappeared or changed markedly when the sample was split between more and less developed countries in a different fashion.

4. It is perhaps one of the peculiar aspects of the tax policy process that the Joint Committee on Taxation (1991) wrote an overview of taxation in an open economy entitled "Factors Affecting the International Competitiveness of the United States" in which one of the principal points is that international competitiveness as the term is commonly used is not meaningful.

5. There has recently been some interest in the notion of "strategic trade theory," which suggests a country could be better off by subsidizing certain industries in order to gain market position and monopoly profits. Even were this the case, however, there has been no quantification of such effects. Nor would a subsidy to capital (rather than to all factors of production) be necessarily optimal even were such industries to be identified.

Indeed one of the originators of this theory, Paul Krugman (1987), nevertheless advocates free trade as a policy prescription.

6. This theory is referred to as the Tiebout hypothesis (see Tiebout 1956), and generally speaking, it suggests that as long as individuals can choose between jurisdictions with different levels of taxes and services, the property tax is capitalized into property values.

Chapter 4

1. The revenue raised by the corporate tax should be measured as the difference in receipts from taxing corporate income on a partnership bases to the present system, not the repeal of the corporate tax. See note 1 to chapter 2 for an explanation of arguments made in some recent papers that little tax is collected by capital income taxes or corporate income taxes.

2. To illustrate this important, yet subtle, point: Suppose that there is no inflation, a 34 percent corporate rate, an average 23 percent individual rate, and a 5 percent interest rate. If the corporate tax is applied at its effective rate, the corporation will pay no tax—a dollar of earnings included in profit will be offset by a dollar of deduction, and the corporation must earn a 5 percent rate of return. Thus for $100 borrowed the corporation must earn $5 of profit. It will also receive an offsetting $5 interest deduction, for no tax. The individual then receives an interest payment of $5, pays a tax of $1.15, and receives an after-tax return of $3.85.

   Suppose now that there is a 5 percent inflation. For the individual to receive $3.85 in real return, the after-tax nominal return must be $8.85, which includes $5 to compensate the individual for the loss in value of the principal. The interest rate must be approximately 11.5 percent for an individual to have $8.85 after paying 23 percent in taxes. The after-tax cost of interest to the firm is 7.6 percent—11.5 times (1 – 0.34)—and the after-tax real cost of interest is 2.6 percent. If the corporation pays a tax on the real return, the pretax real return is only 3.9 percent (the amount necessary to yield a 2.6 percent return when paying tax at a 34 percent rate). The effective tax rate overall is only 2 percent (the tax on 3.9 percent to yield the 3.85 percent after-tax real return to the creditor). Inflation can of course raise the effective tax rate at the firm level, but it will not raise it up to a full effective tax rate on the nominal return because the inflationary increase in the value of the real asset is not currently included in income. Rather, it shows up slowly, over time, in a smaller value of depreciation deductions. Moreove there are frequently explicit rules enacted, such as accelerated depreciation, to offset the effects on inflation on the value of tax depreciation.

3. Arguments have been made that it is appropriate to tax corporations more heavily as an exchange for the benefits of limited liability. This argument is not consistent with an efficient tax, however, since the availability of limited liability contributes to efficiency in the organization of investment and production and should not be discouraged.

4. There are small corporations that may be organized and taxed as corporations in order to obtain some other tax benefits that existed in the past, such as lower tax rates under previous rate structures where individual top marginal tax rates were higher than the corporate rate. There were also some advantages to pension plans for corpo-

rate firms in the past. There are also large limited-liability partnerships. Although these large partnerships can avoid the corporate tax, under current tax rules they lead to quite complicated tax compliance procedures, which may explain why they were limited to certain activities (e.g., real estate and oil and gas).

5. The earliest models in Harberger (1966) simply posited two sectors: a corporate and a noncorporate sector. In these early studies, which did not deal with individual level differences, the average corporate tax rate was 45 percent. The empirical applications divided output by industry aggregations into a high-tax sector and a low-tax sector. The low-tax sector has a very low tax rate, that was almost zero (1.4 percent). The high tax sector, however, had a considerable amount of noncorporate production, and when the zero taxes of the noncorporate sector were averaged with the 45 percent tax rate of the corporate sectors, the average was only 34 percent. Thus the tax wedge between the two sectors was much smaller, an important difference since the excess burden rises more rapidly than the tax rate.

6. Since taxpayers have heterogeneous tax rates, models using a representative investor must choose some representative tax rate, which is typically an average weighted by ownership. Pension funds are not subject to tax, and the corporate/noncorporate distortion becomes smaller if the zero tax rate is averaged in, assuming that these pension funds cannot invest in noncorporate equity. At the same time the distortion between corporate debt and equity becomes larger when pension funds are averaged in, because this distortion depends on the discrepancy between the corporate tax rate and the tax rate of the creditors. There is a strong case for not including pension funds because investments in these funds are not likely to be marginal; this issue is discussed in further detail in chapter 8.

7. Using the corporation as a withholding device simply means that the tax would be collected at the corporate level. The shareholder would include corporate income in tax but would also receive a tax credit for his share of corporate income tax paid. This system would be similar to the withholding of income tax on wages, except that it need not be refundable. (If it is not refundable, tax-exempt shareholders will pay tax at the corporate rate.)

Chapter 5

1. This relationship has to do with the compounding of interest. If an asset is to earn a 5 percent rate of return in a noninflationary environment, its value will be $1.05 after a year. If the inflation rate is 3 percent, then the principal return on the asset at the end of a year must be $1.03, and the five percent return earned on the entire amount. Thus, if the asset must earn a real return of 5 percent, it will have to earn $108.15. The $3 is the restatement of value for inflation, the $5 is the return on the original $100, and the extra $0.15 is the 5 percent return on the $3 of increased value due to inflation.

2. See *The Great Depreciation Hoax* (1971).

3. When the relative cost of goods is changing, LIFO works imperfectly. If the price is rising, LIFO causes the gain in value to go untaxed, while if prices are falling, it allows the loss to go unrecognized.

4. A more technical discussion of these nonneutralities can be found in Gravelle (1982). The particular form of subsidy that is nonneutral is one that increases in present value for long-lived assets in a way related to the longevity. The simplest form, which will be discussed subsequently, is partial expensing.

5. These numerical illustrations also demonstrate why Auerbach and Kotlikoff (1983) were able to conclude that investment incentives have the potential to be self-financing (i.e., the savings stimulated by the tax change would so expand income in the future that revenues could be raised without raising other tax rates. Their model did not account for depreciation. Moreover it assumed an unreasonably low growth rate (only 1 percent); as a result the present value of new savings is only 14 percent of the total of new savings and existing capital, again using a 7 percent growth rate. (Their model also tends to predict a very large savings response, especially in the short run.)

Chapter 6

1. These numbers reflect only the response due to the reduction in lock-in. Both estimates also included an offset for the likelihood that individuals would shift assets from taxable uses into less taxed uses (e.g., substituting capital gains for dividends) which would reduce revenue. The Bush administration proposed a 30 percent exclusion, but that exclusion was modified by the different treatment of assets held for short periods of time and for taxing the part of the gain on depreciable assets that reflected depreciation already taken as ordinary income. Also the exclusion would be included in income for purposes of the alternative minimum tax, discussed in the following chapter.

2. For a typical holding period for corporate stock, the deferral advantage is about half as large as the benefit from the exclusion; the advantage is somewhat larger for real estate. If realizations were drawn proportionally from faster turnover and from selling of assets held until death, the welfare gains might be overstated by 10 percent or so; if they are drawn from more frequent sale, the gains might be half as large.

Chapter 7

1. The Treasury tax reform study (1984) expressed concern about this issue but elected to restrict its recommendations to taxing large limited partnerships as corporations. At least some critics believe that one reason for introducing the passive loss restriction was to raise revenue by taxing existing tax shelters in order to pay for the rate cut.

2. These calculations should not be interpreted as indicating the overall effects of TRA on residential rental investment. First, the effects on taxpayers of more modest circumstances would be smaller. Second, these calculations assume no offsetting changes in interest rates as a result of TRA. In a general equilibrium analysis rents would rise by less because the contraction in the demand for capital would cause the interest rate to fall.

3. Steuerle (1985) discusses the role of borrowing in tax shelter operations and tax arbitrage. Note that although indexation of interest would probably result in an efficiency gain, it would not do so necessarily because it would increase overall corporate tax burdens and aggravate the corporate/noncorporate distortion. It could be combined, however, with some offsetting relief for taxes on corporate equity.

Chapter 8

1. A firm that is funded in terms of ongoing liability (benefits to be paid to workers on their projected salaries for all their past and future years of service) can be overfunded in terms of termination liability (benefits based on current salaries for past years of service). Employer can terminate the plan, use excess funds (reversions) for investment, and create a successor plan with minimum funding.

2. One time series study was used to argue that IRAs increased savings. Carroll and Summers (1987) argued that the divergence in savings rates between Canada and the United States could be attributed in part to more generous tax favored retirement vehicles in Canada. There was no evidence, however, that IRAs in the United States increased savings. Altig (1990) subsequently found this relationship to disappear when controls for wealth were incorporated.

3. Manegold and Joines performed some regressions, controlling for assets, income, and other variables. But these statistical studies did not produce very reliable results, for they explained virtually none of the variance in savings rates. While their coefficient showed that savings increased by a third of IRA contributions (about the amount of the tax savings), the coefficient was not statistically significant. They also divided the sample into individuals with non-IRA assets below and above $25,000. Savings increased by about two-thirds of IRAs for those below and decreased by about two thirds for those above. The first was statistically significant, but the second was not: Neither regression explained very much of the variation in savings. There are several problems with their statistical analysis. If individuals otherwise were identical in savings, individuals not eligible for IRAs would have had larger amounts of non-IRA assets. Thus there may be a correlation between non-IRA assets and the change in the IRA limit. In addition there was no clear reason for choosing the particular division of the sample.

4. Of course there may be an argument for funding social security (building up reserves in a trust fund much as occurs with private pensions), but such an approach would again entail reducing the deficit or even running surpluses. Actually it is not clear whether social security reduces private savings, since social security could have substituted for transfers between families rather than private savings for retirement. Or it could have encouraged early retirement rather than reduced savings. As with so much of the empirical evidence on savings, there is no clear proof that social security has reduced savings.

Chapter 9

1. Much of the debate over the tax treatment of purchased intangibles has been over the issue of the "correct" treatment of intangibles which depreciate over different periods. Gravelle and Taylor (1992) showed that there is no reason to tie the depreciation of these intangibles to useful life to obtain neutral taxation, since replacement expenditures (equivalent to depreciation) will be expensed in any case. This treatment automatically results in uniform treatment for all assets. A common write-off period would be appropriate to neutrality across different types of assets (as well as being administratively simple); the generosity of that period would affect the degree of lock-in and the tax burden on investment given some expectation of future sale.

2. Gordon and Metcalf (1991) suggest borrowing costs might not necessarily fall because states and localities could use the option of tax finance, and taxpayers would pay for these expenditures at an after-tax interest rate. The issue of course is how readily states are willing to substitute financing capital expenditures out of current taxes rather than out of borrowing. Such a substitution might be difficult given the political constraints of borrowing, particularly in states with transient populations.

3. One possible reason for such a bias is the possibility of a transient population combined with a repayment schedule for capital borrowing that is too rapid in comparison with the flow of services from the investment. Taxpayers would be less willing to make capital expenditures under those circumstances.

4. These purposes include airports, wharves, and docks; mass transit; furnishing of water, electricity, gas, waste disposal, or heating and cooling facilities; residential rental facilities, home mortgages, student loans, redevelopment, and nonprofit enterprises.

5. Some of these rules relate to "advance refunding." These are circumstances when a state or local authority might wish to issue replacement bonds in advance of the retirement data, investing them in other securities in the interim. There may be legitimate reasons for doing so (temporarily low interest rates), but such advance refunding mechanisms can also be used to yield arbitrage profits. Ultimately advance refunding was completely denied for most private activity bonds and allowed only one time for other bonds.

6. The technique for measuring income is similar to the method of measuring depreciation—the change in value of asset should be added to income. See Kiefer (1985) for an article that discusses this application to a future cost.

Chapter 10

1. See Musgrave (1975) for a discussion of this concept. A frequently cited paper by Horst (1980) appears to suggest that capital export neutrality is not efficient when savings is responsive to the rate of return. This view arises because lower foreign taxes might lead to more savings. This approach is not very meaningful, since, given an equal revenue constraint, a capital export neutrality system would always be more efficient.

2. This system of taxing only dividends also gives rise to an analytical problem similar to that of the effect of a dividend tax on stockholders, as discussed in chapter 4, except in this case it is difficult to ascertain an intrinsic value of dividends (for signaling or agency cost reasons) because the firms are actually the same firms. That is, there can be a "new view" of dividends in this case as well. This argument, advanced by Hartman (1985), suggests that once a corporation has actually established a subsidiary, an investment financed out of retained earnings will not be affected by any excess tax of the country of ownership. This view means an even more powerful effect of deferral in establishing a territorially based tax system.

3. There is also a special rule discussed in that study, called the *title passage rule*. This rule allows the sourcing of part of the income from the sale of inventory to occur in the location where title passes. To some extent this rule encourages the production of goods for export.

References

Aaron, Henry J., Frank S. Russek, and Neil M. Singer. 1972. Tax changes and the composition of fixed investment: An aggregate simulation. *Review of Economics and Statistics* 54 (November): 343–56.

Agria, Susan. 1969. Special tax treatment of the minerals industry. In *The Taxation of Income From Capital*, edited by Arnold C. Harberger. Washington: Brookings Institution.

Altig, David. 1990. The case of the missing interest deductions: Will tax reform increase U.S. savings rates? *Federal Reserve Bank of Cleveland Economic Review* 26 (4): 22–34.

Altonji, Joseph G., Fumio Hayashi, and Laurence J. Kotlikoff. 1992. Is the extended family altruistically linked? *American Economic Review* 82 (December): 1177–98.

Altschuler, Rosanne. 1988. A dynamic analysis of the research and experimentation credit. *National Tax Journal* 41 (December): 453–66.

Andersen, Arthur. 1992. Why the focus on corporate AMT? Washington: Office of Federal Tax Services Alert, March 11.

Ang, James, and David Peterson. 1986. Optimal debt versus debt capacity: A disequilibrium model of corporate behavior. In *Research in Finance*, vol. 6, edited by A. Chen. Greenwich, CT: JAI Press, pp. 51–72.

Atrostic, B. K., and Leonard E. Burman. 1990. Allocative effects of fringe benefit taxation. Photocopy.

Auerbach, Alan J. 1991. Retrospective capital gains taxation. *American Economic Review* 81 (March): 167–78.

Auerbach, Alan J. 1989a. Capital gains taxation and tax reform. *National Tax Journal* 42 (September): 391–401.

Auerbach, Alan J. 1989b. The deadweight loss from "nonneutral" capital income taxation. *Journal of Public Economics* 40 (October): 1–36.

Auerbach, Alan J. 1985. Real determinants of corporate leverage. In *Corporate Capital Structures in the United States*, edited by Benjamin Friedman. Chicago: University of Chicago Press, pp. 301–22.

Auerbach, Alan J. 1984. Taxes, firm financial policy, and the cost of capital: An empirical analysis. *Journal of Public Economics* 23 (February): 27–57.

Auerbach, Alan J. 1979a. Share valuation and corporate equity policy. *Journal of Public Economics* 11 (June): 291–305.

Auerbach, Alan J. 1979b. Wealth maximization and the cost of capital. *Quarterly Journal of Economics* 93 (August): 433–46.

Auerbach, Alan J., and Kevin Hassett. 1991. Recent U.S. investment behavior and the Tax Reform Act of 1986: A disaggregate view. *Carnegie-Rochester Conference Series on Public Policy* 35 (Autumn): 185–216.

Auerbach, Alan J., and Kevin Hassett. 1990. Investment, tax policy, and the Tax Reform Act of 1986. In *Do Taxes Matter? The Impact of the Tax Reform Act of 1986*, edited by Joel Slemrod. Cambridge: MIT Press, pp. 13–49.

Auerbach, Alan J., Kevin Hassett, and Stephen D. Oliner. 1992. Reassessing the social returns to equipment investment. Board of Governors of the Federal Reserve Working Paper 129. December 1992 (Revised April 1993). Revised version also printed as National Bureau of Economic Research Working Paper 4405, July 1993, forthcoming, *Quarterly Journal of Economics*.

Auerbach, Alan J., and Laurence J. Kotlikoff. 1987. *Dynamic Fiscal Policy*. Cambridge: Cambridge University Press.

Auerbach, Alan J., and Laurence J. Kotlikoff. 1983. Investment versus savings incentives: The size of the bang for the buck and the potential for self-financing business tax cuts. In *The Economic Consequences of Government Deficits*, edited by Laurence H. Meyer. Norwell, MA: Kluwer Nijhiff, pp. 121–48.

Auten, Gerald E. 1980. Capital gains taxes and realizations: Can a tax cut pay for itself? *Policy Studies Journal* 9 (Autumn): 53–60.

Auten, Gerald E., Leonard E. Burman, and William C. Randolph. 1989. Estimation and interpretation of capital gains realization behavior: Evidence from panel data. *National Tax Journal* 42 (September): 353–74. (This study was also released by the Treasury Department as OTA Paper 67, May 1989.)

Auten, Gerald E., and Charles Clotfelter. 1982. Permanent vs. transitory effects and the realization of capital gains. *Quarterly Journal of Economics* 96 (November): 613–32.

Auten, Gerald E., and Joseph Cordes. 1991. Cutting capital gains taxes. *Journal of Economic Perspectives* 5 (Winter): 181–92.

Auten, Gerald E., and William B. Trautman. 1991. The efficiency cost of the tax exempt bond subsidy to state and local governments. Presented at the Atlantic Economic Society Meetings, October 4.

Bagwell, Laurie S., and John B. Shoven. 1989. Cash distributions to shareholders. *Journal of Economic Perspectives* 3 (Winter): 129–40.

Bailey, Martin J. 1969. Capital gains and income taxation. In *Taxation of Income from Capital*, edited by Arnold C. Harberger. Washington: Brookings Institution, pp. 11–49.

Baily, Martin Neil, and Robert Z. Lawrence. 1992. Tax incentives for R&D: What do the data tell us. Paper commissioned by the Council on Research and Technology. April.

Baily, Martin Neil, and Robert Z. Lawrence. 1987. Tax policies for innovation and competitiveness, Paper commissioned by the Council on Research and Technology. April.

Ballard, Charles L. 1993. Taxation and saving. In *Taxation Issues in the 1990s*, edited by John G. Head. Sydney Australia: Australian Tax Research Foundation.

Ballard, Charles L. 1990. On the specification of simulation models for evaluating income and consumption taxes. In *Heidelberg Conference on Taxing Consumption*, edited by Manfred Rose. Berlin: Springer-Verlag, pp. 147–88.

Ballard, Charles L., Don Fullerton, John D. Shoven, and John Whalley. 1985. *A General Equilibrium Model for Tax Policy Evaluation*. Chicago: University of Chicago Press.

Baumol, William J., and Wallace E. Oates. 1975. *The Theory of Environmental Policy*. Englewood Cliffs, NJ: Prentice Hall.

Becker, Gary S. 1964. *Human Capital: A Theoretical and Empirical Analysis*. New York: Columbia University Press.

Beidleman, Carl R. 1976. Economic depreciation in the capital goods industry. *National Tax Journal* 32 (December): 379–90.

Berkovec, James, and Don Fullerton. 1992. A general equilibrium model of housing, taxes, and portfolio choice. *Journal of Political Economy* 100 (April): 390–429.

Bernheim, B. Douglas. 1991. Tax policy and the dividend puzzle. *Rand Journal of Economics* 22 (Winter): 455–76.

Bernheim, B. Douglas. 1989. Incentive effects of the corporate alternative minimum tax. In *Tax Policy and the Economy*, vol. 3, edited by Lawrence Summers. National Bureau of Economic Research. Cambridge: MIT Press, pp. 69–95.

Bernheim, B. Douglas. 1987. Ricardian equivalence: An evaluation of theory and evidence. *NBER Macroeconomics Annual 1987*. Cambridge: MIT Press, 263–304.

Bernstein, Jeffrey I., and M. Ishaq Nadiri. 1989. Research and development, spillovers and adjustment costs: An application of dynamic duality at the firm level. *Review of Economic Studies* 56: 249–69.

Bernstein, Jeffrey I., and M. Ishaq Nadiri. 1988. Interindustry R&D spillovers, rates of return and production in high tech industries. *American Economic Review* 78 (June): 429–34.

Bernstein, Jeffrey I., and M. Ishaq Nadiri. 1984. Rates of return on physical and R&D capital and structure of the production process: Cross section and time series evidence. Working Paper 84–06. Carleton University (Canada).

Bhattacharya, Sudipto. 1979. Imperfect information, dividend policy, and the bird in the hand fallacy. *Bell Journal of Economics* 10 (Spring): 259–70.

Bickley, James M. 1990. Should credit unions be taxed? Congressional Research Service Report 90–498 E. Library of Congress. October 16.

Bischoff, Charles W. 1971. The effective of alternative lag distributions. In *Tax Incentives and Capital Spending*, edited by Gary Fromm. Washington: Brookings Institution, pp. 61–130.

Blair, Margaret, and Robert E. Litan. 1990. Corporate leverage and leveraged buyouts in the eighties. In *Debt, Taxes, and Corporate Restructuring*, edited by John B. Shoven and Joel Waldfogel. Washington: Brookings Institution, pp. 43–89.

Bloom, David E., and Richard B. Freeman. 1992. The fall in private pension coverage in the U.S. National Bureau of Economic Research Working Paper 3973. January.

Board of Governors of the Federal Reserve System. 1953–1991. *Balance Sheets for the U.S. Economy.*

Boskin, Michael. 1978. Taxation, savings, and the rate of interest. *Journal of Political Economy* 86 (January): s3–s27.

Boskin, Michael, and William G. Gale. 1987. New results on the effects of tax policy on the international location of investment. In *The Effects of Taxation on Capital Accumulation,* edited by Martin Feldstein. Chicago: University of Chicago Press, pp. 201–19.

Bosworth, Barry. 1989. There's no simple explanation for the collapse in savings. *Challenge* 32 (July–August): 27–32.

Bosworth, Barry. 1984. *Tax Incentives and Economic Growth.* Washington: Brookings Institution.

Bovenberg, A. Lans. 1989. Tax policy and national savings in the United States: A Survey. *National Tax Journal* 42 (June): 123–38.

Bradford, David F. 1986. *Untangling the Income Tax.* Committee for Economic Development. Cambridge: Harvard University Press.

Bradford, David F. 1981. The incidence and allocation effects of a tax on corporate distributions. *Journal of Public Economics* 30 (February): 1–22.

Bradford, David F. 1980. The case for a personal consumption tax. In *What Should Be Taxed: Income or Expenditure,* edited by Joseph A. Pechman. Washington: Brookings Institution, pp. 75–113.

Brannon, Gerard M. 1974a. The effect of tax deductibility on the level of charitable contributions and variations on the theme; the lock-in problem for capital gains: An analysis of the 1970–71 experience. *Buildings and the Income Tax.* Washington: Fund for Public Policy Research.

Brannon, Gerard M. 1974b. *Energy Taxes and Subsidies.* Cambridge, MA: Ballinger.

Brannon, Gerard M. 1972. The effects of tax incentives for business investment: A survey of the economic evidence. In *The Economics of Federal Subsidy Programs.* Joint Economic Committee, 92d Cong. 2d Sess. July 15. Washington: GPO, pp. 245–68.

Brazer, Harvey E. 1973. The income tax in the federal revenue system. In *Broad Based Taxes: New Options and Sources,* edited by Richard A. Musgrave. Baltimore: Johns Hopkins University Press, pp. 133–54.

Brimmer, Andrew, and Allen Sinai. 1976. The effects of tax policy on capital formation, corporate liquidity and the availability of investible funds: A simulation study. *The Journal of Finance* 31 (May): 287–308.

Brinner, Roger. 1973. Inflation, deferral and the neutral taxation of capital gains. *National Tax Journal* 26 (December): 565–73.

Brinner, Roger, and Alicia Munnell. 1974. Taxation of capital gains: Inflation and other problems. Federal Reserve Bank of Boston, *New England Economic Review,* (September–October): pp. 3–21.

Brittain, John. 1966. *Corporate Dividend Policy*. Washington: Brookings Institution.

Brown, Charles, James Hamilton, and James Medoff. 1990. *Employers Large and Small*. Cambridge: Harvard University Press.

Brumbaugh, David. 1991. Federal taxes and foreign investment in the United States: An assessment. Congressional Research Service Report 91–582 E. Library of Congress. July 29.

Bulow, Jeremy I., and Lawrence H. Summers. 1984. The taxation of risky assets. *Journal of Political Economy* 92 (February): 20–39.

Burman, Leonard E. 1991. Theoretical determinants of aggregate capital gains realizations. Photocopy. July.

Burman, Leonard E. 1990. Why capital gains tax cuts (probably) don't pay for themselves. *Tax Notes*, April 2, pp. 109–10.

Burman, Leonard E., Joseph Cordes, and Larry Ozanne. 1990. IRAs and national savings. *National Tax Journal* 43 (September): 123–28.

Burman, Leonard E., Thomas S. Neubig, and D. Gordon Wilson. 1987. The use and abuse of rental project models. *Compendium of Tax Research 1987*. Office of Tax Analysis, Department of the Treasury. Washington: GPO, pp. 307–48.

Burman, Leonard E., and William C. Randolph. 1992. Measuring permanent responses to capital gains tax changes in panel data. Photocopy. February. Forthcoming, *American Economic Review*.

Cagan, Philip. 1965. *The Effect of Pension Plans on Aggregate Savings*. National Bureau of Economic Research. New York: Columbia University Press.

Caplin, Mortimer. 1969. Taxing the net margins of cooperatives. *Georgetown Law Journal* 58 (October): 6–45.

Carlino, Gerald A. 1982. Interest rate effects and temporary consumption. *Journal of Monetary Economics* 9 (March): 223–34.

Carroll, Chris, and Lawrence H. Summers. 1987. Why have private savings rates in the U.S. and Canada diverged? *Journal of Monetary Economics* 20 (September): 249–80.

Caton, Christopher, Otto Eckstein, and Allen Sinai. 1977. Tax reform studies. *Data Resources Review of the U.S. Economy* (August): 1.10–1.19.

Chamley, Christophe. 1981. The welfare cost of capital income taxation in a growing economy. *Journal of Political Economy* 89 (June): 468–96.

Chang, Angela. 1991. Explanations for the trend away from defined benefit pension plans. Congressional Research Service Report 91–647. Library of Congress. August 25.

Charles River Associates, Inc. 1985. *An Assessment of Options for Restructuring the R&D Tax Credit to Reduce the Dilution of Its Marginal Incentives*. No. 820.05. Prepared for the National Science Foundation, Boston. February.

Clark, Peter K. 1993. Tax incentives for equipment investment in the United States: Lessons from the past and considerations for the future. Presented to the Brookings Panel on Economic Activity. April 1–2.

Clark, Peter K. 1979. Investment in the 1970s: Theory, performance, and prediction. *Brookings Papers on Economic Activity* 1: 73–124.

Clotfelter, Charles. 1992. The distributional consequences of the nonprofit sector. In *Who Benefits from the Nonprofit Sector?* edited by Charles Clotfelter. Chicago: University of Chicago Press, pp. 1–23.

Coen, Robert M. 1971. The effect of cash flow on the speed of adjustment. In *Tax Incentives and Capital Spending*, edited by Gary Fromm. Washington: Brookings Institution, pp. 131–46.

Coen, Robert M. 1969. Tax policy and investment behavior: Comment. *American Economic Review* 59 (June): 370–79.

Cordes, Joseph. 1989. Tax incentives for R&D spending: A review of the evidence. *Research Policy* 18: 119–33.

Cordes, Joseph, and Harvey Galper. 1985. Tax shelter activity: Twenty years of experience. *National Tax Journal* 39 (September): 305–24.

Cordes, Joseph, Harry Watson, and Scott Hauger. 1987. Effects of tax reform on high technology firms. *National Tax Journal* 40 (September): 373–91.

Corlett, W. J., and D. C. Hague. 1953–54. Complimentarity and the excess burden of taxation. *Review of Economic Studies* 21: 21–30.

Cummins, Jason G., and Kevin G. Hassett. 1992. The effects of taxation on investment: New evidence from firm level panel data. *National Tax Journal* 45 (September): 243–51.

Darby, Michael, Robert Gillingham, and John S. Greenlees. 1988. The direct revenue effects of capital gains taxation: A reconsideration of the time series evidence. U.S. Department of Treasury, *Treasury Bulletin* (June): pp. 2–2.8.

Davidson, Paul. 1978–79. The United States Internal Revenue Service: Fourteenth member of OPEC. *Journal of Post Keynesian Economics* 1 (Winter): 47–58.

Davis, Albert J. 1991. Measuring the distributional effects of tax changes for the congress. *National Tax Journal* 44 (September): 257–68.

De Long, J. Bradford, and Lawrence Summers. 1991. Equipment investment and economic growth. *Quarterly Journal of Economics* 106 (May): 445–502.

Diamond, Peter. 1975. Inflation and the comprehensive tax base. *Journal of Public Economics* 4 (August): 227–44.

Dildine, Larry. 1988. Evaluating the impact of the corporate alternative minimum tax on equipment leasing. *1987 Proceedings of the National Tax Association–Tax Institute of America.* Columbus: National Tax Association, pp. 145–47.

Domar, Evsey D., and Richard A. Musgrave. 1944. Proportional income taxation and risk-taking. *Quarterly Journal of Economics* 58 (May): 387–422.

Drexel-Burnham-Lambert Decision Makers Poll. January 16, 1990.

Duerr, Michael G. 1972. *Tax Allocations and International Business.* New York: Conference Board.

References   317

Dworin, Lowell. 1986. An analysis of partnership activity, 1981–1983. U.S. Department of Treasury, Internal Revenue Service, *Statistics of Income Bulletin* 5 (Spring): 63–74.

Dworin, Lowell. 1987a. Impact of the corporate alternative minimum tax. *National Tax Journal* 40 (September): 505–13.

Dworin, Lowell. 1987b. Impact of the corporate alternative minimum tax: A Monte Carlo simulation study. *Compendium of Tax Research 1987*. Office of Tax Analysis, Department of the Treasury. Washington: GPO, pp. 253–78.

Ebrill, Liam P., and David G. Hartman. 1982. On the incidence and excess burden of the corporation income tax. *Public Finance* 37: 48–58.

Eisner, Robert. 1980. Capital gains and income: real changes in the value of capital in the United States, 1946–1977. In *The Measurement of Capital*, edited by Dan Usher. Chicago: University of Chicago Press, pp. 145–72.

Eisner, Robert. 1969. Tax policy and investment behavior: Comment. *American Economic Review* 59 (June): 379–88.

Evans, Owen J. 1983. Tax policy, the interest elasticity of saving, and capital accumulation: Numerical analysis of theoretical models. *American Economic Review* 73 (June): 398–410.

Feenberg, Daniel, and Jonathan Skinner. 1989. Sources of IRA savings. In *Tax Policy and the Economy*, vol. 3, edited by Lawrence H. Summers. Cambridge: MIT Press, pp. 25–46.

Feldstein, Martin S. 1970a. Corporate taxation and dividend behavior. *Review of Economic Studies* 37 (January): 57–72.

Feldstein, Martin. 1970b. Inflation, specification bias, and the impact of interest rates. *Journal of Political Economy* 78 (November–December): 1325–39.

Feldstein, Martin, and Phillipe Bacchetta. 1991. National saving and international investment. In *National Saving and Economic Performance*, edited by B. Douglas Bernheim and John B. Shoven. National Bureau of Economic Research. Chicago: University of Chicago Press, pp. 201–20.

Feldstein, Martin, and David Hartman. 1979. The optimal taxation of foreign source income. *Quarterly Journal Of Economics* 93 (November): 613–30.

Feldstein, Martin, and Charles Horioka. 1980. Domestic savings and international capital flows. *Economic Journal* 90 (June): 314–29.

Feldstein, Martin, Joel Slemrod, and Shlomo Yitzhaki. 1980. The effects of taxation on the selling of corporate stock and the realization of capital gains. *Quarterly Journal of Economics* 94 (June): 777–91.

Fredland, Eric J., John A. Gray, and Emil Sunley. 1968. The six-month holding period for capital gains: An empirical analysis of its effect on the timing of gains. *National Tax Journal* 21 (December): 467–78.

Friend, Irwin, and Joel Hasbrouck. 1983. Saving and after tax rates of return. *Review of Economics and Statistics* 65 (November): 537–43.

Frisch, Daniel. 1989. Aspects of the rate of return approach to transfer pricing. *National Tax Journal* 42 (September): pp. 261–71.

Fullerton, Don, Robert Gillette, and James Mackie. 1987. Investment incentives under tax reform. *Compendium of Tax Research 1987*. Office of Tax Analysis, Department of the Treasury. Washington: GPO, pp. 131–71.

Fullerton, Don, and Roger Gordon. 1983. A reexamination of tax distortions in general equilibrium models. In *Behavioral Simulation Methods in Tax Policy Analysis*, edited by Martin Feldstein. Chicago: University of Chicago Press, pp. 369–426.

Fullerton, Don, and Yolanda K. Henderson. 1989. A disaggregate equilibrium model of the tax distortions among assets, sectors, and industries. *International Economic Review* 30 (May): 391–413.

Fullerton, Don, Yolanda K. Henderson, and James Mackie. 1987. Investment allocation and growth under the Tax Reform Act of 1986. In *Compendium of Tax Research 1987*. U.S. Department of Treasury, Office of Tax Analysis. Washington: GPO, pp. 173–201.

Fullerton, Don, and Andrew B. Lyon. 1988. Tax neutrality and intangible capital. In *Tax Policy and the Economy*, vol. 2, edited by Lawrence Summers. National Bureau of Economic Research. Cambridge: MIT Press, pp. 63–88.

Fullerton, Don, and James Mackie. 1989. Economic efficiency in recent tax reform history: Policy reversals or consistent improvements? *National Tax Journal* 42 (March): 1–14.

Fullerton, Don, and Diane Lim Rogers. 1993. *Who Bears the Lifetime Tax Burden?* Washington: Brookings Institution.

Gale, William G., and John Karl Scholz. 1990. IRAs and household savings. July. Forthcoming, *American Economic Review*.

Galper, Harvey, and Charles Byce. 1986. Individual retirement accounts: Facts and issues. *Tax Notes*, June 2, pp. 917–21.

Galper, Harvey, Lucke, Robert, and Toder, Eric. 1988. A general equilibrium analysis of tax reform. In *Uneasy Compromise: Problems of a Hybrid Income Consumption Tax*, edited by Henry J. Aaron, Harvey Galper, and Joseph Pechman. Washington: Brookings Institution, pp. 59–108.

Gerardi, Geraldine, Hudson Milner, and Gerald Silverstein. 1992. Temporal aspects of the corporate minimum tax: Results of corporate panel data for 1987–1990. Photocopy.

Gertler, Mark, and R. Glenn Hubbard. 1990. Taxation, corporate capital structure, and financial distress. In *Tax Policy and the Economy*, vol. 4, edited by Lawrence Summers. Cambridge: MIT Press, pp. 43–71.

Gillingham, Robert, John S. Greenlees, and Kimberly D. Zieschang. 1989. New estimates of capital gains realization behavior: Evidence from pooled cross-section data. U.S. Department of Treasury, Office of Tax Analysis Paper 66, May.

Goode, Richard. 1980. The superiority of the income tax. The case for a personal consumption tax. In *What Should Be Taxed: Income or Expenditure?* edited by Joseph A. Pechman. Washington: Brookings Institution, pp. 75–113.

Gordon, Roger. 1992. Can capital income taxes survive in open economies? *Journal of Finance* 47 (July): 1159–80.

Gordon, Roger H. 1985. Taxation of corporate capital income: Tax revenues versus tax distortions. *Quarterly Journal of Economics* 100 (February): 1–27.

Gordon, Roger, and David F. Bradford. 1980. Taxation and the stock market valuation of capital gains and dividends: Theory and empirical results. *Journal of Public Economics* 14 (October): 109–36.

Gordon, Roger H., James R. Hines Jr., and Lawrence H. Summers. 1987. Notes on the tax treatment of structures. In *The Effects of Taxation on Capital Accumulation*, edited by Martin A. Feldstein. National Bureau of Economic Research. Chicago: University of Chicago Press, pp. 223–58.

Gordon, Roger, and Dale Jorgenson. 1975. Policy alternatives for the investment tax credit. In *Joint Seminars on Encouraging Capital Formation through the Tax Code*, before the Committee on the Budget, United States Senate, September 18, 1975. Washington: GPO, pp. 15–84.

Gordon, Roger, and Jeffrey K. MacKie-Mason. 1991. Taxes and the choice of organizational form. National Bureau of Economic Research Working Paper 3781. July.

Gordon, Roger, and Jeffrey K. MacKie-Mason. 1990. Effects of the Tax Reform Act of 1986 on corporate financial policy and organizational form. In *Do Taxes Matter?: The Impact of the Tax Reform Act of 1986*, edited by Joel Slemrod. Cambridge: MIT Press, pp. 91–131.

Gordon, Roger, and Burton Malkiel. 1981. Corporation finance. In *How Taxes Affect Economic Behavior*, edited by Henry J. Aaron and Joseph A. Pechman. Washington: Brookings Institution, pp. 131–98.

Gordon, Roger H., and Gilbert Metcalf. 1991. Do tax exempt bonds really subsidize municipal capital? *National Tax Journal* 44 (December pt. 1): pp. 71–80.

Gordon, Roger H., and Joel Slemrod. 1988. Do we collect any revenue from taxing capital income? *Tax Policy and the Economy* vol. 2, edited by Lawrence Summers. National Bureau of Economic Research. Cambridge: MIT Press, pp. 89–103.

Gordon, Roger H., and John Douglas Wilson. 1989. Measuring the efficiency cost of taxing risky capital income. *American Economic Review* 79 (June): 427–39.

Gradison, Bill. 1989. America's competitiveness—Sense and nonsense. *AEI Economist*. (August).

Graetz, Michael J., and Emil M. Sunley. 1988. Minimum taxes and comprehensive tax reform. In *Uneasy Compromise: Problems of a Hybrid Income-Consumption Tax*, edited by Henry J. Aaron, Harvey Galper, and Joseph A. Pechman. Washington: Brookings Institution, pp. 385–419.

Gravelle, Jane G. 1994. Corporate tax incidence in an open economy. Forthcoming in *1993 Proceedings of the National Tax Association–Tax Insititute of America*. Columbus: National Tax Association.

Gravelle, Jane G. 1993a. Estimating long run revenue effects of tax law changes. *Eastern Economic Journal* 19 (Fall): 481–94.

Gravelle, Jane G. 1993b. Small business tax subsidy proposals. Congressional Research Service Report No. 93–316. Library of Congress. March.

Gravelle, Jane G. 1993c. What can private investment incentives accomplish? The case of the investment tax credit. *National Tax Journal* 46 (September): 275–90.

Gravelle, Jane G. 1992a. Equity effects of the Tax Reform Act of 1986. *Journal of Economic Perspectives* 6 (Winter): 27–44.

Gravelle, Jane G. 1992b. New tax proposals: Flat, VAT, and variations. Congressional Research Service Report 92–386. Library of Congress. April 27.

Gravelle, Jane G. 1991a. Corporate tax integration: Issues and options. Congressional Research Service Report 91–482 RCO. Library of Congress. June 14.

Gravelle, Jane G. 1991b. Income, consumption and wage taxation in a life cycle model: separating efficiency from redistribution. *American Economic Review* 81 (September): 985–95.

Gravelle, Jane G. 1991c. Do individual retirement accounts increase savings? *Journal of Economic Perspectives* 5 (Spring): 133–48.

Gravelle, Jane G. 1991d. Limits to capital gains feedback effects. Congressional Research Service Report 91–250. Library of Congress. March 15. (Reprinted in *Tax Notes*, April 22, pp. 363–71.)

Gravelle, Jane G. 1991e. Taxation and the allocation of capital: The experience of the 1980s. In *1990 Proceedings of the National Tax Association–Tax Institute of America.* Columbus: National Tax Association, p. 27–36.

Gravelle, Jane G. 1990. Can a capital gains tax cut pay for itself? Congressional Research Service Report 90–161. Library of Congress. March 23. (Reprinted in *Tax Notes*, July 9, 1990, pp. 209–19.)

Gravelle, Jane G. 1989. Differential taxation of capital income: Another look at the 1986 Tax Reform Act. *National Tax Journal* 42 (December): pp. 441–65.

Gravelle, Jane G. 1988. Comment on minimum taxes and comprehensive tax reform. In *Uneasy Compromise: Problems of a Hybrid Income-Consumption Tax*, edited by Henry J. Aaron, Harvey Galper, and Joseph A. Pechman. Washington: Brookings Institution, pp. 419–28.

Gravelle, Jane G. 1987a. The effect of the passive loss restriction in the Tax Reform Act of 1986 on investment in real estate. Photocopy.

Gravelle, Jane G. 1987b. Tax policy and rental housing: An economic analysis. Congressional Research Service Report 87–536. Library of Congress. June 25.

Gravelle, Jane G. 1986. International tax competition: Does it make a difference for tax policy? *National Tax Journal* 39 (September): 375–84.

Gravelle, Jane G. 1985. The tax credit for research and development: An analysis. Congressional Research Service Report No. 85–6. Library of Congress. January.

Gravelle, Jane G. 1983. Capital income taxation and efficiency in the allocation of investment. *National Tax Journal* 36 (September): 297–306.

Gravelle, Jane G. 1982. Effects of the 1981 depreciation revisions on the taxation of income from business capital. *National Tax Journal* 35 (March): 1–20.

Gravelle, Jane G. 1981. The social cost of nonneutral taxation: Estimates for nonresidential capital. In *Depreciation, Inflation, and the Taxation of Income from Capital*, edited by Charles R. Hulten. Washington: The Urban Institute Press, pp. 239–50.

Gravelle, Jane G. 1979. The capital cost recovery system and the corporate income tax. Congressional Research Service Report No. 79–230 E. Library of Congress. November.

Gravelle, Jane G., and Laurence J. Kotlikoff. 1993. Corporate tax incidence and inefficiency when corporate and noncorporate goods are close substitutes. *Economic Inquiry* 31 (October): 501–16.

Gravelle, Jane G., and Laurence J. Kotlikoff. 1989a. Corporate taxation and the efficiency gains of the 1986 Tax Reform Act. National Bureau of Economic Research Working Paper 3142, October.

Gravelle, Jane G., and Laurence J. Kotlikoff. 1989b. The incidence and efficiency costs of corporate taxation when corporate and noncorporate firms produce the same goods. *Journal of Political Economy* 97 (August): 749–90.

Gravelle, Jane G., and James B. Mackie III. 1992. The real and financial efficiency costs from corporate tax integration: Results from three simulation models. In *1991 Proceedings of the National Tax Association—Tax Institute of America*. Columbus: National Tax Association, pp. 140–47.

Gravelle, Jane G., and Jack Taylor. 1992. Tax neutrality and the tax treatment of purchased intangibles. *National Tax Journal* 45 (March): 77–88.

"The Great Depreciation Hoax." *Industry Week*, May 10, 1971, pp. 29–31.

Gylfason, Thorvaldur. 1981. Interest rates, inflation, and the aggregate consumption function. *Review of Economics and Statistics* 63 (May): 233–45.

Hall, Bronwyn H. 1993. R&D tax policy during the 1980s: Success or failure? In *Tax Policy and the Economy*, vol. 7, edited by James M. Poterba. National Bureau of Economic Research. Cambridge: MIT Press, pp. 1–36.

Hall, Robert E., and Dale W. Jorgenson. 1971. Application of the theory of optimum capital accumulation. In *Tax Incentives and Capital Spending*, edited by Gary Fromm. Washington: Brooking Institution, pp. 9–60.

Hall, Robert E., and Dale W. Jorgenson. 1969. Tax policy and investment behavior: Reply and further results. *American Economic Review* 59 (June): 388–400.

Hall, Robert E., and Dale W. Jorgenson. 1967. Tax policy and investment behavior. *American Economic Review* 58 (June): 391–414.

Hall, Robert E., and Alvin Rabushka. 1986. *The Flat Tax*. Stanford: Hoover Institution Press.

Hall, Robert E., and Dale W. Jorgenson. 1967. Tax policy and investment behavior. *American Economic Review* 58 (June): 391–414.

Halperin, Daniel, and Eugene Steuerle. 1988. Indexing the tax system for inflation. In *Uneasy Compromise: Problems of a Hybrid Income-Consumption Tax*, edited by Henry J. Aaron, Harvey Galper, and Joseph A. Pechman. Washington: Brookings Institution, pp. 347–84.

Hansmann, Henry. 1987. Economic theories of non-profit organization. In *The Non-Profit Sector: A Research Handbook*, edited by Walter W. Powell. New Haven: Yale University Press, pp. 27–42.

Harberger, Arnold C. 1966. Efficiency effects of taxes on income from capital. In *Effects of the Corporation Income Tax*, edited by Marian Krzyzaniak. Detroit: Wayne State University Press, pp. 107–17.

Harberger, Arnold C. 1962. The incidence of the corporation income tax. *Journal of Political Economy* 70 (June): 215–40.

Harter, Gilbert. 1986. How tax reform would affect companies with different growth and profitability characteristics. *Tax Notes*, April 21, pp. 297–301.

Hartman, David. 1985. Tax policy and foreign direct investment. *Journal of Public Economics* 26 (January): 107–21.

Hartman, David. 1984. Tax policy and foreign direct investment in the United States. *National Tax Journal* 37 (December): 475–88.

Heien, Dale. 1980. Demographic effects and the multi-period consumption function. *Journal of Political Economy* 88 (January–February): 125–88.

Hendershott, Patric, and Sheng Cheng Hu. 1981. Investment in producer's durable equipment. In *How Taxes Affect Economic Behavior*, edited by Henry J. Aaron and Joseph A. Pechman. Washington: Brookings Institution, pp. 85–126.

Hendershott, Patric, and David C. Ling. 1984. Trading and the tax shelter value of depreciable real estate. *National Tax Journal* 37 (June): 213–24.

Hinrichs, Harley H. 1963. An empirical measure of investors' responsiveness to differentials in capital gains tax rates among income groups. *National Tax Journal* 16 (September): 224–29.

Hoerner, J. Andrew. ed. 1992a. *The Capital Gains Controversy: A Tax Analyst's Reader*. Arlington, VA: Tax Analysts.

Hoerner, J. Andrew. 1992b. Fairness, growth, neither or both: Dueling visions of the passive loss restriction. *Tax Notes*, April 6, pp. 14–17.

Holik, Dan, Susan Hostetter, and John Labate. 1989. 1985 sales of capital assets. Draft paper prepared for presentation at the 150th Annual Meeting of the American Statistical Association. August 6–10.

Holt, Charles C., and John P. Shelton. 1962. The lock-in effect of the capital gains tax. *National Tax Journal* 15 (December): 357–62.

Horst, Thomas. 1980. A note on the optimal taxation of international investment income. *Quarterly Journal of Economics* 93 (June): 793–98.

Howrey, E. Philip, and Saul H. Hymans. 1978. The measurement and determination of loanable funds savings. *Brookings Papers on Economic Activity* 3: 655–705.

Hubbard, R. Glenn. 1993 Corporate tax integration: A view from the Treasury Department. *Journal of Economic Perspectives* 7 (Winter): 115–32.

Hubbard, R. Glenn. 1984. Do IRAs and Keoghs increase savings? *National Tax Journal* 37 (March): 43–54.

Hulten, Charles R., and Frank C. Wykoff. 1981. The measurement of economic depreciation. In *Depreciation, Inflation, and the Taxation of Income From Capital*, edited by Charles R. Hulten. Washington: Urban Institute Press, pp. 45–60.

Ippolito, Richard. 1991 How recent tax legislation has affected pension plans. *National Tax Journal* 46 (September): 405–17.

Jensen, Michael. 1986. Agency costs of free cash flow, corporate finance, and takeovers. *AER Papers and Proceedings* 76 (May): 323–29.

Jensen, Michael, and William Meckling. 1976. Theory of the firm: Managerial behavior, agency costs, and ownership structures. *Journal of Financial Economics* 3 (September): 305–60.

Jones, Jonathan D. 1989. An analysis of aggregate time series capital gains equations. U.S. Department of Treasury, Office of Tax Analysis Paper 65. May.

Jorgenson, Dale, and Kun-Young Yun. 1990. Tax reform and U.S. economic growth. *Journal of Political Economy* 98 (October, pt. 2): s151–93.

Judd, Kenneth L. 1987. The welfare cost of factor taxation in a perfect foresight model. *Journal of Political Economy* 65 (August): 675–709.

Jun, Joosung. 1990. U.S. tax policy and direct investment abroad. In *Taxation in the Global Economy*, edited by Assaf Razin and Joel Slemrod. National Bureau of Economic Research. Chicago: University of Chicago Press, pp. 55–78.

Kahn, Alfred H. 1973. Consumption and net worth taxes. In *Broad Based Taxes: New Options and Sources*, edited by Richard A. Musgrave. Baltimore: Johns Hopkins University Press, pp. 133–54.

Katona, George. 1965. *Private Pensions and Individual Savings*. Survey Research Center, Institute for Social Research. Ann Arbor: University of Michigan Press.

Kenyon, Daphne. 1991. Effects of volume caps on state and local borrowing. *National Tax Journal* 44 (December, pt. 1): 81–92.

Kiefer, Donald W. 1990. Lock-in effect within a simple model of corporate stock trading. *National Tax Journal* 43 (March): 75–95.

Kiefer, Donald W. 1985. The tax treatment of a "reverse investment." *Tax Notes*, March 4, pp. 925–32.

Kiley, Michael T. 1993. Social and private rates of return to research and development in industry. Congressional Research Service Report 93–770. Library of Congress. August 27.

King, Mervyn A. 1977. *Public Policy and the Corporation*. London: Chapman and Hall.

Klein, Lawrence W., and Paul Taubman. 1971. Estimating effects within a complete econometric model. In *Tax Incentives and Capital Spending*, edited by Gary Fromm. Washington: Brookings Institution, pp. 197–242.

Kotlikoff, Laurence J. 1992. *Generational Accounting*. Detroit: Free Press.

Kotlikoff, Laurence J. 1990. The crisis in U.S. saving and proposals to address the crisis. *National Tax Journal* 43 (September): 233–46.

Krause, Lawrence B., and Kenneth W. Dam. 1964. *Federal Tax Treatment of Foreign Income*. Washington: Brookings Institution.

Krouse, Clement G. 1990. *Theory of Industrial Organization*. Cambridge, MA: Blackwell.

Krugman, Paul R. 1987. Is free trade passe? *Journal of Economic Perspectives* 1 (Fall): 131–44.

Laidler, David. 1969. Income tax incentives for owner-occupied housing. In *The Taxation of Income from Capital*, edited by Arnold C. Harberger and Martin Bailey. Washington: Brookings Institution, pp. 50–76.

Leigh, Wilhelmina A. 1980. Economic depreciation of the residential housing stock of the United States, 1950–1970. *Review of Economics and Statistics* 62 (May): 200–206.

Lindsey, Larry. 1986. Capital gains: Rates, realizations, and revenues. National Bureau of Economic Research Working Paper 1893. April.

Lipton, Richard M. 1992. The application of section 469 to real estate developers: The search for a solution to a problem that should not exist. *Tax Notes*, March 16, pp. 1429–32.

Lucke, Robert, Mark Eisenach, and Larry Dildine. 1986. The Senate alternative minimum tax: Does it snare only the tax abusers? *Tax Notes*, August 18, pp. 681–90.

Lyon, Andrew. 1992a. Tax neutrality under parallel tax systems. *Public Finance Quarterly* 20 (July): 338–58.

Lyon, Andrew. 1992b. Why a minimum tax? *1991 Proceedings of the Canadian Tax Foundation*. Toronto: Canadian Tax Foundation, pp. 18.1–10.

Lyon, Andrew. 1991. The alternative minimum tax: Equity, efficiency and incentive effects. In *Economic Effects of the Alternative Minimum Tax*. Washington: American Council for Capital Formation, Center for Policy Research, pp. 52–82.

Lyon, Andrew. 1990. Investment incentives under the alternative minimum tax. *National Tax Journal* 43 (December): 451–65.

Makin, John, and Kenneth A. Couch. 1989. Savings, pension contributions, and the real interest rate. *The Review of Economics and Statistics* 71 (August): 401–407.

Manegold, James G., and Douglas H. Joines. 1991. IRAs and savings: Evidence from a panel of taxpayers. Photocopy. September.

Mansfield, Edwin, John Rapoport, Anthony Romeo, Samuel Wagner, and George Beardsley. 1977. Social and private rates of return from industrial innovations. *Quarterly Journal of Economics* 41 (May): 221–40.

McDonald, Stephen. 1963. *Federal Tax Treatment of Income from Oil and Gas*. Washington: Brookings Institution.

McLure, Charles E., Jr. 1988. The 1986 Act: Tax reform's finest hour or death throes of the income tax? *National Tax Journal* 41 (September): 303–15.

McLure, Charles E., Jr. 1979. *Must Corporate Income Be Taxed Twice?* Washington: Brookings Institution.

McLure, Charles E., Jr., Jack Mutti, Victor Thuronyi, and George R. Zodrow. 1990. *The Taxation of Income from Business Capital in Columbia.* Chapel Hill: Duke University Press.

Menchik, Paul L., and Martin David. 1983. Income distribution, lifetime savings and bequests. *American Economic Review* 73 (September): 672–90.

Metcalf, Gilbert. 1990. Arbitrage and the savings behavior of state governments. *Review of Economics and Statistics* 72 (August): 390–96.

Miller, Merton H., and Kevin Rock. 1985. Dividend policy under asymmetric information. *Journal of Finance* 40 (September): 1031–51.

Minarik, Joseph. 1984. The effects of taxation on the selling of corporate stock and the realization of capital gains: Comment. *Quarterly Journal of Economics* 98 (February): 93–110.

Minarik, Joseph. 1983. Capital gains. In *How Taxes Affect Economic Behavior*, edited by Henry J. Aaron and Joseph A. Pechman. Washington: Brookings Institution, pp. 241–77.

Mossin, Jan. 1968. Taxation and risk-taking: An expected utility approach. *Economica* 35 (February): 74–82.

Mundstock, George. 1990. Franchises, intangible capital, and assets. *National Tax Journal* 43 (September): 299–305.

Munnell, Alicia. 1992. Current taxation of qualified plans: Has the time come? *New England Economic Review*, Federal Reserve Bank of Boston (March–April): 12–25.

Munnell, Alicia. 1991. Are pensions worth the cost? *National Tax Journal* 44 (September): 406–17.

Munnell, Alicia. 1987. The impact of public and private pension schemes on saving and capital formation. In *Conjugating Public and Private: The Case of Pensions*. Studies and Research 24. Geneva: International Social Security Association, pp. 219–36.

Munnell, Alicia. 1976. Private pensions and saving: New evidence. *Journal of Political Economy* 84 (October): 1013–32.

Munnell, Alicia. 1974. *The Effect of Social Security on Personal Saving.* Cambridge, MA: Ballinger.

Musgrave, Peggy Brewer. 1975. *Direct Investment Abroad and the Multinationals: Effects on the United States Economy.* Senate Foreign Relations Committee Print. 94th Cong. 1st sess. August. Washington: GPO.

Nadeau, Serge. 1988. A model to measure the effects of taxes on the real and financial decisions of the firm. *National Tax Journal* 41 (December): 467–81.

Nadiri, M. Ishaq. 1980. Contributions and determinants of research and development expenditures in U.S. manufacturing industries. In *Capital, Efficiency, and Growth*, edited by George M. von Furstenberg. Cambridge, MA: Ballinger, pp. 361–92.

Navin, John C. 1992. An assessment of tax policy in models with endogenous financial behavior. Ph.D. dissertation. Michigan State University.

Nelson, Richard, and Michael Krashinsky. 1973. Two major issues of public policy: Public policy and organization of supply. In *Public Subsidy for Day Care of Young Children*, edited by Richard Nelson and Dennis Young. Lexington, MA: D. C. Heath, pp. 47–69.

Nelson, Susan. 1985 Taxes paid by high-income taxpayers and the growth of partnerships. U.S. Department of Treasury, Internal Revenue Service, *Statistics of Income Bulletin* 5 (Fall): 31–39.

Nelson, Susan, and Tom Petska. 1989–1990. Partnerships, passive losses, and tax reform. U.S. Department of Treasury, Internal Revenue Service, *Statistics of Income Bulletin* 9 (Winter): 55–60.

Odendahl, Teresa. 1990. *Charity Begins at Home: Generosity and Self Interest among the Philanthropic Elite*. New York: Basic Books.

Ott, David J., and Allan H. Meltzer. 1963. *Federal Tax Treatment of State and Local Securities*. Washington: Brookings Institution.

Papke, Leslie. 1993. What do we know about enterprise zones? *Tax Policy and the Economy*, vol. 7, edited by James M. Poterba. National Bureau of Economic Research. Cambridge: MIT Press, pp. 1–36.

Pechman, Joseph. 1987. *Federal Tax Policy*. 3d ed. Washington: Brookings Institution.

Peek, Joe, and James A. Wilcox. 1986. Tax rates and interest rates on tax-exempt securities. Federal Reserve Bank of Boston, *New England Economic Review* (January–February): 29–41.

Peterson, Frederick M. 1975. Two externalities in petroleum exploration. In *Studies in Energy Tax Policy*, edited by Gerard M. Brannon. Cambridge, MA: Ballinger, pp. 101–14.

Petska, Tom. 1992. Partnerships, partners, and tax shelters after tax reform, 1987–1989. U.S. Department of Treasury, Internal Revenue Service, *Statistics of Income Bulletin* 12 (Summer): 8–24.

Poterba, James M. 1990. Taxation and housing markets: Preliminary evidence on the effects of recent tax reforms. In *Do Taxes Matter? The Effect of the Tax Reform Act of 1986*, edited by Joel Slemrod. Cambridge: MIT Press, pp. 141–60.

Poterba, James. 1989. Venture capital and capital gains taxation. In *Tax Policy and the Economy*, vol. 3, edited by Lawrence H. Summers. National Bureau of Economic Research. Cambridge: MIT Press, pp. 47–68.

Poterba, James M. 1987. Tax policy and corporate saving. *Brookings Papers on Economic Activity* 2: 455–515.

Poterba, James M., and Lawrence H. Summers. 1985. The economic effects of dividend taxation. In *Recent Advances in Corporate Finance*, edited by E. Altman and M. Subrahmanyam. Homewood, IL: Irwin Press, pp. 227–84.

Ramsey, Frank P. 1927. A contribution to the theory of taxation. *Economic Journal* 37 (March): 47–61.

Richman, Peggy Brewer. 1963. *Taxation of Foreign Investment Income: An Economic Analysis*. Baltimore: Johns Hopkins University Press.

Rosen, Harvey S. 1979. Housing decisions and the U.S. income tax: An econometric analysis. *Journal of Public Economics* 11 (February): 1–23.

Schrader, Lee F., and Ray A. Goldberg. 1975. *Farmers Cooperatives and Federal Income Taxes*. Cambridge, MA: Ballinger.

Seater, John J. 1993. Ricardian equivalence. *Journal of Economic Literature* 31 (March): 142–90.

Seltzer, Lawrence H. 1951. *The Nature and Tax Treatment of Capital Gains and Losses*. National Bureau of Economic Research.

Shoven, John. 1991. Using the corporate cash flow tax to integrate corporate and personal taxes. *National Tax Association–Tax Institute of America Proceedings*. Columbus: National Tax Association, pp. 19–27.

Shoven, John B. 1976. The incidence and efficiency effects of taxes on income from capital. *Journal of Political Economy* 84 (December): 1261–83.

Sinn, Hans Werner. 1991. Taxation and the cost of capital: the "old" view, the "new" view, and another view. In *Tax Policy and the Economy*, vol. 5, edited by David F. Bradford. National Bureau of Economic Research. Cambridge: MIT Press, pp. 25–54.

Skinner, Jonathan. 1992. Individual retirement accounts: A review of the evidence. *Tax Notes*, January 13, pp. 201–12.

Skinner, Jonathan, and Daniel Feenberg. 1991. The impact of the 1986 tax reform on personal saving. In *Do Taxes Matter? The Impact of the Effect of the Tax Reform Act of 1986*, edited by Joel Slemrod. Cambridge: MIT Press, pp. 50–79.

Slemrod, Joel. 1990. Tax effects on foreign direct investment in the U.S. In *Taxation in the Global Economy*, edited by Assaf Razin and Joel Slemrod. National Bureau of Economic Research. Chicago: University of Chicago Press, pp. 79–117.

Slemrod, Joel. 1988. Effects of taxation with international capital mobility. In *Uneasy Compromise: Problems of a Hybrid Income-Consumption Tax*, edited by Henry J. Aaron, Harvey Galper, and Joseph A. Pechman. Washington: Brookings Institution, pp. 115–56.

Slemrod, Joel, and William Shobe. 1990. The tax elasticity of capital gains realizations: Evidence from a panel of taxpayers. National Bureau of Economic Research Working Paper 3737. January.

Springer, W. L. 1975. Did the 1968 surcharge really work? *American Economic Review* 65 (September): 664–79.

Steuerle, C. Eugene. 1991. *The Tax Decade*. Washington: Urban Institute.

Steuerle, C. Eugene. 1985. *Taxes, Loans, and Inflation: How the Nation's Wealth Becomes Misallocated*. Washington: Brookings Institution.

Stiglitz, Joseph E. 1969. The effects of income, wealth, and capital gains taxation on risk-taking. *Quarterly Journal of Economics* 83 (May): 263–83.

Summers, Lawrence. 1981. Capital income taxation and accumulation in a life cycle model. *American Economic Review* 71 (September): 533–44.

Taubman, Paul. 1973. The investment tax credit, once more. *Boston College Industrial and Commercial Law Review* 14 (May): 871–90.

Taubman, Paul, and Robert Rasche. 1969. Economic and tax depreciation of office buildings. *National Tax Journal* 25 (September): 334–46.

Taylor, Lester. 1971. Savings out of different types of income. *Brookings Papers on Economic Activity* 2: 383–413.

Tiebout, Charles M. 1956. A pure theory of local expenditures. *Journal of Political Economy* 64 (October): 416–24.

U.S. Congress. Congressional Budget Office. 1992a. The cost-effectiveness of the low-income housing tax credit compared with housing vouchers. Staff Working Paper. Prepared by Leonard Burman. Washington: GPO. April.

U.S. Congress. Congressional Budget Office. 1992b. *Effects of Adopting a Value Added Tax.* Prepared by Jon Hakken. Washington: GPO.

U.S. Congress. Congressional Budget Office. 1990. *Indexing Capital Gains.* Prepared by Leonard Burman and Larry Ozanne. Washington: GPO. August.

U.S. Congress. Congressional Budget Office. 1988. *How Capital Gains Tax Rates Affect Revenues: The Historical Evidence.* Prepared by Eric Toder and Larry Ozanne. Washington: GPO. March.

U.S. Congress. 1987a. Congressional Budget Office. *The Changing Distribution of Federal Taxes: 1975–1990.* Prepared by Richard Kasten and Frank Sammartino. Washington: GPO.

U.S. Congress. Congressional Budget Office. 1987b. *Tax Policy for Pensions and Other Retirement Savings.* Prepared by David Lindeman and Larry Ozanne. Washington: GPO. April.

U.S. Congress. Congressional Budget Office. 1986. Effects of the 1981 Act on the Distribution of Income and Taxes Paid. Staff Working Paper. Washington: GPO. August.

U.S. Congress. Congressional Budget Office. 1984. *Federal Support for R&D and Innovation.* Washington: GPO. April.

U.S. Congress. Joint Committee on Taxation. 1993. *Methodology and Issues in Measuring Changes in the Distribution of Tax Burdens.* Joint Committee Print. Washington: GPO. June 14.

U.S. Congress. Joint Committee on Taxation. 1992. *Staff Description and Analysis of Tax Provisions Expiring in 1992.* Washington: GPO. January 24.

U.S. Congress. Joint Committee on Taxation. 1991. *Factors Affecting the International Competitiveness of the United States.* Joint Committee Print. Washington: GPO. May 30.

U.S. Congress. Joint Economic Committee. 1985. *The R&D Tax Credit: An Evaluation of Evidence on its Effectiveness,* August 23. 99th Cong, 1st sess. Senate Report 99–73. Washington: GPO.

U.S. Congress. Senate Budget Committee. 1992. *Tax Expenditures: Compendium of Background Material on Individual Provisions.* November 1992. Prepared by the

Congressional Research Service. Senate Committee on the Budget, 102d Cong. 2d sess. Washington: GPO.

U.S. Department of Commerce. Bureau of the Census. 1991. *Money Income of Households, Families and Persons in the United States 1990*. Current Population Reports, Consumer Income, Series P–60, No. 174. Washington: GPO.

U.S. Department of Commerce. Bureau of Economic Analysis. *Survey of Current Business*, various issues.

U.S. Department of Labor. Pension and Welfare Benefits Administration. 1989. *Trends in Pensions*. Washington: GPO.

U.S. Department of Treasury. 1992. *Report on Integration of the Individual and Corporate Tax Systems*. Washington: GPO. January.

U.S. Department of Treasury. 1991. *Report to Congress on the Effect of the Full Funding Limit on Pension Benefit Security*. Washington: GPO. May.

U.S. Department of Treasury. 1989. *Final Report to the Congress on Life Insurance Taxation, Department of the Treasury*. Washington: GPO. August.

U.S. Department of Treasury. 1988. A study of intercompany pricing. Discussion Draft. October 18.

U.S. Department of Treasury. 1985. *Report to the Congress on the Capital Gains Tax Reductions of 1978*. Washington: GPO. September.

U.S. Department of Treasury. 1984. *Tax Reform for Fairness, Simplicity and Economic Growth*. Washington: GPO.

U.S. Department of Treasury. 1977. *Blueprints for Basic Tax Reform*. Washington: GPO.

U.S. Department of Treasury. 1971. *Asset Depreciation Range (ADR) System*. Washington: GPO. June.

U.S. General Accounting Office. 1992. *Effects of Changing the Tax Treatment of Fringe Benefits*. Washington: GPO. April.

U.S. General Accounting Office. 1990. *Additional Petroleum Production Tax Incentives Are of Questionable Merit*. Washington: GPO. July.

U.S. General Accounting Office. 1989a. *Allocation of Taxes within the Life Insurance Industry*. Washington: GPO. October.

U.S. General Accounting Office. 1989b. *The Research Tax Credit Has Stimulated Some Additional Research Spending*. Washington: GPO. September.

Utgoff, Kathleen. 1991. Public policy and pension regulation. *National Tax Journal* 44 (September): 383–91.

Venti, Steven F., and David A. Wise. 1990. Have IRAs increased U.S. savings? *Quarterly Journal of Economics* 105 (August): 661–98.

Vickrey, William. 1939. Averaging income for income tax purposes. *Journal of Political Economy* 47 (June): 379–97.

Weber, Warren. 1975. Interest rates, inflation and consumer expenditures. *American Economic Review* 65 (December): 843–58.

Weber, Warren. 1970. The effect of interest rates on aggregate consumption. *American Economic Review* 60 (September): 591–600.

Weisbrod, Burton A. 1988. *The Nonprofit Economy.* Cambridge: Harvard University Press.

Weisbrod, Burton A. 1974. Toward a theory of the voluntary non-profit sector in a three sector economy. In *Altruism, Morality, and Economic Theory,* edited by Edmund Phelps. New York: Russell Sage, pp. 171–96.

Wetzler, James W. 1977. Capital gains and losses. In *Comprehensive Income Taxation,* edited by Joseph Pechman. Washington: Brookings Institution, pp. 115–62.

White, Melvin, and Anne White. 1977. Tax deductibility of interest on consumer debt. *Public Finance Quarterly* 5 (January): 3–6.

Wright, Colin. 1969. Savings and the rate of interest. In *The Taxation of Income from Capital,* edited by Arnold C. Harberger and Martin Bailey. Washington: Brookings Institution, pp. 275–300.

Young, Kan H. 1988. The effects of taxes and rates of return on foreign direct investment in the United States. *National Tax Journal* 41 (March): 109–21.

Zimmerman, Dennis. 1991a. *The Private Use of Tax–Exempt Bonds.* Washington: Urban Institute Press.

Zimmerman, Dennis. 1991b. Tax policy and nonprofit organizations. *National Tax Journal* 44 (September): 341–49.

Zodrow, George R. 1991. On the "traditional" and "new" views of dividend taxation. *National Tax Journal* 45 (December): 497–510.

Index

Accelerated depreciation, 114, 164–165
    capital gain and, 128
    effective marginal tax rate and, 16, 19, 21
    methods, 264, 265
Accelerator, 120
Accrual-based taxation, 70
ACE (adjusted current earnings), 163, 170, 272
Add-on minimum tax, 272
Adjusted current earnings (ACE), 163, 170, 272
Administration tax, 70–71
ADR (asset depreciation range), 265–266
ADRS (asset depreciation range system), 103, 265–266
Advertising, 207, 210
Agency cost, 66, 83
Agriculture, 106
Alternative minimum tax (AMT). *See also* Minimum tax
    base, 162–163, 170, 272
    corporate, 161, 162
    efficiency, 167–172
    equity, 175–176
    historical basis, 164–167
    policy options, 176–178
American Chicle Company v. *U.S.*, 282
Amortization. *See* Tax depreciation
AMT. *See* Alternative minimum tax (AMT)
Asset depreciation range system (ADRS), 103, 265–266
Assets
    capital gains and, 129–130

capital gains taxes and, 133–136
    depreciable, 105
    depreciation of, 115–116, 133–136
    nondepreciable, 131–133

Bankruptcy risk, 83
Banks, taxation of, 279. *See also* Financial institutions
Blueprints for Basic Tax Reform for 1977, 12
Bonds, tax-exempt, 212–215, 278–279
Bureau of Economic Analysis, 104
Business transfer tax, 46. *See also* Value-added tax (VAT)

Cafeteria plans, 274
Capital cost recovery. *See* Depreciation
Capital export neutrality, 229–230, 231, 236–237, 248–249
Capital gains, sources of, 126–130
Capital gains taxes, 58–59, 77, 123
    accrual equivalent taxation, 157–158
    allocation of investments and, 141–143
    corporate/noncorporate capital allocations and, 124
    on corporate stock, 89
    cutting, 252, 253–255
    at death, 156–157
    depreciable assets and, 133–136, 158
    distributional effects, 152–154, 159
    economic efficiency and, 124–126, 141–151
    effective marginal rates, 130–136
    equity, 151–154
    exclusion, 154–156